The Rule of Law in Europe

María Elósegui • Alina Miron • Iulia Motoc
Editors

The Rule of Law in Europe

Recent Challenges and Judicial Responses

Springer

Editors
María Elósegui
Judge at European Court of Human Rights
Strasbourg, France

Alina Miron
Professor at University of Angers
Angers, France

Iulia Motoc
Judge at European Court of Human Rights
Strasbourg, France

ISBN 978-3-030-56000-3 ISBN 978-3-030-56001-0 (eBook)
https://doi.org/10.1007/978-3-030-56001-0

This Springer imprint is published by the registered company Springer Nature Switzerland AG.
The registered company address is: Gewerbestrasse 11, 6330 Cham, Switzerland

Preface

The former Chief Prosecutor of the National Anticorruption Directorate of Romania was removed from her position on account that her critics of new legislation had "skewed the opinions of European and international forums in respect of Romania, [had] triggered evaluation mechanisms never before used against our country, threatening the fulfilment of the objectives assumed and endangering the rule of law" (ECtHR, *Kövesi v. Romania*, 5 March 2020, No. 3594/19, para. 18 quoting a report of the Romanian Ministry of Justice). In its judgement, the European Court of Human Rights held "that no evidence [had] been brought to show that the impugned measure served the aim of protecting the rule of law" (*ibid*, para. 196) and considered that the independence of the prosecutor and access to a court were the real cornerstones of the rule of law. Is this the new *Kramer vs Kramer*? Has the rule of law become a mere slogan, a concept so much overused that it has lost its true meaning to its incantatory shadow? Or is this case a further illustration of the opposition between the "thin" and "thick" notions of the rule of law?

It is true that the concept of the rule of law (*Etat de droit*, *Rechstaat*, *Estado de derecho*, *Stato di diritto*) is as widely used as polysemic. There is however a consensual distinction between the formal and the substantive approaches to the rule of the law. According to the formal conception, "*un Etat de droit est un Etat au sein duquel chacun, y compris l'Etat lui-même, est soumis au droit*" [O. Corten, *L'Etat de droit en droit international*, Pedone (2009), p. 11]. Within this meaning, the rule of law addresses "the manner in which the law was promulgated (...), the clarity of the ensuing norm (...); and the temporal dimension of the enacted norm (was it prospective). Formal conceptions of the rule of law do not however seek to pass judgment upon the actual content of the law itself. They are not concerned with whether the law was in that sense a good law or a bad law, provided that the formal precepts of the rule of law were themselves met. Those who espouse substantive conceptions of the rule of law seek to go beyond this". [Craig, "Formal and Substantive Conceptions of the Rule of Law" (1997), p. 467]

According to the substantive conception, there must be an adequacy between the content of the law and the imperative of justice. Some core human rights and the main democracy principles give thus content to the transnational concept of the rule of law. The ECtHR's jurisprudence is greatly insisting upon the substantive dimension:

> In laying down that any deprivation of liberty must be 'lawful' and be effected 'in accordance with a procedure prescribed by law', Article 5 § 1 does not merely refer back to domestic law; like the expressions 'in accordance with the law' and 'prescribed by law' in the second paragraphs of Articles 8 to 11, it also relates to the quality of the law, requiring it to be compatible with the rule of law, a concept inherent in all the Articles of the Convention. (ECtHR, Judgment, 20 March 2018, *Şahin Alpay v. Turkey*, No. 16538/17, para. 116)

Rather than providing for yet another theoretical analysis over the concept, this book makes an inquiry into the recent challenges to the rule of law. The European regimes have for long been presented as a model of protection of the rule of law within its substantive dimension. Yet, in the past decade, it was put under strain by external and internal factors. Among the external factors, the terrorist threat, the migration crisis and now a pandemic have triggered the application of emergency regimes in many European states. The internal challenges come from the rise of populist movements, some of which won the elections in several European countries. If these regimes proclaim their attachment to a formal conception of the rule of law, its substantive dimension is easily left aside. A further risk comes from the fact that the emergency regimes may lose their temporary character to become the new state of law.

Therefore, the book aims at identifying particular fields in which the rule of law has been put considerably under stress, often in an indirect yet insidious manner. Its focus is upon the responses brought by the courts (domestic and regional) to these threats. When the big waves are rising, courts might prove the ultimate ramparts against the flood. The stress-test of the rule of law might indeed be safeguarding the judicial guarantees designed to protect core European values beyond the discretion of government.

This book is also the result of two conferences held in 2018–2019. The first one, on the *Challenges to the Rule of Law*, was co-organized by Judge Iulia Motoc of the ECtHR and Professor Alina Miron of the University of Angers (Centre Jean Bodin). It was held in the premises of the Court in Strasbourg, on 14 December 2018, in the particular atmosphere of a city not celebrating the popular winter holidays but saddened by a terrorist attack which had taken place a few days before. The second one, held on the 26 and 27 April 2019, dealt with the *Freedom of Expression and Its Balancing with the Right of Respect for Private Life*. It was organized by judges Elósegui, Wojtyczek and Chanturia and of the ECtHR, in collaboration with the International Institute of Human Rights - Fondation René Cassin and the Alexander von Humboldt Foundation. The organizers wish to address their special gratitude to the Humboldt Foundation and to Steffen Mehlich, Director Sponsorship and Network Department of the Humboldt Foundation, who participated with all his enthusiasm in the seminar in the Court.

The book is therefore structured in three parts. The first one deals with *Defending the Rule of Law in Emergency Regimes*. Indeed, as Advocate-General Poiares Maduro wrote in his opinion in the first *Kadi* case,

> Certainly, extraordinary circumstances may justify restrictions on individual freedom that would be unacceptable under normal conditions. However, that should not induce us to say that 'there are cases in which a veil should be drawn for a while over liberty, as it was customary to cover the statues of the gods'. (Montesquieu, *De l'Esprit des Lois*, Book XII) (. . .) On the contrary, when the risks to public security are believed to be extraordinarily high, the pressure is particularly strong to take measures that disregard individual rights, especially in respect of individuals who have little or no access to the political process. Therefore, in those instances, the courts should fulfil their duty to uphold the rule of law with increased vigilance. (ECJ, Opinion of the Advocate-General Poiares Maduro, 16 Jan. 2008, *Yassin Abdullah Kadi and Al Barakaat International Foundation v Council of the European Union and Commission of the European Communities*, Joined cases C-402/05 P and C-415/05 P)

Since judges are the regular guardians of the rule of law and possibly the ultimate ramparts against the reign of the arbitrary, the second part of the book deals with the *Challenges and Safeguards of the Independence of Justice*. As the Court recently reiterated,

> one can scarcely conceive of the rule of law without there being a possibility of having access to the courts. The principle whereby a civil claim must be capable of being submitted to a judge ranks as one of the universally 'recognised' fundamental principles of law; the same is true of the principle of international law which forbids the denial of justice. (*Kövesi v. Romania*, 5 March 2020, No. 3594/19, para. 145)

We have lately witnessed an increasing tendency to put in question the authority of the judiciary or to undermine its independence through various legislative reforms. The jurisprudence of the ECtHR aimed at supporting and consolidating the domestic judiciary. It reminds that

> For another court to call into question the powers conferred on a constitutional court to give final and binding judgments on individual applications runs counter to the fundamental principles of the rule of law and legal certainty. The Court reiterates that these principles, inherent in the protection afforded by Article 5 of the Convention, are the cornerstones of the guarantees against arbitrariness. (ECtHR, 20 March 2018, *Şahin Alpay v. Turkey*, No. 16538/17, para. 118)

Finally, the third part of the book deals finally with *Freedom of Expression*. The limitation of power through the guarantee of rights is, as we know, an inherently liberal political philosophy. And freedom of expression is part of the triad of values that it enshrines, alongside the separation of powers and the independence of the judiciary, which are indispensable for containing state arbitrariness. Particular attention is devoted to the freedom of the press. This is certainly a special form of freedom of expression, but it is much more than just individual freedom (the freedom to transmit and receive information): it is a structuring component of democratic life. It is thus at once a public freedom, a collective good and a cog in the wheel of democracy. For a long time, the Court has summed up this scholarly idea in a colourful expression—that of the press the watchdog of democracy. The book attempts to clarify the legal regime by underscoring not only the particular positive obligations which States have towards journalist, but also by identifying the restrictive limitations acceptable in democratic regimes.

Before ending by wishing you a pleasant or instructive reading, the editors of the book would like to express their gratitude to all of the contributors, but also to Leila Bezdrob, a trainee at the ECtHR, for her help in formatting some of the contributions.

Strasbourg, France María Elósegui
Angers, France Alina Miron
Strasbourg, France Iulia Motoc

Contents

Part I Defending the Rule of Law in Emergency Regimes

The Rule of Law Principle in the Jurisprudence of the Court of Justice of the European Union 3
Dean Spielmann

How State of Emergency Affects Democracy: Fair Trial for Political Activists 21
Dmitry Dedov

La Défense de l'Etat de Droit en Période d'Exception : l'Exemple Récent de la France sous Etat d'Urgence 33
Peggy Ducoulombier

The Rule of Law and Property 49
Vladimíra Pejchalová Grünwaldová

Part II Challenges and Safeguards of the Independence of Justice

The Independence of Judiciary Within the Political Dimension 61
Armen Harutyunyan

The Independence of the Judiciary in the Jurisprudence of the European Court of Human Rights: The Case of *Baka v. Hungary* 69
María Elósegui

Judges' Freedom of Expression and Their Independence: An Ambivalent Relationship 89
Anja Seibert-Fohr

UN Actions and Programs in Safeguarding the Independence of Judges 111
Ida Caracciolo

Social Media Communication by Judges: Assessing Guidelines and New Challenges for Free Speech and Judicial Duties in the Light of the Convention 137
Jannika Jahn

Part III Freedom of Expression

The Strasbourg Case Law on the Limits of Free Speech: A Few Legal-Theoretical Issues 157
Krzysztof Wojtyczek

Freedom of Expression, Offences to Religion and Public Morals in Strasbourg Case Law 171
Javier Martínez-Torrón

The Responsibility of Internet Portal Providers for Readers' Comments. Argumentation and Balancing in the Case of *Delfi AS v. Estonia* 199
Robert Alexy

***Axel Springer AG v. Germany*, or: How to Perform Limited Review** 215
Martin Borowski

***Satakunnan Markkinapörssi Oy and Satamedia Oy v. Finland*, Conflict of Rights, and the Notion of Responsible Journalism** 229
Peggy Ducoulombier

The Right to Respect for a Journalist's Private Life: Combined Analysis of Articles 8 and 10 of the Convention. Case *Khadija Ismayilova v. Azerbaijan* 249
Beata Jurik

Freedom of Expression, Sliding-Scales, and Fake News 265
Alessio Sardo

Part I
Defending the Rule of Law in Emergency Regimes

The Rule of Law Principle in the Jurisprudence of the Court of Justice of the European Union

Dean Spielmann

Contents

1 Introduction 3
2 The Member States of the Union: The Rule of Law As a Tool Guaranteeing the Primacy of EU Law and Mutual Trust Between Member States 6
2.1 Rule of Law and Effective Judicial Protection 6
2.1.1 Preliminary References and Actions for Failure to Fulfil Obligations 6
2.1.2 Interim Measures 10
2.2 Rule of Law and Mutual Trust 11
3 The Rule of Law and the Common Foreign and Security Policy 14
4 Conclusion 18
References 19

1 Introduction

Understanding the role and function of the "rule of law" principle in the jurisprudence of the Court of Justice of the European Union ("CJEU" or "the Court") requires an analysis that is far from self-evident. Its complexity is twofold.

First, the very broad nature of this concept must be considered. In general, it refers to the pre-eminence of the law over political decisions, in the context of a

This contribution is based on a paper given to a colloquium under the title "International and European law and the Challenges to the Rule of Law", organised on 14 December 2018 at the European Court of Human Rights by Judge Iulia Motoc and Professor Alina Miron of Angers University. An initial version of the paper was published in French in *In Memoriam Stavros Tsakyrakis*, edited by Lucy Kiousopoulou, Marialena Tsirli and Panayotis Voyatzis (Nomiki Vivliothiki, Athens, 2020). The author wishes to thank for their precious help Panayotis Voyatzis and Linus Hoffmann, respectively *référendaire* and trainee in his *cabinet*. Any opinions expressed are personal to the author.

D. Spielmann (✉)
European Court of Human Rights, Strasbourg, France
e-mail: Dean.Spielmann@curia.europa.eu

M. Elósegui et al. (eds.), *The Rule of Law in Europe*,
https://doi.org/10.1007/978-3-030-56001-0_1

democratic society, in particular to guarantee that the majority in power is unable to oppress minorities. Aristotle reflected this idea in the following passage of *Politics*:

> And the rule of the law, it is argued, is preferable to that of any individual. On the same principle, even if it be better for certain individuals to govern, they should be made only guardians and ministers of the law.[1]

The rule of law principle is thus rendered in French as "*prééminence du droit*",[2] a term used almost synonymously with "*État de droit*" (itself closer to the German "*Rechtsstaat*").[3] At the same time, the concept of the rule of law has been given substance in the form of a large number of criteria, guarantees and individual rights, which all make up the framework in which any genuine democracy should function, in order to protect minorities from any oppression by the will of the majority. The key principles thus include legality, legal certainty, preventing abuse of power, equality before the law and access to justice.[4]

In addition, it must be said that the singular physiognomy of the legal order of the European Union (EU) and therefore of the CJEU, complicates the understanding of the rule of law in this context. Firstly, unlike the ECtHR, the CJEU is not an international court whose *sole purpose* is to protect fundamental rights—values which lie at the heart of the rule of law concept. Placed as it is at the top of a supranational and autonomous legal order, the CJEU is the ultimate interpreter of EU law, having the principal function of ensuring that its effectiveness and primacy are always upheld by the Member States. The Court's use of the rule of law concept must therefore always be placed in the specific context of the structure of the EU's legal order: the CJEU does not invoke the concept in the abstract. Recourse to the

---

[1]Aristotle, *Politics*, Book III, Part 16 (translated by Benjamin Jowett, Kitchener: Batoche Books, 1999).

[2]The European Court of Human Rights ("ECtHR") has played a major role in giving effect to the rule of law through its case-law. By way of example, in *Klass* it found that "[t]he rule of law implies, *inter alia*, that an interference by the executive authorities with an individual's rights should be subject to an effective control which should normally be assured by the judiciary, at least in the last resort, judicial control offering the best guarantees of independence, impartiality and a proper procedure" (ECtHR judgment, *Klass and Others v. Germany*, no. 5029/71, 6 September 1978, para. 55). See also Spielmann (2009), pp. 179–188; Nußberger (2017), p. 173.

[3]See Heuschling (2002), *passim.*

[4]The recent work of the Venice Commission for democracy through law (the "Venice Commission") is highly pertinent in this connection. See, esp., Venice Commission, Rule of Law Checklist, adopted at its 106th Plenary Session (Venice, 11–12 March 2016). While emphasising that the Checklist is "neither exhaustive nor final" and that "it could change over time" (para. 30), the Commission summarises the concept as follows: "the notion of the Rule of Law requires a system of certain and foreseeable law, where everyone has the right to be treated by all decision-makers with dignity, equality and rationality and in accordance with the laws, and to have the opportunity to challenge decisions before independent and impartial courts through fair procedures" (para. 15). It points out the need to "take into account the whole context, and avoid any mechanical application of specific elements of the checklist" (para. 27). The Venice Commission also stresses that the "[f]ull achievement of the Rule of Law remains an on-going task, even in the well-established democracies" (para. 29). See also Drzemczewski (2017), pp. 14–18.

rule of law always serves the purpose of guaranteeing the primacy of the EU legal order over the orders of the Member States, in respect of acts which implement the law of the Union.[5]

In addition, the rule of law is closely associated with the principle of mutual trust, which has been established by the CJEU as a constitutional principle of the EU. The CJEU has taken the view that mutual trust between Member States is based on the premiss of a unified constitutional area governed by the same values. As it expressly observed in Opinion 2/13 on accession of the European Union to the European Convention on Human Rights,[6] the law of the Union is a structured network of principles which are all based on

> the fundamental premiss that each Member State shares with all the other Member States, and recognises that they share with it, a set of common values on which the EU is founded, as stated in Article 2 TEU. That premiss implies and justifies the existence of mutual trust between the Member States that those values will be recognised and, therefore, that the law of the EU that implements them will be respected.[7]

The rule of law is thus a fundamental value which lays the foundation for a unified constitutional area being built by and between the Member States.

Secondly, the rule of law plays a prominent role in the implementation by the EU of its Common Foreign and Security Policy. More specifically, restrictive measures constitute an essential instrument of that policy. They are used by the EU in the context of an integrated and holistic action, seeking to bring about a change of policy or conduct on the part of the individuals or entities concerned, in order to promote the aims of the policy, including, pursuant to Article 21 of the Treaty on European Union ("TEU"), to "consolidate and support democracy, the rule of law, human rights and the principles of international law".

In the following lines, the role of the rule of law in the case-law of the CJEU will be examined under these two main heads. It will first be examined how the rule of law is deployed in the case-law to develop the primacy of EU law and mutual trust, principles which form the cornerstone of the scrutiny exercised by this Court. Attention will then be turned to the role of the rule of law in the EU's application of its Common Foreign and Security Policy, and in particular to the case-law on restrictive measures.

---

[5] See, in this connection, Spielmann and Voyatzis (2017), pp. 904–907.

[6] CJEU, Opinion 2/13 of 18 December 2014, EU:C:2014:2454.

[7] *Ibid.*, para. 168.

2 The Member States of the Union: The Rule of Law As a Tool Guaranteeing the Primacy of EU Law and Mutual Trust Between Member States

2.1 *Rule of Law and Effective Judicial Protection*

2.1.1 Preliminary References and Actions for Failure to Fulfil Obligations

In the wake of the Single European Act of 1986, which in particular ushered in a new European political cooperation, the Court's judgment in *Parti écologiste "Les Verts" v. European Parliament* described the European Economic Community as "a Community based on the rule of law,"[8] specifically referring to that fundamental principle of the organisation now known as the European Union. The principle has since been expressly enshrined in Article 2 TEU in 2009, providing that:

> The Union is founded on the values of respect for human dignity, freedom, democracy, equality, the rule of law and respect for human rights, including the rights of persons belonging to minorities.[9]

In addition, Article 7 TEU enables the Council to "determine the existence of a serious and persistent breach by a Member State of the values referred to in Article 2" and accordingly to restrict some of the State's rights under the treaties.[10] The responsibility for ensuring that the rule of law is upheld by the Member States lies with the CJEU under Article 19 TEU, which more generally entrusts the Court with the task of ensuring that the law is observed in the interpretation and application of the Treaties. As the Court has found, "Article 19 TEU... gives concrete expression to the value of the rule of law stated in Article 2 TEU."[11] The provisions of Articles 2 and 19 TEU thus represent the foundations of the Court's jurisdiction.

In the above-mentioned judgment, *Parti écologiste "Les Verts" v. European Parliament*, the Court explained that by the concept of a "Community based on the rule of law" it meant that:

---

[8]CJEU, *Parti écologiste "Les Verts" v. European Parliament*, Judgment of 23 April 1986, C-294/83, EU:C:1986:166, para. 23.

[9]Article 2 TEU. This Article is identical to Article I-2 of the 2004 Treaty Establishing a Constitution for Europe.

[10]Article 7 TEU. One of the possible sanctions is the suspension of the voting rights of the representative of the government of the Member State in the Council, but Article 7 provides that other rights arising from the treaties may be suspended, without expressly identifying them. The Council thus has a degree of freedom in deciding on the type of sanctions. To date the Council has not yet imposed sanctions on Member States under Article 7, and this can be explained in particular by the requirement of a unanimous vote to initiate that procedure.

[11]CJEU, *Associação Sindical dos Juízes Portugueses*, Judgment of 27 February 2018, C-64/16, EU:C:2018:117, para. 32.

> neither its Member States nor its institutions can avoid a review of the question whether the measures adopted by them are in conformity with the basic constitutional charter, the Treaty. In particular, in Articles 173 [Article 263 TFEU] and 184 [Article 277 TFEU], on the one hand, and in Article 177 [new Article 267 TFEU], on the other, the Treaty established a complete system of legal remedies and procedures designed to permit the Court of Justice to review the legality of measures adopted by the institutions.[12]

It is thus a Union based on the rule of law as a result of the primacy of EU law, which is binding on the Union's own institutions, but also on those of the Member States.

The primacy of EU law relies on the effective capacity of citizens to have their treaty rights upheld in the national courts and in the Union's own court. This is the thrust of Article 47 of the EU's Charter of Fundamental Rights (the "Charter") which asserts the principle of effective judicial protection. In the Court's own words, this provision requires

> that any person whose rights and freedoms guaranteed by EU law are violated should have the right to an effective remedy before a tribunal in compliance with the conditions laid down in that article.... [T]he very existence of effective judicial review designed to ensure compliance with provisions of EU law is of the essence of the rule of law.[13]

The concept of the rule of law is considered by the Court in each situation with a twofold imperative in mind: first the obligation for Member States to uphold the primacy of EU law and secondly the obligation to have a system of effective remedies in order to guarantee that primacy. The case of *Associação Sindical dos Juízes Portugueses (Tribunal de Contas)* provides a very pertinent example of this conception and of the way in which the Court associates the rule of law and the independence of national courts with the effective functioning of the preliminary reference mechanism under Article 267 TFEU. In that case the Portuguese Government had adopted measures to reduce the remuneration of the judges of the *Tribunal de Contas* (Court of Auditors) in the context of the budgetary austerity imposed on Portugal and the financial assistance granted by the EU. The question referred to the Court was whether or not the measures taken by the Portuguese Government were compatible with the principle of judicial independence.

The CJEU began by finding that to give concrete expression to the value of the rule of law as stated in Article 2 TEU, the responsibility for judicial review was entrusted not only to the Court of Justice but also to national courts and tribunals.[14] Consequently, it was for the Member States to ensure that EU law was applied and

---

[12]CJEU, *Parti écologiste "Les Verts" v European Parliament*, Judgment of 23 April 1986, C-294/83, EU:C:1986:166, para. 23. More generally, the General Court of the European Union, as an administrative court reviewing the acts of the EU's institutions, organs and bodies, plays a fundamental role in terms if effective judicial protection.

[13]CJEU, *Rosneft*, Judgment of 28 March 2017, C-72/15, EU:C:2017:236, para. 73.

[14]CJEU, *Associação Sindical dos Juízes Portugueses*, Judgment of 27 February 2018, C-64/16, EU:C:2018:117, para. 32.

upheld in their respective territories with a guarantee of effective judicial protection.[15] It explained that principle as:

> a general principle of EU law stemming from the constitutional traditions common to the Member States, which has been enshrined in Articles 6 and 13 of the European Convention for the Protection of Human Rights and Fundamental Freedoms,... and which is now reaffirmed by Article 47 of the Charter.[16]

The Court went on to find that:

> The very existence of effective judicial review designed to ensure compliance with EU law is of the essence of the rule of law
>
> and that:
>
> [i]t follows that every Member State must ensure that the bodies which, as 'courts or tribunals' within the meaning of EU law, come within its judicial system in the fields covered by that law, meet the requirements of effective judicial protection.[17]

As to the question whether the reduction in the remuneration of national judges could prove problematic in relation to the requirement of independence and protection against removal from office, the CJEU pointed out that the concept of independence presupposed, in particular, that the body concerned exercised its judicial functions wholly autonomously, without being subject to any hierarchical constraint or subordinated to any other body and without taking orders or instructions from any source whatsoever, and that it was thus protected against external interventions or pressure liable to impair the independent judgment of its members and to influence their decisions.[18] In that case it concluded that the principle of judicial independence did not preclude general salary-reduction measures, such as those at issue in the main proceedings, linked to requirements to eliminate an excessive budget deficit and to an EU financial assistance programme, from being applied to the members of the Tribunal de Contas.

The CJEU has followed the same approach in the more recent case of *Commission v Poland (Independence of the Supreme Court)* in which the Commission had

---

[15] *Ibid.*, paras. 34 and 35.

[16] *Ibid.*, para. 35.

[17] CJEU, *Associação Sindical dos Juízes Portugueses*, Judgment of 27 February 2018, C-64/16, EU:C:2018:117, paras. 36 and 37.

[18] *Ibid.*, paras. 44 and 45. See also *Wilson*, Judgment of 19 September 2006, C-506/04, EU:C:2006:587, para. 51, and of *Margarit Panicello*, Judgment of 16 February 2017, C-503/15, EU:C:2017:126, para. 37 and the case-law cited. It should also be observed that the primary aim of the principle of judicial independence is to guarantee the separation of powers. The objective of this principle is to protect the courts from pressure on the part of the executive. To ensure this structural independence, the Venice Commission has drawn attention to the need for "objective procedures and criteria for judicial appointments, tenure and discipline and removals", which must be enshrined in the Constitution rather than ordinary legislation (Venice Commission, Rule of Law Checklist, p. 33). In order to determine the level of independence of the judiciary, the ECtHR has found that "regard must be had, *inter alia*, to the manner of appointment of its members and their term of office, the existence of safeguards against outside pressures and the question whether it presents an appearance of independence" (ECtHR, *Incal v. Turkey*, Judgment of 9 June 1998, No. 22678/93, para. 65).

brought an action against the Republic of Poland for failure to fulfil its obligations under Article 258 TFEU, alleging that Poland had infringed the second sub-paragraph of Article 19(1) TEU, on the ground that the New Law on the Supreme Court (*Sąd Najwyższy*) provided that a measure lowering the retirement age of judges of the Supreme Court was to apply to judges in post who had been appointed to that court before the date on which that Law entered into force. The Commission argued that this constituted a breach of the principle of judicial independence and, in particular, of the principle of the irrevocability of judges.

In keeping with its findings in *Associação Sindical dos Juízes Portugueses (Tribunal de Contas),* the CJEU pointed out that Article 19 TEU

> [gave] concrete expression to the value of the rule of law affirmed in Article 2 TEU, [and] entrust[ed] the responsibility for ensuring the full application of EU law in all Member States and judicial protection of the rights of individuals under that law to national courts and tribunals and to the Court of Justice.[19]

Moreover, the Court took the view that the requirement that courts be independent, which was inherent in the task of adjudication, formed part of the essence of the right to effective judicial protection and the fundamental right to a fair trial, which was of cardinal importance as a guarantee that all the rights which individuals derived from EU law would be protected and that the values common to the Member States set out in Article 2 TEU, in particular the value of the rule of law, would be safeguarded.[20]

On the merits, the Court took the view that the measure lowering the retirement age of the judges of the Supreme Court who were in post at the time of the entry into force of the New Law concerning that court, together with a mechanism granting the President of the Republic of Poland the discretion to extend the period of judicial activity of judges of that court beyond the newly fixed retirement age, were capable of raising reasonable doubt in the minds of individuals as to the imperviousness of the Supreme Court to external factors and its neutrality with respect to the interests before it.[21]

These judgments demonstrate the willingness of the CJEU to assess domestic measures which might undermine the independence of the national judiciary, which is seen as an integral part of the EU judicature on the basis of the primary law of the Union. It can clearly be seen from the Court's reasoning that Article 19 TEU should apply—and thus should engage the duty to uphold the rule of law—in every case where a national court interprets or applies EU law.[22]

In addition, those two cases reveal that the Court's examination of questions concerning the upholding of the rule of law by the Member States may be carried out

---

[19]CJEU, *Commission v. Poland (Independence of the Supreme Court),* Judgment of 24 June 2019, C-619/18, EU:C:2019:531, para. 47.

[20]*Ibid.,* para. 58.

[21]*Ibid.,* para. 71–97.

[22]Bonelli and Claes (2018), p. 636.

both directly and indirectly.[23] Through the preliminary reference procedure, the Court enters into a direct dialogue with the domestic courts of the Member States; while through an action for failure to fulfil obligations, it is the Commission which brings allegations before the CJEU about any failure by a State to uphold the rule of law in connection with its obligations under EU law.

2.1.2 Interim Measures

The effective application of EU law, as a component of the rule of law, is also reflected in the CJEU's case-law on provisional measures. In this scenario, the effectiveness of the legal remedies exercised before the CJEU depends on the proper enforcement of judicial decisions.[24] The Court has thus established the possibility of complementing interim measures under Article 279 TFEU with pecuniary sanctions in cases of failure to fulfil obligations, even though this is not expressly provided for in the Article itself. In its Order of 20 November 2017 in a case concerning a measure prohibiting Poland from continuing clearance of an area of one of the best preserved natural forests in Europe, the Court decided as follows:

> The purpose of seeking to ensure that a Member State complies with interim measures adopted by the Court hearing an application for such measures by providing for the imposition of a periodic penalty payment in the event of non-compliance with those measures is to guarantee the effective application of EU law, such application being an essential component of the rule of law, a value enshrined in Article 2 TEU and on which the European Union is founded.[25]

It added:

> if the Court hearing an application for interim measures considers that the circumstances of the case require additional measures to be taken in order to ensure the effectiveness of the measures requested, it has power under Article 279 TFEU, *inter alia*, to provide for a

---

[23]K. Lenaerts, "La jurisprudence de la Cour de Justice de l'Union européenne concernant l'État de droit", speech delivered on 23 May 2019 during the visit of the diplomatic conference of the Grand Duchy of Luxembourg.

[24]In this context it is useful to refer to the case-law of the ECtHR. In *Hirschhorn v. Romania*, it took the view that "[the] right [to a court] would be illusory if a Contracting State's domestic legal system allowed a final, binding judicial decision to remain inoperative" (*Hirschhorn v. Romania* No. 29294/02, Judgment of 26 July 2002, para. 49). Similarly, in the *Hornsby* judgment, the ECtHR had already made a connection between the right of access to a court and the proper enforcement of judgments: it has found that "the right of access, that is the right to institute proceedings before courts in civil matters,... would be illusory if a Contracting State's domestic legal system allowed a final, binding judicial decision to remain inoperative to the detriment of one party. [This] would be likely to lead to situations incompatible with the principle of the rule of law which the Contracting States undertook to respect when they ratified the Convention" (*Hornsby v. Greece*, Judgment of 19 March 1997, *Reports* 1997-II, p. 510, para. 40).

[25]CJEU, *Commission v Poland (Forest of Białowieża),* Order of 20 November 2017, C-441/17 R, EU:C:2017:877, paras. 102 and 104. See Wennerås (2019), pp. 541–558.

> periodic penalty payment to be imposed on a Member State in the event that that Member State fails to comply with the interim measures ordered.[26]

Similarly, in the case cited above of *Commission v. Poland (Independence of the Supreme Court),* the Commission had asked the Court to order the Republic of Poland, pending the judgment on the merits, to adopt interim measures, such as the suspension of national legislation on the reduction in retirement age of Supreme Court judges. The Court's Vice-President ordered Poland to adopt the interim measures proposed by the Commission referring to the effective right of access to an independent tribunal:

> if the action for failure to fulfil an obligation is ultimately upheld, the immediate application of these provisions would be likely to cause irreparable damage to the fundamental right of access to an independent tribunal, as enshrined in Article 47, second paragraph, of the Charter. In those circumstances it is appropriate, in the interest of the proper administration of justice, to order the interim measures sought by the Commission, pending the adoption of the order terminating the proceedings for interim measures.[27]

Moreover, in the same case, under Article 23a of the Statute of the Court and Article 133 of the Rules of Procedure, the Commission had also requested that the case be determined pursuant to the expedited procedure, and the President granted that request with express reference to the rule of law:

> a response from the Court within a short time is such as, for the purposes of legal certainty, in the interest of both the European Union and the Member State concerned, to remove the uncertainties relating to fundamental questions of EU law and concerning in particular the existence of possible interference with certain fundamental rights safeguarded by EU law and the effects which the interpretation of that law is likely to have as regards the actual composition and working conditions of the supreme court of that Member State.[28]

2.2 *Rule of Law and Mutual Trust*

The principle of mutual trust does not consist in a vertical relationship between the EU's legal order and that of the Member States, but rather relates to a dialogue between the Member States when it comes to applying EU law. With the gradual extension of the EU's remit in areas which raise an increasing number of questions involving the protection of fundamental rights, for example in the area of freedom, security and justice, the principle of the rule of law, a foundational value of the EU, has seen more frequent reference in case-law.[29]

---

[26] *Ibid.*

[27] CJEU, *Commission v. Poland (Independence of the Supreme Court),* Order of the Vice-President of the Court of 19 October 2018, C-619/18 R, EU:C:2018:852 para. 25 (free translation). See also Zoll and Wortham (2019), pp. 920 ff.

[28] CJEU, *Commission v. Poland (Independence of the Supreme Court),* Order of the President of the Court of 15 November 2018, C-619/18, EU:C:2018:910, para. 25.

[29] Spielmann and Voyatzis (2017), p. 911; Platon (2019), pp. 16–22.

In the *Aranyosi and Căldăraru* judgment, the Court explained that this principle

> require[d], particularly with regard to the area of freedom, security and justice, each of those States, save in exceptional circumstances, to consider all the other Member States to be complying with EU law and particularly with the fundamental rights recognised by EU law.[30]

As Judge Marek Safjan notes, the principle of mutual trust and the area of freedom, security and justice are seriously undermined even if only one Member State fails to uphold the principle of the rule of law. The EU itself may thus be affected by legislative changes within the Member States which could be regarded by some as purely internal and not falling within the remit of the CJEU.[31]

This is what the Court emphasised in *Commission v. Poland (Independence of the Supreme Court)* referring to the common values adhered to by the States, when they become members of the EU, and to the mutual trust between the Member States in terms of respect for those values:

> As is apparent from Article 49 TEU, which provides the possibility for any European State to apply to become a member of the European Union, the European Union is composed of States which have freely and voluntarily committed themselves to the common values referred to in Article 2 TEU, which respect those values and which undertake to promote them, EU law being based on the fundamental premiss that each Member State shares with all the other Member States, and recognises that those Member States share with it, those same values (see, to that effect, judgment of 10 December 2018, *Wightman and Others*, C-621/18, EU:C:2018:999, paragraph 63 and the case-law cited).[32]
>
> That premiss both entails and justifies the existence of mutual trust between the Member States and, in particular, their courts that those values upon which the European Union is founded, including the rule of law, will be recognised, and therefore that the EU law that implements those values will be respected (see, to that effect, judgments of 27 February 2018, *Associação Sindical dos Juízes Portugueses*, C-64/16, EU:C:2018:117, paragraph 30, and of 25 July 2018, *Minister for Justice and Equality (Deficiencies in the system of justice)*, C-216/18 PPU, EU:C:2018:586, paragraph 35).[33]

It has already been observed that the Court may address questions concerning the level of protection of the rule of law in a Member State directly or indirectly: respectively, through the preliminary reference procedure or an action against a State for failure to fulfil its obligations. The case of *Minister for Justice and Equality* provides an additional variant, as it was a preliminary ruling requested by a national authority raising fundamental questions about the independence of the justice system in another Member State. More specifically, the High Court of Ireland had asked the CJEU whether a Member State could refuse to enforce a European arrest warrant issued by the issuing judicial authority (in this case, Polish) on account of

---

[30]CJEU, *Aranyosi and Căldăraru,* Judgment of 5 April 2016, C-404/15 and C-659/15 PPU, EU: C:2016:198, para. 78.

[31]Safjan (2018), pp. 552–560.

[32]CJEU, *Commission v. Poland (Independence of the Supreme Court),* Judgment of 24 June 2019, C-619/18, para. 42.

[33]*Ibid.*, para. 43.

shortcomings in the national justice system, in a context where the executing judicial authority had material, such as that set out in a reasoned proposal of the Commission adopted pursuant to Article 7(1) TEU, indicating that there was a real risk of a breach of the fundamental right to a fair trial.

The Court referred to the cardinal function of "mutual trust" in the EU's legal order:

> Both the principle of mutual trust between the Member States and the principle of mutual recognition, which is itself based on the mutual trust between the latter (see, to that effect, judgment of 10 August 2017, *Tupikas*, C-270/17 PPU, EU:C:2017:628, paragraph 49 and the case-law cited), are, in EU law, of fundamental importance given that they allow an area without internal borders to be created and maintained. More specifically, the principle of mutual trust requires, particularly as regards the area of freedom, security and justice, each of those States, save in exceptional circumstances, to consider all the other Member States to be complying with EU law and particularly with the fundamental rights recognised by EU law (judgment of 10 November 2016, *Poltorak*, C-452/16 PPU, EU:C:2016:858, paragraph 26 and the case-law cited).[34]

It also took the view that:

> the requirement of judicial independence forms part of the essence of the fundamental right to a fair trial, a right which is of cardinal importance as a guarantee that all the rights which individuals derive from EU law will be protected and that the values common to the Member States set out in Article 2 TEU, in particular the value of the rule of law, will be safeguarded.[35]

The Court followed the methodology from the *Aranyosi and Căldăraru* judgment, which required the domestic court to assess, on the basis of material that was "objective, reliable, specific and properly updated", whether there was a risk for the person in respect of whom the warrant had been issued. It found that where there was a real risk of a breach of that person's fundamental right to an independent tribunal and, therefore, of his or her fundamental right to a fair trial, the executing judicial authority could refrain from giving effect to the European arrest warrant.

The judgment in *Minister for Justice and Equality* is particularly important because it shows that respect for the rule of law is not examined by the CJEU through the preliminary reference mechanism solely according to a vertical configuration, in which the domestic court of a Member State refers questions about respect for the rule of law in its own State's legal system. Having regard to the principle of mutual trust and the imperative of cooperation between Member States in the implementation of migration or security policies, a State is thus also able, through a request for a preliminary ruling, to express doubts as to whether the rule of law is upheld in the legal system of another Member State. This possibility thus injects a significant element of horizontality into the structure of the EU's legal order, allowing for inter-State control, through the intermediary of the CJEU, as to the level of protection of the rule of law within the Union.

---

[34]CJEU, *Minister for Justice and Equality*, Judgment of 25 July 2018, C-216/18 PPU, EU:C:2018:586, para. 36. See Konstadinides (2019), pp. 743–770.

[35]*Ibid.*, para. 48.

3 The Rule of Law and the Common Foreign and Security Policy

The interpretation of the rule of law in the area of the Common Foreign and Security Policy (CFSP) takes place in a very different context from that of disputes concerning respect for the rule of law by the Member States. Article 3 § 5 TEU provides that "[i]n its relations with the wider world, the Union shall uphold and promote its values and interests and contribute to the protection of its citizens."[36]

As a fundamental value of the EU contained in Article 2 TEU, the value of the rule of law thus also guides its actions under the CFSP.[37] As has already been noted, the restrictive measures are among the tools available to the EU in order to promote the objectives of this policy, namely peace, democracy and respect for the rule of law, human rights and international law.[38] Such measures are always part of an overall policy approach involving political dialogue and complementary actions. The EU-imposed sanctions do not seek to punish but rather to bring about a change in policy or actions on the part of the country concerned or the targeted entities or individuals; thus always being directed at such policies and actions, the means used to achieve them and the individuals responsible for them.[39]

The most frequent restrictive measures are arms embargos, the freezing of assets, and visa or travel bans. An arms embargo usually covers the sale, supply and transport of the goods included in the EU common military list. Related technical and financial assistance is normally also included. An asset freeze concerns funds and economic resources owned or controlled by targeted individuals or entities. Lastly, persons targeted by a travel ban will be denied entry to the EU at the external borders. If visas are required for entering the EU, they will not be granted to persons subject to such restrictions on admissions.[40]

The recent and voluminous case-law on restrictive measures against individuals in the context of the CFSP has given the Court of Justice and General Court an opportunity to review the legality of the acts introducing such measures and to rule on the concept of the rule of law.[41] In those judgments the Court has asserted its competence to uphold the rule of law, whether directly or implicitly, when it decides

[36]See also Article 21 para. 1 TEU.

[37]EU General Court, *Mabrouk v Council of the European Union*, Judgment of 5 October 2017, T-175/15, EU:T:2017:694, para. 64; see also, for example: Article 2 (c) of the Common Position 98/350/CFSP, 25 May 1998, defined by the Council on the basis of Article J.2 of the Treaty on European Union, concerning human rights, democratic principles, the rule of law and good governance in Africa, OJ L158, 2 June 1998, p.1.

[38]Aumond (2011), pp. 365–385. On the general historical development, see Candela Soriano (2005) pp. 5–42.

[39]Council of the European Union, Factsheet on EU restrictive mesures, 29 April 2014, at: https://www.consilium.europa.eu/uedocs/cms_data/docs/pressdata/EN/foraff/135804.pdf.

[40]*Ibid.*

[41]See Bertrand (2015), pp. 555–577.

on the legality of intervention by the Council in the name of the rule of law. Thus, not only is the rule of law directly invoked, the Court also proceeds with an implicit review of the proper application of this concept by the Union's institutions. It may thus be argued that disputes over restrictive measures have allowed the Court of Justice and General Court to clarify and "standardise" the concept in concrete and varied situations.

Accordingly, in the *Klyuyev* case, in the context of restrictive measures related to the situation in Ukraine following the suppression of demonstrations on Independence Square in Kiev in February 2014, the name of the applicant, former Head of Administration of the Ukrainian President, had been added to an asset-freezing list on the grounds that he was a "[p]erson subject to criminal proceedings in Ukraine to investigate crimes in connection with the embezzlement of Ukrainian State funds and their illegal transfer outside Ukraine".

The General Court expressly referred to the content of the rule of law when it examined the legality of the applicant's inclusion on that list:

> The case-law of the Court and of the European Court of Human Rights, and the work of the Council of Europe, by means of the European Commission for Democracy through Law, provide a non-exhaustive list of principles and standards which may fall within the concept of the rule of law. That list includes: the principles of legality and legal certainty and the prohibition of arbitrary exercise of power by the executive; independent and impartial courts; effective judicial review, extending to respect for fundamental rights and equality before the law (see, in that regard, the rule of law checklist adopted by the European Commission for Democracy through Law at its 106th Plenary Session (Venice, 11-12 March 2016)). Further, in the context of European Union external action, a number of legal instruments include reference to the fight against corruption as a principle within the scope of the concept of the rule of law (see, for example, Regulation (EC) No 1638/2006 of the European Parliament and of the Council of 24 October 2006 laying down general provisions establishing a European Neighbourhood and Partnership Instrument (OJ 2006 L 310, p. 1)).[42]

The General Court further stated that "it [was] evident, as acknowledged by the Council in its written pleadings, that the restrictive measures against the applicant [had been] adopted solely with the objective of consolidating and supporting the rule of law in Ukraine."[43] And it went on to find as follows:

> Before it can be established that a misappropriation of public funds is capable of justifying European Union action under the CFSP, based on the objective of consolidating and supporting the rule of law, it is, at the very least, necessary that the disputed acts should be such as to undermine the legal and institutional foundations of the country concerned.[44]

The General Court concluded that the misappropriation of certain State funds or public assets might be

[42]EU General Court, *Klyuyev v. Council of the European Union*, Judgment of 15 September 2016, T-340/14, EU:T:2016:496, para. 88.

[43]*Ibid.*, para. 83.

[44]*Ibid.*, para. 89.

> such as to undermine the legal and institutional foundations of Ukraine, and in particular the principles of legality, prohibition of arbitrary exercise of power by the executive, effective judicial review and equality before the law and, ultimately, to undermine respect for the rule of law in that country.[45]

In the *Yanukovych* case, concerning the freezing of funds imposed on the former President of Ukraine, the General Court found:

> it is evident, first, that the listing criterion relies, as far as the applicant is concerned, on offences constituting ‘misappropriation of public funds’ and, second, that that criterion exists within a legal framework that is clearly circumscribed by Decision 2014/119 and the pursuit of the relevant objective of the EU Treaty to which it refers, stated in recital (2) of that decision, namely that of consolidating and supporting the rule of law in Ukraine.[46]

However, the Court did not then give *carte blanche* to the Council to impose restrictive measures on an individual in the name of the rule of law in any situation of misappropriation of public funds:

> [W]hile it is conceivable that certain conduct pertaining to acts classifiable as misappropriation of public funds may be capable of undermining the rule of law, it cannot be accepted that any act classifiable as misappropriation of public funds, committed in a third country, justifies European Union action with the objective of consolidating and supporting the rule of law in that country, using the powers of the Union under the CFSP. Before it can be established that a misappropriation of public funds is capable of justifying European Union action under the CFSP, based on the objective of consolidating and supporting the rule of law, it is, at the very least, necessary that the disputed acts should be such as to undermine the legal and institutional foundations of the country concerned.[47]

In the *Mabrouk* case, in the context of the restrictive measures taken by the Council of the European Union against certain individuals and entities following political developments in Tunisia in December 2010 and January 2011, the General Court, after declaring that compliance with the rule of law was “required of all actions of the European Union, including actions under the CFSP,”[48] took the view that the principle that proceedings should be concluded within a reasonable time formed part of the right to a fair trial, which was safeguarded by the provisions of a number of binding instruments of international law.[49] On that basis, the General Court found as follows:

> [I]t cannot be ruled out that, where there is objective, reliable, specific and consistent evidence such as to raise legitimate questions concerning observance of an applicant’s right to have his case heard within a reasonable time in the context of the ongoing judicial

---

[45] *Ibid.*, para. 91.

[46] EU General Court, *Yanukovych v. Council of the European Union*, judgment of 15 September 2016, T-346/14, EU:T:2016:497, para. 96.

[47] *Ibid.*, para. 99.

[48] EU General Court, *Mabrouk v. Council of the European Union*, Judgment of 5 October 2017, T-175/15, ECLI:EU:T:2017:694, para. 64.

[49] *Ibid.*, para. 64.

investigation concerning him, which serves as the basis for the freezing of his assets in the European Union, the Council may be required to carry out the necessary verifications.[50]

Moreover, in the *Azarov* case, concerning restrictive measures imposed on the Prime Minister of Ukraine in 2014, the Court took a further step forward by confirming the Council's responsibility to verify that the decisions of third States on which it based the inclusion of a person or entity on a list of persons whose assets were to be frozen had been taken in accordance with that person's procedural rights, thus securing the safeguards which lay at the heart of the rule of law:

> [T]he requirement for the Council to verify that the decisions of third States on which it bases the entry of a person or entity on a list of persons or entities whose assets are to be frozen have been taken in accordance with those rights is designed to ensure that they are included on that list only on a sufficiently solid factual basis and, thus, to protect the persons or entities concerned (see, to that effect, judgment of 26 July 2017, *Council* v *LTTE*, C-599/14 P, EU:C:2017:583, paragraph 26).
>
> The Court has also held that the Council must refer, if only briefly, in the statement of reasons relating to a decision to include a person or entity on a list of persons or entities whose assets are to be frozen and to subsequent decisions, to the reasons why it considers the decision of the third State on which it intends to rely to have been adopted in accordance with the rights of the defence and the right to effective judicial protection (see, to that effect, judgment of 26 July 2017, *Council* v *LTTE*, C-599/14 P, EU:C:2017:583, paragraphs 31 and 33).
>
> Thus it is for the Council, in order to fulfil its obligation to state reasons, to show, in the decision imposing the restrictive measures, that it has verified that the decision of the third State on which those measures are based was taken in accordance with those rights (see, to that effect, judgment of 26 July 2017, *Council* v *LTTE*, C-599/14 P, EU:C:2017:583, paragraph 37).[51]

This recent case-law, strengthening the requirements of the protection of fundamental rights in third States, shows that compliance with the rule of law is relevant at three different levels in the area of restrictive measures. *Firstly*, the European Union, through its political action in promoting the rule of law, imposes restrictive measures. *Secondly*, the European Union is itself subject to the rule of law in terms of having to provide a sophisticated recourse system, including before its administrative court, namely the General Court. *Thirdly*—and it is here that the *Azarov* case

[50] *Ibid.*, para. 65.

[51] CJEU, *Azarov v. Council of the European Union*, Judgment of 19 December 2018, C-530/17 P, EU:C:2018:1031, paras. 28- 30. See also EU General Court *Yanukovych v. Council of the European Union*, Judgment of 11 July 2019, T-244/16 and T-285/17, EU:T:2019:502; *Yanukovych v. Council of the European Union*, T-245/16 and T-286/17, EU:T:2019:505; *Klymenko v. Council of the European Union*, T-274/18, EU:T:2019:509; *Arbuzov v. Council of the European Union*, Judgment of 11 July 2019, T-284/18, EU:T:2019:511; *Pshonka v. Council of the European Union*, T-285/18, EU:T:2019:512; *Klyuyev v. Council of the European Union*, Judgment of 11 July 2019, T-305/18, EU:T:2019:506. The General Court, applying the jurisprudential principles from the Court of Justice's judgment in *Azarov v. Council of the European Union*, took the view that the reasoning of Council acts extending restrictive measures did not include the slightest reference to any verification of compliance with such rights.

contained a novel solution—the EU will henceforth be required to conduct an in-depth review of respect for fundamental rights by a third State, i.e. one which receives the political support of the Union.

Lastly, it should be observed that, in the area of restrictive measures, one can also see the very close relationship between the principles of democracy, human rights and the rule of law in the European jurisprudence. The General Court and the Court of Justice very often rely on the three principles put together, thus showing that they are indissociable.[52] The EU courts in fact regularly refer to the European Convention on Human Rights, thus demonstrating a willingness to foster a trend of convergence with the ECtHR as regards the "standardisation" of the rule of law through its case-law.[53]

4 Conclusion

Against the backdrop of an economic, political and migratory crisis, which is still ongoing in a number of European Union Member States, and which in some States has turned into a real crisis of democracy itself, the CJEU's role as guarantor of the rule of law, involving its two branches (the Court of Justice and the General Court), has become considerably more important. The principle of the rule of law is not only at the heart of the constitutional debate among the Member States, it is also one of the constitutional foundations of the Union, thus empowering the European judiciary to take the lead in interpreting the concept. To use the words of one commentator, "with the EU judicature's involvement in consolidating and safeguarding principles such as legality, legal certainty and proportionality, the rule of law is being reinforced dynamically throughout Europe."[54]

It must be said that the emergence of the rule of law in the Court's case-law should not be a surprise. The rule of law is the substance without which law in general would be a hollow shell. By defending the rule of law and ruling on cases which go to the heart of the Member States' constitutional arrangements, the Court is merely defending the vision of a liberal democracy, of which—let's not forget—the Court is itself the offspring. In this context its case-law converges with that of the European Court of Human Rights. However, as has already been observed, the route that the CJEU is obliged to follow, in order to arrive at the point where it is able to hand down decisions on the rule of law in a given State, is longer, more complex and

---

[52]See, for example, EU General Court, *CW v. Council of the European Union*, Judgment of 30 June 2016, T-224/14, EU:T:2016:375, para. 69; *Tomana and others v. Council and Commission*, Judgment of 28 July 2016, C-330/15 P, EU:C:2016:601, para. 48; *Rotenberg v. Council of the European Union*, Judgment of 30 November 2016, T-720/14, EU:T:2016:689, para. 176.

[53]See, for example, *Yanukovych v. Council of the European Union*, T-346/14, para. 97; *Klyuyev v. Council of the European Union*, T-340/14, para. 87.

[54]Mede (2018), p. 589 [our translation].

more convoluted than the path open to the ECtHR, whose natural remit is to interpret fundamental rights, or even the rule of law.

That being said, when confronted with "illiberal democracies", urgent action may be called for.[55] The Court has a duty to intervene, since the majority principle alone does not guarantee the existence of a just society in which fundamental rights are secured. The current political situation in a fair number of western democracies reminds us that the tyranny of the majority is not a distant and improbable dystopia. It is precisely for this reason that the rule of law is not just one value among others but the fundamental principle which underpins the very existence of the European Union as a community based on the rule of law. It is only with a system of effective remedies, in the context of a State governed meaningfully by the rule of law, that it is possible to guarantee the fundamental rights of all citizens, and not only those of the political majority. As rightly emphasised by S. Carrera and P. Bárd, "[i]f EU institutions do not respond meaningfully to rule of law backsliding and systematic violations of EU values, this will weaken the very fabric of the EU legal order and challenge the nature of the European integration project as we know it."[56]

At the same time the Court must remain vigilant in its use of Article 2 TEU, since the rule of law concept, on account of its considerable variability and uncertain parameters, has the potential to become an ultra-powerful tool. There is a great temptation to use the concept exponentially, as it enables the Court to deal with very different situations and to intervene in constitutional debates—debates which hitherto tended to fall within the exclusive remit of the Member States. Excessive reliance on the concept could be seen as an over-intrusive means of interference in national issues, and this would only be fodder for the populist movements with their strong rhetoric of national sovereignty—movements which are precisely the source of all our concerns. The Court must certainly be careful not to open this Pandora's Box.

References

Aumond F (2011) La participation de l'Union européenne à la préservation de la paix et de la sécurité internationales par l'adoption de mesures restrictives. In: Lamblin-Gourdin A-S, Mondielli E (eds) Le droit des relations extérieures de l'Union européenne après le traité de Lisbonne. Bruylant, Brussels, pp 365–385

Bertrand B (2015) La particularité du contrôle juridictionnel des mesures restrictives : Les considérations impérieuses touchant à la sûreté ou à la conduite des relations internationales de l'Union et des États membres. Revue Trimestrielle de Droit Européen:555–577

Bonelli M, Claes M (2018) Judicial serendipity: how Portuguese judges came to the rescue of the Polish judiciary. Eur Const Law Rev 14(3):622–643

[55] See, among many others, Mounk (2018); Waelbroeck and Oliver (2017), pp. 299–342; Labayle (2018), pp. 485–496.

[56] Carrera and Bárd (2018).

Candela Soriano M (2005) Analyse de l'évolution de l'action extérieure de l'UE dans le domaine des droits de l'homme, de la démocratie et de l'État de droit. Revue de la Faculté de Liège:5–42

Carrera S, Bárd P (2018) The European Parliament vote on Article 7 TEU against the Hungarian government: too late, too little, too political?. CEPS Commentaries. www.ceps.eu/publications/european-parliament-vote-article-7-teu-against-hungarian-government-too-late-too-little. Accessed 15 Mar 2020

Drzemczewski A (2017) Le Conseil de l'Europe et l'État de droit : à propos de la liste des critères de l'État de droit élaborée par la Commission de Venise. Revue Universelle des Droits de l'Homme 23:14–18

Heuschling L (2002) État de droit, Rechtsstaat, Rule of Law. Dalloz, Paris, pp 1–739

Konstadinides T (2019) Judicial independence and the rule of law in the context of non-execution of a European Arrest Warrant. Common Market Law Rev 56(3):743–769

Labayle H (2018) Winter is coming : l'État de droit devant les institutions de l'Union. Remarques sur les crises polonaises et hongroises. Revue des affaires européennes 3:485–496

Mede L (2018) L'État de droit à l'épreuve de l'intégration européenne. Revue de l'Union européenne 622:589–597

Mounk Y (2018) The people vs. democracy: why our freedom is in danger and how to save it. Harvard University Press, Cambridge

Nußberger A (2017) The European Court of Human Rights and rule of law – a tale of hopes and disillusions. In: Zubik M (ed) Essays in Honour of Professor Leszek Garlicki. Wydawnictwo Sejmowe, Warsaw, pp 162–173

Platon S (2019) Confiance mutuelle et crise de l'État de droit dans l'Union européenne. L'observateur de Bruxelles 115:16–22

Safjan M (2018) Domestic infringements of the rule of law as a European Union problem. Osteuropa Recht 64:552–560

Spielmann D (2009) La jurisprudence de la Cour européenne des droits de l'homme sur l'État de droit. In: Société Française pour le Droit International (ed) Colloque de Bruxelles, L'État de droit en droit international. Pedone, Paris, pp 179–188

Spielmann D, Voyatzis P (2017) L'étendue du contrôle du respect des droits fondamentaux à l'aune de l'expérience juridique comparée. Revue trimestrielle des droits de l'homme 112:897–952

Waelbroeck M, Oliver P (2017) La crise de l'État de droit dans l'Union européenne : que faire ? Cahiers de droit européen:299–342

Wennerås P (2019) Saving a forest and the rule of law: Commission v. Poland. Common Market Law Rev 56(2):541–558

Zoll F, Wortham L (2019) Judicial independence and accountability: withstanding political stress in Poland. Fordham Int Law J 42:875–948

Dean Spielmann is a Judge and Chamber President of the General Court of the European Union and Former President of the European Court of Human Rights. He was a lawyer at the Luxembourg Bar (1989–2004) and a Judge (2004–2015), Section President (2011–2012), Vice-President (2012), then President (2012–2015), of the European Court of Human Rights. Since 13 April 2016, he has been a Judge of the General Court of the European Union and a Chamber President of the General Court of the European Union since 30 September 2019. He was also associate lecturer at the University of Luxembourg (1996–2006) and lecturer at the University of Nancy 2 (1997–2009); member of the Grand-Ducal Institute, Moral and Political Science Section (since 2002); Honorary Fellow, Fitzwilliam College, University of Cambridge (since 2013); Honorary Bencher of Gray's Inn, London (since 2013); Honorary Professor, University College London (since 2013); member of scientific committees of several legal journals; author of numerous publications.

How State of Emergency Affects Democracy: Fair Trial for Political Activists

Dmitry Dedov

Contents

1 Anatomy of the Political Power ... 21
2 Emergency Situations: No Explicit Definition ... 24
3 Social Unrest and Lack of Fair Trial ... 25
4 Conclusion ... 31
References ... 31

1 Anatomy of the Political Power

In fact, we know very little about democracy. I was surprised by opinions of some experts who said that Venezuela is the most democratic country[1] or others who claimed that the economic development in China was achieved without any democratic reforms. In the United States the democrats cannot accept that they lost their power after Donald Trump was elected the President and they constantly challenge his legitimacy. The style of governance was quite different in Russia from a liberal approach in 2001 to a conservative one in 2012 and afterwards. In the long term and a broader perspective, the authoritarian sovereign power dominated initially before the shift to liberal governance commenced.[2] Today the situation has changed again: the democratic institutions can for some time demonstrate anti-democratic measures or reactions. It depends on the circumstances relating to the retention of power.

As you know, the key element of the liberal regime is a freedom, whereas the key element of the authoritarian regime is coercion. The European Court of Human Rights ("the Court") dealt with the conflict of those approaches in many cases. The

[1] Swift (2010).

[2] On this subject, see, for example, Foucault (1979, 2007); Dean (2010).

D. Dedov (✉)
European Court of Human Rights, Strasbourg, France
e-mail: dmitry.dedov@echr.coe.int

M. Elósegui et al. (eds.), *The Rule of Law in Europe*,
https://doi.org/10.1007/978-3-030-56001-0_2

conflict is based on different values. I would like to demonstrate such a conflict based on the *Khoroshenko* case,[3] concerning the limitation of family visits for long term prisoners. The Russian Constitutional Court defended the position that the limitation of the family visits is a part of the criminal punishment motivated by the isolation of prisoners, whereas the Court stated that the deprivation of liberty itself constitutes a criminal punishment without any other elements of coercion. Obviously, both courts elaborated their positions while being oriented towards different political regimes.

Today, there are elements of both regimes in modern states. The problem arises with disproportionate dominance of those elements in the spheres of dependency, decision making, ideology, monopoly, subordination. Equally, we can presume that the democratic institutions exist in each of the countries mentioned above, but their influence on decision making process could be different due to the imbalance between the State and the civil society.

Indeed, without certain theoretical remarks it would be difficult to explain the sources of the emergency regime during the conflict situation between the power and the opposition. In my view, there is a difference between the traditional power and the democratic power. Traditionally the political power was associated with the privileges to impose taxes and to spend the public funds and other resources controlled by State officials and not by private individuals. The power is naturally interested to maintain the order and security in the society, but finally in the interest of the power. So, the diagnosis is clear: people should serve to the power, and the power controls the society.

In the democratic society the nature of political power has been changed completely: now the power should serve the people. This brings power under control of the society, including the public expenditure (effectiveness, necessity, information) and the decision-making process. The power becomes responsible before the society.

In addition to traditional functions, the democratic power is concentrating on the improvement of the quality of life of people. This creates the basis for new functions: to identify the problems, to find appropriate measures, to response to the general demand for sustainable development. These new democratic functions change the political landscape in favour of the competition. Those who better understand the problems and who can propose the most adequate ways to respond to the modern challenges, will win at the elections and get the right to allocate the public funds (I prefer not to use the word "power" here). According to the rules of the political competition, the dominant position (to enjoy the power in the traditional sense of this term) will come to an end, sooner or later, which means temporary character of the political power.

Here are, in my view, the main features of the democratic power: responsibility, control by the society (via independent mass media and other watchdogs), necessity and proportionality of measures, the new function to improve the quality of life,

[3]ECtHR, *Khoroshenko v. Russia*, Judgment of 30 June 2015, No. 41418/04.

effective democratic institutions. All these features are antagonists of the traditional power. Therefore, any conclusion about the abuse of the power is in fact a reaction on hostile measures against any of the above features of the democratic ruling. The abuse of power is always a demonstration of the traditionalist way of ruling.

For example, in the real competition the power usually does not see the problems arising from its policy. This explains the victory of far right "populists" in Europe or the defeat of democrats in the United States of America. Donald Trump revealed the deficiencies of the economic policy which the democrats justified and defended saying that there will always be losers in the new global economy. These are examples of the victory of democracy and its basic value—political pluralism and free choice of voters.

The anti-democratic regime pursues another purpose—to keep the power and the control over natural resources. This makes the regime less flexible, demonstrating almost no reaction to the needs of the society. It listens to the opposition and it tries to minimize the dissatisfaction of people with the authorities with only one purpose—to keep the power. When the opposition indicates a certain problem and the authorities start to deal with the problem, making public declarations, but the measures usually do not become effective, because there is no priority to resolve the problem.

Obviously, in the anti-democratic regime, the power tries to reduce the effectiveness of the political competition and democratic institutions. When we speak about the abuse of power or about the abuse of the dominant position, the democratic institutions again become under attack. Any abuse of the power, occasional or systematic, is incompatible with democratic values and principles.

The democratic institutions are always the first victims. Independent judges could be deprived of their mandates after their retiring age was reduced or their court was reorganized. Independent members of the parliament could be deprived of the opportunity to take their seats due to miscalculation of votes. Independent journalists are fired or criminally persecuted under false charges. Opposition leaders and their supporters are arrested during peaceful gatherings. The power will remain unchanged if the political competition is distorted and the democratic institutions are weak and artificial.

Weak institutions are usually justified by traditional functions of the authorities: their dependence and ineffectiveness should be compensated by the stability and security—traditional functions. This concept contradicts to the democratic values because it does not leave any space to the freedom. Public order and security should always be subordinated to democratic institutions including the freedom of expression and the right to a peaceful assembly. Public order and security should serve to the fundamental rights and freedoms. In contrary, we would face with the abuse of power and anti-democratic regime. Since the law enforcement and security authorities serve to them, paradoxically they are interested in violence, so they start to provoke the violence to justify the distortion of democratic values and institutions. This is how the state of emergency could be provoked by the power itself.

2 Emergency Situations: No Explicit Definition

A state of emergency is an extreme situation when the life and security of the whole nation is under threat. It happens during a natural disaster, mass disorder, civil unrest, or armed conflict. The list of such situations could be continued to include poverty, hunger, terrorist attacks, mass violations of fundamental rights and freedoms, in other words, they include everything that leads to the destabilization of normal life and goes against progress and sustainable development. Such situations are not rare. In contrary, they happen every day in different parts of the world. I will concentrate on emergency situations when the people demonstrate that they are not satisfied with the State authorities when they disregard the fundamental rights and freedoms. That is the domain of democracy, the sphere of social life, and it is interesting to see how and why the state of emergency could arise since the normal and peaceful life of the society is ignored by power.

There are so many problems around such situations. States of emergency can be used as a rationale or pretext for suspending rights and freedoms guaranteed under a country's constitution or basic law. The authorities should declare such state under domestic law or its international obligations. In reality States prefer not to do that in order to be free to apply any measures without restrictions, especially in the domain of democracy. It is noteworthy that the derogation in time of emergence governed by Article 15 of the European Convention for the protection of fundamental rights and freedoms requires that a High Contracting Party may take measures derogating from its obligations under this Convention to the extent strictly required by the exigencies of the situation, provided that such measures are not inconsistent with its other obligations under international law.

Therefore, the measures of the State should be limited in all aspects of proportionality (strictly necessary, limited in time and consistent with other obligations to pursue core rights and freedoms). The national authorities usually try to avoid any restrictions by refusing to recognize any application of Article 15. In the case of *Hassan*, the respondent Government submitted to the Court that "the inclusion of Article 15 in the Convention in no sense indicated that, in time of war or public emergency threatening the life of the nation, obligations under the Convention would at all times be interpreted in exactly the same way as in peacetime."[4] The Court echoed to the Government:

> Article 15 of the Convention provides that '[i]n time of war or other public emergency threatening the life of the nation', a Contracting State may take measures derogating from certain of its obligations under the Convention, including Article 5. In the present case, the United Kingdom did not purport to derogate under Article 15 from any of its obligations under Article 5.[5]

[4]ECtHR, *Hassan v. the United Kingdom*, Judgment of 16 September 2014, No. 29750/09, para. 90.
[5]*Ibid.*, para. 98.

The derogation from fundamental rights and freedoms is always sensitive, and the derogation from democracy is even dangerous for the reputation of those in power. The level of unpredictability and enforceability of the social unrest is high, especially in the new undeveloped democracies where the democratic institutions are so weak that they are not able to strike the balance between the branches of power and to protect democratic values and to promote the democratic manner of a decision making. The main task of the State is to predict an emergency situation. The object of research could be easily simplified and analyzed if it resulted from a natural disaster or enemies who are motivated to launch the war. It is much more difficult to assess when it is related to social unrest, when the power has to face with a lot of actors: opposition activists, journalists, bloggers, intellectuals, and political parties, social and professional groups. They all are free to criticize the Government. The criticism becomes annoying when the freedom of expression goes far beyond the limits of peaceful discussion; it becomes shocking, provocative, reaching general dissatisfaction and hate speech.

It is always difficult to agree with the opinions of others or to recognize your own mistakes. It requires a lot of training or a special state of mind to achieve such ability for any individual, especially for those who have the power. The situation becomes worse when people go out on the streets to demonstrate their dissatisfaction. Even in case of a peaceful demonstration, the authorities might believe that mass disorder is inevitable.

Lack of dialogue, absence of tradition of a rational public debate, lack of transparency, monopolization and centralization of power, superficial perception of the situation in the society, temptation to keep the power—all these factors create fear and trigger disproportional reaction on the criticism. Inadequate reaction to social demands could trigger an inadequate assessment of any threat to the stability of state and power which almost automatically leads to measures to enhance power or to avoid losing the power belonging to a political stratum. The emergency situation is considered as a threat to the power, not to the society, and it triggers the power to take measures against any criticism. As a result, the power itself creates a threat to the rule of law and finally to serious and mass violations of human rights, including the freedom of expression, the right to liberty and the right to a fair trial.

3 Social Unrest and Lack of Fair Trial

There are many examples of social unrest provoked by the authorities themselves. Recent *coup d'Etat* in Turkey provoked mass persecution and lustration of intellectuals and thousands of complaints to the national Constitutional Court and to the Court. There was a lustration of thousands government officials in Ukraine after the revolution in 2014. In Russia during the so-called Bolotnaya manifestation ("March of millions") the police provoked clashes with demonstrators which lead to mass arrests and imprisonment for violence against police. The social unrest was provoked by a ruling party who had organized the recalculation of votes and falsification of the election results during the parliamentary elections in 2011. The ECtHR has received hundreds of repetitive applications similar to those already examined by the Court in the judgments of *Frumkin v. Russia, Davydov and Others v. Russia and Navalnyy v. Russia.*[6]

Other examples concern the lustration of judges in Hungary, Ukraine and Poland,[7] through the lowering of the retirement age for judges, arbitrary dismissal of judges and presidents of the courts before expiry of their terms of office, unconditionally and without proper reasoning or any right of appeal. They also relate to unlimited and discretionary power of the executive power and of members of parliament to extend or to early terminate the performance of duties of judges.

The scenario is typical in all cases: abuse of power—protests—persecution of activists and supporters accompanied by unlawful arrests—arbitrary criminal persecution and lustration without fair trial. The above-mentioned cases demonstrate that the power uses the following anti-fair trial technics in such emergency situations which are also typical in nature:

- no right to complain to the authorised independent body to protect the rights under Articles 10 and 11 of the Convention; only political parties can lodge the complaint about violation of election laws during parliamentary elections; individual voters are excluded;
- no competent body to examine the complaints (electoral commissions; prosecutors; domestic courts);
- no effective remedies, administrative or criminal;[8]
- arbitrary criminal conviction of the bloggers and journalists regardless of any damages;
- witness statements of co-accused who agreed to "cooperate" with investigators;[9]
- no consideration of complaints in substance by the national court;
- refusal to consider complaints on merits;
- the national court did not accept any evidence proposed by the defense (violation of equality of arms);

---

[6]ECtHR, *Frumkin v. Russia*, Judgment of 5 January 2016, No. 74568/12; *Davydov and Others v. Russia*, Judgment of 30 May 2017, No. 75947/11; and *Navalnyy v. Russia* [GC], Judgment of 15 November 2018, Nos. 29580/12 and 4 others.

[7]ECtHR, *Baka v. Hungary*, Judgment of 23 June 2016, No. 20261/12; *Oleksandr Volkov v. Ukraine*, Judgment of 9 Jan. 2013, No. 21722/11; CJEU, *European Commission v. Poland*, Judgment of 24 June 2019, C-619/18; and ECtHR, *Broda and Bojara v. Poland,* Communicated cases No. 26691/18 and 27367/18.

[8]ECtHR, *Davydov and Others v. Russia*, Judgment of 30 May 2017, No. 75947/11, paras. 335–337.

[9]ECtHR, *Navalnyy and Ofitserov v. Russia*, Judgment of 23 February 2016, Nos. 46632/13 and 28671/14 (the "*Kirovles*" case); *Navalnyy v. Russia*, Judgment of 17 October 2017, No. 101/15 (the "*Yves Rocher*" case), *Ilgar Mammadov v. Azerbaijan*, Judgment of 22 May 2014, No. 15172/13; *Ilgar Mammadov v. Azerbaijan (No. 2)*, Judgment of 16 November 2017, No. 919/15; *Rasul Jafarov v. Azerbaijan*, Judgment of 17 March 2016, No. 69981/14; *Yagublu v. Azerbaijan*, Judgment of 5 November 2015, No. 31709/13.

- arbitrary detention which make impossible to perform the duties of a member of the parliament and a leader of the opposition party.[10]

The Court reminded in the *Navalnyy* judgment that "political pluralism. . .forms part of 'effective political democracy' governed by 'the rule of law'. . . [I]n the context of Articles 10 and 11, pluralism, tolerance and broadmindedness are hallmarks of a 'democratic society'. (. . .) Although individual interests must on occasion be subordinated to those of a group, democracy does not simply mean that the views of a majority must always prevail: a balance must be achieved which ensures the fair and proper treatment of people from minorities and avoids abuse of a dominant position."[11]

As the Court reiterated in the *Karácsony* judgment, the democracy constitutes a fundamental element of the "European public order", and that the rights guaranteed under Article 3 of Protocol No. 1 are crucial to establishing and maintaining the foundations of an effective and meaningful democracy governed by the rule of law. The Court therefore prefers to protect effective and meaningful democracy against any derogation from it through arbitrariness and distortion of democratic institutions or values regardless of whether there was an abuse of dominant position. The abuse of power could be added in terms of violation of Article 5 of the Convention when the power means the coercion which should be applied in a strictly limited manner. The power itself does not have any recognizable interest.

In the *Davydov* case, the applicants alleged that the organisation and conduct of elections for two legislative bodies (the regional Legislative Assembly of St Petersburg and the national State Duma) breached Article 3 of Protocol No. 1 to the Convention, in several polling stations in St Petersburg in December 2011. They had taken part in the elections in different capacities: all of them were registered voters; some of them were candidates while others were members of electoral commissions or observers. They contended, during the proceedings before the ECtHR, as well as in their various unsuccessful challenges before various national authorities, that there had been serious irregularities in the procedure in which votes had been recounted, which resulted in more votes being assigned following the recounts to the ruling party and its candidates to the detriment of the opposition parties and their candidates. They alleged that the domestic authorities had failed to ensure an effective review of their complaints.

The Court partially satisfied their complaints.[12] It confirmed that the right of individual voters to appeal against the results of voting may be subject to reasonable

---

[10]ECtHR, *Selahattin Demirtaş v. Turkey (No. 2)*, Judgment of 20 November 2018, No. 14305/17.

[11]*Navalnyy v. Russia* [GC], Judgment of 15 Nov. 2018, Nos. 29580/12 and 4 others, para. 175. See also, among other authorities, ECtHR, *Young, James and Webster v. the United Kingdom*, Judgment of 13 August 1981, para. 63, Series A no. 44; *Gorzelik and Others v. Poland* [GC], Judgment of 17 Feb. 2004, No. 44158/98, para. 90; *Leyla Şahin v. Turkey* [GC], Judgment of 10 Nov. 2005, No. 44774/98, para. 108; and *Karácsony and Others v. Hungary* [GC], Judgment of 15 May 2016, Nos. 42461/13 and 44357/13, para. 147.

[12]*Davydov and Others v. Russia*, Judgment of 30 May 2017, No. 75947/11.

limitations in the domestic legal order. Nevertheless, where serious irregularities in the process of counting and tabulation of votes can lead to a gross distortion of the voters' intentions, such complaints should receive an effective examination by the domestic authorities. A failure to ensure the effective examination of such complaints would constitute a violation of individuals' right to free elections guaranteed under Article 3 of Protocol No. 1 to the Convention, in its active and passive aspects. The suspicion of unfairness was strongly supported by absence of any procedure for recounting, large extent of the recounting, the unclear reasons for ordering it, the lack of transparency and the breaches of procedural guarantees in carrying it out, as well as the results whereby the ruling party gained large numbers of votes.

Similar complaints were raised before different State authorities which could, at least potentially, be regarded as effective and accessible remedies. In particular, the courts were empowered to consider complaints from participants in the electoral process, to obtain and examine relevant evidence and, if the irregularities were sufficiently serious, to overturn the decisions of the relevant electoral commissions. However, none of the avenues employed by the applicants afforded them a review which would provide sufficient guarantees against arbitrariness. The Court has found a violation of Article 3 of Protocol No. 1 to the Convention in so far as the applicants have been denied an effective examination of their complaints of serious irregularities in the procedure in which the votes were recounted.[13]

According to the circumstances of the *Kirovles* case,[14] in January 2009 the Governor of the region of Kirov invited Mr. Navalnyy to be a volunteer consultant on enhancing the transparency of the region's property management. One of his projects was to help steer the region's loss-making timber industry out of crisis. He discussed the financial and logistical problems of the State enterprise Kirovles, whose commercial activities consisted, in particular, of timber processing, with its director, X. On Mr. Navalnyy's suggestion, X agreed that the company join forces with a timber trading company to bring in customers and curtail the Kirovles timber mills' practice of direct sales for cash bypassing Kirovles' accounts. Contacted by Mr. Navalnyy, Mr. Ofitserov set up a timber trading company, VLK. In April 2009 Kirovles, represented by X, concluded a framework contract with VLK, represented by Mr. Ofitserov. In particular, the contract provided for non-exclusive sales by Kirovles to VLK, which would then sell goods on to customers at 7% commission.

During 2010, Mr. Navalnyy pursued an anti-corruption campaign and published a number of articles and documents exposing high ranking officials' involvement in large-scale fraud. In particular, in one article published in November 2010, he claimed that at least four billion US dollars of State funds had been misappropriated during the construction of the East Siberia-Pacific Ocean oil pipeline. In December 2010 the Kirov Regional department of the Investigative Committee of the Prosecutor's Office (later replaced by the Investigative Committee of the Russian

[13] *Ibid.*

[14] ECtHR, *Navalnyy and Ofitserov v. Russia*, Judgment of 23 February 2016, Nos. 46632/13 and 28671/14 (the "*Kirovles*" case).

Federation—"the Investigative Committee") opened an inquiry on suspicion that the applicants had defrauded Kirovles by inducing its director to enter into a loss-making transaction. Initially the Investigative Committee decided in three consecutive decisions not to open a criminal investigation against them for lack of *corpus delicti*—that is, for lack of a criminal act to be investigated—but in May 2011 a criminal investigation was opened in their respect on suspicion of deception and abuse of trust of the Kirovles director.

After a number of witnesses had been questioned—including X and several former employees of Kirovles—and Kirovles' and VLK's accounts had been examined, the investigators found that there was no case against the applicants. In April 2012 the Investigative Committee closed the criminal investigation. However, the Committee subsequently reversed its decision. On 30 July 2012 the Investigative Committee opened a criminal investigation against X—on suspicion that he had conspired with unknown individuals to dissipate Kirovles' assets through VLK—which was joined with the criminal case against the applicants. Subsequently the three men were charged with conspiring to dissipate Kirovles' assets.

In September 2012 the Deputy Prosecutor General granted X's request to conclude a plea-bargaining agreement and to have his criminal case examined in accelerated proceedings. As a condition, X undertook to provide the investigation with information about "Mr. Ofitserov and Mr. Navalnyy's involvement in the misappropriation [of assets]" and "their roles in the commission of the crime". In October 2012 the case against X was disjoined from the applicants' case. Subsequently Mr. Navalnyy complained that the plea-bargaining agreement had breached his procedural rights and the right to fair trial because the charge against X had been directly relevant to the applicants' case.

In those circumstances it would have been essential for safeguards to be in place to ensure that decisions taken in the proceedings against X would not undermine the fairness of the subsequent proceedings against the applicants. However, the Court came to the conclusion that the two basic requirements for guaranteeing the fairness of proceedings, when co-accused were being tried in separate sets of proceedings, had not been fulfilled. Notably, contrary to the courts' obligation to refrain from any statements that might have had a prejudicial effect on the pending proceedings, the trial court convicting X had worded its judgment of December 2012 in respect of X in a manner that no doubt could remain as regards the applicants' identities or their involvement in the crime of which X was convicted. It had expressed its findings in terms which could not be defined as anything but prejudicial.[15]

Second, contrary to the courts' obligation not to treat as *res judicata*—that is, a matter already judged—any facts admitted in a case to which the applicants had not been party, the circumstances established in the judgment against X had in effect had the force of *res judicata*. The Russian Government had argued that in the applicants' case the trial court had been obliged to examine all evidence and witnesses and to base its assessment exclusively on the material and testimony presented at the

[15] *Ibid.*, paras. 96–104.

hearing. However, the Court considered that the trial court had had an obvious interest in remaining concordant, because any conflicting findings made in related cases could have undermined the validity of both judgments issued by the same court. The risk of issuing contradictory judgments was a factor that had discouraged the judges from finding out the truth and had diminished their capacity to administer justice.[16]

Similarly, X's conviction with the use of plea-bargaining and accelerated proceedings had compromised his competence as a witness in the applicants' case. His conviction had been based on the version of events formulated by the prosecution and the accused in the plea-bargaining process, and it had not been required that that account be verified or corroborated by other evidence. Standing later as a witness, X had been compelled to repeat his statements made as an accused during plea-bargaining. Moreover, by allowing X's earlier statements to be read out at the trial before the defense could cross-examine him as a witness, the court could give an independent observer the impression that it had encouraged the witness to maintain a particular version of the events. The Court stated that it was essential for safeguards to be in place to ensure that the procedural steps and decisions taken in the proceedings against X would not undermine the fairness of the hearing in the subsequent proceedings against the applicants. This was particularly so, given that the applicants were legally precluded from any form of participation in the disjoined proceedings, as they had not been granted any status which would have allowed them to challenge the decisions and findings made therein.[17]

The most obvious guarantee to be secured when co-accused are tried in separate sets of proceedings is the courts' obligation to refrain from any statements that may have a prejudicial effect on the pending proceedings, even if they are not binding. If the nature of the charges makes it unavoidable for the involvement of third parties to be established in one set of proceedings and those findings would be consequential on the assessment of the legal responsibility of the third parties tried separately, this should be considered as a serious obstacle for disjoining the cases. Any decision to examine cases with such strong factual ties in separate criminal proceedings must be based on a careful assessment of all countervailing interests, and the co-accused must be given an opportunity to object to the cases being separated. Therefore, the risk of issuing contradictory judgments was a factor that discouraged the judges from finding out the truth and diminished their capacity to administer justice, thus causing irreparable damage to the court's independence, impartiality and, more generally, its ability to ensure a fair hearing.

In the *Ilgar Mammadov* cases the Court was informed that the applicant, political blogger and journalist, heavily criticised the authorities during the civil riots in the country. The Court has concluded that the applicant was arrested and charged without a reasonable suspicion and subsequently was deprived of a fair trial. Therefore, the Court found violations of Articles 5, 6 and 18. It stated that the

[16]*Ibid.*, paras. 105–107.

[17]*Ibid.*, para. 109.

applicant's rights to a reasoned judgment and to examine witnesses were infringed. His conviction was based on flawed or misrepresented evidence and his objections in this respect were inadequately addressed. The evidence favourable to the applicant was systematically dismissed in an inadequately reasoned or manifestly unreasonable manner.[18]

4 Conclusion

It seems that the world has changed completely. The international community did not pay much attention to the derogation from democracy some time ago. Today the situation is different: any anti-democratic attempts to save or to enhance the power, to abuse the power, to apply the power in the arbitrary manner or to undermine the independency of the democratic institutions like judiciary, mass media, NGO and other "watchdogs"—may lead to a peaceful (and furious at the same time) protest or even to civil unrest if the measure would contradict to the well comprehended and widespread values of the democratic society. The democracy is now better and better understood by the society (ordinary people) as one of the most important elements of social life. The democracy becomes an important element of the quality of life because it includes the respect of dignity of the person as a member of the society. Any large-scale anti-democratic measures become so sensitive that they put the society in danger and they lead to the situation of emergency.

References

Dean M (2010) Governmentality. Power and rule in modern society. SAGE, London
Foucault M (1979) On governmentality. Ideol Conscious 6:5–22
Foucault M (2007) Security, territory, population. Palgrave, London
Swift R (2010) The no-nonsense guide to democracy. New Internationalist Publications Ltd, Oxford

Dmitry Dedov is a judge of the European Court of human rights elected in respect of the Russian Federation. Before that he was a professor at the Moscow State University for 18 years and the judge of the Russian Supreme Commercial Court for five years. The subject of his academic research relates to the general principles of law.

[18] *Ilgar Mammadov (No. 2)*, Judgment of 16 November 2017, No. 919/15, para. 237.

La Défense de l'Etat de Droit en Période d'Exception : l'Exemple Récent de la France sous Etat d'Urgence

Peggy Ducoulombier

Contents

1 Introduction ... 33
2 La Défense par le Parlement : une Défense plus que Limitée ... 36
3 La Défense par les Juges : une Défense Contestée ... 39
4 Conclusion ... 46
Références ... 48

1 Introduction

L'état d'urgence français, régi par la loi du 3 avril 1955, implique une augmentation des pouvoirs de police des autorités administratives.[1] Il n'entraîne pas une suspension généralisée des droits et libertés mais la mise en œuvre, dans certains domaines, de règles dérogeant aux règles habituelles et entraînant des restrictions plus importantes aux droits et libertés. Par conséquent, on peut estimer qu'il ne remet

[1]L'état d'urgence a permis le recours à 12 types de mesures de police administrative selon le rapport parlementaire de contrôle d'un an d'état d'urgence: restrictions à la liberté d'aller et venir, perquisitions administratives, assignations à résidence, remises d'armes, réquisitions de personnes et de biens, fermetures de lieux de réunions ; interdictions de cortèges ; contrôles d'identité et fouilles de bagages et de véhicules; blocages de sites internet; dissolutions d'associations. Voir D. Raimbourg et J.-F. Poisson, *Rapport sur le contrôle parlementaire de l'état d'urgence*, Doc. AN, n° 3784, 25 mai 2016, p. 8. En raison d'un régime insuffisamment protecteur certains articles de la loi ont été abrogés par les décisions du Conseil constitutionnel, comme par exemple ceux relatifs à l'établissement des zones de protection et de sécurité (CC, déc. n° 2017-684 QPC du 11 janvier 2018, *Associations La cabane juridique / Legal Shelter et autre* [Zones de protection ou de sécurité dans le cadre de l'état d'urgence]) ainsi qu'aux contrôle d'identité et fouilles des véhicules (CC, déc. n° 2017-677 QPC du 1er décembre 2017, *Ligue des droits de l'Homme* [Contrôles d'identité, fouilles de bagages et visites de véhicules dans le cadre de l'état d'urgence]).

P. Ducoulombier (✉)
University of Strasbourg, Strasbourg, France
e-mail: ducoulombier@unistra.fr

M. Elósegui et al. (eds.), *The Rule of Law in Europe*,
https://doi.org/10.1007/978-3-030-56001-0_3

pas en cause l'Etat de droit même si un débat doctrinal existe sur cette question.[2] Toutefois, afin que l'Etat de droit soit préservé encore faut-il que le régime mis en place ne porte pas atteinte à sa substance. En effet, selon l'article 16 de la Déclaration des Droits de l'Homme et du Citoyen de 1789, "toute société dans laquelle la garantie des droits n'est pas assurée, ni la séparation des pouvoirs déterminée, n'a point de Constitution." Les mesures applicables grâce au régime de l'état d'urgence doivent ainsi restées proportionnées à l'objectif légitime poursuivi. Par ailleurs, l'article 15 de la Convention européenne des droits de l'Homme (ci-après la Convention ou la CEDH), qui a été utilisé par la France, implique qu'elles ne peuvent déroger à la protection habituelle des libertés que dans la stricte mesure où la situation l'exige et uniquement pour les droits qui ne sont pas considérés comme indérogeables.[3] Par ailleurs, la séparation des pouvoirs doit être garantie afin notamment de permettre la réalisation d'un contrôle efficace sur ces mesures restrictives des libertés. Or, celle-ci n'est pas remise en cause par la loi de 1955 contrairement à ce qui peut exister dans d'autres régimes d'exception.[4]

Malgré cette garantie, l'épreuve que la France a traversée a constitué un véritable "stress test" de la force de l'Etat de droit dans notre pays. En effet, jamais l'état d'urgence n'avait été si longuement appliqué, plus de 700 jours.[5] Cette durée inédite a ainsi donné lieu à l'application de très nombreuses mesures,[6] ayant elles-mêmes

---

[2]Voir, par exemple, A. Roblot-Troizier (2016), pp. 426–426.

[3]Article 15 CEDH: "1. En cas de guerre ou en cas d'autre danger public menaçant la vie de la nation, toute Haute Partie contractante peut prendre des mesures dérogeant aux obligations prévues par la présente Convention, dans la stricte mesure où la situation l'exige et à la condition que ces mesures ne soient pas en contradiction avec les autres obligations découlant du droit international. 2. La disposition précédente n'autorise aucune dérogation à l'article 2, sauf pour le cas de décès résultant d'actes licites de guerre, et aux articles 3, 4 (paragraphe 1) et 7. [...]". A cette liste, il faut ajouter l'interdiction de la peine de mort en vertu des protocoles 6 et 13 et le principe du *ne bis in idem* en vertu de l'article du 4 protocole 7.

[4]Qu'il s'agisse d'une comparaison interne (par exemple, par rapport à l'article 16 de la Constitution) ou avec des régimes étrangers (par exemple, la Turquie). Par ailleurs, concernant la répartition des compétences entre pouvoir civil et militaire, l'article 12 de la loi de 1955 a été abrogé par la loi du 20 novembre 2015 afin de mettre un terme à la possibilité de recourir à la compétence des tribunaux militaires pour le jugement de certains crimes et délits, distinguant ainsi mieux état d'urgence et état de siège.

[5]L'état d'urgence a été prorogé à 6 reprises, par les lois du 20 novembre 2015, 19 février 2016, 20 mai 2016, 21 juillet 2016, 19 décembre 2016 et 11 juillet 2017. Sur la question du temps et de l'état d'urgence, voir D. Baranger (2016), pp. 447–454.

[6]Selon les chiffres du Ministère de l'Intérieur (Sortie de l'état d'urgence, un bilan et des chiffres-clés, disponible à https://www.interieur.gouv.fr/Espace-presse/Dossiers-de-presse/Sortie-de-l-etat-d-urgence-un-bilan-et-des-chiffres-cles, dernière consultation le 31/08/2019), on recense environ 6000 mesures (4444 perquisitions administratives – les plus nombreuses – , 754 assignations à résidence, 6 remises d'armes, 59 zones de protection, 29 fermeture des lieux de culte et autres). Ne sont pas mentionnées les interdictions de séjour ou les contrôles d'identité par exemple. Toutefois, le contrôle parlementaire permet de comptabiliser 656 interdictions de séjour et 5229 contrôles d'identité et fouilles de véhicules. L'état d'urgence aurait ainsi donné lieu à plus de 10000 mesures administratives.

suscité un contentieux non négligeable quoique quantitativement limité.[7] Par ailleurs, la prorogation de cet état d'urgence par le Parlement lui a également donné l'occasion de modifier (de "moderniser" selon lui) son régime.[8] La durée d'application de l'état d'urgence, alors que cet état devrait être temporaire par définition,[9] ainsi que sa redéfinition, ont suscité de nombreuses critiques. Les critiques sur la durée de l'état d'urgence sont peut-être les plus sérieuses, particulièrement si on les lie à la question de la transformation du temporaire en permanent, de l'exceptionnel en commun. On aboutirait ainsi à une banalisation de ce régime d'exception. Il n'est donc pas inutile d'examiner les mécanismes qui ont été à l'œuvre pendant cette période pour protéger les libertés individuelles des excès de pouvoir des autorités. La question posée est de savoir si la séparation des pouvoirs a permis au Parlement et au Juge d'exercer la fonction de contrôle nécessaire à la préservation de l'Etat de droit en période de trouble. Si la définition d'un juste équilibre entre liberté et sécurité par le législateur est une condition nécessaire de la défense de l'Etat de droit, elle n'est pas suffisante et celui-ci impose des mécanismes de contrôle efficaces et qui sont dépendants de la culture démocratique prévalant dans le pays.[10] Or, le bilan est contrasté qu'il s'agisse du rôle joué par le Parlement comme par le Juge.

---

[7]Selon S. Hennette-Vauchez, seul 10% des mesures prises aurait fait l'objet d'un contrôle contentieux (S. Hennette-Vauchez (2018), p. 59). Par exemple, selon le contrôle parlementaire, sur la période allant du 14 novembre au 18 juillet 2016, sur 3594 perquisitions administratives, on recense 70 contentieux de l'annulation et 22 contentieux indemnitaire; sur 554 assignations à résidence, on dénombre 210 référés-liberté et 14 recours pour excès de pouvoir. Seules 15 mesures ont été annulées. Sur 540 interdictions de séjour, on dénombre 25 recours (dont 13 suspensions). Ces chiffres démontrent une importante variation dans le contentieux des différentes mesures, qui s'explique notamment par le fait que le référé-liberté ou le référé-suspension ne peuvent être utilisés contre les perquisitions administratives.

[8]A cet égard, il convient de relever que la loi a été modifiée afin de supprimer le pouvoir des autorités administratives de prendre toutes mesures pour assurer le contrôle de la presse et des publications de toute nature ainsi que celui des émissions radiophoniques, des projections cinématographiques et des représentations théâtrales.

[9]La Cour européenne des droits de l'Homme ne semble pas lier l'application de l'article 15 au caractère temporaire de la menace ni des mesures prises. Voir CEDH [GC], *A et autres c. Royaume-Uni*, 19 février 2018, No. 3455/05.

[10]Comme met en garde V. Champeil-Desplats: "Il se pourrait donc bien que l'expérience de l'état d'urgence soit un des laboratoires testant le degré jusqu'auquel les sociétés des États de droit contemporains sont capables d'accepter des limitations aux droits et libertés au nom d'exigences sécuritaires". Voir V. Champeil-Desplats (2018), p. 33.

2 La Défense par le Parlement : une Défense plus que Limitée

La première des protections offerte par le régime français est que l'état d'urgence, décrété en conseil des ministres, ne peut être prorogé au-delà de 12 jours sans le vote d'une loi et donc l'intervention du Parlement, représentant de la Nation et garant des libertés publiques.[11]

Il faut souligner que cette disposition est le résultat d'une modification de la loi en 1960. Initialement, il revenait au Parlement de déclencher l'état d'urgence. Ainsi est-il passé de décideur à contrôleur. Mais on peut estimer que les circonstances qui président au déclenchement de cet état justifient une réactivité plus grande et le rôle de décideur du pouvoir exécutif n'apparaît pas illégitime, même si d'autres Etats confient au Parlement le rôle d'accepter le déclenchement de l'état d'urgence.[12]

Toutefois, l'intervention du Parlement a-t-elle permis d'encadrer, de contenir les atteintes aux droits et libertés ? Au regard du fait que la France est restée du 14 novembre 2015 au 1er novembre 2017 en état d'urgence, le constat est que l'intervention du Parlement ne semble pas constituer une protection particulièrement forte contre un éventuel excès dans l'application de ce régime. On peut notamment s'inquiéter de ce que la loi ne prévoit pas de durée maximale d'application de cet état d'urgence, ce qui peut retarder de manière importante la consultation du Parlement, ni de limite au nombre de renouvellements successifs. La durée de l'état d'urgence a fait l'objet d'importantes critiques de la société civile, du monde universitaire, des instances de protection des droits de l'Homme nationales et internationales, mais également du Conseil d'Etat dans son rôle de conseil du gouvernement, soulignant que la protection de l'Etat de droit nécessite que la mesure demeure temporaire.[13]

L'absence de limite dans le temps de cet état d'urgence pose d'autant plus question que le contrôle du juge administratif sur ce point est minimal, laissant au Président de la République un important pouvoir d'appréciation quant à la décision de mettre un terme par anticipation à l'état d'urgence comme la loi l'y autorise.[14] Les

---

[11]Art. 3 de la loi de 1955. Le Conseil constitutionnel a estimé qu'aucune disposition constitutionnelle ne s'opposait à ce que le Parlement se voit confier le rôle de réaliser la conciliation de la sauvegarde de l'ordre public et des libertés dans le cadre d'un régime d'urgence. Voir CC, déc. n° 85-187 DC du 25 janvier 1985, *Loi relative à l'état d'urgence en Nouvelle-Calédonie*. Pour autant, en période d'état d'urgence et contrairement à la période d'application de l'article 16, le Parlement ne se réunit pas de plein droit.

[12]Voir P. Türk (2016), pp. 455–465.

[13]Le Conseil d'Etat a rappelé, dans son avis rendu le 18 juillet 2016 sur le projet de loi de prorogation de l'état d'urgence, que "même dans les circonstances résultant de l'attentat commis à Nice, [. . .] les renouvellements de l'état d'urgence ne sauraient se succéder indéfiniment et que l'état d'urgence doit demeurer temporaire. Les menaces durables ou permanentes doivent être traitées, dans le cadre de l'Etat de droit, par des moyens permanents [. . .]".

[14]CE, ord., *Ligue des droits de l'Homme et autres*, 27 janvier 2016, n° 396220: "Considérant qu'il résulte de l'instruction que le péril imminent résultant d'atteintes graves à l'ordre public qui a conduit, à la suite d'attentats d'une nature et d'une gravité exceptionnelles, à déclarer l'état

réalités politiques expliquent que le contrôle parlementaire ait été limité. On peut toutefois espérer qu'un abus clair dans la volonté de proroger l'état d'urgence, alors que les circonstances ayant présidé à son déclenchement n'existeraient plus, serait sanctionné par un refus du Parlement.[15] On peut estimer que la situation française n'a pas caractérisé une telle hypothèse, même si des débats ont eu lieu sur la nécessité de renouveler cet état d'urgence, dès lors que l'on était passé d'une réaction face à la commission d'attentats à la lutte contre une menace dont l'existence est malheureusement permanente. Les divergences de vues sur la nécessité de maintenir l'état d'urgence révèlent ainsi la question centrale du recours à des mesures censées être exceptionnelles pour lutter contre une menace permanente.

Ce que la situation française a également mis en lumière c'est que la révision constitutionnelle n'est pas interdite en période d'état d'urgence.[16] Le projet avorté de constitutionnalisation de l'état d'urgence couplé aux débats sur la déchéance de

---

d'urgence n'a pas disparu [...] ; que les mesures qui ont été arrêtées, sous le contrôle du juge administratif, à qui il appartient de s'assurer qu'elles sont adaptées, nécessaires et proportionnées à la finalité qu'elles poursuivent, ont permis d'atteindre des résultats significatifs ; que, si leur utilisation est moindre que dans les jours qui ont suivi la déclaration de l'état d'urgence, il résulte tant de l'instruction écrite que des débats au cours de l'audience publique qu'en se fondant, dans l'exercice du pouvoir d'appréciation étendu qui est le sien, pour s'abstenir de prendre un décret mettant fin à l'état d'urgence, sur ce que leur prolongation, leur renouvellement ou le prononcé d'autres mesures contribuent à prévenir le péril imminent auquel le pays est exposé, sans qu'il soit aujourd'hui possible de distinguer entre les mesures prévues par les articles 6, 8 et 11 de la loi du 3 avril 1955, le Président de la République n'a pas porté une atteinte grave et manifestement illégale à une liberté fondamentale qui justifierait que le juge des référés fasse usage des pouvoirs qu'il tient de l'article L. 521-2 du code de justice administrative [...]". Voir également CE, ord., *Allouache*, 9 décembre 2005, n° 287777: "Considérant qu'ainsi qu'il a été précédemment indiqué, l'article 3 de la loi prévoit cependant qu'il peut être mis fin à l'état d'urgence "par décret en conseil des ministres" avant l'expiration du délai de trois mois; que le silence de la loi sur les conditions de mise en œuvre de la faculté ainsi reconnue au Président de la République ne saurait être interprété, eu égard à la circonstance qu'un régime de pouvoirs exceptionnels a des effets qui dans un Etat de droit sont par nature limités dans le temps et dans l'espace, comme faisant échapper ses modalités de mise en œuvre à tout contrôle de la part du juge de la légalité; Considérant en l'espèce, qu'en raison notamment des conditions dans lesquelles se sont développées les violences urbaines à partir du 27 octobre 2005, de la soudaineté de leur propagation, de l'éventualité de leur recrudescence à l'occasion des rassemblements sur la voie publique lors des fêtes de fin d'année et de l'impératif de prévention inhérent à tout régime de police administrative, il ne saurait être valablement soutenu qu'en décidant de ne pas mettre fin dès à présent à la déclaration de l'état d'urgence, le chef de l'Etat aurait, dans l'exercice du pouvoir d'appréciation étendu qui est le sien, pris une décision qui serait entachée d'une illégalité manifeste, alors même que, comme le soulignent les requérants, les circonstances qui ont justifié la déclaration d'urgence, ont sensiblement évolué".

[15]Il semble moins probable que la résistance aille jusqu'au vote d'une motion de censure, du moins initialement. A cet égard, il faut souligner que l'article 4 de la loi prévoit que la loi de prorogation de l'état d'urgence est caduque à l'issue d'un délai de 15 jours suivant la dissolution de l'Assemblée nationale, au cas où le Président déciderait, face au refus de proroger une nouvelle fois l'état d'urgence, de recourir à l'article 12 de la Constitution.

[16]Voir l'article 89 al. 4 de la Constitution de 1958 qui mentionne uniquement qu'"[a]ucune procédure de révision ne peut être engagée ou poursuivie lorsqu'il est porté atteinte à l'intégrité du territoire".

nationalité[17] (qui pourtant ne nous semblait pas nécessiter de révision constitutionnelle) démontre qu'une telle possibilité n'est pas pertinente, la sérénité nécessaire aux discussions relatives aux révisions constitutionnelles n'étant pas réunie et le temps du Parlement détourné alors qu'il devrait se concentrer sur ses autres missions, dont le contrôle de l'état d'urgence. Toutefois, cette constitutionnalisation aurait pu améliorer l'équilibre entre sécurité et liberté en rendant plus difficile les modifications du régime.[18]

Outre le fait que le Parlement a toujours consenti à la prorogation, il a accompagné sans grande résistance les projets du gouvernement sur la modification de la loi de 1955 et donc des mesures pouvant être prises dans le cadre de l'état d'urgence. Il apparaît même que plusieurs mesures restrictives des libertés résultent du débat parlementaire.[19] Par ailleurs, l'intervention du Parlement ne s'est pas limitée à la mise à jour du texte de 1955 mais il a également saisi cette occasion pour modifier d'autres textes de droit commun afin de renforcer les mesures pénales ou administratives de lutte contre le terrorisme.[20]

Toutefois, il convient de relever qu'à l'occasion de l'adoption de la loi du 20 novembre 2015, première loi de prorogation, le Parlement a étendu son pouvoir de contrôle,[21] en ajoutant un article 4-1 qui énonce, dans sa rédaction issue de la loi du 21 juillet 2016 que

> L'Assemblée nationale et le Sénat sont informés sans délai des mesures prises par le gouvernement pendant l'état d'urgence. Les autorités administratives leur transmettent sans délai copie de tous les actes qu'elles prennent en application de la présente loi. Ils peuvent requérir toute information complémentaire dans le cadre du contrôle et de l'évaluation de ces mesures.

Ce contrôle a donné lieu à des auditions (souvent à huis-clos pour des raisons de sécurité), des communiqués de presse, rapports et autres publications sur les mesures

---

[17]Projet de loi constitutionnelle de protection de la Nation n° 3381, enregistré à la présidence de l'Assemblée nationale le 23 décembre 2015.

[18]On peut regretter que, l'état d'urgence une fois levé, le débat sur l'intérêt et les modalités d'une éventuelle constitutionnalisation disparaisse.

[19]Ainsi, le projet de loi de prorogation de l'état d'urgence de 2015 mentionnait une durée maximale de l'assignation à résidence de 8 heures. Le débat parlementaire a amené à augmenter cette durée à 12 heures au maximum. Comparez l'article 4 du projet de loi avec l'article 4 de la loi du 20 novembre 2015, modifiant l'article 6 de la loi de 1955. Dossier législatif disponible à https://www.legifrance.gouv.fr/affichLoiPubliee.do?idDocument=JORFDOLE000031493228&type=general&legislature=14%E2%80%8E, dernière consultation le 31/08/2019. Pour une analyse éclairante du renforcement du régime de l'état d'urgence par le Parlement, voir S. Hennette-Vauchez (2018), pp. 59–74.

[20]La loi du 20 juillet 2016 est ainsi une loi de prorogation de l'état d'urgence mais également une loi qui porte mesures de renforcement de la lutte contre le terrorisme et qui, à cet effet, modifie le code pénal ainsi que le code de la sécurité intérieure. On peut également citer le vote de la loi du 3 juin 2016 renforçant la lutte contre le crime organisé, le terrorisme et leur financement, et améliorant l'efficacité et les garanties de la procédure pénale.

[21]Démontrant que le rôle du Parlement relève aujourd'hui plus du contrôle-information que du contrôle-sanction.

prises dans le cadre de l'état d'urgence, constituant une source précieuse d'information[22] et qui ont, par exemple, souligné la perte de sens de la prorogation de l'état d'urgence face à la diminution du recours aux mesures qu'il autorise, ou le faible taux de poursuite judiciaire en lien avec le terrorisme réalisée à leur suite.[23]

Toutefois, il est un pouvoir dont le Parlement n'a pas fait usage, c'est celui de déférer au contrôle du Conseil constitutionnel la constitutionnalité des lois amendant le contenu de l'état d'urgence. Alors que l'article 61 de la Constitution ouvre l'accès du Conseil à l'opposition (et que le recours à l'urgence pouvait réduire le délai d'examen du Conseil), même celle-ci n'a pas voulu prendre de risque à cet égard,[24] alors que la possibilité d'une inconstitutionnalité de la loi avait été évoquée par le Premier ministre, laissant aux associations, avocats, individus, le soin d'utiliser les mécanismes juridictionnels pour contrôler d'éventuels abus. Toutefois, cette absence de contrôle *a priori* implique le risque, confirmé par la suite, que certaines mesures inconstitutionnelles soient appliquées, comme ce fut le cas du régime initial des perquisitions administratives, jugé contraire à la Constitution grâce à une question prioritaire de constitutionnalité (ci-après QPC) en date du 23 septembre 2016,[25] illustrant le rôle central des "juges"[26] dans la protection des libertés en état d'urgence.

3 La Défense par les Juges : une Défense Contestée

L'état d'urgence a d'abord révélé l'importance du nouveau mécanisme de la QPC, qui est venu compenser, malheureusement parfois tardivement,[27] l'absence de contrôle *a priori* de la loi. Ce contrôle a toutefois été critiqué par certains comme étant trop tolérant à l'égard des ingérences dans les libertés prévues par le

---

[22]Consultez http://www2.assemblee-nationale.fr/14/commissions-permanentes/commission-des-lois/controle-parlementaire-de-l-etat-d-urgence/controle-parlementaire-de-l-etat-d-urgence/(block)/27358.

[23]Voir D. Raimbourg et J.-F. Poisson, *Rapport sur le contrôle parlementaire de l'état d'urgence*, préc. Ainsi, on peut prendre en exemple la décrue dans le recours aux perquisitions administratives, passant de 890 perquisitions par jour, entre le 14 et 20 novembre 2015, à, au maximum, 30 par jour sur la période allant jusqu'en mai 2016; d'après le rapport du CREDOF (2018), on compte 3427 perquisitions jusqu'en février 2016, puis on passe à 167 sur la période allant jusqu'en mai 2016.

[24]L'opposition, lors du déclenchement et de la plupart des renouvellements, étant de droite, sa position sur les questions de sécurité peut expliquer l'absence de saisine du Conseil constitutionnel.

[25]CC, déc. n° 2016-567/568 QPC du 23 septembre 2016, *Georges F. et a.* [perquisitions administratives dans le cadre de l'état d'urgence II].

[26]Nous incluons dans cette catégorie le Conseil constitutionnel bien qu'il ne soit pas composé de juges.

[27]Car intervenant après la levée de l'état d'urgence. Voir, par exemple, CC, déc. n° 2017-677 QPC du 1er décembre 2017, *Ligue des droits de l'Homme* [Contrôles d'identité, fouilles de bagages et visites de véhicules dans le cadre de l'état d'urgence].

législateur.[28] A été notamment critiquée la conception trop restrictive du Conseil constitutionnel de la notion de liberté individuelle, mentionnée à l'article 66 de la Constitution et qui prévoit que l'autorité judiciaire en est la gardienne.[29] Cette notion est centrale dans la répartition des compétences juridictionnelles entre juge judiciaire et juge administratif en France. Toutefois, l'interprétation du Conseil n'est pas nouvelle[30] et le rôle accru du juge administratif qui en découle n'est donc ni surprenant ni même illégitime. Il n'existe pas de principe constitutionnel faisant du juge judiciaire le seul et exclusif gardien des libertés individuelles, la Constitution ne mentionne que son rôle de gardien de *la* liberté individuelle, comprise comme la sûreté. Le juge judiciaire entre ainsi en jeu en cas de privation de liberté. L'accroissement du rôle du juge administratif n'est ainsi pas la conséquence d'une modification directe de la répartition des compétences entre les deux ordres de juridiction par la loi relative à l'état d'urgence, qui déciderait du transfert de compétences au profit du juge administratif dans des domaines ne relevant pas de sa compétence habituelle, mais le résultat de l'application des critères classiques de cette répartition.[31]

La compétence du juge administratif est accrue parce que la loi sur l'état d'urgence étend les pouvoirs de police administrative[32] et donc le contrôle de ce juge sur l'exercice de ces pouvoirs. Ainsi, le Conseil constitutionnel a, par exemple, estimé que le régime des assignations à résidence, dans la limite de 12 heures par jour, ne relevait pas d'une privation de liberté mais d'une restriction des libertés, notamment la liberté d'aller et venir, pouvant ainsi demeurer sous le contrôle du juge administratif.[33]

Malgré les critiques, le contrôle du Conseil constitutionnel a existé. Par exemple, le Conseil a constaté que le régime des perquisitions administratives, antérieur aux modifications introduites par la loi de 2015, était contraire à la Constitution.[34] De

---

[28]Voir, par exemple, A. Roblot-Troizier (2016) qui parle de contrôle "superficiel", p. 432.

[29]Voir, par exemple, B. Louvel (2016).

[30]Elle résulte de différentes décisions débutant à la fin des années 1990. Voir, par exemple, CC, déc. n° 99-411 DC du 16 juin 1999, *Loi portant diverses mesures relatives à la sécurité routière et aux infractions sur les agents des exploitants de réseau de transport public de voyageurs*, détachant la liberté d'aller et venir de l'article 66 de la Constitution.

[31]Sur ce sujet, voir O. Le Bot (2016), pp. 436–446.

[32]Notion qui a, par ailleurs, tendance à être interprétée plus largement par le juge et le législateur. Voir, par exemple, CE, ord., *Société les productions de la plume*, 9 janvier 2014, n° 374508. Voir, par exemple, la Loi n° 2015-912 du 24 juillet 2015 relative au renseignement qui augmente les pouvoirs de l'administration d'intervenir préventivement pour empêcher la commission d'une infraction. Voir CC, déc. n° 2015-513 DC du 23 juillet 2015, *Loi relative au renseignement.*

[33]CC, déc. n° 2015-527 QPC du 22 décembre 2015, *M. Cédric D.* [Assignations à résidence dans le cadre de l'état d'urgence].

[34]CC, déc. n° 2016-567/568 QPC du 23 septembre 2016, *Georges F. et a.* [Perquisitions administratives dans le cadre de l'état d'urgence II].

même, il a censuré le régime du renouvellement au-delà de 12 mois des assignations à résidence,[35] celui de l'exploitation des données saisies lors d'une perquisition administrative et de leur conservation,[36] il a encadré le régime des interdictions de séjour,[37] ou encore a abrogé l'article 8-1 de la loi fondant la possibilité de contrôle d'identité et de fouilles de véhicules sur décision préfectorale[38] ainsi que la possibilité d'instituer des zones de sécurité où le séjour des personnes est réglementé.[39]

Il faut cependant souligner que les censures ont porté sur les disproportions les plus manifestes. Cela ne constitue pas une surprise. Tout d'abord parce que l'objet même de l'état d'urgence est d'autoriser des ingérences plus importantes dans les droits et libertés, ce qui se traduit par un contrôle moins intrusif dans lequel l'importance de l'objectif de sauvegarde de l'ordre public pèse lourdement. Par ailleurs, le Conseil constitutionnel n'est pas connu pour être particulièrement sévère à l'égard du Parlement concernant le contrôle des textes dits "sécuritaires".[40] Le Conseil constitutionnel a, de longue date, développé une jurisprudence qui souligne que, dans ce domaine comme dans d'autres, il ne jouit pas d'un pouvoir d'appréciation identique à celui du Parlement, laissant au législateur une marge de manœuvre importante[41]. Le contrôle des modifications législatives liées à l'état d'urgence poursuit donc une tendance générale.

Par ailleurs, le caractère tardif de certaines QPC a privé d'effet utile les censures prononcées. Ainsi, certaines décisions ont été rendues alors que l'état d'urgence avait été levé comme, par exemple, la décision abrogeant l'article 8-1 relatif au

---

[35]CC, déc. n° 2017-624 QPC du 16 mars 2017, *M. Sofiyan I.* [Assignations à résidence dans le cadre de l'état d'urgence n° II]. Cela ne s'est pas forcément traduit par une meilleure protection des libertés, le renouvellement relevant alors seulement de la décision du ministre de l'Intérieur sous le contrôle *a posteriori* du juge administratif.

[36]CC, déc. n° 2016-536 QPC du 19 février 2016, *Ligue des droits de l'Homme*; CC, déc. n° 2016-600 QPC du 2 décembre 2016, *Raïme A.* [*Perquisitions administratives dans le cadre de l'état d'urgence III*].

[37]CC, déc. n° 2017-635 QPC du 9 juin 2017, *Emile L.* [Interdiction de séjour dans le cadre de l'état d'urgence].

[38]CC, déc. n° 2017-677 QPC du 1er décembre 2017, *Ligue des droits de l'Homme* [Contrôles d'identité, fouilles de bagages et visites de véhicules dans le cadre de l'état d'urgence].

[39]CC, déc. n° 2017-684 QPC du 11 janvier 2018, *Associations La cabane juridique / Legal Shelter et autre* [Zones de protection ou de sécurité dans le cadre de l'état d'urgence].

[40]Voir K. Roudier (2016), pp. 37–50.

[41]Voir, pour un exemple récent concernant la pénalisation des clients de personnes se livrant à la prostitution, CC, déc. n° 2018-761 QPC du 1er février 2019, *Association Médecins du monde et autres*, para.12: "[. . .] l'article 61-1 de la Constitution ne confère pas au Conseil constitutionnel un pouvoir général d'appréciation et de décision de même nature que celui du Parlement mais lui donne seulement compétence pour se prononcer sur la conformité à la Constitution des lois déférées à son examen [. . .]". Voir également CC, déc. n° 2018-706 QPC du 18 mai 2018, *M. Jean-Marc R.* [Délit d'apologie d'actes de terrorisme].

contrôle d'identité et fouilles de véhicules rendue le 1er décembre 2017.[42] L'utilisation par le Conseil de son pouvoir de modulation dans le temps des effets de ses décisions a également pu venir limiter l'intérêt des déclarations d'inconstitutionnalité pour les personnes concernées et ainsi "couvrir", au nom de la sauvegarde de l'ordre public, des inconstitutionnalités. Par exemple, dans sa décision du 23 septembre 2016,[43] portant sur le régime des perquisitions administratives utilisé entre le 14 et le 20 novembre 2015 (période pendant laquelle cette mesure a été la plus utilisée), après avoir constaté l'inconstitutionnalité totale du 1er alinéa de l'article 11 de la loi,[44] le Conseil rappelle que la loi du 20 novembre 2015 a modifié le texte, ce qui n'impose pas que soit reportée la prise d'effet de la déclaration contestée. Mais il poursuit en énonçant que "la remise en cause des actes de procédure pénale consécutifs à une mesure prise sur le fondement des dispositions déclarées contraires à la Constitution méconnaîtrait l'objectif de valeur constitutionnelle de sauvegarde de l'ordre public et aurait des conséquences manifestement excessives. Par suite, les mesures prises sur le fondement des dispositions déclarées contraires à la Constitution ne peuvent, dans le cadre de l'ensemble des procédures pénales qui leur sont consécutives, être contestées sur le fondement de cette inconstitutionnalité".[45]

Le Conseil constitutionnel a, par ailleurs, été critiqué comme se reposant trop sur le contrôle exercé par le juge administratif pour estimer que les dispositions législatives réalisaient un équilibre satisfaisant entre l'ordre public et les libertés. Or, le contrôle du juge administratif, qui a été, de plus, quantitativement limité,[46] a également fait l'objet de critiques et d'interrogations de la part du pouvoir judiciaire,

---

[42]CC, déc. n° 2017-677 QPC du 1er décembre 2017, *Ligue des droits de l'Homme* [Contrôles d'identité, fouilles de bagages et visites de véhicules dans le cadre de l'état d'urgence], points 6 et 7: "en prévoyant que ces opérations peuvent être autorisées en tout lieu dans les zones où s'applique l'état d'urgence, le législateur a permis leur mise en œuvre sans que celles-ci soient nécessairement justifiées par des circonstances particulières établissant le risque d'atteinte à l'ordre public dans les lieux en cause. Dès lors, le législateur n'a pas assuré une conciliation équilibrée entre, d'une part, l'objectif de valeur constitutionnelle de sauvegarde de l'ordre public, et, d'autre part, la liberté d'aller et de venir et le droit au respect de la vie privée. Par conséquent, et sans qu'il soit besoin d'examiner les autres griefs, les dispositions contestées doivent être déclarées contraires à la Constitution". Par ailleurs, l'abrogation est reportée au 30 juin 2018 (ce qui permet de couvrir des poursuites pénales engagées sur ce fondement).

[43]CC, déc. n° 2016-567/568 QPC, préc.

[44]Le texte visait simplement à "Conférer aux autorités administratives visées à l'article 8 [ministre de l'Intérieur et préfet de département sur le territoire couvert par l'application de l'état d'urgence] le pouvoir d'ordonner des perquisitions à domicile de jour et de nuit". Point 8: "en ne soumettant le recours aux perquisitions à aucune condition et en n'encadrant leur mise en œuvre d'aucune garantie, le législateur n'a pas assuré une conciliation équilibrée entre l'objectif de valeur constitutionnelle de sauvegarde de l'ordre public et le droit au respect de la vie privée".

[45]Point 11.

[46]Le rapport du CREDOF estime qu'environ 10% des mesures administratives prises ont été contestées devant le juge administratif (S. Hennette-Vauchez (2018), p. 59 et S. Hennette-Vauchez et al. (2018), p. 177).

estimant que son rôle de gardien de la liberté individuelle était injustement affaibli,[47] et d'une partie de la doctrine.[48] On retrouve ici la critique récurrente s'exerçant à l'encontre du juge administratif, qui serait trop proche de l'administration active et manquerait d'indépendance à l'égard de l'Exécutif. Pourtant, grâce notamment aux procédures de référé (référé-liberté, référé-suspension), le recours au contrôle de proportionnalité, la contribution du juge administratif à la protection des libertés s'est indéniablement développée depuis plusieurs années. Le référé-liberté a été ainsi particulièrement utile et utilisé pour contester, par exemple, les assignations à résidence. Par ailleurs, l'intensité du contrôle du juge administratif sur les mesures prises par les autorités s'est progressivement améliorée et dans ses ordonnances du 11 décembre 2015 rendues contre des assignations à résidence, le juge administratif a non seulement présumé la réalisation de la condition d'urgence mais aussi affirmé exercer un contrôle entier en recourant à un contrôle de proportionnalité.[49] Le contrôle du recours à l'état d'urgence et de la décision d'y mettre un terme reste, au contraire, logiquement minimal sans que cela ne semble devoir susciter de critiques particulières, notamment au regard de la jurisprudence de la Cour européenne qui laisse sur cette question une grande marge d'appréciation aux Etats.[50]

D'après le Conseil d'Etat, environ 30% des mesures prises ont été annulées soit par les autorités administratives elles-mêmes, soit par la voie du contrôle contentieux. Pour autant, cela ne suffit pas à écarter les interrogations concernant le contrôle du juge administratif.[51] Deux points problématiques ont été principalement relevés par la doctrine.[52]

[47]Dans son discours de l'audience solennelle de rentrée de la Cour de cassation du 14 janvier 2016, le président Louvel s'interrogeait sur les raisons qui amenaient les pouvoirs publics à "éviter" l'autorité judiciaire. Voir également I. Boucobza (2018) qui estime que "l'analyse des décisions juridictionnelles montre clairement l'existence d'une alliance entre le juge constitutionnel et le juge administratif au détriment du juge judiciaire", p. 76.

[48]Voir, par exemple, A. Roblot-Troizier (2016), p. 433, qui parle d'"impuissance du juge à protéger efficacement les droits et libertés", tout en reconnaissant l'amélioration globale du contrôle du juge administratif sur les actes administratifs pris dans le cadre de l'état d'urgence. Pour une position nuancée, voir P. Wachsmann (2016), p. 473: "le dessaisissement du juge judiciaire ne signifie nullement un crépuscule des libertés publiques. Les garanties offertes par les deux ordres de juridiction sont en effet équivalentes au regard des normes définissant l'équité du procès." L'auteur relève cependant que le pouvoir d'autorisation préalable fait défaut au juge administratif ce qui justifierait, en l'absence d'intervention législative, de restaurer la compétence de l'autorité judiciaire.

[49]Si le juge adhère au moins en parole au contrôle de proportionnalité, il n'est pas certain que, dans toutes les affaires, ce contrôle soit effectivement réalisé. Notamment lorsque l'on voit les éléments de preuve qui sont parfois retenus par le juge au soutien de sa décision, on peut douter du caractère très poussé de l'analyse.

[50]Pour un exemple récent, voir CEDH, *Şahin Alpay c. Turquie* et *Mehmet Hasan Altan c. Turquie*, 20 mars 2018, Nos 13237/17 et 16538/17.

[51]Par ailleurs, le rapport du CREDOF conteste ce taux. Voir note 46.

[52]Pour un examen d'ensemble des différentes problématiques, voir X. Vandendriesche (2018), pp. 1322–1333.

Tout d'abord, l'admission de la légitimité des mesures restrictives de liberté par "répercussion" de l'état d'urgence. L'état d'urgence a été mis en place et prolongé à la suite de la commission d'attentats islamistes sur le territoire. Il n'est donc pas surprenant que les motivations de la plupart des mesures prises l'aient été sur des fondements liés à l'implication des personnes concernées dans ces réseaux. Pourtant, il faut constater que d'autres mesures ont concerné des publics différents. Ainsi, les ordonnances du Conseil d'Etat du 11 décembre 2015 ont été critiquées car le contrôle n'a pas abouti à la suspension des assignations à résidence contestées.[53] Or, ces assignations à résidence ne concernaient pas des personnes soupçonnées d'activités en lien avec une entreprise terroriste mais des militants dans le cadre de la tenue de la COP 21. Le Conseil d'Etat, se reposant sur la rédaction de l'article 6 qui mentionne que la mesure peut être prise contre toute personne à l'égard de laquelle il existe des "raisons sérieuses de penser que son comportement constitue une menace pour la sécurité et l'ordre publics" rappelle que les dispositions de la loi "n'établissent pas de lien entre la nature du péril imminent ou de la calamité publique ayant conduit à ce que soit déclaré l'état d'urgence et la nature de la menace pour la sécurité et l'ordre publics susceptible de justifier une mesure d'assignation à résidence."[54]

L'argument mis en avant par les autorités, et qui peut être entendu, est que les forces de l'ordre, engagées sur d'autres terrains, ne peuvent se voir détournées de leur mission pour le contrôle ordinaire de l'ordre public, justifiant que d'éventuels fauteurs de trouble soient "neutralisés" par des interdictions de séjour, interdiction de manifester ou assignations à résidence. Or, si un tel raisonnement nous semble justifiable face à l'organisation de manifestations d'ampleur (qui, pourtant, ont été rarement interdites alors même que la plupart des manifestations sont aujourd'hui accompagnées de troubles à l'ordre public), cela pourrait sembler moins pertinent concernant des mesures individuelles plus attentatoires aux libertés comme les assignations à résidence, sauf à ce que ces assignations permettent, en écartant des personnes connues pour leur dangerosité, que les manifestations puissent se tenir. Ainsi, l'assignation à résidence ou l'interdiction de séjour de certains devient la mesure la moins intrusive pour la liberté de manifestation de la majorité.

Ensuite, les éléments de preuve retenus dans certaines affaires et la charge de la preuve soulèvent des interrogations.[55] A ainsi été critiqué le fait que les décisions de l'administration se fondaient souvent sur des notes blanches. Ces éléments de preuve sont acceptés par le juge administratif,[56] et ce en dehors même du contentieux de

---

[53]Voir, par exemple, A. Roblot-Troizier (2016), p. 428; S. Hennette-Vauchez et al. (2018), pp. 207–213.

[54]Voir, par exemple, CE, ord., 11 décembre 2015, *Cédric Domenjoud*, n° 395009.

[55]Voir X. Vandendriesche (2018); S. Hennette-Vauchez et al. (2018), pp. 226–231.

[56]CE, ord., 11 décembre 2015, n° 395009, para. 28: "aucune disposition législative ni aucun principe ne s'oppose à ce que les faits relatés par les "notes blanches" produites par le ministre, qui ont été versées au débat contradictoire et ne sont pas sérieusement contestées par le requérant, soient susceptibles d'être pris en considération par le juge administratif".

l'état d'urgence. Le juge exerce un contrôle sur leur caractère probant, contrôle qui est toutefois difficile et par nature assez subjectif. Toutefois, ces documents sont soumis à un débat contradictoire ce qui est une garantie pour les libertés individuelles. Ainsi, des éléments imprécis, trop indirects,[57] de simples suspicions non corroborées par des faits ont pu amener le juge administratif à ordonner la suspension des mesures prises, notamment des assignations à résidence.[58] Mais, dans d'autres, cas la doctrine a pu critiquer le renversement de la charge de la preuve au détriment du requérant pouvant être en peine de prouver le caractère non dangereux pour l'ordre public de ses actions ou intentions, notamment lorsqu'il pratique un islam radical.[59] Le rôle du juge administratif est difficile et il a souvent préféré errer du côté de la prudence et donc de la sécurité plutôt que de la liberté.

Par ailleurs, pour certaines mesures, les procédures de référé ne peuvent être utilisées, ne laissant aux personnes concernées que la voie du recours pour excès de pouvoir et une action en responsabilité pour faute.[60] C'est le cas en matière de perquisitions administratives alors qu'il s'agit des mesures qui ont été les plus utilisées[61] et que le traumatisme que représente une perquisition administrative[62] réalisée par erreur est difficilement réparable. Même si le taux d'annulation par le juge administratif est plus important que pour les assignations à résidence,

[57]La menace pour la sécurité "par association" est toutefois souvent retenue (par exemple dans l'ordonnance du 11 décembre 2015, préc., note 56, c'est le fait que le requérant a par le passé été poursuivi – mais on ne dit pas qu'il a été condamné – et a participé à des manifestations violentes, qui emporte la conviction du juge, ou le fait, dans d'autres affaires d'être lié par des liens familiaux à une personne dangereuse).

[58]CE, ord., 22 janvier 2016, *M. B.*, n° 396116. Les éléments retenus contre la personne étaient qu'elle appartenait à la mouvance islamiste radicale, qu'elle avait été aperçue à proximité du domicile d'une personnalité en train de prendre des photos et aurait été impliquée dans un trafic de véhicules avec des membres de la même mouvance. Les débats ont permis de révéler que les autorités n'avaient pas d'éléments étayant son appartenance à la mouvance islamiste, qu'il avait pu justifier de sa présence sur les lieux mentionnés (sa mère y habite, l'utilisation de face time confirmée par les appels a pu être confondue avec une prise de photo) et son implication dans le trafic de véhicules se limite à avoir été auditionné comme témoin et aucun élément ne soutient l'existence d'un contexte islamiste radical en relation avec cette infraction. Voir également CE, ord., 23 février 2016, *M. A.*, n° 396872, dans laquelle le Conseil d'Etat estime que, malgré l'appartenance à la mouvance radicale et la condamnation du requérant pour des faits liés au terrorisme (présence en Afghanistan), les éléments du dossier ne justifient plus le maintien de l'assignation, notamment en l'absence d'éléments sur les contacts du requérant et des activités de prosélytisme visant au départ pour le Jihad.

[59]Voir notamment S. Hennette-Vauchez et al. (2018).

[60]CE, avis contentieux, 6 juillet 2016, n° 398234.

[61]Par ailleurs, avant la modification de la loi, on pouvait réaliser les perquisitions de nuit. Aujourd'hui, il faut une motivation spéciale.

[62]La gravité de l'ingérence dans les libertés que les perquisitions administratives représentent est soulignée par le fait que les pouvoirs publics doivent expressément signifier qu'ils entendent utiliser la mesure de l'article 11 de la loi.

l'intervention *a posteriori* du juge peut ne pas apparaître comme suffisante à la protection des libertés, sans être pour autant nécessairement inconstitutionnelle ou inconventionnelle. D'aucuns militent ainsi pour un contrôle *a priori* du juge administratif[63] ou pour une dérogation à la répartition classique des compétences pour permettre un contrôle *a priori* du juge judiciaire.[64]

4 Conclusion

Le bilan que nous pouvons tirer de ce bref survol est que le régime français de l'état d'urgence est un régime qui paraît, en théorie, équilibré mais qui, en pratique, se révèle trop facilement susceptible d'abus. Il est par ailleurs le révélateur, voire l'accélérateur, de tendances générales, qu'il s'agisse des directions prises par le législateur en termes d'équilibre, ou de déséquilibre, entre sécurité et libertés ou de l'intensité du contrôle des juges sur ces mesures. Cette brève présentation souligne ainsi que l'efficacité des mécanismes de défense de l'Etat de droit, contrôle parlementaire ou juridictionnel, reflète l'état général de la culture de l'Etat de droit des pouvoirs constitutionnels et des requérants. Si la culture de l'Etat de droit est forte, l'existence de garde-fous n'est pas un vain mot alors qu'en présence d'une culture de l'Etat de droit plus faible, l'effectivité de ces mêmes mécanismes peut être sujette à caution.

Ainsi, le contrôle du Conseil constitutionnel demanderait à être renforcé, notamment par l'utilisation du contrôle *a priori*, particulièrement au regard de la faiblesse du recours au juge administratif ou du manque d'efficacité de son contrôle pour certaines mesures. Les autorités administratives devraient aussi être plus prudentes dans l'utilisation des pouvoirs que la loi leur confie. Or, sur ce point, il faut constater que le régime de l'état d'urgence a été utilisé au-delà de la lutte contre le terrorisme, le principe de précaution ayant lourdement fait pencher la balance du côté de la sécurité. Le rapport parlementaire de contrôle de l'état d'urgence a, par ailleurs, souligné la difficulté de sortir de cet état alors que les mesures qu'il permettait avaient été, euphémisme intéressant, "apprivoisées" par les services de police. En ce qui concerne l'Etat de droit, il nous semble que les effets les plus importants et les questionnements que l'état d'urgence peut soulever sur la défense des libertés sont à rechercher dans ses répercussions au-delà de son application. En effet, l'urgence peut justifier une réaction qui fait prévaloir la sécurité sur la liberté, même si cette prévalence doit s'estomper au fur et à mesure du passage du temps.

Ce qui interroge plus est le fait qu'un recours excessif à cet état exceptionnel peut engendrer des modifications de longue durée, plus problématiques quant à l'état du

[63]Voir P. Wachsmann (2016).

[64]Voir O. Le Bot (2016), pp. 444–446.

droit commun et la défense des libertés.[65] Au nom de la logique selon laquelle on ne peut rester indéfiniment en état d'urgence et qu'on ne peut lutter contre des risques permanents par des mesures temporaires,[66] nous sommes sortis de l'état d'urgence par le vote d'une nouvelle loi sur la sécurité intérieure et le terrorisme, laquelle a adapté, en les encadrant et en les limitant à la lutte contre le terrorisme, certaines mesures développées par les amendements successifs de la loi de 1955.[67] Ces mesures ont fait l'objet d'un contrôle du Conseil constitutionnel par le biais de QPC donnant lieu à des décisions de non-conformité partielle limitées.[68] La plupart des mesures ont ainsi été déclarées constitutionnelles, sous certaines réserves visant à limiter d'éventuels excès pour les libertés. Toutefois, le risque de glisser vers des mesures toujours plus restrictives des libertés est présent, particulièrement lorsque l'on sait que les lois de lutte contre le terrorisme sont souvent l'antichambre de ce qui

[65]Voir V. Champeil-Desplats (2016), pp. 33: "l'application de régimes d'exception dans le cadre de l'État de droit est facteur de porosité, de flou et de brouillage entre le droit relevant de l'exception et le droit commun, et ce tant sur les plans pratique que conceptuel [...]".

[66]Voir l'avis consultatif du Conseil d'Etat en date du 22 juin 2017 concernant la dernière loi de prorogation qui souligne ce lien entre sortie de l'état d'urgence et transformation du droit commun pour s'adapter à la menace terroriste. Ainsi, le Conseil d'Etat relève que "le Gouvernement souligne dans l'exposé des motifs du projet de loi renforçant la sécurité intérieure et la lutte contre le terrorisme examiné le même jour que plusieurs mesures permanentes de ce texte visant à prévenir de manière plus efficace les actes de terrorisme – protection de lieux et d'évènements soumis à un tel risque, fermeture temporaire de lieux de culte, surveillance des personnes, visites et saisies – "*permettront une sortie maîtrisée de l'état d'urgence*" et qu'il pourra y être mis fin par décret en Conseil des ministres avant le terme de la prorogation si la loi renforçant la sécurité intérieure et la lutte contre le terrorisme est publiée avant cette date. Les menaces durables ou permanentes pourront être traitées dans le cadre du droit commun: - par les instruments juridiques de la lutte contre le terrorisme, significativement renforcés par les lois adoptées ces dernières années dans le domaine du renseignement, de la police administrative et de la procédure pénale, complétés par les mesures mentionnées ci-dessus", para.4 (nous soulignons).

[67]Loi n° 2017-1510 du 30 octobre 2017 renforçant la sécurité intérieure et la lutte contre le terrorisme.

[68]CC, déc. n° 2017-691 QPC du 16 février 2018, *M. Farouk B.* [Mesure administrative d'assignation à résidence aux fins de lutte contre le terrorisme]. Le Conseil constitutionnel a estimé que le délai d'un mois pour introduire un recours en excès de pouvoir contre une telle mesure et le délai de deux mois laissé au juge pour statuer portent atteinte au droit de recours juridictionnel effectif. Il a également censuré les conditions de renouvellement de la mesure au-delà de trois mois. Il émet également une réserve d'interprétation sur la mesure pour la limiter à une durée totale cumulée de 12 mois. CC, déc. n°2017-695 QPC du 29 mars 2018, *M. Rouchdi B. et a.* [Mesures administratives de lutte contre le terrorisme]. La décision concerne les périmètres de protection, l'accès à ces périmètres et les fouilles avec consentement nécessaires pour y accéder et l'impossibilité d'y accéder en cas de refus, la fermeture des lieux de culte, l'assignation sur territoire déterminé et les obligations l'accompagnant, et les visites domiciliaires et saisies. Le Conseil constitutionnel émet des réserves d'interprétation sur certains points (par exemple, l'absence de discrimination lors des fouilles, une durée ne dépassant pas 12 mois pour les assignations sur un territoire). En revanche, il sanctionne pour atteinte au droit de propriété l'imprécision des dispositions sur les saisies concernant la conservation et la restitution des objets et documents. Par ailleurs, il constate (avec effet différé) la violation de l'article 16 de la Déclaration des Droits de l'Homme et du Citoyen pour avoir laissé au juge administratif 4 mois pour statuer sur le recours contre la décision de ne pas se trouver en relation avec certaines personnes.

se développe ensuite dans la lutte contre la criminalité de droit commun. Les temps difficiles que nous traversons appellent à la fois la vigilance en ce qui concerne la défense des libertés et à la responsabilité en ce qui concerne la sécurité.

Références

Baranger D (2016) L'état d'urgence dans la durée. Revue française de droit administratif:447–454

Boucobza I (2018) Quel juge pour l'état d'urgence ?. In Ce qui reste(ra) toujours de l'urgence, ed. CREDOF, available online https://www.defenseurdesdroits.fr/sites/default/files/atoms/files/rapport_defenseur_des_droits_-_ce_qui_restera_toujours_de_lurgence.pdf. Accessed 16 April 2020

Champeil-Desplats V (2018) Aspects théoriques: Ce que l'état d'urgence fait à l'état de droit. In: Ce qui reste(ra) toujours de l'urgence, ed. CREDOF, available online https://www.defenseurdesdroits.fr/sites/default/files/atoms/files/rapport_defenseur_des_droits_-_ce_qui_restera_toujours_de_lurgence.pdf. Accessed 16 April 2020

Hennette-Vauchez S (2018) La fabrique législative de l'état d'urgence: lorsque, par la disposition des choses le pouvoir n'arrête pas le pouvoir. In: Ce qui reste(ra) toujours de l'urgence, ed. CREDOF. Available at https://www.defenseurdesdroits.fr/sites/default/files/atoms/files/rapport_defenseur_des_droits_-_ce_qui_restera_toujours_de_lurgence.pdf. Accessed 16 April 2020

Hennette-Vauchez S et al (2018) L'état d'urgence au prisme du contentieux: analyse transversale de corpus. In: Ce qui reste(ra) toujours de l'urgence, ed. CREDOF, available online https://www.defenseurdesdroits.fr/sites/default/files/atoms/files/rapport_defenseur_des_droits_-_ce_qui_restera_toujours_de_lurgence.pdf. Accessed 16 April 2020

Le Bot O (2016) Etat d'urgence et compétences juridictionnelles. Revue française de droit administratif:436–446

Louvel B (2016) L'autorité judiciaire, gardienne de la liberté individuelle ou des libertés individuelles ?. Available at: https://www.courdecassation.fr/publications_26/prises_parole_2039/discours_2202/premier_president_7084/. Accessed 16 April 2020

Roblot-Troizier A (2016) Etat d'urgence et protection des libertés. Revue française de droit administratif:424–435

Roudier K (2016) Le Conseil constitutionnel face à l'avènement d'une politique sécuritaire. Nouveaux Cahiers du Conseil constitutionnel 51:37–50

Türk P (2016) Les commissions parlementaires et l'état d'urgence. Revue française de droit administratif:455–465

Vandendriesche X (2018) Le contrôle du Conseil d'Etat sur les mesures prises au titre de l'état d'urgence. Actualité juridique droit administratif:1322–1333

Wachsmann P (2016) De la marginalisation du juge judiciaire en matière de libertés et des moyens d'y remédier. Recueil Dalloz 2016:473–476

Peggy Ducoulombier is Professor of Public Law at the University of Strasbourg. She holds a PhD from the University of Strasbourg. She previously worked as a Lecturer for the University of Keele (UK), Aberdeen (UK) and as Professor at the University of Perpignan (France). Her main area of expertise is the European Convention on Human Rights. She is the author of *Les conflits de droits fondamentaux devant la Cour européenne des droits de l'Homme*, published by Bruylant, in 2011.

The Rule of Law and Property

Vladimíra Pejchalová Grünwaldová

Contents

1 Introduction 49
2 The Problem Outline 50
3 The Concept of the Rule of Law 51
4 The Essence of Private Property 52
5 Private Property as a Fundamental Right 53
6 Conclusion 56
References 57

1 Introduction

The Rule of Law is first and foremost commonly perceived as a formal conception comprising principles of a formal and procedural character. But there is generally controversy as to whether the idea of the Rule of Law comprises a substantive dimension, and so, more concretely, whether its scope may embrace also the protection of property as a fundamental right. Property, for its part, is often associated with individual liberty. But it cannot be contested that property serves also a social function which entails limitations of property rights in the public interest. The protection of property as a fundamental right embraces, apart from the protection of the proprietary freedom of an individual vis-à-vis the state, the protection of legitimate proprietary claims in cases of conflicting interests to the same resource between individuals or between an individual and the state. Consequently, it entails weighing of competing interests within a given social context and the interpretation of particular fundamental rights in the light of social goals and aspirations, such as social justice, equality, or human dignity. The weighing of competing interests encompasses the weighing of individual interests against public interests, such as

V. Pejchalová Grünwaldová (✉)
University of West Bohemia, Pilsen, Czech Republic
e-mail: pejchalo@kmp.zcu.cz

M. Elósegui et al. (eds.), *The Rule of Law in Europe*,
https://doi.org/10.1007/978-3-030-56001-0_4

in cases of expropriation or limitation of property, in the framework of which competing interests to the same resource between an individual and the state are assessed.

On this account, it is suggested that the formal and procedural dimensions of the Rule of Law are not sufficient as guiding principles in the process of assessment of property limitation cases that entail balancing of competing interests, and that in this context the social function of property requires that the substantive dimension of the Rule of Law embodying the fundamental rights protection rules be acknowledged.

2 The Problem Outline

The issue of the relationship between the Rule of Law and property may be set forth by having resort to a couple of case examples, both of which were dealt with by the European Court of Human Rights. Imagine, you own a land, you cultivate it and pay the taxes and duties provided for by the legislation on land ownership. One day the government decides to create a nature reserve on your land. The government declares that your land is needed for public purposes and authorises 'the immediate taking of possession' of half of your land by the state. A legislative decree is adopted on the basis of which the state takes immediate possession of half of your land without compensation. On the other half of your land the government prohibits any construction and any change in the use of the land for environmental reasons.[1] Or imagine you are a property developer who acquired a land for building purposes but your construction plans are hindered by a land-use plan later developed by the municipal council which follows newly adopted environmental regulations.[2] As a

[1]See, for example, the judgment of the European Court of Human Rights in the case of *Matos e Silva, Lda., and Others v. Portugal*, Judgment of 27 August 1996, Reports 1996-IV. The Portugese government declared that a half of Matos e Silva's land was needed for public purposes. This public-interest declaration was preliminary to expropriating the land with a view to building an aquacultural research station on it. Later the Government made another public-interest declaration with a view to expropriating the other half of Matos e Silva's land in order to set up a single nature reserve for the protection of migrant birds and other important species. The order authorised 'the immediate taking of possession' of the land by the state. Furthermore, by decree the Government withdrew the applicant's concession to work all the parcels of land. The withdrawal was to be effected in the manner in which expropriation was permitted by the decree and the state was to take immediate possession of the land without any formalities or compensation except for compensation payable for necessary and useful improvements made on the property. By another decree the government created the Ria Formosa Nature Reserve on the Algarve and adopted rules for the protection of the area's ecosystem. Among other things, these rules prohibited, in addition to all building, any change in the use of the land and the starting up of any new agricultural and fish-farming activities without permission.

[2]See, for example, the judgment of the European Court of Human Rights in the case of *Katte Klitsche de la Grange v. Italy*, 27 October 1994, Series A no. 293-B. The applicant owned a large portion of a park. A land-use plan developed by the District Council excluded part of the applicant's land from the area intended for residential construction. The applicant complained that the land-use

consequence, your land is excluded from the area intended for residential construction and you are deprived of the right to build without compensation. This renders your property worthless. These concrete situations clearly involve a conflict and balancing between private property and environmental regulations.

The question which suggests itself for consideration is whether these restrictions of property rights may be looked at as being contrary to the Rule of Law or whether the Rule of Law requires that the environmental law be implemented. Should private property be protected by the Rule of Law in such situations? We are confronted with property rights that were acquired and exercised in keeping with the law and that are protected by the constitutional property clause, on the one hand, and constitutionally conform environmental regulations that limit those property rights, on the other hand. When balancing on the scales, which interest shall prevail from the point of view of the Rule of Law? First of all, let us deal with the notion of the Rule of Law.

3 The Concept of the Rule of Law

When we speak about the Rule of Law, we might first of all think of lawfulness—public authorities and all men are expected to act within the limits of law. So, the Rule of Law in this understanding means unconditional compliance with the law. In addition, the idea of lawfulness entails certain requirements as regards the quality of law, which we denote as the formal legality, such as intelligibility, predictability, foreseeability, or accessibility of both substantive law and legal procedures. At this point I shall refer to Lon Fuller who, in his *The Morality of Law*, identified eight principles of legality that have been widely accepted, such as: generality, publicity, prospectivity, clarity, noncontradiction, compliability, stability, and congruence between formulation and implementation. These principles must go hand in hand with the independence of the judiciary which ensures that judges will be impartial in making their decisions.

So far, we have dealt with the formal and procedural principles of the Rule of Law. But the notion of the Rule of Law is more complex than that and is not only about legality. Although copiously used, it is a term that is not easy to define, for it is rather an ideal that we endeavour to achieve. The Rule of Law is not a straightforward idea but rather a multifaceted one.

Suppose that the environmental regulations comply with the formal and procedural principles of the Rule of Law. This, however, does not appear to be enough to answer the question whether private property should be afforded protection against the given implications of the environmental regulations. If we limit ourselves only to

plan had unfairly deprived him of the right to build on a part of the park and of the lack of compensation for the damage he had sustained. The ECtHR held that the mere approval of the land-use plan was sufficient to restrict the applicants' excercise of his right to the peaceful enjoyment of his possessions.

the formal conception of the Rule of Law, we may find ourselves stranded in a standoff in resolving this clash between property law and regulatory law from a formal perspective. If the law is general, prospective, clear and stable, if it is promulgated, and if the procedures are observed, then the Rule of Law is complied with. This is what seems to have happened in the discussed environmental regulations cases. But impartial application of properly enacted laws to individual property cases does not render the state action 'trespass-safe'. Having lived a part of my life in communist Czechoslovakia, I can assert that, based on my own experience, many bad laws can be produced by authoritarian regimes that follow the formal principles of the Rule of Law. A vital question therefore is whether the Rule of Law protects property or economic freedom in general.

For that purpose it is necessary to go beyond the Rule of Law as a formal and procedural idea and reach for the substantive conception of the Rule of Law. The substantive dimension of the Rule of Law means that individuals are endowed with rights and duties, that are recognized in positive law, vis-à-vis one another and vis-à-vis the state.[3] Although there are some legal theorists, such as Joseph Raz, who insist that the Rule of Law cannot be confused with human rights or social justice,[4] suppose that the substantive dimension of the Rule of Law embraces the preservation of property as a fundamental right and related aspects such as dignity and social welfare. If we accept that the Rule of Law comprises the protection of human rights within its scope, the view on the discussed environmental regulations cases changes from when we look at the Rule of Law only as a formal and procedural concept. It is because the rights dimension comes in and provides content to the formal understanding of the Rule of Law.

If we accept that there is a connexion between the Rule of Law and private property, on this account, the Rule of Law would be associated with the protection of private property as a human right incorporated as a substantive dimension of the Rule of Law. What exactly does such a substantive dimension of the Rule of Law involve?

4 The Essence of Private Property

The essence of private property can be described, in general, as a series of relationships between private individuals over the control and use of resources. Every society, democratic or totalitarian, develops its own system of property as a basic instrument for survival. It is beyond dispute that property is not only a legal institution but also a social and economic one, which can be generally perceived as a system of rules governing the allocation and control of the use of material resources for the purpose of satisfying human needs. The fundamental

[3]See Tamanaha (2004), p. 102.

[4]See Raz (1979), p. 211.

presupposition for the existence of private property is that the rest of society accepts that its members are allocated elements of material resources and that the rest of society is prepared to abide by property rules.

Intrinsic to property are competing claims and interests over external resources. It is the inherent allocative nature of property that brings about inequalities and legitimises restrictions of property, and, thus, less protection. It is the allocative nature of property that is the driving force behind the recognition of property as a social institution which entails an obligation to balance out inequalities brought about by this nature of property. It follows that property is not absolute and is always judged in relation to public policy.

For their existence to be secured, private property rights need to be recognized and protected by the government. Their existence thus depends on the state and their enforcement requires state action. It is inevitable that the enforcement of property rights generates disparities, as property interests of some will always be protected at the expense of identical interests of others, for legal protection of someone's property rights in resources is always to someone else's exclusion or detriment. As Joseph Singer puts it, "the grant of a property right to one person leaves others vulnerable to the will of the owner; conversely, the refusal to grant a property right leaves the claimant the vulnerable one".[5]

Since the existence of property rights depends on the willingness of the government to recognise and protect them, it implies that the government also has the inherent power to restrict or otherwise interfere with property rights, provided that the limits of their protection laid down in fundamental laws are not transgressed. So, the Rule of Law, operating in the framework of a social contract, allows that, for example, environmental regulations limit property of one to secure liberty or property of the other. The extent to which this may be done is delimited by the standards laid down by the social contract, or, in other words, it depends on the nature of the political regime (democratic, totalitarian) within which the Rule of Law operates and the level up to which its legislature, executive and judiciary adhere to the protection of property as a fundamental right.

5 Private Property as a Fundamental Right

Accordingly, property as a fundamental right may be conceived as serving two different essential functions. The first one is an individual function whereby the sphere of liberty of action of the individual is secured. Property is thus interconnected with freedom. This conception of property "may be thought to constitute the core substantive meaning of property in the liberal tradition."[6] The

[5]See Singer (1991), p. 41.

[6]See Alexander (1999), p. 89.

second one is a social function whereby property serves to advance the public good in society.

The idea that property rights should have their share of social responsibility is transposed in the constitutionally permitted restrictions of the right of property, or, in other words, in duties connected with property rights. The scope of constitutionally acknowledged duties connected with property varies, as the social function of property depends in practice on the political and economic interests that prevail in a specific country and society. Today, it is widely acknowledged that property serves individual as well as social function which has udergone an evolution, especially over the past century. The conception of property as a social function today stands quite apart from the classical understanding of the limitation of rights in exchange for their recognition and enforcement. It relates to the advent of social (or welfare) liberalism and its impingement throughout the twentieth century. With the development of Western societies, from the eighteenth-century revolutions directed against absolutist monarchies to established liberal democracies and stabilised legal relations under constitutional imperatives, classical liberalism started losing ground in Europe in favour of an advancing stream of social liberalism that appeared on stage in the late nineteenth century to be present, side by side, with classical liberalism. Advocating state interventions for the enhancement of personal liberty, social liberalism accentuates the protection of civil and political rights and proposes to replace the individualistic conception of property by a social one. Free society does not need extensive private property rights any more. Instead, in modern societies the interests of community often take precedence over individual rights, as opposed to the insistence of classical liberals on the importance of strong and extensive private property to protect freedom and promote efficient economic transactions.

It is evident that the manner of perception of property has been under constant motion along with the evolution of society. It is, therefore, not possible to conceive of property only from the point of view of an individual, as a full legal power over a thing, for there may be many different rights to its utilization. It is the utility on behalf of society that influences the modern understanding of property. In this respect, J.W. Harris, for example, has given an apposite account of the relation between ownership and property-limitation rules. Departing from the premise that ownership is not absolute, for owners are not free to do anything they like to or with their things, he claims that property-limitation rules and expropriation rules are typically part of the minimal structure of ownership and that ownership must comprise them.[7] He, thus, advances the claim that limitations of property are an inherent part of the notion of property, including the constitutional one.

---

[7]Harris (1996), pp. 29, 33–34. The author presumes that ownership is determined by, first, the "trespassory rules", by which he means any social rules which purport to impose obligations on all members of society, other than the owner who is taken to have some form of open-ended relationship to a thing, not to make use of property without the consent of the owner, and, second, by "ownership spectrum" meaning open-ended relationships presupposed and protected by trespassory rules. In other words, according to Harris, ownership is defined by the negative obligation of other persons not to interfere with property of the owner, and by particular ownership

Having this in mind, let us take the example of Article 1 of Protocol No. 1 to the European Convention on Human Rights (hereinafter the "Convention") which guarantees the protection of property. When we take the text of this provision[8] we can see that the first sentence of the first paragraph expresses the fundamental nature of the right of property which represents the personal function of the right of property—"every natural or legal person is entitled to the peaceful enjoyment of his possessions". The personal function of property secures an area of freedom for the individual; property is closely connected with individual liberty. Article 1 of Protocol No. 1 also reflects that individuals are, at the same time, deeply enmeshed in social relations. The social context of an individual's freedom results in the second aspect of the property guarantee enshrined in the Convention, the social function of property. Article 1 of Protocol No. 1 refers to the function of property to serve public good by acknowledging the power of states to interfere with property in the general, or public, interest. The personal and the social aspects of property represent the core functions of constitutional property and form the ideological backbone of Article 1 of Protocol No. 1. The personal function of property represents the freedom of an individual owner from external interferences with his property that is necessary for his self-realization, whereas the social function of property implies that the individual owner has obligations vis-à-vis society that has recognized his area of autonomy.

We can discern that the philosophical conception of the right of property in the Convention is clearly a projection of liberal political thought of the twentieth century, which is a blend of classical and social liberalism. Article 1 of Protocol No. 1 contains justification of private property of individuals (freedom from interference), as well as that of the welfare regulatory power of states (authorization of interference). It comprises seemingly contradictory norms that are, in fact, from the liberal philosophical stance, complementary to one another, as an individual owner's freedom cannot stand without a social and economic context and the "blessing"of the society that, in turn, cannot be created and function otherwise but by the endeavour of individuals.

So, the implications of the empowered social dimension of property are reflected in limitations of property rights that are permitted by fundamental laws. In this respect, the European Court of Human Rights has adopted certain interpretative criteria justifying interferences with property with regard to the property guarantee in Article 1 of Protocol No. 1 to the Convention. Namely, it applies the criteria of

---

relations. He alleges that these twin constituents of ownership may be superimposed by 'property limitation rules' and 'expropriation rules' whereby ownership rights (privileges and powers) are curtailed or taken away.

[8]Article 1 of Protocol No. 1 reads as follows: "Every natural or legal person is entitled to the peaceful enjoyment of his possessions. No one shall be deprived of his possessions except in the public interest and subject to the conditions provided for by law and by the general principles of international law.

The preceding provisions shall not, however, in any way impair the right of a State to enforce such laws as it deems necessary to control the use of property in accordance with the general interest or to secure the payment of taxes or other contributions or penalties."

legality, legitimacy, proportionality, and compensation. Many of the national constitutional jurisdictions follow the same path. If we take a look, for example, at the Czech, the French, the Russian or the Swiss constitutional property clauses as interpreted by the respective constitutional jurisdictions, we can find that the general criteria of justification of interferences with property are basically congruent and comply with the standards laid down by the Convention and the interpretative practice of the European Court of Human Rights.

It follows that the premise that the substantive Rule of Law embraces the protection of property as a fundamental right implies that it also permits limitations of property rights within the limits of the safeguards provided for by respective national constitutions as interpreted by respective national constitutional jurisdictions and, on European level, by the Convention as interpreted by the European Court of Human Rights.

6 Conclusion

Considering that the protection of property as a fundamental right may be conceived as forming the substantive dimension of the Rule of Law, any interference with property, such as the discussed environmental regulations, may be contested by virtue of the argument of its incompatibility with the Rule of Law. Under this understanding, not only must the government act through law which must comply with the requirements of formal legality but it must also see to preserving the fundamental rights it undertook to safeguard. It is both the formal and substantive principles of the Rule of Law that need to be followed so that private property be protected against arbitrary regulations and discretionary state action.

For our environmental regulations cases, the substantive Rule of Law represent the fundamental private property protection clauses—safeguards against arbitrary restrictions and takings of property provided for in national constitutions and in the European Convention on Human Rights on European level, within the meaning of the interpretative practice of the respective jurisdictions. When we take a look at our environmental regulations cases through the lens of these fundamental justificatory standards, although the public authorities might have followed the letter of the law which was properly enacted, we can observe that they did not provide at least any compensation for the interferences with property, notwithstanding that the particular laws did not require it. The substantive conception of the Rule of Law requires a constitutionally conform action from the part of public authorities and, of course, individuals.

Now we are ready to answer our questions. The restrictions of property rights under scrutiny, such as the exclusion of a land from the area intended for residential construction, do not have to be contrary to the Rule of Law, provided that the environmental regulations comply with both the formal/procedural and substantive principles of the Rule of Law as to their form, contents and the procedures through which they were enacted. In case to the contrary, they would infringe on private property rights.

References

Alexander GS (1999) Constitutionalising property: two experiences, two dilemmas. In: McLean J (ed) Property and the constitution. Hart, Oxford, pp 88–108
Harris JW (1996) Property and Justice. Oxford University Press, Oxford
Raz J (1979) The authority of law: essays on law and morality. Clarendon Press, Oxford
Singer JW (1991) Sovereignty and property. Northwest Univ Law Rev:1–41
Tamanaha B (2004) On the rule of law: history, politics, theory. Cambridge University Press, Cambridge

Vladimíra Pejchalová Grünwaldová is a lecturer in private international law at the University of West Bohemia, the Czech Republic, and at the Business Institute in Prague, the Czech Republic. She also lectures on comparative human rights law at the University of Strasbourg, France. She is an arbitrator at the Arbitration Court attached to the Economic Chamber of the Czech Republic and the Agricultural Chamber of the Czech Republic. She holds a Ph.D. in public law from the University of Strasbourg, France; an LL.M. in European law from the University of London (Queen Mary and Westfield College/University College London), the United Kingdom; and a Master of Laws (Mgr.) degree from Masaryk University, the Czech Republic.

Part II
Challenges and Safeguards of the Independence of Justice

The Independence of Judiciary Within the Political Dimension

Armen Harutyunyan

Contents

1 Introduction: Independence of the Judiciary Beyond Positive Law 61
2 Independence of the Judiciary from a Sociological Perspective 62
3 The Independence of the Judiciary Within a Political System 64
4 European Guarantees for the Independence of the Judiciary 66
5 Conclusion 67
References 68

1 Introduction: Independence of the Judiciary Beyond Positive Law

When analysing the independence of judiciary very often we examine the system of checks and balances in the framework of state power. It is a methodological mistake. That is why very often we limit ourselves to the formal side of the issue. Formally, from the legal point of view everything seems to be fine, but in point of fact there is no independence of judiciary.

It is important to always look at the bigger picture and then move towards the smaller one, which is the environment in which state institutions function. Many democracies in transition are borrowing their system of checks and balances from the positive law of western democracies without taking into account their realities. So that very often by constitution (written text) such countries can be considered as semi-presidential republics (Russia, Ukraine), but de facto they are superpresidential

A. Harutyunyan (✉)
European Court of Human Rights, Strasbourg, France
e-mail: armen.harutyunyan@echr.coe.int

M. Elósegui et al. (eds.), *The Rule of Law in Europe*,
https://doi.org/10.1007/978-3-030-56001-0_5

ones, where instead of a system of checks and balances is functioning a system of domination by the presidential institution.[1]

There are two levels of objective regulations, which must be taken into account, for forming the positive law. First, there are the universal "rules" for all type of human societies; these are about human being. The second ones concern the particularities of a given society: political and legal traditions, history, legal cultures etc.

Independence of judiciary is impossible without the separation of powers. But the fundamental problems of this conception can be found and solved not in the narrow scopes of state powers, but within the organisation and functioning of the whole political system.[2] We should say, that this is even wider than just political system. We agree with N.W. Barber, who wrote:

> The principles of constitutionalism relate directly to the institutional structure of the state but there are other, wider, moral principles that also help determine how the state should act.[3]

That is why it is necessary to go beyond the framework of positive law, analyse the objective regulations of the development of human society and form a positive law on their basis. Only then the positive law will not be "stillborn".

2 Independence of the Judiciary from a Sociological Perspective

One of those regularities is the law of small numbers. The concept of this law is that the so-called locomotive of the society is always an active and creative minority. In political science this law is reflected in the theory of elites. The elite, political, scientific, financial and so on is the active part of the society, capable of generating ideas and pulls the society. What is the elite is the society too. Democracy and the rule of law are not able to change this objective regularity, but, by contrast with the authoritarian regimes, they restrain the elite from becoming closed and dictatorial. There is constant interaction of the elite and society. Speaking from a sociological perspective, constitutional law guarantees the existence of social lifts.

Unfortunately, the situation of social lifts is warning everywhere, including in the "old" democracies. The educational system, the possibility to make career, to run business depends more and more on where you are from (your social class). Social hierarchy is getting stronger and more separated. Public institutions are losing their possibilities to balance this. Gifted young men and women are facing more

[1]See for example: Holmes (1994), pp. 36–39.

[2]This approach is not new one. See for instance Vile (1998), pp. 1–22; 362–367.

[3]Barber (2018), p. 11.

difficulties to make a career. Society is risking losing them, as potential leaders in a particular sphere.[4]

The global system of checks and balances relies on elites' balancing each other. The distinctive feature of our time is that the mentioned balances have been shattered, if not broken. Today, financial elites dominate over political, military, scientific and other elites. It is the financial elite that sets the agenda. Every elite has its own priorities, system of values and this is normal. What is not normal is when elites stop balancing each other. In some cases, financial elites act as political elites as well. This phenomenon is called the oligarchic system of government. The result is that the balances in the system of values and the system of human needs have been broken. The consumer philosophy pushed aside others: spiritual, scientific and so on. The "material" man won, whereas human rights and liberties are first and foremost spiritual values.

The result is that comfort and convenience became "higher" values than liberties and dignity. People became very dependent on privileges, salary, career advancement. Comfort and convenience keep pushing away liberty and dignity. It is more and more rare for the man to be ready to challenge comfort for dignity and is unable to leave his comfort zone for freedom. The difference between a "prosperous" society and "non-prosperous" one resides more and more in the fact that, in prosperous societies, everyone has his "beefsteak" whereas in non-prosperous ones there is one "beefsteak" for 10 people. But all the same, the struggle in both types of societies turns around a "beefsteak". That is why more and more often we see the subconscious challenge of the "street" towards authorities in prosperous countries.

That is what was meant by the world-famous philosopher M.K. Mamardashvili, who raised the issue of an anthropological catastrophe, even during USSR period. He considered that:

> In order to set up the tone of thoughts, one can characterize their nerve in such a way. This is a feeling that from all the varieties of catastrophes that the twentieth century is famous for and threatens us with, the major one and often hidden from our mind is the anthropological catastrophe, which becomes apparent not in such a colourful, spectacular phenomena as the supposed explosion of a nearby supernova or the clash of the Earth with a large asteroid, and not in a dramatic exhaustion of natural resources of the Earth or overpopulation, and not even in ecological or 'brighter than a thousand suns' nuclear tragedies. I mean an event that happening with the human itself and connected to the civilization in the sense that something vital can be irreversibly broken directly depending on destruction or just on absence civilizational foundations of the process of life and communication. And this event is already underway.[5]

People more and more withdraw into themselves and the world becomes more materialistic. The great Sufis Shams says:

> The world is a huge cauldron and something big is cooking in it. We don't know what yet. Everything we do, we feel, or think is an ingredient in that mixture. We need to ask ourselves

---

[4]Harutyunyan (2013), pp. 78–82.

[5]Mamardashvili (2011), pp. 7–8.

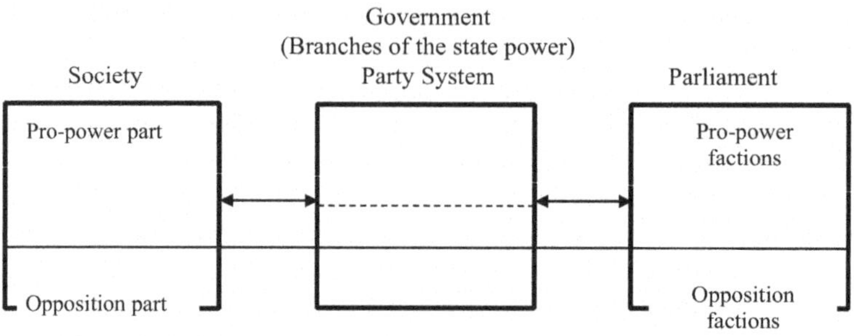

Fig. 1 Democratic system

> what we are adding to the cauldron. Are we adding resentments, animosities, anger and violence? Or are we adding love and harmony?[6]

The judges are the same as we are. We cannot demand justice from judges, unless it corresponds to the imperative of the inner values of the individual and to the external values of society. The first step that should be done towards the impartial judicial system is the step towards the inner freedom of an individual. The next step is to distinguish inner space from spirituality in our busy life.

3 The Independence of the Judiciary Within a Political System

The courts are formed by the political authorities. Judges are appointed by political authorities. The constitution and the laws may be formalized to an absurd level. The party-system is an active institution, which is functioning between society and state. It is reflecting the situation of the society and reproduces inside itself as a model of majority and minority via oppositional and governmental bodies. But in case of falsification of election, the party-system is not able to reflect the real situation. Majority and minority within the party-system and subsequently in Parliament don't have anything to do with the real situation in society. The party-system is thus losing its role as a middle institution between the society and the state, opening the door to clashes. It is the cold war between them, but it can easily turn into hot one.[7] Such a distortion of reality is impacting judiciary very negatively (see below Figs. 1 and 2).

In the theory of constitutional law and political science a number of scientists have expressed the idea according to which the existence and types of democracy depend on certain criteria. Based on these criteria democratic countries can be

[6]Shafak (2010), p. 146.

[7]Harutyunyan (2013), pp. 125–127.

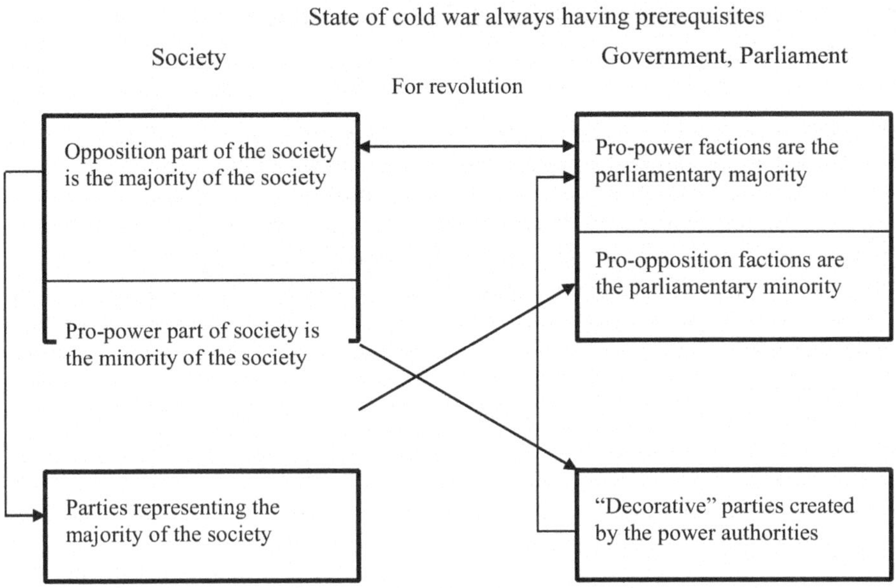

Fig. 2 Anti-democratic system

qualified as: maximum and minimum democracies,[8] but other qualifications could be given to the "minimum" democracies, such as "hybrid regimes", "competitive authoritarianism", "semi-autoritarianism" and so on.[9] However, the core of the problem is that the dynamics of the modern global, including pan-European, processes reveal a situation where a challenge to human rights and democracy is wrapped up in a democratic package. This means that anti-democratic democracies and the anti-constitutional constitutionalism are emerging.[10] All types of illiberal democracies, which are "semi-democracies" by their nature, are challenging the democracy.

[8]See for instance Sodaro (2008), pp. 177–178.

[9]See Levitsky and Way (2010); see also Ottaway (2003).

[10]Harutyunyan (2019), pp. 221–227.

4 European Guarantees for the Independence of the Judiciary

What democracy is like, justice is like also.[11] The European Convention of Human Rights and the case law of the European Court of Human Rights (hereafter the Court) set out minimum standards of guarantees and protect human rights that ensure consensus of member states. It can be said that they are in a way cultural and civilizational references, uniting forty-seven maximum and minimum democracies. Maximum justice is possible only in maximum democracies. Where is the red line after which the minimum democracy ceases to exist? Will the institutions and values of the twentieth century survive in the twenty-first century? A rhetorical question, but a cruel reality.

The test under the European Convention of Human Rights regarding the independence of tribunals consists of two parts: one institutional, the other individual. The institutional side is about whether there is a real separation of powers and a real system of checks and balances. The case law on Article 6 of the Court provides detailed rules about the independence of the judiciary, which are designed to protect it from external pressures and guarantee neutrality.[12] These rules cover the manner of appointing the members of the tribunal, the duration of their terms of office, and the existence of guarantees against outside pressure. This test consists of four elements:

- The manner of appointment of its members;
- The duration of their term of office;
- The existence of guarantees against outside pressure;
- Whether the body presents an appearance of independence.

This objective test was formulated in *Campbell and Fell v. the United Kingdom*:

> In determining whether a body can be considered to be 'independent' - notably of the executive and of the parties to the case (see, inter alia, the *Le Compte, Van Leuven and De Meyere* judgment of 23 June 1981, Series A no. 43, p. 24, para. 55) -, the Court has had regard to the manner of appointment of its members and the duration of their term of office (*ibid.*, pp. 24-25, para. 57), the existence of guarantees against outside pressures (see the *Piersack* judgment of 1 October 1982, Series A no. 53, p. 13, para. 27) and the question whether the body presents an appearance of independence (see the *Delcourt* judgment of 17 January 1970, Series A no. 11, p. 17, para. 31).[13]

[11]In this article we are speaking only about democracies. It is pointless to talk about independence of judiciary outside democracies.

[12]For further details on the right to a fair and public hearing by a competent independent and impartial tribunal, see UN, Committee on Human Rights (HRC) (2007), General Comment 32, 23 August 2007, paras. 19–23.

[13]ECtHR, *Campbell and Fell v. the United Kingdom*, 28 June 1984, Nos. 7819/77 and 7878/77, para. 78.

It was thereafter reiterated by the Court several times, as for instance in *Maktouf and Damjanovic v. Bosnia and Herzegovina*:

> The Court reiterates that in determining in previous cases whether a body could be considered as "independent" – notably of the executive and of the parties to the case – it has had regard to such factors as the manner of appointment of its members, the duration of their term of office, the existence of guarantees against outside pressures and the question whether the body presents an appearance of independence (see, for example, *Campbell and Fell v. the United Kingdom*, 28 June 1984, § 78, Series A no. 80, and Brudnicka and Others v. Poland, no. 54723/00, § 38, ECHR 2005-II).[14]

More recently, in *Ramos Nunes de Carvalho e sa v. Portugal*, the Court held:

> In order to establish whether a tribunal can be considered to be 'independent' within the meaning of Article 6 § 1, regard must be had, inter alia, to the manner of appointment of its members and their term of office, the existence of guarantees against outside pressures and the question whether the body presents an appearance of independence (see *Findlay v. the United Kingdom*, 25 February 1997, § 73, Reports of Judgments and Decisions 1997I, and *Tsanova-Gecheva*, cited above, § 106, 15 September 2015).[15]

The dynamics of modern worldwide (including pan-European) processes reveals a situation where the challenges to the independence of judiciary and democracy are presented in a democratic "packaging". Thus an anti-democratic democracy and anti-constitutional constitutionalism are formed.

5 Conclusion

Thus, nowadays we are facing crisis of constitutional state. The legal system and the constitution at its heart would not be able to be effective without minimum ethics. But what is the level of ethics nowadays? Our question here is different from ones, which concern the mechanism of the living instrument. The problem is not how to reflect in the constitution, in the legal position of courts, including of the European Court of Human Rights, the new tendencies and the new values of the society. The problem is what to do if the dynamics of values is degrading. We witness thus the decline in the level of education, culture, rise of nationalism, religious radicalism and terrorism. The manipulated man has replaced the free one, all institutions that ensure the integrity of a person—family, culture, relationship between parents and children, etc.—are targeted. The needy person is a fragmented person, a person who is easily influenced, a person who is ready for anything in order to gain wealth.

Societies are more and more heterogeneous, and social values of different segments are about to reach the level of the conflict. The process of reconsideration

[14]ECtHR [GC], *Maktouf and Damjanović v. Bosnia and Herzegovina*, 18 July 2013, Nos. 2312/08 and 34179/08, para. 49.

[15]ECtHR [GC], *Ramos Nunes de Carvalho E Sá v. Portugal*, 6 Nov. 2018, Nos. 55391/13, 57728/13 and 74041/13, para 144.

of the family and of its values is a great example of it. How should courts perceive these changes? Judges are facing objective difficulties while being responsible during the process of inclusion of external values in the constitution. This is a task which requires a decision to be made by political institutions. Political unity is an imperative of the constitutional state. Political institutions must form a relevant agenda that will ensure both political unity and the frame of values, which constitute a consensus for the society. Only under such conditions it is possible for the courts to function independently.

References

Barber N (2018) The principles of constitutionalism. Oxford University Press, Oxford

Harutyunyan A (2013) Constitutionalism: Problems of Postsoviet Realities. Norma, Moscow. (in Russian)

Harutyunyan A (2019) Anti-constitutional constitutionalism: minority against minority (its impact on international law). In: de Albuquerque PP, Wojtyczek K (eds) Judicial power in a globalized world. Springer, Cham

Holmes S (1994) The postcommunist presidency. East Eur Const Rev 3(1):36–39

Levitsky S, Way LA (2010) Competitive authoritarianism: hybrid regimes after the cold war. Cambridge University Press

Mamardashvili MK (2011) Conscious and Civilization. Azbuka, Saint Petersburg. (in Russian)

Ottaway M (2003) Democracy challenged: the rise of semi-authoritarianism. Carnegie Endowment for Int'l Peace

Shafak E (2010) The Fourty rules of love. Penguin Books, London

Sodaro MJ (2008) Comparative politics: a global introduction, 3rd edn. McGraw-Hill, New York

Vile MJC (1998) Constitutionalism and the separation of powers. Liberty Fund, Inc [Previous edition: Vile MJC (1967) Constitutionalism and the separation of powers. Clarendon Press, Oxford University Press, Oxford, London]

Armen Harutyunyan is a Judge of the European Court of Human Rights, Doctor of Law, Professor. Apart from academic professional activity which he started in 1986, he has held a number of different responsible positions both on national and international level. These, among other things, include Human Rights Defender (Ombudsman) of Armenia (2006–2011), Deputy Representative of Armenia, European Commission for Democracy through Law (Venice Commission) (2002–2011), Member of the Board of European Ombudsman Institute (2008–2011) (external member (2011–2015)), Regional Representative at the Regional Office for Central Asia of the Office of the UN High Commissioner for Human Rights (2011–2014), Head of the UN Human Rights Monitoring Mission in Ukraine (2014–2015).

The Independence of the Judiciary in the Jurisprudence of the European Court of Human Rights: The Case of *Baka* *v. Hungary*

María Elósegui

Contents

1 Introduction 69
2 The Right to Freedom of Expression of Judges 72
3 Violation of Article 10 (Freedom of Expression) and Removal as a Consequence of Expressing Legitimate Opinions in Public 75
4 General Principles on the Freedom of Expression of Judges and Their Special Duty of Discretion 76
5 The Irremovability of Judges and the Right to the Procedural Safeguards of Article 6, Paragraph 1 of the Convention 79
6 The *Eskelinen* Test and Civil Servants Facing Destitution *Ad Hoc* 80
7 The Execution of the *Baka* Judgment 83
References 86

1 Introduction

First I would like to express my thanks to Judge Iulia Motoc for this invitation to co-edit this publication. Secondly, I would recommend a document prepared by the Registry of the European Court of Human Rights about cases concerning the authority of the judiciary, stemming from a seminar held in 2018.[1] Moreover Kevin Aquilina did a complete study of all the cases before the Strasbourg Court in which the applicants were judges.[2] The present contribution will focus on the independence of judges (in relation to the other two powers) and the freedom of

[1]ECtHR [the Registry] (2018).
[2]Aquilina (2019).

M. Elósegui (✉)
European Court of Human Rights, Strasbourg, France
e-mail: elosegui@unizar.es

M. Elósegui et al. (eds.), *The Rule of Law in Europe*,
https://doi.org/10.1007/978-3-030-56001-0_6

expression of judges, analysing the leading case of *Baka v. Hungary*.[3] This judgment contains also a summary of the most important criteria relating to the independence of judges as they appear in the jurisprudence of the European Court of Human Rights. More recently, these principles were applied in two Grand Chamber cases, *Denisov v. Ukraine*[4] and *Ramos Nunes Carvalho e Sá v. Portugal*.[5] The cases of *Baka* and *Denisov* are related to the applicants' removal from administrative positions, as presidents of the Supreme Court, without termination of their judicial tenure.

The *Baka* case concerns the limits to the freedom of expression of Judge Baka, a former president of the Supreme Court of Hungary, and his access to a judicial process. The case was examined first by a Chamber of the Second Section of the ECtHR, resulting in an initial judgment of 27 May 2014. The Chamber itself concluded unanimously that there had been a violation of Articles 6 and 10 of the Convention in respect of Judge Baka, because of his removal as President of the Supreme Court.[6] The Government of Hungary requested the referral of the case to the Grand Chamber. A panel of five judges of the Grand Chamber accepted the referral request, under Article 43 of the European Convention on Human Rights. The public hearing took place on 17 June 2015.[7] The Grand Chamber adopted its final judgment on 14 March 2016, which was delivered at a public hearing by its President on 23 June 2016.

As stated in the above-mentioned paper compiled by the Court's registry on "The authority of the judiciary":[8]

> International standards affirm that a necessary condition of an independent judiciary is that judges enjoy security of tenure and are not subject to arbitrary removal from office. Accordingly, the Court must scrutinize very carefully allegations that mandates have been prematurely terminated because of views and criticisms publicly expressed in a judge's professional capacity.

In *Baka* the applicant had been elected President of the Hungarian Supreme Court for a six-year term. By a new legislation, the Hungarian government had terminated his term of office three and a half years early. He alleged that he had been denied

---

[3]ECtHR [GC], *Baka v. Hungary*, 23 June 2016, No. 20261/12. See Kosař and Šipulová (2018), pp. 83–110.

[4]ECtHR [GC], *Denisov v. Ukraine*, 25 September 2018, No. 76639/11.

[5]ECtHR [GC], *Ramos Nunes de Carvalho e Sá v. Portugal*, 6 Nov. 2018, Nos. 55391/13 and 2 others.

[6]For a summary of the facts and a critical comment on the changes in the Constitutional law in Hungary see Cannoot (2016).

[7]I had the opportunity to attend the hearing, owing to the fact that at the time I was an expert in the Commission against Racism and Intolerance of the Council of Europe and happened to be in Strasbourg. The hearing in the presence of Judge Baka had a great impact on me, also because Judge Baka had been a judge of the European Court of Human Rights for many years, from 1991 to 2008. In order to preserve independence, not one of the judges sitting in the Grand Chamber composition had previously been a colleague of his at the Court.

[8]ECtHR [the Registry] (2018), p. 6.

access to a tribunal to contest the premature termination. He also complained that this termination was due to views and positions that he had expressed publicly, in his official capacity, concerning legislative reforms affecting the judiciary. He relied on Article 6, paragraph 1 and on Article 10 of the Convention. The new legislation, which did not seem compatible with the requirements of the rule of law, prevented the review of the premature termination by any bodies exercising judicial powers. The Grand Chamber held that the respondent State had impaired the very essence of the applicant's right of access to a court.

In relation to the exercise of the right to freedom of expression by a judge, a balance has to be struck between the separation of powers and the right enjoyed by every citizen. However, the exercise of this right by judges is subject to many restrictions. The problem begins when the political power uses the possible disciplinary sanctions against judges in an arbitrary manner, precisely to restrict their freedom of expression, beyond what is necessary. These limits are not always clear and this is reflected in the fact that most of the judgments of the European Court of Human Rights about judges have been accompanied by dissenting or other separate opinions.

The Court has repeatedly addressed the importance of the separation of powers as a relevant point in, *inter alia*, judicial appointments.[9] Judges must be independent of other organs of the State; this is crucial in a democracy. The Court indicated in *Stafford v. the United Kingdom* that the separation of powers between the executive and the judiciary was a "notion which ha[d] assumed growing importance in the case-law of the Court."[10]

As has been pointed out, it may be legitimate for the State to impose upon judges a special duty of discretion due to their status.[11] But in special circumstances, judges can play an important role in matters that concern the judiciary, the courts or the administration of justice. Fear of sanctions for speaking openly in favour of the independence and impartiality of judges could produce an undesirable "chilling effect".

The Court's examination began as usual with an analysis of Article 6, concerning access to a court, then turned to Article 10 on freedom of expression. Nevertheless, as my approach is to look at the independence of judges in relation to the two other powers and consider their possibilities of criticism and public speaking, I would start reverse the analysis, moving from the right to freedom of expression to the procedural safeguards against the removal of a judge afforded by Article 6, paragraph 1. I will do so because the principles of independence and irremovability of judges are mainstream principles which have to be seen from the perspective of Convention

[9]To quote Halmai (2017), p. 488: "And the aim of the Hungarian government with the reduction of the retirement age of the judges was exactly to get rid of the most of the court presidents, and replace them with new ones, loyal to the government." See also Halmai (2012).

[10]See ECtHR [GC], *Stafford v. the United Kingdom*, no. 46295/99, para. 78, ECtHR 2002-IV; and ECtHR [The registry], p. 3.

[11]See A. Seibert-Fohr in the present book. Also Dijkstra (2017), pp. 11–14.

rights, in this case under Articles 6 and 10, but they are not autonomous rights protected by the Convention. I agree with the conclusions of a previous article written by Cano Palomares about this judgment, where he said:

> The ECtHR analyzed the alleged violations of the ECtHR (arts. 6 and 10) in the light of the principles of irremovability and judicial independence, but did not reach the explicit conclusion that Mr. Baka's subjective right to his own judicial independence had been violated. This is because the applicant had not specifically invoked this right before the Court and, above all, the ECtHR does not recognize as such the subjective right of the judge to be independent. Judicial independence is only guaranteed from the point of view of the trial [art. 6paragraph1 ECtHR: 'Everyone is entitled to a fair and public hearing . . . by an independent and impartial tribunal'], but not for the judge.[12]

This means that the litigants are the ones protected by Article 6 and not the judges themselves. Yet it is true at the same time that judges could find themselves in the position of a litigant or applicant when they go to court to defend their own case. However, Judge Baka was not allowed to have access to a court in his country.

2 The Right to Freedom of Expression of Judges

The Court examines the right to freedom of expression as applied to State officials and members of the judiciary.[13] In cases related to disciplinary procedures, as well as the appointment or dismissal of judges, the Court analyses whether this measure interferes with the exercise of the right to freedom of expression.

The ECtHR has established several criteria to distinguish between, on the one hand, their spheres of legitimate independence and freedom and, on the other, disciplinary sanctions due to the fact that a judge did not respect his obligations, for example of impartiality, neutrality, confidentiality and secrecy of deliberations. It will be necessary to examine whether these sanctions are legal or on the contrary whether they seek to limit the freedom of expression in an illegal manner.[14]

In the reasoning of its judgments, the Court takes into account in such cases the specific legislation of the country and the concrete facts. In the *Baka* case, the Court started by analysing its own case-law. In particular, it looked at the case of *Wille v Liechtenstein*, where the applicant, the Presiding Judge of the Liechtenstein Administrative Court, considered that a letter from the Prince of Liechtenstein announcing his intention not to renew him in the post of public office constituted "a reprimand for the previous exercise of freedom of expression by the applicant."[15] In that letter, the Prince had announced the intention to sanction this judge for expressing his

---

[12]Cano Palomares (2018), p. 128.

[13]See *Baka v. Hungary* [GC], para. 140.

[14]See an in-depth analysis of these cases and the difficulties in making the distinction in Dijkstra (2017), pp. 12–13.

[15]ECtHR [GC], *Wille v. Liechtenstein*, 28 Oct. 1999, No. 28396/95, paras. 41–42.

opinion at a public conference on certain issues of constitutional law relating to the powers of the Constitutional Court. In that case, the Court concluded that the impugned conduct was protected by Article 10 of the Convention and that the interference with the applicant's freedom of expression constituted a violation of his right.[16] The Court characterised the letter as an unjustified interference with the judge's freedom of expression, finding that at no time had the judge been accused of a lack of professionalism in performing his duties and that the sanction could not be a disciplinary measure of dismissal.[17]

In the Court's view, there is no right as such under the Convention to hold a public position in the administration of justice.[18] But Article 10 affords to judges protection from disproportionate or ill-founded sanctions. In the case of *Olga Kudeshkina*,[19] the ECtHR found that there had been a violation of Article 10. The applicant had been dismissed from her post as judge as a result of her statements to the media. The ECtHR found that the disciplinary sanction, the most serious available, was disproportionate and that it had been imposed without adequate procedural safeguards.

A case in which the ECtHR considered that the government's proposal to dismiss a public official had been made in a reasonable manner is that of *Harabin v. Slovakia* (2004). Harabin was the President of the Supreme Court of Slovakia and his dismissal was based on a report from the Ministry of Justice on his professional qualifications and his personal qualities for the performance of that position, explaining that he lacked the requisite skills for the exercise of his functions. The problematic areas in which he had showed a lack of professionalism included the application of professional criteria when proposing candidates to assume positions in the Supreme Court and his inhibition in not taking disciplinary measures against a judge of that court who had attacked an official of the Ministry of Justice.[20] Judge Harabin had also expressed, in a draft about the possible amendment of the Constitution, his concerns about the separation of powers and judicial independence, but none of this was actually the reason for his dismissal. In fact, the sanction procedure was the result of his refusal to subject his court to an audit of its accounts by the competent officials from the Ministry of Finance.

In *Baka v. Hungary*, the applicant, in his professional capacity as President of the Supreme Court and the National Council of Justice, publicly expressed his views on a number of legislative reforms concerning the judiciary. As a result, he was dismissed prematurely from his position as President of the Supreme Court.[21] The

---

[16]See *Baka v. Hungary* [GC], para. 141 and ECtHR [The Registry] (2018), p. 7.

[17]Unlike the case of *Kayasu v. Turkey,* 13 Nov. 2008, Nos. 64119/00 and 76292/01, paras. 77–79 (about the disciplinary dismissal of a prosecutor).

[18]*Harabin v. Slovakia*, Decision, 29 June 2004, No. 62584/00 (dismissed as manifestly ill-founded).

[19]See *Kudeshkina c. Russia*, 26 February 2009, No. 29492/05, para.79.

[20]Cited in *Baka v. Hungary* [GC], para. 142.

[21]Halmai (2017), p. 488.

ECtHR considered that this action by the Hungarian government could dissuade judges from participating in the debate on legislative reforms or on issues related to the independence of the judiciary.

The ECtHR proceeded with an analysis of the proven facts presented by the parties. In the *Baka* case, *the standard of proof beyond reasonable doubt* acquired special relevance, since there had been no judicial domestic decisions on this case, nor on the applicant's allegations and reasons for the termination of his post as President of the Supreme Court.[22] This is one of the key points in situations where the dismissal of public officials precisely does not allow for the possibility of judicial supervision. In those cases, in the absence of domestic judicial procedures, the ECtHR cannot make use of the arguments of the domestic courts and does not have evidence or facts usually collected in those instances. This is a difficulty added to the task that the ECtHR must carry out in order to gather evidence on whether or not the dismissal was likely to have been arbitrary (an aspect which will be analysed later).

The ECtHR took into account the entire sequence of events. The relevant facts were the following: on 12 February 2011, the applicant's press officer explained to a newspaper his concern about an annulment law ordering the nullity of final judicial decisions on a 2006 demonstration, which in his opinion violated the right of the judges to assess the evidence with due freedom. In March 2011, Judge Baka gave a speech in Parliament on various aspects of the draft of the new Constitution of Hungary.[23] On 7 April 2011, together with other presidents of courts, he addressed a letter to the Prime Minister criticising the draft of the Constitution, which sought to reduce the judges' retirement age from 70 to 62.[24] Four days later, he sent another letter in which he emphasised that this proposal was humiliating and that it undermined the principle of independence and irremovability of the judges.

On 14 April 2011, this time in his position as President of the National Council of Justice, and together with the full Supreme Court and other presidents of courts, he made a public statement on the proposal to modify the presiding body, and suggested that the fact that the new regulation of the retirement age and the impossibility of raising any appeal of unconstitutionality against it before the Constitutional Court, was motivated by political reasons. Later, on 3 November 2011, he criticised the

---

[22]*Baka v. Hungary*, para. 144.

[23]Scheppele (2015), pp. 111–124.

[24]Gyulavári and Hős (2013), p. 289. Summary: The retirement age of Hungarian judges was lowered by a new law from 70 to 62 years at the beginning of 2012. This generated heated legal and political debates both at national and European level. Firstly, in mid-2012 the Hungarian Constitutional Court stated its unconstitutionality based on the principle of judicial independence (33/2012. (VII. 17.) AB decision). Secondly, in November 2012 the Court of Justice (Court of Justice or CJEU) established the violation of EU age discrimination provisions of Directive 2000/78/EC (Directive), on the grounds that the introduction of the automatic retirement scheme was in breach with the principle of proportionality (C-286/12 *European Commission v Hungary*, judgment of 6 December 2012). Also Halmai (2017), pp. 471–488.

project to replace the National Council of Justice with a body external to the judiciary that would be responsible for the administration of the courts.[25]

Reacting to these criticisms, two MPs from the majority party declared in two interviews (of 14 April and 19 October 2011) that the President of the Supreme Court would remain as president of the new organisation called *Kúria* and that only the name of the institution would be changed. The reality was that in between 19 and 23 November 2011 the proposal to terminate his office was made public. It would take effect from 1 January 2012, the date on which the new Constitution would come into effect and the new *Kúria* would substitute the Supreme Court.

In addition, the legislation on the organisation and administration of the courts was amended by introducing a new criterion according to which a candidate to be president of the *Kúria*, must have served for at least five consecutive years as a judge in Hungary. This excluded the time served as a judge in an international court.[26] András Baka, who had been a judge in the European Court of Human Rights for sixteen years (1991–2008), was de facto excluded by this new criterion. In the opinion of the ECtHR, this criterion was actually decided *ad hominem*.

3 Violation of Article 10 (Freedom of Expression) and Removal as a Consequence of Expressing Legitimate Opinions in Public

For the ECtHR there had been a proven causal link between the exercise of freedom of expression by Judge Baka and the termination of his office. That opinion was already shared, prior to this ruling of the ECtHR, by other institutions of the Council of Europe, such as the Supervisory Committee of the Parliamentary Assembly and the Venice Commission.[27] The ECtHR accepted the applicant's version *prima facie* and stated that the burden of proving the true reasons for his dismissal was in the hands of the Government, as there had been no opportunity for the applicant to gain access to a court or independent body. The act of termination did not give reasons for the premature termination of Judge Baka's term as President of the Supreme Court, whereas in previous statements, the government asserted that the entry into force of the new legislation did not entail the end of the President's term. To be clear, "neither the applicant's ability to exercise his functions as president of the supreme judicial body nor his professional conduct were called into question by the domestic authorities."[28]

[25]See *Baka v. Hungary* [GC], para. 145.

[26]*Ibid.*, para. 147. See Vincze (2015), p. 3.

[27]*Ibid.*, para. 148.

[28]*Ibid.*, para. 149. See by contrast *Harabin v. Slovakia*, 20 November 2012, No. 58688/11, paras. 150–153.

As Judge Baka held two posts, as president of the Supreme Court and as president of the National Council of Justice, the Government sought to justify his dismissal on the grounds that the latter body had disappeared with the legal reform. However, this argument did not convince the ECtHR, for two reasons: on the one hand, the powers of the new judicial institution (the *Kúria*) did not seem so different from those of the old court presided over by the applicant; and on the other hand, the fact that, under the new legislation, the administrative or non-judicial functions of the President of the Supreme Court were no longer devolved to the President of the new *Kúria*, did not affect in principle the capacity of the applicant to continue exercising the rest of the functions as President of the Supreme Court.[29] In sum, "the ECtHR considers that the applicant has been able to prove in an indifferent way the cause-effect relationship between the exercise of his right to freedom of expression (the criticisms expressed through speeches before Parliament, letters and communiqués) and his dismissal as President."[30]

The Court examined whether this interference was justified. In order to do so, it applied the proportionality test, examining the "prescribed by law", "legitimate aim" and "necessity in a democratic society" criteria, to reach the conclusion that the interference was not justified.

4 General Principles on the Freedom of Expression of Judges and Their Special Duty of Discretion

The ECtHR has developed general principles or criteria through its jurisprudence on the special limits that apply to public officials and judges in exercising their freedom of expression.

In principle, in the case of public officials[31]—and more so in the case of judges—those rights are particularly restricted, due to their obligations and duties as public officials, in the exercise of their functions.[32] On the other hand, the legitimate interests of the society must be taken into account. In the case of judges, it is essential that, in their public statements, they be neutral and that their independence in relation to the other two powers should be clear. The right of the citizens to know that their judges will do justice in an objective way is also crucial. However, the question of the possibility for the judges to be affiliated with political parties is another difficult topic, which I am not going to develop in the present article,

[29]Cano Palomares (2018), pp. 124–125.

[30]*Ibid.*, p. 124.

[31]ECtHR, *Vogt v. Germany* [GC], 26 Sept. 1995, No. 17851/91.

[32]ECtHR, *Albayrak v. Turkey*, 31 Jan. 2008, No. 38406/97 and *Pitkevich v. Russia*, 8 Feb. 2001, No. 47936/99.

although I would refer to the contribution of Professor and Judge Anja Seibert-Forh in the present publication.[33]

In the case of *Albayrak v. Turkey*, the applicant was a judge in 1995 when the authorities instituted disciplinary proceedings against him, among other things because he was reading legal publications of the PKK and watching a television channel controlled by the PKK. The applicant denied all the accusations, arguing that he believed in the fundamental principles of the State and served it faithfully. The Supreme Council of Judges and Prosecutors considered that the allegations against the applicant were well founded, and as a sanction he was transferred to another court. The Supreme Council of Judges subsequently and repeatedly refused to promote the applicant due to these previous disciplinary sanctions. The ECtHR considered that the interference was not in accordance with the principle of proportionality for the following reasons: there was no evidence that the judge was associated with the PKK or that his conduct in the cases he had to adjudicate would have cast doubt on his ability to act impartially. Consequently, the ECtHR concluded that, by imposing a disciplinary sanction, the authorities had placed excessive weight on the fact that he had read or heard media related to the PKK. Therefore that interference was not "necessary in a democratic society."[34]

In its jurisprudence, the Court has established two other criteria to underline specific topics on which judges should not express themselves publicly. Judges must maintain maximum discretion about the cases they are dealing with, in order to preserve their image as impartial judges. Even when they disseminate objective information, they must do so with restraint and propriety.[35] Moreover, they must not criticise the conduct of other judges in the conduct of pending cases.[36] Furthermore, they cannot express doubts about trust in the judicial system, engage in destructive criticism or call in question the honesty of other judges.[37] A further criterion is that Article 10 protection covers the freedom of expression of the judge when he refers to issues related to the justice system and judicial impartiality.

Taking this case-law into account, the Court recognised that there had been an interference in Judge Baka's freedom of expression. In order to analyse the conformity of this decision with the right protected by the Convention, the Court proceeded with the test of proportionality, in accordance with the three steps provided for in Article 10, paragraph 2. First it had to be seen whether the removal was prescribed by law, second whether it pursued a legitimate aim, and last, whether it was necessary in a democratic society.

---

[33]A. Seibert-Fohr, in this book; and Seibert-Fohr (2012, 2019).

[34]ECtHR, *Albayrak v. Turkey*, 31 January 2008, No. 38406/97.

[35]ECtHR, *Olujic v. Croatia*, 5 Feb. 2009, No 223305/05. See Mahoney (2012). Also Dijkstra (2017), pp. 11–14.

[36]ECtHR, *Kudeshkina v. Russia,* 26 Feb. 2009, No. 29492/05, para. 94.

[37]ECtHR, *Di Giovanni v. Italy,* 9 July 2013, No. 51160/06, para. 81; *Kudeshkina v. Russia*, 26 Feb. 2009, No. 29492/05, para. 86.

In relation to the first point, the Court took it for granted that there was a law about removal, namely section 11(2) of the Transitional Provisions of the Fundamental Law of Hungary and section 185(1) of the Organisation and Administration of the Courts Act, although it must be added that the Court had expressed doubts about the quality of this law with regard to Article 6.[38] In fact, it concluded that this norm was not compatible with the rule of law.[39] However, the existence of this legislation created an assumption that the removal was prescribed by law.[40] Going to the second step, the aim of the removal, the Hungarian Government maintained in its observations that the finality of this legislative change was to reinforce the independence of the judiciary, especially of the president. The Court was not convinced and held, on the contrary, that it was a measure which ran counter to the independence of the judiciary from the legislature, since the measure had been taken as a consequence of the criticisms by Judge Baka and not following the application of a neutral law, meant to improve the organisation of the judiciary.[41]

According to the Court's normal analysis when applying the test of proportionality, if one condition is not fulfilled, it is not necessary to go into the subsequent steps of the test. In the present case, the Court nevertheless proceeded with an analysis of the necessity of this new law. The ECtHR applied the general principles to the present case. First, it found that, as President of the National Council of Justice, Judge Baka did not only have a right, but even a duty to express an opinion on the legislative reforms affecting the judiciary.[42]

Applying all these criteria in the *Baka* case, the Court first concluded that Judge Baka had expressed his views on the legislative reforms that affected the judiciary and that he had used the legal means to do so. In addition, this had been in keeping with his position as President of the National Judicial Council. To be precise, the ECtHR emphasised that, in accordance with paragraph 3 of the Magna Carta of Judges of the Council of Europe, "each judge is responsible for promoting and protecting judicial independence."[43] Secondly, all the Judge Baka's opinions and criticisms had focused on the legislative reforms from a professional point of view

---

[38]See ECtHR [GC], *Baka v. Hungary*, paras. 117–118.

[39]*Ibid.* This lack of analysis of the Court about the rule of law has received many critics by the part of several academics. Among them, Kosař and Šipulová (2018), pp. 83–110. Chronowski and Varju (2016), pp. 271–289.

[40]ECtHR [GC], *Baka v. Hungary*, para. 156.

[41]*Ibid.*, para. 157. According to Halmai (2017), p. 488: "While the former aimed at getting rid of as many aged court leaders, who were presumably not loyal to the government, as possible, the aim of the early termination of the Supreme Court President's term was to replace the head of the entire judiciary, who was critical towards the new judicial system, which curtailed the independence of the judiciary. In this respect, the Baka case was also an issue of judicial independence, threatened by legislative means, even if this was the new Fundamental Law itself."

[42]ECtHR [GC], *Baka v. Hungary*, para. 168.

[43]*Ibid.*

and were of great public interest.[44] Thirdly, they had also dealt with the independence and irrevocability of the judges.[45] Lastly,

> the premature termination of the applicant's mandate [had] undoubtedly had a 'chilling effect' in that it must have discouraged not only him but also other judges and court presidents in future from participating in public debate on legislative reforms affecting the judiciary and more generally on issues concerning the independence of the judiciary.[46]

The Grand Chamber concluded that all this fell within the limits of his freedom of expression and therefore Judge Baka's removal as President of the Supreme Court had constituted a violation of Article 10 of the Convention. It was also a violation of Article 6 paragraph 1, since the principle of judicial irremovability was essential to maintaining of judicial independence, as was said in the cases of *Fruni v. Slovakia*[47] and *Henryk Urban and Ryszard Urban v. Poland*.[48]

5 The Irremovability of Judges and the Right to the Procedural Safeguards of Article 6, Paragraph 1 of the Convention

International standards establish that a necessary condition for judicial independence is that judges must have security in knowing that the maintaining of their position will not be subject to arbitrary changes. For this reason, the European Court of Human Rights conducts special scrutiny in cases where the term of office is ended prematurely because of the points of view and criticisms expressed publicly by judges in their professional capacity. In these cases, of which the *Baka* case is one, the judge affected should have had access to a process in which he could defend himself. As regards the applicability of Article 6 paragraph 1 of the Convention in relation to disputes concerning the judges, it was clear that the judges themselves must be protected by the guarantees of a fair trial.

Judge Baka complained to the ECtHR that he had been denied access to a fair judicial process. For that reason, the ECtHR also examined the possible violation of Article 6 paragraph 1, concluding that there had also been a violation of this provision. As a result of Hungarian legislation, the premature termination of the office could not be reviewed—nor was it open to review—by any judicial body or by any institution. The ECtHR concluded that this was not in accordance with the rule of law. In conclusion, the Hungarian State had violated the universal right of access to a court that protected all citizens, including judges.

---

[44] *Ibid.*, para. 171. Solomon (2012), pp. 909–935.

[45] *Baka v. Hungary* [GC], para. 172. See Sonnevend et al. (2015), pp. 33–110.

[46] *Baka v. Hungary* [GC], para. 173.

[47] ECtHR, *Fruni v. Slovakia*, 21 June 2011, No. 8014/07, para. 145.

[48] ECtHR, *Henryk Urban and Ryszard Urban v. Poland*, 30 Nov. 2010, No. 23614/08.

In *Vilho Eskelinen and Others v. Finland*[49] the Grand Chamber established the criteria to be applied under the civil limb of Article 6 paragraph 1 in disputes related to State employees or public officials. If this protection is to be excluded, the two criteria which must be met are the following: first, that a national law expressly excluded such access to a court for persons occupying that post or for a category of officials; second, the exclusion must be justified by objective reasons to protect the interests of the State.

6 The *Eskelinen* Test and Civil Servants Facing Destitution *Ad Hoc*

The so-called *Eskelinen* test was also applied step by step by the ECtHR in *Baka v. Hungary*.[50] This test had originally been applied to career officials, but the different chambers of the Court soon extended its application to disputes related to judges by creating extensive jurisprudence (see *G v. Finland*,[51] *Oleksandr Volkov v. Ukraine*,[52] *Di Giovanni v. Italy*,[53] *Tsanova-Gecheva v. Bulgaria*,[54] *Olujic v. Croatia*,[55] *Harabin v. Slovakia*,[56] the latter judgment on the disciplinary dismissal of the President of the Supreme Court). Although judges are not ordinary public officials, the European Court of Human Rights considers them to be part of the public service. Thus these criteria began to be applied to multiple disputes relating to both officials and judges, over issues such as recruitment and appointment, career and promotion, change of destination, termination of service, and dismissal of the president of a Supreme Court (see).[57]

The doctrine considers that the *Eskelinen* test means that:

> In order for a State to invoke the status of a plaintiff's public official to avoid the applicability of article 6, two conditions must be met. First, the internal law of the State in question must have expressly excluded access to a court in relation to the category position in question. Second, this exception must be based on objective reasons of interest of the State. In this sense, the State must demonstrate that the object of the dispute is related to the exercise of the authority of the State or calls into question the special link between the official and the Employer State.[58]

[49] ECtHR [GC], *Vilho Eskelinen and Others v. Finland*, 19 April 2007, No. 63235/00.

[50] ECtHR [GC], *Baka v. Hungary*, paras. 107–118.

[51] ECtHR, *G v. Finland*, 27 Jan. 2009, No. 33173/05.

[52] ECtHR, *Oleksandr Volkov v. Ukraine*, 9 Jan. 2013, No. 21722/11.

[53] ECtHR, *Di Giovanni v. Italy*, 9 July 2013, No. 51160/06.

[54] ECtHR, *Tsanova-Gecheva v. Bulgaria*, 15 Sept. 2015, No. 43800/12.

[55] ECtHR, *Olujic v. Croatia*, 5 Feb. 2009, No. 22330/05.

[56] ECtHR, *Harabin v. Slovakia*, 20 Nov. 2012, No.58688/11.

[57] See *Nazsiz v. Turkey*, Decision, 26 May 2009, No 22412/05, on the disciplinary dismissal of a prosecutor, cited in *Baka v. Hungary*, para. 105.

[58] Cano Palomares (2018), p. 121.

In *Olujic v. Croatia* the applicant was President of the Supreme Court of Croatia when the National Council of the Judiciary initiated disciplinary proceedings against him and removed him from his post, terminating his service as a judge. The decisions of the Council were confirmed by the Parliament and by the Constitutional Court. The applicant filed different claims based on Article 6, but the Croatian Government maintained that it was not applicable to a dispute related to the dismissal of a Supreme Court judge, owing to the nature of his role as a public official.[59] In this case, although national legislation had excluded access to a court, the scope of that exclusion was not absolute. Consequently, the Court considered that Article 6 was applicable. Moreover, the fact that the applicant was a judge of the Supreme Court and also its president did not justify the non-application of that Article, in connection with his suspension from both those positions. The Court found a violation of Article 6 paragraph 1 of the Convention on four accounts: the lack of impartiality of the president and two other members of the National Council; the exclusion of public process in the disciplinary proceedings against the applicant; the violation of the principle of equality of arms; and the excessive length of the procedure.

In *Paluda v. Slovakia*,[60] disciplinary proceedings were brought against the applicant, a judge of the Supreme Court, who was temporarily suspended from his duties with immediate effect by the General Judicial Council. The consequence was that his salary was reduced by 50% for the duration of the suspension, which lasted for two years. The applicant filed different claims against the suspension, but without success. Finally, he filed a complaint with the European Court of Human Rights for the impossibility to have access to a court to challenge the suspension. The Court found a violation of Article 6 paragraph 1 of the Convention because the General Judicial Council was not a judicial body and did not provide the institutional and procedural guarantees required by that provision. Further, the Government did not provide any conclusive reason to justify denying the complainant access to judicial protection.

In the *Baka* case, the President of the Supreme Court was elected by the Parliament, in 1999 for a period of six years. According to the rules applicable at that time, the only possible reason for the dismissal was incompetence in the fulfilment of management tasks, in which case the incumbent was entitled to seek judicial review of the dismissal before the Service Tribunal. But in order to avoid this possibility, an *ad hominem* law was actually enacted later, in the form of "Transitory Provisions of the Constitution", that would come into force together with the Constitution on 1 January 2012. These laws prohibited judicial review of the removal of the President of the Supreme Court, and were applied retroactively to a previous appointment that should have been governed by the laws in force at the time the appointment was made.

The reasoning of the Grand Chamber in the *Baka* case adds a clarification to the first criterion of the *Eskelinen* test, by developing two additional steps, to avoid the

[59]Some recent comments by Kosař (2018), p. 80. Also Settem (2016), p. 366.

[60]ECtHR, *Paluda v. Slovakia*, 23 May 2017, No. 33392/12.

stalemate created by arbitrary changes in legislation which result in the suppression of an existing right of access to a court. These two new analytical steps established by the ECtHR consist in examining the legislation in force before the impugned action and after the subsequent enactment. To be precise, this examination in the *Baka* case showed that the State had changed the legislation expressly to prevent that a certain measure become subject to judicial supervision.[61] As Cano Palomares states:

> [T]he national legislation that exempts the right of access to a court must be compatible with the requirements of the rule of law, inherent in all articles of the ECtHR, which implies in this context that it must be a law of general application to a category of officials, and not an *ad hominem* legislation.[62]

The ECtHR concluded that this type of measure would open the way to abuse, allowing States parties to the Convention to prevent access to a court through individual measures concerning public officials, by including these measures in an *ad hoc* statutory provision not subject to judicial review. All this led it to find that Hungary lacked a valid law to support the ban on the president of the Supreme Court to challenge the premature termination of his mandate before a court.

The Grand Chamber carried out an in-depth analysis of the hierarchy of sources of the constitutional legal order of Hungary. Before the legislative change, the previous ordinary legislation, as well as the constitutional principles about the independence and inamovability of judges, protected Judge Baka's right to finish his mandate and even to defend himself in a court if he had been removed without objective reasons. The difficult question for the Grand Chamber was to build its reasoning for the following conclusion. The new law which ordered the removal of Judge Baka as president of the Supreme Court had been enacted with a constitutional status. From the perspective of the primacy of sources of law, the problem is whether a law at a constitutional level, which goes against the rights protected in the Convention, could be accepted by the ECtHR as a valid one. The majority of the Grand Chamber, with one exception, agreed that it could not accept a law which denied access to a court without any objective grounds, even if this law had a constitutional rank. According to the dissenting opinion of Judge Wojtyczek, a subsequent law of constitutional rank could derogate from a prior ordinary norm of inferior rank.[63] By contrast, Judges Pinto de Albuquerque and Dedov wrote a concurring opinion emphasising the direct effect of the Convention and its supraconstitutional status within the hierarchy of sources.[64] The judgment of the Grand Chamber did not go that far,[65] this being a very controversial question in some of the Contracting Parties of the Council of Europe.

[61] *Baka v. Hungary*, para. 116.

[62] Cano Palomares (2018), p. 122. *Baka v. Hungary*, para. 117.

[63] *Baka v. Hungary*, Dissenting opinion of Judge Wojtyczek.

[64] *Baka v. Hungary,* Concurring opinions of Judges Pinto de Alburquerque and Dedov.

[65] Some academics such as Cannoot, *o.c.,* affirm that "The Court clearly attributes direct supraconstitutional effect to the Convention, and more specifically articles 6 para.1 and 10. Indeed,

Given that the Grand Chamber concluded that there was no valid legal basis and thus that the first requirement of the *Eskelinen* test had not been met, the Court would normally consider it unnecessary to examine the second requirement, namely the existence of objective reasons of State interest justifying the restriction of the right of access. However the Grand Chamber judgment did proceed to the second step, hypothesising that if a national law existed stipulating that the applicant in this specific case would not have access to a Court in case of removal, this law would not have met the *Eskelinen* test, because the State would not have shown that such restrictions on civil servants were based on objective reasons of State interest.[66]

It concluded that the protection guaranteed in Article 6 paragraph 1 of the Convention had not been complied with. The limitation had not pursued a legitimate aim and there was no reasonable relationship of proportionality between the end pursued and the means employed. The premature termination of the applicant's mandate as President of the Supreme Court had not been reviewed, and it was not open to a possible review by an ordinary court or other body with judicial power. This lack of access to justice was the result of a norm whose compatibility with the requirements of the principle of legality and the rule of law was very doubtful.[67] The ECtHR emphasised the importance of the instruments of the Council of Europe for enhancing and guaranteeing the fairness of procedures in cases concerning the removal and dismissal of judges, including the intervention of an independent authority of the executive and legislative powers in relation to all decisions affecting the termination of a judge's position. For all these reasons, the Court concluded that in this case there had been a violation of Article 6 paragraph 1 of the Convention.

7 The Execution of the *Baka* Judgment

In the meeting of the Committee of Ministers of 7–9 March 2017, the Government of Hungary presented their action report about the execution of the *Baka* judgment. The first aspect concerned the payment of just satisfaction and individual measures. According to this report:

> The Court awarded just satisfaction for pecuniary and non pecuniary damages of 70,000 euros, as well as 30,000 euros for the costs and expenses incurred before the Court. Just satisfaction was already paid by the Hungarian Government on 14th September 2016.[68]

---

it emphasizes that the applicable provision of the Hungarian Fundamental law and the accessory Transitional Provisions are incompatible with the rule of law, which is inherent to the Convention (para.117)". However, paragraph 117 does not use these words.

[66] *Baka v. Hungary,* Chamber Judgment, 27 May 2014, para. 77.

[67] *Baka v. Hungary* [GC], paras. 120–121.

[68] Committee of Ministers, 1280 Meeting, 7-9 March 2017, Decision following Communication from Hungary concerning the case of *Baka against Hungary*, doc. CM/Del/Dec(2017)1280/H46-15.

The communication continued by affirming that:

> No further individual measures were considered necessary, because (1) no such measure was indicated by the Court; (2) the applicant's original term of office had already expired before the judgment was delivered.[69]

With reference to general measures, the Report emphasised that:

> No further measures were found necessary because the violation found by the Court resulted from a one-time reform of the Hungarian judicial system.[70]

As to the first aspect, certain authors have commented on the lack of efficiency of some international courts because of the length of the proceedings. According to Ahrens, Fischer, Gómez and Nowak "the *Baka* case was dealt with relatively quickly, the Court's judgment is very well drafted"[71] (it took four years). However, the result did not go as far as enabling Judge Baka to recover his old post and even when the judgment was delivered, his term of office as judge in the civil court was already finished and he had retired.

Other judgments where judges were the applicants include *Ermenyi*, a case brought by the vice-president of the Hungarian Supreme Court, who passed away during the proceedings. Even though the judgment found in his favour, he himself was no longer able to enjoy the result. The ECtHR also examined the premature termination of his office.[72] In this case, the situation could be reviewed by the Hungarian Constitutional Court, since the dismissal had been made under the transitory provisions of a law (the Law on the organisation and administration of the courts) and not under the transitory provisions of the Constitution, as was the case for Judge Baka. Although Judge Erményi introduced his claim before the ECtHR under Articles 6, 13 and 14 of the ECtHR and Article 1 of Protocol No. 1, the ECtHR examined it under Article 8 (right to private life), finding that there had been a violation because his legitimate professional expectations had been truncated, thus affecting his private life.

Another example is *Volvok*, where the President of the Ukrainian Supreme Court, who also obtained a judgment in his favour and against his dismissal, but never occupied his position again.[73] These facts show the limited effect of the judgments of

---

[69] *Ibid.*

[70] *Ibid.*

[71] Ahrens et al. (2019), p. 152.

[72] ECtHR, *Erményi v. Hungary*, n° 22254/14, 22 February 2017.

[73] Ahrens et al. (2019), p. 153. See also *ibid.*, p. 153, note 38. "On 4 December 2014 the Committee of Ministers adopted Interim Resolution CM/ResDH(2014) in the *Volkov case*, in which it expressed 'grave concern that despite the efforts deployed by the Ukranian authorities to ensure, by way of a parliamentary resolution, the applicant's reinstatement as required by the Convention, such a resolution has still not been adopted'. In *Supervision of the execution of judgments and decisions of the ECtHR-Annual Report 2017* it is stated that Mr. Volkov was 'reintegrated' into the Supreme Court (p. 201). It would seem, however, that the situation still has not been fully solved, and the Committee of Ministers did not close its examination of this case yet."

the European Court of Human Rights, because of its subsidiary role and the respect for the margin of appreciation of the member States.

If one takes into account the second aspect concerning the general measures, the Agent of the Hungarian State was correct in saying that "no further measures were found necessary because the violation found by the Court resulted from a one-time reform of the Hungarian judicial system."[74] As is well known and has been underlined by some academics like Gábor Halmai:

> In reality, the rule applied in the case of the termination of Baka's term will not be applied ever again, as it was a transitory provision of the Fundamental Law to solve this one concrete case. For this reason, this concrete rule cannot be the subject to a pilot judgment, because this institution aims at changing unacceptable abstract norms in a national legal system, and this is not the case here. As this rule was made a transitory provision, after Baka's dismissal it does not even exist anymore, and therefore even a pilot judgment would have been unable to force the Hungarian government to repeal it.[75]

Other authors such as David Kosař and Katarina Sipulova have been very critical about the conclusion of the *Baka* judgment. According to them the Court has not done enough in order to protect the rule of law and to lay down more limits against abusive constitutionalism.[76]

Subsequent to this ruling, the Grand Chamber delivered its judgment in *Ramos Nunes de Carvalho e sà v. Portugal*, which once again insisted on the above-mentioned general principles:

> In order to establish whether a tribunal can be considered to be 'independent' within the meaning of Article 6 § 1, regard must be had, inter alia, to the manner of appointment of its members and their term of office, the existence of guarantees against outside pressures and the question whether the body presents and appearance of independence.[77]

According to a research done by Aquilina the statistics are as follows:

> In all, there were 39 judgments delivered by the ECtHR in which a violation of the ECtHR was found in respect of twelve Members States cited as respondent states:
>
> (a) One applicant judge in relation to Albania, Armenia, Croatia, Cyprus, Georgia, Portugal, Slovakia and Russia;
> (b) Four applicant judges in all in relation to Hungary and Turkey;
> (c) Seven applicant judges in akk in relation to the Yugoslav Republic of Macedonia; and
> (d) Twenty applicant judges all in relation to Ukraine.[78]

---

[74]Committee of Ministers, 1280 Meeting, 7–9 March 2017, Decision following Communication from Hungary concerning the case of *Baka against Hungary*, doc. CM/Del/Dec(2017)1280/H46-15.

[75]Halmai (2012), p. 486.

[76]Kosař and Šipulová (2018), pp. 83–110.

[77]ECtHR [GC], *Ramos Nunes de Carvalho e sà v. Portugal,* 6 Nov. 2018, Nos. 55391/13 and 2 others.

[78]Aquilina (2019), p. 7.

In conclusion, it is possible to prove with data that, in a range of countries, in the past few years more and more judges have been coming to the ECtHR seeking protection for their rights, especially as regards their independence from the legislature,[79] against arbitrary dismissal, also invoking freedom of expression and procedural safeguards in their own administrative or judicial process.

References

Ahrens H, Fischer H, Gómez V, Nowak M (eds) (2019) Equal access to justice for all and Goal 16 of the Sustainable Development Agenda: challenges for Latin America and Europa. Lit Verlag, Vienna

Aquilina K (2019) The independence of the judiciary in Strasbourg Judicial Disciplinary Case Law: judges as applicants and national judicial councils as factotums of respondent states. In: de Albuquerque PP, Wojtyczek K (eds) Judicial power in a globalized world. Liber Amicorum Vincent De Gaetano. Springer, Heidelberg

Cannoot P (2016) *Baka v. Hungary*: judicial independence at risk in Hungary's new constitutional reality. Strasbourg Observers. Available at: strasbourgobserves.com/2016/07/12/baka-hungary-judicial-independence-at-risk-in-hungary-new-constitutional-reality. Accessed 18 Apr 2020

Cano Palomares G (2018) El caso *Baka c. Hungría* ante el Tribunal Europeo de Derechos Humanos o la Protección de la Independencia Judicial a través del Convenio Europeo de Derechos Humanos. In: Raimondi G et al (eds) Human rights in a global world. Essays in honour of Judge Luis López Guerra. Wolf Legal Publishers, The Netherlands, pp 119–129

Chronowski N, Varju M (2016) Two eras of Hungarian constitutionalism: from the rule of law to rule by law. Hague J Rule Law 8(2):271–289

Dijkstra S (2017) The freedom of the judge to express his personal opinions and convictions under the ECtHR. Utrecht Law Rev 13(1):1–17

ECtHR [The Registry] (2018) Background Paper. The Authority of the Judiciary. Available at: https://www.ECtHR.coe.int/Documents/Seminar_background_paper_2018_ENG.pdf. Accessed 18 Apr 2020

Gyulavári T, Hős N (2013) Retirement of Hungarian judges, age discrimination and judicial independence: a tale of two courts. Ind Law J 42:289–297

Halmai G (2012) From the "rule of law revolution" to the constitutional counter-revolution in Hungary. Eur Yearb Hum Rights:367–384

Halmai G (2017) The early retirement age of the Hungarian judges. In: Nicola F, Davies B (eds) EU law stories. Contextual and critical histories of European jurisprudence. Cambridge University Press, Cambridge, pp 471–488

Kosař D (2012) Policing separation of powers: a new role for the European Court of Human Rights? Eur Const Law Rev 8(1):33–62

Kosař D (2018) The Strasbourg Court and domestic judicial politics. In: Wind M (ed) International courts and domestic politics. University of Copenhagen and Cambridge University Press, Cambridge, pp 71–92

Kosař D, Šipulová K (2018) The Strasbourg Court meets abusive constitutionalism: Baka v. Hungary and the rule of law. Hague J Rule Law 10(1):83–110

Mahoney P (2012) Free speech of civil servants and other public employees. In: Casadevall J et al (eds) Freedom of expression: essays in honour of Nicholas Bratza. Wolf Legal Publishers, The Netherlands, pp 257–276

[79]See Kosař (2012), p. 110.

Scheppele KL (2015) Understanding Hungary's constitutional revolution. In: Von Bogdandy A, Sonnevend P (eds) Constitutional crisis in the European constitutional area. Hart Publishing, Oxford, pp 111–124

Seibert-Fohr A (2012) Introduction. The challenge of transition. In: Seibert-Fohr A (ed) Judicial independence in transition. Springer, Heidelberg, pp 1–15

Seibert-Fohr A (2019) The independence of judges and their freedom of expression: an ambivalent relationship. Springer, Heidelberg

Settem OJ (2016) Application of the "fair hearing" norm in ECtHR Article 6(1) to civil proceedings. With special emphasis on he balance between procedural safeguards and efficiency. Springer, Heidelberg

Solomon PH (2012) The accountability of judges in post communist states: from bureaucratic to professional accountability. In: Seibert-Fohr A (ed) Judicial independence in transition. Springer, Heidelberg, pp 909–935

Sonnevend P, Jakab A, Csink L (2015) The constitution as an instrument of everyday party politics: the basic law of Hungary. In: Von Bogdandy A, Sonnevend P (eds) Constitutional crisis in the European constitutional area. Hart Publishing, Oxford, pp 33–110

Vincze A (2015) Dismissal of the president of the Hungarian Supreme Court: ECtHR Judgment *Baka v. Hungary*. Eur Public Law 21:445–456

María Elósegui is a Judge of the European Court of Human Rights at Strasbourg. Full Professor of Philosophy of Law in the Faculty of Law of the University of Saragossa (Spain). PhD in Law, PhD in Philosophy. Bachelor Degree in Law, Bachelor Degree in Philosophy. MPhil in Law University of Saint Louis of Brussels. MPhil in Philosophy University of Glasgow (Scotland). Humboldt Research Fellow at the Faculty of Law, University Christians Albrecht in Schleswig-Holstein (Germany). Visiting professor of the Max Planck Institute of International Law in Heidelberg (Germany), University of UCLA, University of Chicago, University of Toronto, and Berlin Institute of Human Rights. Member of the European Commission against Racism and Intolerance of the Council of Europe (ECRI) (2013–2017). Expert on women's rights in UN conferences. Research and publications on legal argumentation, human rights and discrimination based on race and gender.

Judges' Freedom of Expression and Their Independence: An Ambivalent Relationship

Anja Seibert-Fohr

Contents

1 Introduction 89
2 Comparative Overview 91
3 The Protection of Judges' Freedom of Expression Under Article 10 (1) of the Convention 94
4 Duties and Responsibilities of Judges (Article 10 (2) of the Convention) 95
5 Balancing the Freedom of Expression with the Independence, Impartiality and Authority of the Judiciary 96
5.1 Different Spheres of Interest 96
5.1.1 Expressions with a Nexus to a Judicial Dispute 97
5.1.2 Expressions Regarding Political Matters 99
5.1.3 Expressions on Behalf of the Judiciary 101
5.2 Criteria for Balancing the Freedom of Expression and the Authority of the Judiciary 106
6 Conclusions 108
References 110

1 Introduction

Judges posting tweets on Twitter, writing columns in newspapers and pronouncing their views in public lectures—all this is a relatively new phenomenon.[1] Whereas judges have traditionally exercised restraint in public pronouncements, there is an increasing expectation nowadays that they explain their decision-making to the

The author thanks Julian Chorus, Julius Brackmann and Anna-Mia Brandau for valuable research assistance and Joschua Klitsch for his thorough help with references and citations.

[1]For a detailed analysis, see J. Jahn (2021), Die Medienöffentlichkeit der Rechtsprechung und ihre Grenzen.

A. Seibert-Fohr (✉)
Heidelberg University, Heidelberg, Germany
e-mail: sekretariat.seiber-fohr@jurs.uni-heidelberg.de

M. Elósegui et al. (eds.), *The Rule of Law in Europe*,
https://doi.org/10.1007/978-3-030-56001-0_7

broader public.[2] Moreover, judges, at times, participate in political debate; they express their views on legislative reforms and take a stance on issues related to the judiciary.[3] This increased visibility and public exposure raise new issues about judicial independence. For example, public pronouncement of personal views may give rise to concerns about a judge's impartiality and the authority of the judiciary more generally. After all, when judges express themselves their pronouncements may be received not only as an individual opinion, but also as an expression of the judiciary as such. Thus, divergent interests are at stake here and need to be weighed against the freedom of expression. How to balance the competing principles is the subject of the following contribution.

Under the European Convention on Human Rights, maintaining the authority and impartiality of the judiciary is one of the reasons for which the freedom of expression may be restricted.[4] According to the European Court, this requires that courts are accepted by the public as the proper forum for the settlement of legal disputes and for the determination of guilt in criminal matters.[5] It explained:

> What is at stake as regards protection of the judiciary's authority is the confidence which the courts in a democratic society must inspire in the accused, as far as criminal proceedings are concerned, and also in the public at large.[6]

This is relevant, when judges express their views in the context of adjudication in criminal proceedings and in civil matters, because the judiciary generally depends on public confidence to carry out its duties successfully.[7] Allowing judges to speak out on pending cases would be irreconcilable with the imperatives of their impartiality and discretion because it would be conceived as prejudicial. Judges are expected not to take sides so that their judgments can be perceived as unbiased and based on law. This is not just a matter of state authority, but a vital precondition for the legitimacy

[2]See e.g. Russian Federation: Article 13 Code of Judicial Ethics 2012: judges should interact with mass media in order to ensure adequate press-coverage of the courts' activities; United Kingdom: Section 2.5 Supreme Court Guide to Judicial Conduct, 2019; France: Conseil supérieur de la magistrature, Rapport annuel 2007, 122.

[3]Ewing (2011), pp. 237–256.

[4]Article 10 (2): The exercise of these freedoms, since it carries with it duties and responsibilities, may be subject to such formalities, conditions, restrictions or penalties as are prescribed by law and are necessary in a democratic society, in the interests of national security, territorial integrity or public safety, for the prevention of disorder or crime, for the protection of health or morals, for the protection of the reputation or rights of others, for preventing the disclosure of information received in confidence, or for maintaining the authority and impartiality of the judiciary.

[5]ECtHR, *Simić v. Bosnia and Herzegovina*, Judgment of 15 November 2016, No. 75255/10, para. 33; *Worm v. Austria*, Judgment of 29 August 1997, Reports 1997-V, para. 40.

[6]*Simić v. Bosnia and Herzegovina*, *supra* note 5, para. 33.

[7]The Court has emphasised on many occasions "the special role in society of the judiciary, which, as the guarantor of justice, a fundamental value in a law-governed State, must enjoy public confidence if it is to be successful in carrying out its duties." See e.g. *Simić v. Bosnia and Herzegovina*, *supra* note 5, para. 33. See also Bangalore Principles of Judicial Conduct, UN Economic and Social Council (ECOSOC), Resolution 2006/23: Strengthening Basic Principles of Judicial Conduct, 27 July 2006, E/RES/2006/23, paras. 1.6 and 3.2.

of judicial decision-making. What is more, and I will come back to this later, judicial independence and impartiality are essential for the right to due process.

However, not all cases are as clear-cut as those in which the expression of opinion relates directly to judicial decision-making. While it is appropriate to limit judges' freedom of expression in respect of pending proceedings, the issue is more difficult when speech is related to a judge's political views in general. Can judges participate in political debate? Are they even allowed to become members of political parties?

Another issue, which came up in the *Baka Case* was the question whether judges may take position with respect to constitutional reform projects.[8] All these issues require a careful balancing exercise, because judges, on the one hand, enjoy the right to freedom of expression just as everyone else in society. On the other hand, their involvement in political affairs may jeopardize the perceived independence and impartiality of the judiciary.[9] Before analyzing these issues under the European Convention on Human Rights, I will give a short comparative overview of how national jurisdictions deal with potential conflicts of freedom of speech and judicial independence.

2 Comparative Overview

Traditionally, judges have been expected to exercise considerable restraint in the exercise of their freedom of expression.[10] This restraint is grounded in both, the interest of judicial independence and the authority of the judiciary.[11] For example, judges must not disclose confidential information concerning a dispute, which come to their knowledge in the course of the performance of judicial office[12] or comment on the merits of pending proceedings.[13] This is in line with the Bangalore Principles

---

[8]ECtHR, *Baka v. Hungary*, Judgment of 23 June 2016, Application No. 20261/12. See also Seibert-Fohr (2018), pp. 241–244.

[9]For a comprehensive account of the relevant standards under the European Convention on Human Rights, see Müller (2015), pp. 21–155. For a detailed account on the standards for impartiality, see Steinfatt (2012).

[10]See e.g. Russian Federation: Article 3 Law on the Status of Judges. For a general overview see Venice Commission, Report on the Freedom of Expression of Judges, 23 June 2015, CDL-AD (2015)018.

[11]See e.g. Germany: Section 39 German Judiciary Act (*Mäßigungsgebot*).

[12]Venice Commission, Report on the Freedom of Expression of Judges, *supra* note 10, para. 17, with reference to Croatia: Arts. 92 to 98 of the Law on Courts; Article 9 Code of Judicial Ethics of Croatia. See also Fleck (2012), pp. 817–818, with reference to Section 28 (2) Act LXVII of 1997: "A judge shall not be permitted to publicly comment on any case that is in progress or has been concluded, particularly cases over which he has presided." and Section 29 Act LXVII of 1997: "Judges may not release any information to the press, radio or television on any case over which they preside." See also Bangalore Principles of Judicial Conduct, *supra* note 7, para. 4.10.

[13]See e.g. Russian Federation: Article 13 (3) Code of Judicial Ethics; Ukraine: Article 12 Code of Judicial Ethics; Croatia: Article 12 Code of Judicial Ethics.

of Judicial Conduct, according to which a judge shall not knowingly, while a proceeding is before, or could come before, the judge, make any comment that might reasonably be expected to affect the outcome of such proceedings or impair the manifest fairness of the process.[14] Some domestic codes of ethics therefore discourage judges from discussing cases that are *sub judice*.[15] Judges are also bound to preserve secrecy with respect to deliberations.[16] As a matter of internal independence, judges should furthermore exercise particular restraint when taking a position with respect to cases pending before or decided by their peers.[17] They should exercise their freedom to talk to the media cautiously and either refrain from answering public criticism of their judicial activities[18] or at least act with moderation and diligence when they reply to public criticism.[19]

Restraint applies not only to their official conduct, but also when judges act in their private capacity. The German Judiciary Act, for example, incorporates a duty of moderation ("Mäßigungsverbot") which is relevant for conduct outside judicial office.[20] However, the applicable standards of restraint vary amongst the Council of Europe Member States with respect to extra-judicial activities. For example, in several states judges may not become members of a political party.[21] In the United Kingdom, for example, judges should not engage politically and avoid any appearance of political ties, e.g. by attending political gatherings.[22] In Germany, Austria and France, however, judges are allowed to become party members and take a more active stance with respect to political matters[23] Still, they may not participate actively in politics while in office and they are expected to draw a line between their personal views and their judicial office.[24] For example, judges should not make use of their judicial position to reinforce the value of their speech when they publicly

[14]Bangalore Principles of Judicial Conduct, *supra* note 7, para. 2.4.

[15]See e.g. Malta: Rules 13 and 28 Code of Ethics for Members of the Judiciary.

[16]See e.g. Germany: Section 43 German Judiciary Act.

[17]German Federal Constitutional Court, Judgment of 30 August 1983, 2 BvR 1334/82. For a summary of this case see Venice Commission, Report on the Freedom of Expression of Judges, *supra* note 10, paras. 50-52. See also United Kingdom: Courts and Tribunals Judiciary, Guide to Judicial Conduct, 2019, 14–15.

[18]*Ibid.*

[19]See e.g. Russian Federation: Article 13 (6) Code of Judicial Ethics.

[20]Section 39 German Judiciary Act.

[21]See e.g. Croatia: Article 60 Croatian Judiciary Act; United Kingdom: Section 3.3 Supreme Court Guide to Judicial Conduct, 2019; Romania: Article 9 (1) Law on the Status of Judges and Prosecutors; Ukraine: Article 16 Code of Judicial Ethics; Malta: Rule 12 Code of Ethics for Members of the Judiciary.

[22]Section 3.3 Supreme Court Guide to Judicial Conduct, 2019; Courts and Tribunals Judiciary, Guide to Judicial Conduct, 2019, 12–13.

[23]Seibert-Fohr (2012), pp. 499–500.

[24]Section 39 German Judiciary Act.

express their political opinions.[25] Their individual views should be distinguishable from their official function in order not to jeopardize public trust in the independent administration of their judicial office.[26] The case is different with respect to legal issues, which they comment on in law reviews and lectures.[27] In most countries, judges are allowed, in some countries even encouraged, to participate in public discussions on the law, the legal system and the functioning of the justice system more generally.[28]

The short overview demonstrates that, despite variances, there are a number of similarities. All countries seek to balance the freedom of expression with the authority, impartiality and independence of the judiciary. For this matter, they distinguish between different spheres: the judicial decision-making sphere, the representative sphere (meaning the presentation of the judiciary in general terms) and the judges' individual sphere. The protection of the freedom of speech is strongest when judges express their views in non-judicial matters which are related to their individual capacity, whereas, in matters related to judicial decision-making, they are expected to exercise more restraint. For example, in Sweden judges are protected comprehensively from any sanctions unless their speech is directly connected to the administration of justice.[29] Publicly expressed opinions by judges are considered a private matter and thus widely protected by the freedom of expression.[30] Nevertheless, they need to be weighed against public interests if public confidence in the judiciary is at stake.[31]

The measures taken to achieve this balance vary. They are not limited to repressive measures, such as reprimand and removal from office, which represent the most serious interference with the freedom of expression. In practical terms, a balance can often be struck by conflict of interest provisions, which allow judges to express their views but prevent them from sitting in cases where their perceived impartiality is at stake.

---

[25]German Federal Administrative Court, Judgment of 29 October 1987, 2 C 72/86 and 2 C 73/86; German Federal Constitutional Court, Judgment of 6 June 1988, 2 BvR 111/88. For a summary of this case see Venice Commission, Report on the Freedom of Expression of Judges, *supra* note 10, paras. 53–55. See also Section 39 German Judiciary Act.

[26]For example, in the United Kingdom judges writing articles for publication should carefully consider to whether it is appropriate to include reference to their judicial position. Courts and Tribunals Judiciary, Guide to Judicial Conduct, 2019, 15.

[27]See e.g. Romania: Article 11 Law on the Status of Judges and Prosecutors. See also Bangalore Principles of Judicial Conduct, *supra* note 7, para. 4.11.1, according to which judges may write, lecture, teach and participate in activities concerning the law, the legal system, the administration of justice or related matters.

[28]See e.g. Croatia: Rule 12 Code of Judicial Ethics; United Kingdom: Courts and Tribunals Judiciary, Guide to Judicial Conduct, 2019, 14–15.

[29]Chapter 3 and Article 5 Chapter 7 of the Freedom of the Press Act.

[30]Venice Commission, Report on the Freedom of Expression of Judges, *supra* note 10, para. 42.

[31]*Ibid.*

3 The Protection of Judges' Freedom of Expression Under Article 10 (1) of the Convention

When I turn now to the jurisprudence of the European Court of Human Rights, it is important to note at the outset that, according to the Court, judges enjoy the right to freedom of expression irrespective of their official function and that this protection applies also to the workplace.[32] This does not only relate to private speech, but also extends to public speech and speech related to judicial office.[33] The Court recognized the broad scope of protection in *Wille v. Liechtenstein*, where a lecture by the President of the Administrative Court was at issue. The applicant had maintained in his lecture that the Constitutional Court of Liechtenstein had the final say over the Prince in constitutional interpretation. When the judge's term expired, the Prince of Liechtenstein refused to reappoint him in reaction to the speech. The Strasbourg Court, when seized with the case by Mr. Wille, held that the applicant was not prevented from commenting on constitutional matters and enjoyed the protection of the freedom of expression despite his position and the political implications of his speech.[34]

There are only few cases, in which the Court has considered a restriction on the freedom of judges as not affecting their freedom of speech.[35] For example, in *Harabin v. Slovakia (2)* it refused to consider the reduction of the President of the Supreme Court's salary as a restriction on Article 10. In this case, the applicant was disciplined after he had refused to allow an official audit.[36] The European Court explained that the disciplinary proceedings against the court president did not concern "any statements or views expressed by him in the context of a public debate or in the media", but only his "professional behaviour in the context of administration of justice".[37] The Court distinguished the case from *Wille v. Liechtenstein,* where it had found that the measures complained of "essentially related to freedom of expression" as they had been prompted by a public lecture.[38] In the case of

---

[32]ECtHR, *Simić v. Bosnia and Herzegovina*, *supra* note 5, para. 32.

[33]ECtHR, *Wille v. Liechtenstein*, Judgment of 28 October 1999, No. 28396/95, para. 64; *Baka v. Hungary*, *supra* note 8, para. 140; ECtHR, *Kudeshkina v. Russia*, Judgment of 26 February 2009, No. 29492/05, para. 95; *Previti v. Italy*, Judgment of 8 December 2009, No. 45291/06.

[34]See also *Harabin v. Slovakia*, Judgment of 20 November 2012, No. 58688/11, para. 149: "The Court reiterates that the status the applicant has enjoyed as President of the Supreme Court does not deprive him of the protection of Article 10 to the extent that the sanction complained of may be qualified as an interference with the exercise of his freedom of expression. In order to determine whether that is the case, the scope of the disciplinary measure must be determined by putting it in the context of the facts of the case and of the relevant legislation."

[35]See e.g. *Harabin v. Slovakia (2)*, Judgment of 29 June 2004, No. 62584/00.

[36]*Ibid.*

[37]*Ibid.*, para. 151.

[38]*Ibid.*, para. 152: "In that respect the present case is to be distinguished from other cases, in which the Court has found that the measures complained of essentially related to freedom of expression, and where such measures had been prompted, for example, by views expressed by the President of

Harabin, however, the *discharge of his duties* as President of the Supreme Court were at issue and not the applicant's freedom of expression.[39]

There is thus a narrow set of cases, which concerns the pure discharge of public office that do not fall within the scope of the freedom of expression.[40] In all other cases, including in *Baka v. Hungary*,[41] the Court has found a restriction on the freedom of expression and subsequently engaged in a balancing analysis.[42] In other words, judges usually enjoy the freedom of expression also in connection with the performance of their judicial functions.[43] But this freedom is subject to limitations.

4 Duties and Responsibilities of Judges (Article 10 (2) of the Convention)

In the exercise of this freedom, judges are bound by the "duties and responsibilities" of their office which are essential for the rule of law and for public confidence in the functioning of the judiciary.[44] The fundamental premise is that judges, due to their official function, are bound by a duty of loyalty and discretion.[45] Albeit the judiciary does not form part of the ordinary civil service, the duty of loyalty and discretion also applies to the third branch of government, given its prominent place among State

the Liechtenstein Administrative Court in the course of a public lecture..., by a judge's statements to the media... or by the form and contents of texts drafted by a public prosecutor and a civil servant then disseminated to the press."

[39] *Ibid.*

[40] See also *ibid.*

[41] In *Baka v. Hungary, supra* note 8, para. 168, the Court considered that "the applicant expressed his views on the legislative reforms at issue in his professional capacity as President of the Supreme Court and of the National Council of Justice." Still he was protected under Article 10 ECtHR.

[42] In some instances, the Court found Article 10 applicable because a member of the judiciary had voiced his or her views not only as public officials but also as simple citizens. See e.g. *Kayasu v. Turkey*, Judgment of 13 November 2008, No. 64119/00, para. 93: "Il s'agit sans aucun doute d'un *débat d'intérêt général*, auquel le requérant a entendu participer en tant que simple citoyen, d'une part, et en tant que procureur, d'autre part." For *Baka v. Hungary* see below.

[43] *Baka v. Hungary, supra* note 8, para. 162; *Pitkevich v. Russia*, Judgment of 8 February 2001, No. 47936/99, 12–13. In this case, the Court held that the opinions expressed by the applicant were covered by Article 10, but the interferences with her rights under Article 10 were justified. See also *Simić v. Bosnia and Herzegovina, supra* note 5, para. 32.

[44] *Wille v. Liechtenstein, supra* note 33, para. 64: "the 'duties and responsibilities' referred to in Article 10 § 2 assume a special significance since it can be expected of public officials serving in the judiciary that they should show restraint in exercising their freedom of expression in all cases where the authority and impartiality of the judiciary are likely to be called in question"; *Kudeshkina v. Russia, supra* note 33, para. 86: "What is at stake as regards protection of the judiciary's authority is the confidence which the courts in a democratic society must inspire... in the public at large."

[45] *Ibid.*, para. 93; *Simić v. Bosnia and Herzegovina, supra* note 5, para. 32.

organs in a democratic society.[46] The Court has repeatedly emphasised that the judiciary "as the guarantor of justice" must enjoy "public confidence if it is to be successful in carrying out its duties."[47]

Thus the scope of judge's freedom of expression is limited to the extent that a fair balance is struck between the individual right to freedom of expression and the legitimate interest of a democratic state in ensuring that its civil service properly furthers the purposes enumerated in Article 10 (2).[48] For this matter the Court needs to determine, whether the independence, impartiality and authority of the judiciary is implicated by a judge's speech.[49] Otherwise, a restriction on free speech is not necessary.[50] If a restriction serves one of these interests, the Court examines whether the restriction is proportionate to the aim pursued.

5 Balancing the Freedom of Expression with the Independence, Impartiality and Authority of the Judiciary

5.1 *Different Spheres of Interest*

Generally speaking, the more an expression relates to a particular judicial dispute, the less demanding are the requirements for a restriction on the freedom of expression since the independence, impartiality and authority of the judiciary carry particular weight. On the other hand, if the expression is of a more general nature and does not relate to a specific legal dispute, a judge's right to freedom of expression carries heavier weight and is more likely to prevail. I will illustrate this by the following three scenarios: expressions with a nexus to an individual judicial dispute, expressions related to political matters and expressions on behalf of the judiciary.

[46] *Pitkevich v. Russia, supra* note 43, 12.

[47] *Simić v. Bosnia and Herzegovina, supra* note 5, para. 33.

[48] *Kudeshkina v. Russia, supra* note 33, para. 86; *Pitkevich v. Russia, supra* note 43, 11.

[49] The Court denied a violation of the principle of impartiality in *Chim and Przywieczerski v. Poland* where a judge had expressed a preference for punishing so-called white-collar mafia. The European Court of Human Rights held that it would have been preferable if the judge had refrained from expressing his views in the media entirely, in order to avoid any possible misgivings about his impartiality. Nevertheless, it denied a violation of the applicant's due process rights in his criminal trial. *Chim and Przywieczerski v. Poland,* ECtHR Application Nos. 36661/07 and 38433/07, Judgment of 12 April 2018.

[50] *Wille v. Liechtenstein, supra* note 33, para. 70; *Albayrak v. Turkey*, ECtHR Application No. 38406/97, Judgment of 31 January 2008, para. 48.

5.1.1 Expressions with a Nexus to a Judicial Dispute

The European Court of Human Rights distinguishes between the expression of views in private life and those expressed in the context of judicial office.[51] For the latter category, it allows the Government a certain margin of appreciation to determine whether an interference with a judge's freedom of expression is necessary for maintaining the authority and impartiality of the judiciary.[52] Therefore, it has ultimately denied a violation of Article 10 in several cases. For example, in *Pitkevich v. Russia*, a judge had prayed publicly during court hearings, had discussed moral and religious issues in court and promised a favorable outcome of their cases to litigants if they joined her church. Since the conduct had called into question her impartiality and had impaired the authority of the judiciary, the Strasbourg Court found that her removal from office was justified as proportionate to a legitimate aim and thus did not amount to a violation of the applicant's freedom of expression.[53]

Admittedly this is an extreme case, where a judge abused her judicial activities for private matters. However, there are also cases in which judges have been disciplined for expressing their views on pending judicial proceeding. According to the European Court of Human Rights, judges are required to exercise maximum discretion in respect of cases with which they deal in order to preserve their image as impartial.[54] For example, in *Lavents v. Latvia*, the Court found a violation of a defendant's right to an independent court because in the course of criminal proceedings the presiding judge had criticized the strategy of the defence in several press interviews and thus caused the applicant to fear that the judge lacked impartiality.[55]

The imperative of discretion applies even if a judge seeks to reply in response to criticism voiced in the media.[56] Judges should avoid making use of the press to

---

[51] *Pitkevich v. Russia, supra* note 43, 12.

[52] *Ibid.*, 11–12; *Prager and Oberschlick v. Austria*, Judgment of 26 April 1995, No. 15974/90, para. 35: "National authorities... enjoy a certain margin of appreciation in determining the existence and extent of the necessity of an interference with the freedom of expression. That assessment is, however, subject to a European supervision embracing both the legislation and the decisions applying it, even those given by an independent court."

[53] *Pitkevich v. Russia, supra* note 43, 12.

[54] *Previti v. Italy, supra* note 33, para. 257: "*Il convient en outre de rappeler que la plus grande discrétion s'impose aux autorités judiciaires lorsqu'elles sont appelées à juger, afin de garantir leur image de juges impartiaux. Cette discrétion doit les amener à ne pas utiliser la presse, même pour répondre à des provocations.*" *Buscemi v. Italy*, Judgment of 16 September 1999, No. 29569/95, para. 67: "The Court stresses, above all, that the judicial authorities are required to exercise maximum discretion with regard to the cases with which they deal in order to preserve their image as impartial judges. That discretion should dissuade them from making use of the press, even when provoked. It is the higher demands of justice and the elevated nature of judicial office which impose that duty."

[55] *Lavents v. Latvia*, Judgment of 28 November 2002, No. 58442/00, paras. 118–119.

[56] *Buscemi v. Italy, supra* note 54, para. 67.

defend themselves even in case of provocation.[57] The Court has explained the necessary discretion with the "higher demands of justice and the elevated nature of judicial office."[58]

This also applies to expressions, which do not relate to a judge personally. Judges are generally expected to exercise restraint if their speech could be seen to compromise their independence. Nevertheless, disciplinary measures in response to such speech may be in violation of Article 10 if they are not proportionate. When the Court balances the freedom of expression with the authority of the judiciary, it takes into account the subject matter of the expression. If a matter is of public interest,[59] the protection of the freedom of speech may carry particular weight.

This was recognized in *Kayasu v. Turkey*. Though this case concerned the rights of a public prosecutor the Court's analysis is also relevant for judges. In this case, a public prosecutor was removed from office because he had announced to the press that he took steps to indict a former army general who had allegedly been involve in a military coup of 1980. The European Court of Human Rights recognized that the notice concerned a debate of general interest, which enjoyed a heightened level of protection under Article 10.[60] When balancing the interest at stake, it recognized that the disputed speech about the amnesty for those involved in the military coup fundamentally served to demonstrate a dysfunction of the democratic regime and thus carried a certain weight.[61] The Court also took note of the chilling effect of the prosecutor's removal from office for other members of the judiciary and concluded that the interference with the applicant's freedom of expression, i.e. removal from the post of the prosecutor and the prohibition to practice as a lawyer, was disproportionate under these circumstances.[62]

Summing up, when judges express views which are related to judicial proceedings or which may compromise their impartiality in respect of pending or future proceedings, they are expected to exercise restraint in order to preserve their authority, independence and impartiality as judges. States have a certain margin of appreciation to determine whether a restriction on the freedom of speech is

---

[57] *Lavents v. Latvia*, *supra* note 55, para. 118; *Previti v. Italy*, *supra* note 33, para. 257; *Prager and Oberschlick v. Austria*, *supra* note 52, para. 34: "Judges who have been criticised are subject to a duty of discretion that precludes them from replying."

[58] *Buscemi v. Italy*, *supra* note 54, para. 67.

[59] *Baka v. Hungary*, *supra* note 8, para. 165.

[60] *Kayasu v. Turkey*, *supra* note 42, para. 93: "*Il s'agit sans aucun doute d'un débat d'intérêt général, auquel le requérant a entendu participer en tant que simple citoyen, d'une part, et en tant que procureur, d'autre part. Elle rappelle à cet égard que la présence d'un sujet d'intérêt général implique un niveau de protection élevé au titre de l'article 10 de la Convention.*"

[61] *Ibid.*, para. 101: "*le discours litigieux servait fondamentalement à* démontrer un dysfonctionnement du régime démocratique."

[62] *Ibid.*, para. 106: "*Il s'ensuit que cet effet dissuasif est un facteur important à prendre en compte pour ménager un juste équilibre entre le droit à la liberté d'expression d'un magistrat et tout autre intérêt légitime concurrent dans le cadre d'une bonne administration de la justice.*" For the chilling effect of the removal of judges see also *Kudeshkina v. Russia*, *supra* note 33, para. 99.

necessary. However, this does not allow disproportionate measures. In balancing the competing interests at stake, the European Court attributes particular weight to the freedom of speech if it concerns matters of public interest.

5.1.2 Expressions Regarding Political Matters

Turning now to the category of cases in which judges have expressed views on political matters, unrelated to a specific legal dispute, it is important to note that, according to the Strasbourg Court, judges are not prevented from making political statement.[63] Nevertheless, they should also show restraint in exercising their freedom of expression when the authority and impartiality of the judiciary are likely to be called in question.[64] Whether this is the case, requires a consideration of all relevant circumstances.[65]

In determining whether a sanction is necessary and proportionate to a legitimate aim, the Court considers the office held by the applicant, the content of the statement, the context in which it is made and the reaction thereto.[66] In the above mentioned case, *Wille v. Liechtenstein*, the Court noted the high judicial office held by the applicant as President of the Administrative Court and thus exercised "close scrutiny" to determine whether his public lecture justified the refusal to reappoint him as President of the Administrative Court.[67] While he denied the Prince's final word in constitutional matters, he had not insulted him or any other high official. Neither had he made any remarks on pending cases nor had his lecture any bearing on his judicial tasks.[68] Therefore, the Court did not consider the interference with the applicant's rights necessary in a democratic society and found a violation of Article 10.

The Court pursued a similar approach in *Albayrak v. Turkey*. The applicant had been transferred to another jurisdiction as a disciplinary measure for reading PKK legal publications and being sympathetic to the PKK. When it assessed the necessity of the disciplinary measure, the Court considered the impact of the judge's conduct on his impartiality and his judicial function as essential factors.[69] The Government had not referred to any incident, which would have suggested that the applicant's conduct had a bearing on his performance as a judge.[70] He had not overtly associated himself with the PKK or behaved in a way, which could call into question his

---

[63] *Wille v. Liechtenstein*, *supra* note 33, para. 67.

[64] *Ibid.*, para. 64; *Kayasu v. Turkey*, *supra* note 42, para. 92; *Kudeshkina v. Russia*, *supra* note 33, para. 86, *Di Giovanni v. Italy*, ECtHR Application No. 5160/60, Judgment of 9 July 2013, para. 71; *Baka v. Hungary*, *supra* note 8, para. 164.

[65] *Kudeshkina v. Russia*, *supra* note 33, para. 82; *Baka v. Hungary*, *supra* note 8, para. 166.

[66] *Wille v. Liechtenstein*, *supra* note 33, para. 63.

[67] *Ibid.*, para. 64; See also *Baka v. Hungary*, *supra* note 8, para. 165.

[68] *Wille v. Liechtenstein*, *supra* note 33, paras. 67, 69.

[69] *Albayrak v. Turkey*, *supra* note 50, para. 46.

[70] *Ibid.*

capacity to deal impartially with related cases coming before him.[71] Therefore, the Court considered that the interference with the applicant's freedom of expression was not based on sufficient reasons to show that the interference complained of was "necessary in a democratic society".[72]

My prediction is that we will see more such cases related to political participation in the future. As mentioned before, judges are increasingly inclined to speak to the media, to partake in social media and to express their views in matters related to society. There is no case yet, in which a judge has challenged the prohibition to become a member of a political party. It is difficult to predict how the Court will decide these matters. Taking into account that there is no pan-European consensus on party membership, the Court may allow States a certain margin of appreciation when determining the proportionality of such prohibitions for judges.[73]

Both judgements, *Wille v. Liechtenstein* and *Albayrak v. Turkey*, demonstrate, however, that States must argue conclusively that the prohibition of party membership would be necessary in a democratic society. In both cases, the Court denied the necessity of an interference with the judges' freedom of expression because the views at issue did not have an impact on their judicial decision-making.

In the context of civil service, the Court held in *Vogt v. Germany* that the dismissal of a teacher on the ground of the mere membership of a communist party was in violation of her freedom of expression. No account had been taken of the context of her breaching the statutory requirements of loyalty. No criticism had been levelled at the way she had actually performed her duties as a teacher.[74] Whether this also applies to the judiciary, remains open. Arguably, the position of the judiciary as the third branch of government is different from ordinary civil service in this respect and requires more distance from political parties.

This is why, in some Council of Europe Member States judges' party membership is perceived as irreconcilable with judicial independence given their historical experience with a politicized judiciary. They seek to avoid similar experiences by preventing judges from getting politically involved. Others, like the Federal Republic of Germany, consider it important for judges to partake in society and to take an interest in issues of public interest. In this case judges should be politically mature and diverse in their views in order to prevent political usurpation of the judiciary. Both views have their pros and cons. It remains to be seen whether the European Court considers restrictions on party membership necessary in a democratic country or allows States a margin of appreciation in this respect.

---

[71] *Ibid.*

[72] *Ibid.*, para. 48.

[73] See e.g. *ibid.*, para. 41.

[74] ECtHR, *Vogt v. Germany*, Judgment of 26 September 1995, No. 17851/91, para. 54.

5.1.3 Expressions on Behalf of the Judiciary

Finally, there is a third category of cases, which has become increasingly relevant over the past years. This is when judges publicly speak out against the government to defend judicial independence.[75] These cases differ from the aforementioned scenarios, because they are neither close to a particular legal dispute nor to a judge's private sphere. They stand out because they relate to judicial matters and at the same time, they are relevant for the judge individually. This scenario is distinguishable from purely political expressions as it relates to judicial office and thus is closer to those cases in which judges express themselves about legal issues. On the other hand, and this is particularly relevant, judges speak out here in the interest of the judiciary in order to maintain their independence. This distinguishes these instances from those in which a government restricts free speech *in the interest* of judicial independence.

The main argument advanced by governments for the interference with the freedom of expression in these cases is usually the authority of the judiciary, which they consider at stake when judges criticize the government for insufficient protection of their independence. In whistle-blowing scenarios, this argument needs to be balanced with the freedom of speech, which is reinforced by the public interest in an independent judiciary.[76]

Generally speaking, the Court recognizes that it is in the interest of democracy and pluralism that judges, in their capacity as experts, express reservations or criticism of Government bills.[77] Such criticism does not undermine the fairness of judicial proceedings.[78] In some jurisdictions, high-level judges are even required *ex officio* to comment on legislation affecting the judiciary.[79] This was the case in *Baka v. Hungary*.[80] The applicant served as the President of the Supreme Court of Hungary and headed the National Council of Justice.[81] In this capacity, he was tasked to comment on any legislation affecting the third branch of government. On several occasions, he publicly voiced concerns over governmental reform proposals affecting the judiciary.[82] Subsequently, legal provisions were introduced into parliament, which led to his removal from the office of President of the Supreme Court three and a half years before the end of his term. He remained in office as judge and

[75] According to the Bangalore Principles, judges may participate in activities concerning the law, the legal system and the administration of justice. Bangalore Principles of Judicial Conduct, *supra* note 7, para. 4.11.1.

[76] See also *Guja v. Modova*, Judgment of 12 February 2008, No. 14277/04.

[77] ECtHR, *Previti v. Italy*, *supra* note 33, para. 253.

[78] *Ibid.*

[79] See *Baka v. Hungary*, *supra* note 8, para. 167.

[80] For the background of this case, see Vincze (2014), pp. 208–211. For a critique of this case see Kosař and Šipulová (2012), p. 83.

[81] *Baka v. Hungary*, *supra* note 8, paras. 12–13.

[82] E.g. the Nullification Bill, the retirement age of judges, the amendments to the Code of Criminal Procedure, and the new Organisation and Administration of the Courts Bill. See *Baka v. Hungary*, *supra* note 8, para. 15. See also Vincze, *supra* note 80, para. 210.

became president of a civil division of the newly established Kúria, the legal successors of the Supreme Court, but a new president was elected to the court.

The Government argued that the termination of the applicant's mandate as President of the Supreme Court was aimed at increasing the independence of the judiciary.[83] However, the Court found that the premature termination of the applicant's mandate, which had been taken because of the judge's critique, "defeated, rather than served" the aim of maintaining the independence of the judiciary.[84] His removal could hardly be reconciled with the function of the judiciary as an independent branch of State power and to the principle of irremovability of judges.[85] Therefore, it did not pursue a legitimate aim and could not justify the restriction on his freedom of speech.

The Court went on in its legal analysis and found that it was neither necessary in a democratic society. It attached a high level of protection to the applicant's freedom of speech because it involved a great public interest.[86] The European judges emphasised in this respect the legitimate interest that the public had in being informed about the issues related to the separation of powers raised by the applicant.[87] It also stressed that, as President of the National Council of Justice, he had a duty to express his opinion on legislative reforms affecting the judiciary.[88]

This argument led to a controversy within the Court. Judge Pejchal took issue with the Court's decision, arguing that official speech was unprotected under the Convention.[89] So did Judge Wojtyczek, who distinguished official from private speech, too,[90] arguing that official speech is not a matter of individual freedom.[91] According to him, the plaintiff had spoken out on behalf of a public authority and not as a matter of personal choice. Therefore, his individual freedom of expression was not implicated.[92] Judge Wojtyczek explained this assertion with the nature of the right, arguing that the notion of freedom of expression presupposes free choice. Such choice was incompatible with an official duty to speak out in defense of public interests.[93] Furthermore, he considered the notion of individual rights at stake if public officials could rely on them in the exercise of their office. This would be

[83] *Baka v. Hungary*, *supra* note 8, para. 155.

[84] *Ibid.*, paras. 156 and 172: "This can hardly be reconciled with the particular consideration to be given to the nature of the judicial function as an independent branch of State power and to the principle of the irremovability of judges."

[85] *Ibid.*, para. 172.

[86] *Ibid.*, para. 171.

[87] *Ibid.*, para. 165.

[88] *Ibid.*, para. 167.

[89] Dissenting Opinion of Judge Pejchal, *ibid.*

[90] Dissenting Opinion of Judge Wojtyczek, *ibid.*, paras. 2, 4, 6.

[91] *Ibid.*, para. 7: "Public office in the judiciary is not a rostrum for the exercise of free speech."

[92] *Ibid.*, para. 4. According to him, neither Art.10 was implicated (paras. 2–8), nor was there an interference with the applicant's rights (para. 10) nor a causal line the applicant's speech and the termination of his mandate.

[93] *Ibid.*, para. 7.

particularly problematic if official speech interfered with the rights of private individuals.[94] Any such balancing of public speech against competing private rights would jeopardize the effective protection of individuals against the State.

A fortiori he took issue with the idea that judges' speech enjoy stronger protection under the Convention if it is in the interest of judicial independence. The guarantee of judicial independence, according to him, is not a matter of individual rights, but a matter of objective law and thus could not be analyzed as an individual right by a judge.[95] On the contrary, judicial integrity and independence could justify stronger interference with judges' rights than in the case of other citizens.[96] Accordingly, he considered the case a public-law dispute between two state organs, which was outside the scope of the European Court's jurisdiction.[97]

The Court's majority, however, took a different approach and found the right to free speech to be applicable not only in purely private matters but also in matters of public concern.[98] Its reference to Mr. Baka's official obligations may not have been particularly persuasive in this respect, but when the role of the judiciary is discussed, it is difficult to separate a judge's private concerns from public concerns, anyway.[99] Measures, such as early retirement, may affect judges not only professionally but also individually in their private sphere. In these instances, it makes sense not to exclude their speech from Article 10 but to protect it comprehensively even when it relates to judicial office unless it constitutes judicial decision-making like in *Harabin v. Slovakia*. Arguably, the better option to deal with the competing interests is when the question about the justification of a restriction is addressed.

The German Federal Constitutional Court pursues a similar approach with respect to whistle-blowing and other matters of public interest. According to the Court, the freedom of expression deserves special protection if it serves the disclosure and examination of shortcomings in public affairs.[100] It considers it as an essential precondition for liberal democracy that anyone, including civil servants, who take

[94]*Ibid.*, para. 8.

[95]*Ibid.*, para. 5. But see Dissenting Opinion of Judge Sicilianos, *ibid.*

[96]Dissenting Opinion of Judge Wojtyczek, *ibid.*, para. 5.

[97]*Ibid.*, para. 18.

[98]*Wille v. Liechtenstein*, *supra* note 33, para. 50.

[99]This is why the European Court considered in *Harabin v. Slovakia* that statements or views expressed in the context of a public debate or in the media are protected under Article 10 while purely "professional behaviour in the context of administration of justice" is not. *Harabin v. Slovakia*, *supra* note 34, para. 151.

[100]German Federal Constitutional Court, Judgment of 20 September 2007, 2 BvR 1047/07. See also German Federal Constitutional Court, Judgment of 28 April 1970, 1 BvR 690/65, BVerfGE 28, 191–206, para. 30: "*Die Aufmerksamkeit und das Verantwortungsbewußtsein des Staatsbürgers, der Mißstände nicht nur zur Kenntnis nimmt, sondern sich auch für deren Abstellung einsetzt, ist eine wesentliche Voraussetzung für den Bestand der freiheitlichen demokratischen Ordnung (vgl. BVerfGE 12, 113 (124 f.)). Das Grundrecht der freien Meinungsäußerung verdient, wenn es diesem Ziel dient, besonderen Schutz; er kann auch dem Träger eines öffentlichen Amts nicht versagt werden. Andererseits kann das Recht zur öffentlichen Rüge des verfassungswidrigen Handelns einer Behörde für deren Angehörige nicht unbeschränkt*

note of shortcoming in the context of their public office, take action thereon.[101] This also applies to political speech by judges in the public area.[102] The Court therefore considers the freedom of expression to be applicable and deals with the public interests involved on the level of justification.[103] For example, it requires public officials to exhaust available remedies available before making shortcomings public.[104] Another example is Sweden, where the Parliamentary Ombudsman has developed the notion of reprisal bans, so that judges and civil servants are not sanctioned for sharing information with the public.[105]

It is thus not surprising that the European Court of Human Rights resorts to Article 10 of the European Convention to deal with cases in which judges voice criticism against public authorities. However, though judges enjoy the right to speak out on issues related to the judiciary under Article 10, this does not give them carte blanche. The Court emphasises that judges are required to exercise maximum discretion in the interest of justice.[106] This is particularly relevant if they make accusations of irregularities by other judges who depend on public confidence to exercise their functions.[107] Therefore, the Court refused to find a violation of the right to freedom of expression in *Di Giovanni v. Italy*. In this case, a judge had been sanctioned with a warning because she had alleged in a press interview that one of the members of a selection committee charged with the recruitment of new judges had influenced the selection procedure on behalf of a relative. The rumor later turned out to be unfounded. The Strasbourg judges stressed the judge's duty of discretion.[108] Taking into account the judicial function of the applicant which demands discretion in order to preserve public confidence in the judiciary and the fact that the

sein. Sie dürfen bei der Abwägung die Rücksicht auf die ihnen anvertrauten öffentlichen Interessen nicht außer Acht lassen."

[101] German Federal Constitutional Court, Judgment of 28 April 1979, 1 BvR 690/65, para. 30; German Federal Constitutional Court, Judgment of 25 January 1961, 1 BvR 9/57, BVerfGE 12, 113, 124-125.

[102] German Federal Constitutional Court, Judgment of 6 June 1988, 2 BvR 111/88; German Federal Constitutional Court, Judgment of 30 August 1983, 2 BvR 1334/82.

[103] The expression is only protected if it is in accordance with Article 33 (5) Basic Law, which provides for the obligation of loyalty. Therefore, judges need to respect the dignity and protect the confidence in their judicial office. This requires restraint, when their personal convictions touch on the standing of the judiciary. They should not use their office to emphasise their political views. German Federal Constitutional Court, Judgment of 6 June 1988, 2 BvR 111/88, paras. 4–5.

[104] German Federal Constitutional Court, Judgment of 28 April 1970, 1 BvR 690/65, BVerfGE 28, 191–206.

[105] Venice Commission, Report on the Freedom of Expression of Judges, *supra* note 10, para. 36.

[106] *Di Giovanni v. Italy*, *supra* note 64, para. 80.

[107] *Ibid.*, para. 81. The European Court of Human Rights emphasised in this case that the applicant had not been sanctioned for her critique of the judicial system in general. *Ibid.*, para. 76.

[108] See also *Kudeshkina v. Russia*, *supra* note 33, para. 86: "the Court has on many occasions emphasised the special role in society of the judiciary, which, as the guarantor of justice, a fundamental value in a law-governed State, must enjoy public confidence if it is to be successful in carrying out its duties."

judge had only received the mildest possible sanction the Court considered the interference with her freedom of expression to be proportionate and necessary in a democratic society.[109] A similar approach was taken in *Simić v. Bosnia and Herzegovina*, where the Court denied a violation because the applicant had damaged the reputation of the Constitutional Court and the reputation of a fellow judge and his speech had given rise to reasonable suspicion as to his impartiality and independence.[110] It explained its decision with the need to protect the confidence in the judiciary against destructive attacks, which are essentially unfounded.[111]

The careful balancing of the Court in these cases demonstrates that it is a matter of nuance. Several factors need to be taken into account in order to determine whether a restriction of a judge's freedom of speech is necessary. For example, in *Kudeshkina v. Russia* the Court took into account not only the subject matter of the speech, but also its mode, context and the gravity of the sanction.[112] The applicant, Ms. Kudeshkina, was a Russian judge at the Moscow City Court who was removed from a high-profile corruption trial. When she subsequently requested a suspension of her judicial functions in order to campaign for a seat in the Russian Duma, she harshly criticized the Russian judicial system and questioned its independence in a number of interviews. She referred to pressure from a court's president that she had experienced in the earlier corruption case. When her campaign failed to succeed, she was initially reinstated in her previous office, but later removed from judicial office with the argument that she had disclosed confidential information and deliberately spread falsehoods.

In this case, a narrow majority of the Court found the removal from office disproportionate for a number of reasons. Though judges owe a duty of loyalty and discretion and are expected to exercise restraint so as not to give rise to doubts regarding the authority and impartiality of the judiciary,[113] the Court found a violation because of the vital public interest in the handling of a high-profile corruption case by judicial officials "which should be open to free debate in a democratic society".[114] The majority concluded that the applicant was entitled to bring the matter at issue to the public's attention.[115] They added that Ms. Kudeshkina had not divulged classified information of which she had become aware in the course of her work. She had described merely her experience as a judge when she alleged that courts were under pressure from various officials.[116] For all these reasons, the Court concluded that the authorities had failed to strike the right

[109] *Di Giovanni v. Italy*, *supra* note 64, para. 85.
[110] *Simić v. Bosnia and Herzegovina*, *supra* note 5, para. 35.
[111] *Ibid.*, para. 33.
[112] For an analysis of this case, see Jean (2010), p. 179.
[113] *Kudeshkina v. Russia*, *supra* note 33, paras. 85–86.
[114] *Ibid.*, para. 94.
[115] *Ibid.*, para. 99.
[116] *Ibid.*, para. 91.

balance between the need to protect the authority of the judiciary and the need to protect the applicant's right to freedom to expression.[117]

The case was different from *Di Giovanni v. Italy* because Ms. Kudeshkina had voiced general criticism of the functioning of the judicial system more generally by questioning its independence from outside pressure and her accusations had been confirmed by witnesses.[118] Furthermore, she had expressed her views in the context of her electoral campaign for a seat in the Duma[119] and was later sanctioned for this expression with the removal from her judicial poste.[120] However, a narrow minority of the judges could not agree, arguing with the harsh criticism that Ms. Kudeshkina had voiced as not in line with her duty of loyalty and discretion.

Irrespective of the outcome, all three cases demonstrate that there is only a fine line between justified critique and impermissible corrosion of the authority of the judiciary.[121] This requires the consideration of several different aspects and a careful balancing of the competing interests which shall be outlined in the following.[122]

5.2 *Criteria for Balancing the Freedom of Expression and the Authority of the Judiciary*

The most relevant criteria for balancing the freedom of expression and the authority, independence and impartiality of the judiciary are the subject matter, the manner,[123] the motive and the context of the speech,[124] the rank of judicial office[125] and the gravity of the interference.[126] With respect to the subject matter, the Court takes into

[117]*Ibid.*, para. 101.

[118]*Di Giovanni v. Italy*, *supra* note 64, para. 84.

[119]The Court attributed particular significance to the unhindered exercise of freedom of speech by candidates. *Kudeshkina v. Russia*, *supra* note 33, para. 87.

[120]*Ibid.*, para. 98.

[121]See also Nußberger (2012), p. 902.

[122]See also Venice Commission, Report on the Freedom of Expression of Judges, *supra* note 10, paras. 61–79; Dijkstra (2017), pp. 6–10.

[123]The views expressed should not be insulting. The dissemination of even accurate information must be carried out with moderation and propriety, see *Kudeshkina v. Russia*, *supra* note 33, para. 93: "duty of loyalty and discretion owed by civil servants, and particularly the judiciary, requires that the dissemination of even accurate information is carried out with moderation and propriety"; *Baka v. Hungary*, *supra* note 8, para. 164.

[124]*Kudeshkina v. Russia*, *supra* note 33, para. 87: "In the context of election debates, on the other hand, the Court has attributed particular significance to the unhindered exercise of freedom of speech by candidates."

[125]*Baka v. Hungary*, *supra* note 8, para. 167: "the applicant expressed his views on the legislative reforms at issue in his professional capacity as President of the Supreme Court and of the National Council of Justice."

[126]*Ibid.*, para. 166; *Di Giovanni v. Italy*, *supra* note 64, para. 75: "*Quant à la question de savoir si l'ingérence était 'nécessaire dans une société démocratique', la Cour attache une importance*

account whether the content of the speech is of public interest (i.e. political speech enjoys special protection[127]) and represents a fair comment.[128] In order to determine whether a sanction is proportionate,[129] the Court also considers whether it has the effect of discouraging other judges from making statements critical of public institutions or policies in the future.[130] Such chilling effects on other judges wishing to participate in public debate would work to the detriment of society as a whole.[131]

An expression purely motivated by personal antagonism or the expectation of personal advantage would not justify a high level of protection.[132] According to the Court, the proportionality of an interference may also depend on whether there exists sufficient factual basis for a statement. Even a value judgment without any factual basis to support it may be excessive.[133] Therefore, speech should not be entirely devoid of any factual grounds.[134] It may be necessary to protect the confidence in the judiciary against destructive attacks, which are essentially unfounded.[135] Furthermore, disclosure of information obtained in the course of judicial work should be strictly restricted.[136]

The relevant factors of assessing the proportionality of an interference include also the fairness of the proceedings leading to a restriction (e.g. disciplinary proceedings), the procedural guarantees afforded[137] and the nature and severity of the penalties imposed.[138] In the case of Baka, the Court criticized that effective and adequate safeguards against abuse did not accompany the restriction on his speech.[139]

---

particulière à la fonction occupée par la requérante, à la teneur des propos litigieux et aux circonstances dans lesquelles ceux-ci ont été divulgués."

[127] *Kudeshkina v. Russia, supra* note 33, para. 95.

[128] *Ibid.*

[129] *Di Giovanni v. Italy, supra* note 64, para. 85.

[130] *Kudeshkina v. Russia, supra* note 33, paras. 98-99. See also *Wille v. Liechtenstein, supra* note 33, para. 50; *Baka v. Hungary, supra* note 8, para. 160.

[131] *Kudeshkina v. Russia, supra* note 33, para. 99; *Baka v. Hungary, supra* note 8, para. 167.

[132] *Kudeshkina v. Russia, supra* note 33, para. 95.

[133] *Ibid.*, para. 84.

[134] *Ibid.*, para. 95.

[135] *Ibid.*, para. 86; *Simić v. Bosnia and Herzegovina, supra* note 5, para. 33.

[136] *Ibid.*, para. 32.

[137] *Baka v. Hungary, supra* note 8, para. 161. See also *Kudeshkina v. Russia, supra* note 33, para. 83: "In addition, the Court reiterates that the fairness of the proceedings, the procedural guarantees afforded... and the nature and severity of the penalties imposed... are factors to be taken into account when assessing the proportionality of an interference with the freedom of expression guaranteed by Article 10."; *ibid.*, para. 97: "the manner in which the disciplinary sanction was imposed on the applicant fell short of securing important procedural guarantees."

[138] *Baka v. Hungary, supra* note 8, para. 160: "The Court reiterates that the nature and severity of the sanctions imposed are also factors to be taken into account when assessing the proportionality of the interference."

[139] *Ibid.*, para. 174.

These criteria work like balancing weights. When the freedom of expression is balanced against the standing of the judiciary, the weight of the competing interests needs to be measured. On the judicial scale, we need to weigh the value of the speech and the seriousness of its restriction on the one hand. On the other one, we consider the importance of the interest, which is affected by the speech and the degree to which it is compromised.

The value of the speech is determined by its subject matter, context, manner, motive, foundation, the function of the author and the interests involved. The higher the public interest and the more the speech is based on factual grounds and objectively expressed, the heavier is the weight of the expression. Furthermore, the more serious the sanction, the higher are the expectations for its justification.

On the other side of the scale, the authority of the judiciary, its impartiality and independence may be at stake. These interests weigh particularly high if litigants' right to due process is implicated, for example, if judges disclose confident information or express views, which are prejudicial to the outcome of legal proceedings. This is why the restriction on views, which concern a judicial dispute, on balance are more likely to be justified than expressions, which relate to matters that are more general.

6 Conclusions

Judicial independence and the freedom of expression represent cornerstones of the European legal order. Both are protected under the European Convention on Human Rights. Nevertheless, their relationship is not without tensions. When judges express their views in a way that raises concerns about their independence and impartiality, restrictions may be appropriate to preserve the rule of law and the due process rights of litigants. In other words, judges, who express their views, are expected to exercise self-restraint when their authority and independence is likely to be called into question.[140] They should act with moderation and propriety.[141]

The outcome of a case depends *inter alia,* on whether a dispute is closer related to the private sphere of a judge or to the judicial sphere. In other words, in order to determine whether a restriction is justified, the nexus to and impact on judicial authority becomes relevant. Freedom of expression and judicial independence may even be mutually reinforcing. When judges raise their voice to protect their judicial independence, they do not solely act in their individual interest and in pursuit of their

[140] *Wille v. Liechtenstein, supra* note 33, para. 64.

[141] *Kudeshkina v. Russia, supra* note 33, para. 93. See also Bangalore Principles of Judicial Conduct, *supra* note 7, para. 4.6: "A judge, like any other citizen, is entitled to freedom of expression, belief, association and assembly, but, in exercising such rights, a judge shall always conduct himself or herself in such a manner as to preserve the dignity of the judicial office and the impartiality and independence of the judiciary."

freedom of expression, but also in the interest of the litigants and the rule of law more generally.

All three above named category of cases -expressions with a nexus to a judicial dispute, expressions regarding political matters and expressions on behalf of the judiciary- demonstrate that the relationship of judicial independence and the freedom of expression is ambivalent. This ambivalence is relevant for the balancing exercise. When judges express their opinions, there are different legal interests at stake, which weigh for or against their restriction. Not only are personal interests involved, but also the interest to protect the authority and legitimacy of the judiciary and the litigant's right to due process.

The European Court of Human Rights leaves Respondent states a certain margin of appreciation when it considers whether a restriction on the freedom of expression is necessary in a democratic society for maintaining the authority and impartiality of the judiciary.[142] This is due to variances amongst the Council of Europe's participating states. There is, for example, no pan-European consensus as to whether judges may become members of political parties. What is more, the question whether the judiciary's authority, impartiality and independence requires a restriction in a particular case is a matter, which in many instances can be assessed best at the domestic level. After all: "Not only must Justice be done; it must also be seen to be done."[143] In other words, public perception is an important criterion for the authority, impartiality and independence of the judiciary. In some cases, local stakeholders may be situated better to assess this perception. It is therefore with good reasons that the Court accords Council of Europe States a margin of appreciation.[144]

However, there are limits to this margin. The European Court of Human Rights applies a narrow margin of appreciation for cases in which freedom of expression and judicial independence are mutually reinforcing (e.g. remarks on the functioning of the judiciary).[145] In this case, the rule of law and the rights of litigants to due process, both fundamental principles for the protection of European human rights, lead to a narrow margin of appreciation, and call for close scrutiny of any

[142] *Baka v. Hungary*, *supra* note 8, para. 162; *Wille v. Liechtenstein*, *supra* note 33, para. 62; *Vogt v. Germany*, *supra* note 74, para. 53; *Albayrak v. Turkey*, *supra* note 50, para. 41; *Prager and Oberschlick v. Austria*, *supra* note 52, para. 35: "national authorities... enjoy a certain margin of appreciation in determining the existence and extent of the necessity of an interference with the freedom of expression. That assessment is, however, subject to a European supervision embracing both the legislation and the decisions applying it, even those given by an independent court."

[143] See Bangalore Principles of Judicial Conduct, *supra* note 7, paras. 1.6 and 3.2.

[144] *Albayrak v. Turkey*, *supra* note 50, para. 41.

[145] *Baka v. Hungary*, *supra* note 8, paras. 159 and 171: "Accordingly, the Court considers that the applicant's position and statements, which clearly fell within the context of a debate on matters of great public interest, called for a high degree of protection for his freedom of expression and strict scrutiny of any interference, with a correspondingly narrow margin of appreciation being afforded to the authorities of the respondent State." According to Dijkstra, the margin is narrowed when the expression forms part of a political debate. S. Dijkstra, *supra* note 122, 6.

interference with the freedom of expression.[146] This is so because Article 10 (2) of the Convention only allows restrictions, which are *necessary in a democratic society*. This requirement is an important yardstick for the Court to balance the freedom of expression with judicial independence and will continue to be so in the years to come.

References

Dijkstra S (2017) The Freedom of the Judge to Express his personal Opinions and Convictions under the ECtHR. Utrecht Law Rev 13(1):6–10

Ewing K (2011) Judges and free speech in the United Kingdom. In: Lee HP (ed) Judiciaries in comparative perspective. Cambridge University, Cambridge, pp 237–256

Fleck Z (2012) Judicial independence in Hungary. In: Seibert-Fohr A (ed) Judicial independence in transition. Springer, London, pp 793–833

Jahn J (2021) Die Medienöffentlichkeit der Rechtsprechung und ihre Grenzen, Nomos, Baden-Baden

Jean JP (2010) La liberté des juges de critique publiquement le fonctionnement du sysème judiciaire. Revue trimestrielle des droits de l'homme:179

Kosař D, Šipulová K (2012) The Strasbourg court meets abusive constitutionalism: Baka v. Hungary and the rule of law. Hague J Rule Law 10:83–110

Müller LF (2015) Richterliche Unabhängigkeit und Unparteilichkeit nach Art. 6 EMRK. Duncker & Humblot, Berlin

Nußberger A (2012) Judicial reforms in post-soviet countries – good intentions with flawed results?. In judicial independence in Germany. In: Seibert-Fohr A (ed) Judicial independence in Transition. Springer, Berlin, pp 885–907

Seibert-Fohr A (2012) Judicial independence in Germany. In: Seibert-Fohr A (ed) Judicial independence in transition. Springer, Berlin, pp 447–519

Seibert-Fohr A (2018) Die Europäische Menschenrechtskonvention als Verfassungskorrektiv? Chancen und Grenzen einer Konventionalisierung des Verfassungsrechts. In: Darák P et al (eds) Freiheit und Verantwortung: Verfassung und Menschenrechte im Wandel der Zeit in Ungarn und in Deutschland. Universitätsverlag Winter GmbH, Heidelberg, pp 231–244

Steinfatt G (2012) Die Unparteilichkeit des Richters in Europa im Lichte der Rechtsprechung des Europäischen Gerichtshofs für Menschenrechte. Nomos, Baden-Baden

Vincze A (2014) Judicial Independence and its Guarantees beyond the Nation State. J Indian Law Institute 56(2):202–215

Anja Seibert-Fohr is judge of the European Court of Human Rights elected in respect of Germany. Until her election in 2019 the former member and Vice-Chair of the UN Human Rights Committee (2013–2018) was the Hengstberger Professor of Public Law, International Law and Human Rights and Director of the Institute for Constitutional Law, Constitutional Theory and Philosophy of Law at the University of Heidelberg.

[146] *Baka v. Hungary*, *supra* note 8, para. 165: "the growing importance attached to the separation of powers and the importance of safeguarding the independence of the judiciary, any interference with the freedom of expression of a judge in a position such as the applicant's calls for close scrutiny on the part of the Court."

UN Actions and Programs in Safeguarding the Independence of Judges

Ida Caracciolo

Contents

1 Introduction 111
2 Establishing the Principle of the Independence of Judges: Art. 10 of the Universal Declaration of Human Rights and Art. 14(1) of the International Covenant on Civil and Political Rights 113
3 Interpreting the Principle of the Independency of Judges: General Comment No. 32/2007 and the 'Jurisprudence' of the UN Human Rights Committee 116
4 Detailing the Principle of the Independence of Judges Through Soft Law 122
5 Improving the Principle of Independence of Judges: The Practice of the Special Rapporteur on the Independence of Judges and Lawyers 128
6 Sustaining the Independence of Judges As a Means Towards Economic Growth: The Assistance by the World Bank 132
7 Conclusion 134
References 135

1 Introduction

The organisation of justice is one of the foundations of the rule of law since the exercise of justice guarantees the respect of human rights. Wherein the principle of the independence of judges legitimises their role in modern society and enhances citizens' confidence in democracy; the independence of judges ensures the equality of citizens before the law and the effectiveness of the judicial protection of human rights.

The United Nations (UN) have always considered this inherent link between the rule of law[1] and the independence of the judiciary as indispensable to the protection

[1]On the concept and the uncertainty of its contents see Chesterman (2012), pp. 1014–1222.

I. Caracciolo (✉)
Università della Campania Luigi Vanvitelli, Viale Ellittico, Caserta, Italy
e-mail: ida.caracciolo@unicampania.it

M. Elósegui et al. (eds.), *The Rule of Law in Europe*,
https://doi.org/10.1007/978-3-030-56001-0_8

of human rights and the maintenance of international peace and security. In particular, the UN General Assembly has repeated several times that both the rule of law and the proper administration of justice play a central role in the promotion and protection of human rights and that the administration of justice, and especially, an independent judiciary in full conformity with applicable standards contained in international human rights instruments "are essential to the full non-discriminatory realization of human rights and indispensable to democratization processes and sustainable development."[2]

In 2004, in his Report to the UN Security Council, the UN Secretary General wrote that:

> the rule of law as a concept refers to a principle of governance in which all persons, institutions and entities, public and private, including the State itself, are accountable to laws that are publicly promulgated, equally enforced and independently adjudicated, and which are consistent with international human rights norms and standards. It requires measures to ensure adherence to the principles of supremacy of the law, equality before the law, accountability to the law, fairness in the application of the law, separation of powers, participation in decision-making, legal certainty, avoidance of arbitrariness, and procedural and legal transparency.[3]

The UN Secretary General has not only underlined the importance of the concept of rule of law in the action of the United Nations, but has also tried to define the concept, listing its constituent elements, among them, the need that all persons must be independently adjudicated. Furthermore, the principle requires measures to ensure adherence to a number of additional principles, namely, *inter alia*, the separation of powers.

The UN have also qualified the independence of the judiciary as a fundamental requisite of democracy. In Resolution 59/201, the UN General Assembly has declared "that the essential elements of democracy include respect [. . .] for the rule of law, the separation of powers, the independence of the judiciary" and finally, has invited the United Nations system

> to identify, develop and coordinate effective policies of assistance in the field of democracy and, in this context, to support programmes of technical assistance to States, upon their request, aimed at: (*a*) Developing a competent, independent and impartial judiciary.[4]

Some years later, in 2012, the Declaration adopted by the UN General Assembly on the rule of law has emphasized that the independence of the judicial system, along with its impartiality and integrity, is an essential prerequisite for upholding the rule of law and ensuring that there is no discrimination in the administration of justice.[5]

---

[2]UNGA, Resolutions 50/181 of 22 December 1995 and 48/137 of 20 December 1993.

[3]Report of the UN Secretary General to the Security Council, The Rule of Law and Transnational Justice in Conflict and Post-conflict Societies, S/2004/616, 23 August 2004. Fitschen (2008), pp. 347–380.

[4]UNGA Resolution, A/RES/59/201, 25 March 2005, respectively, paras. 1 and 14.

[5]UNGA Resolution, A/RES/67/1, 30 November 2012, Declaration of the High-level Meeting of the General Assembly on the Rule of Law at the National and International Levels, para. 13.

According to this Declaration, "human rights, the rule of law and democracy are interlinked and mutually reinforcing and [...] they belong to the universal and indivisible core values and principles of the United Nations."[6]

In order to promote, develop, and implement the principle of independence and impartiality of judges, the United Nations have operated at different levels and through various instruments. In particular, a wide variety of tools: legislative, operational and also financial have been utilised and several UN organs—from the UN General Assembly to the High Commissioner for Human Rights, from the UN Economic and Social Committee to the UN Human Rights Council and the UN Human Rights Committee (HR Committee)—have been engaged to this end. Some UN offices and organs, such as the UN Office on Drugs and Crime and the Special Rapporteur on the Independence of the Judiciary and Lawyers, have the lead in this issue which is included respectively in their institutional functions, goals and mandate, while some UN agencies deal with this issue following a sector-based approach, as it is the case of the World Bank, which approaches the topic under the perspective of the economic assistance to development. All these activities respond to several main goals: to establish the principle of the independence of the judiciary; to define in a detailed manner the principle in order to have precise and common standards for the assessment of its respect; to strengthen the implementation by States of the principle and finally to financially support its implementation by States.

This study analyses the various actions taken within the UN system to create an 'international' notion of judicial independence and 'international' standards and requirements of independence, to promote their universalisation and respect, and to operationally support their implementation in domestic law in situations where serious deficiencies, political, economic or structural, make this task particularly difficult.

2 Establishing the Principle of the Independence of Judges: Art. 10 of the Universal Declaration of Human Rights and Art. 14(1) of the International Covenant on Civil and Political Rights

A large part of efforts by the United Nations in the field of safeguarding the independence of the judiciary have been focused on establishing the principle itself or, in other words, on universalising and objectivising it. This result was firstly achieved through the production of soft and hard law, namely through Art. 10 of the Universal Declaration of Human Rights of 1948 and through Art. 14(1) of the International Covenant on Civil and Political Rights of 1966 (ICCPR).

---

[6] *Ibid*, para. 5.

The attempt to subordinate the different political, social and cultural structures of the States to uniform rules on the protection of human rights has been slow and, understandably and obviously, much less easy than at the European level. So, if the Declaration was rapidly adopted as an immediate expression of the reaction to the sufferings and atrocities caused by the Second World War, the laborious elaboration of the two UN Covenants of 1966 (not only the Covenant on Civil and Political Rights but also the Covenant on Economic, Social and Cultural Rights), concluded 14 years after the start of the negotiations, and entered into force 10 years after their signature, practically represents the States' reluctance and caution as well as the differences, both political and legal, between them on the protection of human rights.

Art. 10 of the Universal Declaration on Human Rights provides that:

> Everyone is entitled in full equality to a fair and public hearing by an independent and impartial tribunal, in the determination of his rights and obligations and of any criminal charge against him.

The reference to an 'independent tribunal' is inserted in the right to a fair trial which, as the European Court of Human Rights already noted in the judgment of 1975 in the Case *Golder v. The United Kingdom*, consists in a set of distinct, although interrelated, rights which "taken together, make up a single right not specifically defined".[7]

The disposition is rather concise so that nothing is specified on the requirements of the independency of judges. This even though the conditions of service of judges, including their economic conditions, the methods of their appointments, whether they are immovable or not, and their legal and physical protection from external pressure and threats, are all elements that contribute to the qualification of the concept of independence. Nevertheless, considering the variety of existing judicial systems and their very different degrees of development, it has been a success that the reference to the independence of the judiciary, as well as to impartiality, has been included in Art. 10.[8]

However, Art. 10 is not devoid of value; the Universal Declaration is still nowadays influential because of its universal and general nature, which puts it above all historical and contingent dimensions and at the origin of the development process of the principles of fair trial with all its components, including the independence of the judiciary.[9]

More elaborated is Art. 14(1) of the ICCPR which states that:

> All persons shall be equal before the courts and tribunals. In the determination of any criminal charge against him, or of his rights and obligations in a suit at law, everyone shall be entitled to a fair and public hearing by a competent, independent and impartial tribunal established by law.

---

[7]ECtHR, *Golder v. The United Kingdom*, 21 Feb. 1975, p. 13.

[8]Lehtimaja and Matti (1999), pp. 223–240.

[9]Leanza and Caracciolo (2010), pp. 62–65.

Also in the ICCPR, the principle of the judges' independence is one of the fair trial rights; rights which are usually classified into three parts: basic rules, minimum guarantees and other provisions. Basic rules of fair trial rights are provided by paragraphs one and two; paragraph three refers to minimum guarantees while other provisions are contained in the rest of Art. 14 and Art. 15.[10] Therefore the principle of the independence of the judiciary, along with those of competence and impartiality, falls within the category of the basic rules.[11] In short, the ICCPR elucidates *inter alia* the requirement of independence and it implies an obligation on States to create conditions for judges to adjudicate independently. Under this perspective, the rights to a fair trial impose to the ICCPR States Parties an obligation not only to respect and ensure those rights to all individuals but, most importantly, to adopt such laws or other measures necessary to give effect to the same rights, following their constitutional processes (Art. 2(2) ICCPR).

The establishment of the principle of the independence of the judiciary in the ICCPR has resulted in obliging all States Parties to adopt and implement this principle in their justice systems in accordance with their constitutional process and domestic practice. It has also resulted in the obligation for these States to guarantee the independence of the judiciary because of the duty of all governmental and other institutions to respect and observe this independence. Indeed, over the years the principle has been accepted by rather all legal systems throughout the world and subsequently most States have enshrined it in their constitutions. Thus, formally Art. 14(1) has reached its purpose even if divergence has remained in numerous States all around the world between written norms and actual practice.

Nevertheless, this provision does not provide for more details and information on the contents and standards of independency of the judiciary.[12] The problem is not merely theoretical but also practical since the definition of certain standards of independency is necessary to ascertain the compliance by States with this principle.

---

[10]Zhang (2009), pp. 39–43.

[11]Similar rules are contained, *inter alia*, in Art. 6 of the European Convention on Human Rights and Fundamental Freedoms, Arts. 2(3) and 14 of the International Covenant on Civil and Political Rights, Art. 8 of the American Convention on Human Rights, Art. 5 of the International Convention on the Elimination of All Forms of Racial Discrimination and Art. 7 of the African Charter on Human and Peoples' Rights. Moreover, guarantees of the independence and impartiality of domestic courts and judges may be found in many conventional instruments outside the principal civil and political rights conventions, e.g. under Art. 17(1)(a) of the ICC Statute, the fact that the domestic tribunal satisfies the international requirements of independence and impartiality is also relevant to the issue of the admissibility of proceedings.

[12]Other dispositions of the ICCPR entail the independence and impartiality of the judiciary as Art. 2 (claims of violation of a right recognized by the Covenant are to be "determined by competent judicial, administrative or legislative authorities, or by any other competent authority provided for by the legal system of the State", and Art. 26 ("all persons are equal before the law and are entitled without any discrimination to the equal protection of the law"). See, on this point Olbourne (2003), p. 99. For comments see Nowak (2005).

3 Interpreting the Principle of the Independency of Judges: General Comment No. 32/2007 and the 'Jurisprudence' of the UN Human Rights Committee

While the ICCPR does not further elaborate on the content of judicial independence, the UN Human Rights Committee (HR Committee) has suggested a more detailed range of requirements of the principle, mainly in its General Comments No. 13 of 1984 and No. 32 of 2007 and in its case-law.[13] The HR Committee's interpretative activity is particularly relevant because of its authoritative value even if, as well known, the views and comments by the Committee have no binding force on States Parties.

The first Comment contains rather generic explanations, nevertheless of primary importance, since they were provided following the lack of information contained in numerous States' reports on the implementation of the principles of fair trial. In particular, General Comment No. 13 focuses on the scope of application of these principles; to begin with, these principles must apply not only to procedures for the determination of criminal charges against individuals but also to procedures to determine their rights and obligations in a suit at law;[14] secondly, they apply to all courts and tribunals whether ordinary or specialized.[15] According to the Committee:

> the existence, in many countries, of military or special courts which try civilians [. . .] could present serious problems as far as the equitable, impartial and independent administration of justice is concerned. Quite often the reason for the establishment of such courts is to enable exceptional procedures to be applied which do not comply with normal standards of justice.[16]

More extended is General Comments No. 32 which also interprets thoroughly Art. 14 as far as the independency of the judiciary is concerned. The Committee dwells on several elements of the principle of independency: namely in which cases the principle applies; which is the notion of tribunal and the nature of the requirement of independence, along with those of being competent and established by the law.

Before analysing the observations on the independence of judges by the HR Committee, it is worth reminding that the UN body clarified that even if Art. 14 is not included in the list of non-derogable rights under Art. 4(2) of the Covenant:

> States derogating from normal procedures required under article 14 in circumstances of a public emergency should ensure that such derogations do not exceed those strictly required by the exigencies of the actual situation. The guarantees of fair trial may never be made

[13] HRC, General Comment No. 13, Art. 14 (Administration of justice). HRC, General Comment No. 32, Article 14 (Right to equality before courts and tribunals and to a fair trial) (CCPR/C/GC/32, 23 August 2007).

[14] HRC, General Comment No. 13, Art. 14 (Administration of justice), para. 2.

[15] *Ibid.*, para. 4.

[16] *Ibid.*, para. 4.

subject to measures of derogation that would circumvent the protection of non-derogable rights.[17]

With specific reference to the requirement of competence, independence and impartiality of a tribunal, the Committee clearly concludes that "[...] is an absolute right that is not subject to any exception."[18]

Indeed, the impossibility to derogate to the competence, independence and impartiality of judges seems to stem from the fact that the right to a fair trial not only is a guarantee for the individual but also a general public interest in itself.[19] In other words, the right to have the criminal charges or a suit at law heard by an impartial and independent judge is an institutional guarantee for the proper administration of justice and a prerequisite for the protection of any other right established in the Covenant. Therefore, it is a fundamental principle of a fair trial from which it is forbidden to deviate.

Concerning when the principle of the independency of the judiciary applies, the Committee seeks to identify a common standard, in particular with regard to civil proceedings, whose definition appear to be rather vague also because of the differences between legal systems. On this point, the Committee clarifies that:

> Criminal charges relate in principle to acts declared to be punishable under domestic criminal law. The notion may also extend to acts that are criminal in nature with sanctions that, regardless of their qualification in domestic law, must be regarded as penal because of their purpose, character or severity.[20]

While the concept of '[...] a 'suit at law' or its equivalents

> is based on the nature of the right in question rather than on the status of one of the parties or the particular forum provided by domestic legal systems for the determination of particular rights.[21]

The Committee exemplifies also a series of hypotheses of suits at law to which, however, it attributes non-exhaustive value and suggests a case by case assessment taking into consideration the nature of the right at stake.[22] The failure of a State Party to the ICCPR to establish a competent tribunal would already amount to a violation of Art. 14. Contrarily, the right to access a court or tribunal does not apply where domestic law does not grant any entitlement to the person concerned.[23]

With regard to the definition of tribunal or court, the Committee observes that:

---

[17] HRC, General Comment No. 32, Article 14 (Right to equality before courts and tribunals and to a fair trial) (CCPR/C/GC/32, 23 August 2007), para. 6.

[18] *Ibid.*, para. 19. HRC, Communication No. 263/1987, 19 October 1987, *Miguel González del Río v. Peru*, para. 5.2.

[19] E.g., ECtHR, *Engels v. The Netherlands*, 8 Jun. 1976, para. 58.

[20] HRC, General Comment No. 32, para.15.

[21] *Ibid.*, para.16.

[22] *Ibid.*, para.16.

[23] *Ibid.*, para.17.

> [It] designates a body, regardless of its denomination, that is established by law, independent of the executive and legislative branches of government or enjoys in specific cases judicial independence in deciding legal matters in proceedings that are judicial in nature.[24]

Therefore, it can be said that the Committee gives an autonomous meaning of tribunal for the purpose of the ICCPR. For the Committee, the term 'tribunal' refers to all civil and criminal courts provided for in a particular legal order. However, since the legal systems of the ICCPR States Parties are significantly different, it cannot be excluded that a State Party creates bodies which, although not specifically qualified as courts or tribunals, have nevertheless their legal nature. In these cases, the autonomous definition of 'tribunal' contained in General Comment No. 35 nonetheless imposes to that State the obligation to respect the requirements of competence, independence and impartiality.[25]

These requirements must be complied with also by military tribunals, special tribunals, courts based on customary law and religious courts.[26] Reiterating the considerations expressed in General Comment No. 13, the Committee specifies that even if the ICCPR does not prohibit the trial of civilians in military or special courts,

> it requires that such trials are in full conformity with the requirements of Article 14 and that its guarantees cannot be limited or modified because of the military or special character of the court concerned. The Committee also notes that the trial of civilians in military or special courts may raise serious problems as far as the equitable, impartial and independent administration of justice is concerned.[27]

Notably, trials of civilians by military or special courts are not automatically excluded by the Covenant but they should be exceptional; on the contrary special tribunals of 'faceless judges' composed of anonymous judges "do not satisfy basic standards of fair trial and, in particular, the requirement that the tribunal must be independent and impartial."[28]

The fact that trials of civilians by military tribunals should be exceptional means that:

> the State party must demonstrate, with regard to the specific class of individuals at issue, that the regular civilian courts are unable to undertake the trials, that other alternative forms of special or high-security civilian courts are inadequate for the task and that recourse to military courts is unavoidable. The State party must further demonstrate how military courts ensure the full protection of the rights of the accused pursuant to Article 14.[29]

---

[24] *Ibid.*, para.18.

[25] According to Nowak, "[o]n the one hand it is not enough for the national legislature to designate an authority as a court if it does not correspond to Article 14(1)'s requirements of independence and impartiality. On the other hands administrative authorities that are largely independent and free of directives may, under certain circumstances, satisfy the requirements of a tribunal pursuant to Article 14." (Nowak 2005, p. 319).

[26] HRC, General Comment No. 32, paras. 22–24.

[27] *Ibid.*, para.22. See Report of the Special Rapporteur on the independence of judges and lawyers (A/68/285, 7 August 2013).

[28] *Ibid.*, para. 23.

[29] HRC, Communication No. 1813/2008, 22 March 2011, *Ebenezer Derek Mbongo Akwanga v. Cameroon*, para. 7 (CCPR/C/101/D/1813/2008, 19 May 2011).

In conclusion, the HR Committee does not propose in General Comment No. 32 a 'classic' definition of court or tribunal, but sets out a substantial and dynamic view whereby whatever the *nomen juris* is, what counts is that the tribunal or court respects the principles of jurisdiction, impartiality, independence and to be established by law. More recently in the case *Gabriel Osío Zamora v. Venezuela*, the HR Committee has better defined its position on this point, stating that:

> whenever domestic law entrusts a judicial body with a judicial task, the guarantees provided for in the first sentence of Article 14 (1) of the ICCPR are applicable, namely the right to equality before courts and tribunals and thus the principles of impartiality, fairness and equality, as enshrined in that provision, must be respected.[30]

Finally, the requirement of independence applies also to jury. The ICCPR retains that:

> it is important that all the jurors be placed in a position in which they may assess the facts and the evidence in an objective manner, so as to be able to return a just verdict. On the other hand, the HR Committee recalls that where attempts at jury tampering come to the knowledge of either of the parties, these alleged improprieties should have been challenged before the court.[31]

Concerning, the requirement of the independence of the judges, the HR Committee seeks to render this principle in practical terms by identifying its components and standards. According to the UN body:

> The requirement of independence refers, in particular, to the procedure and qualifications for the appointment of judges, and guarantees relating to their security of tenure until a mandatory retirement age or the expiry of their term of office, where such exist, the conditions governing promotion, transfer, suspension and cessation of their functions [. . .].[32]

Furthermore, the safeguard of judges' independence cannot but be secured by law and in particular: the status of judges, including their term of office, their independence, security, adequate remuneration, conditions of service, pensions and the age of retirement.[33] In short terms, from the appointment to the retirement, all aspects of the judges' career should be established by the law and be settled in order to guarantee their independence.

The HR Committee has also elaborated on the dismissal of judges which proves to be a very delicate issue. On this point the UN body observes that:

> Judges may be dismissed only on serious grounds of misconduct or incompetence, in accordance with fair procedures ensuring objectivity and impartiality set out in the

[30]HRC, Communication No. 2203/2012, 20 November 2017, *Gabriel Osío Zamora v. Venezuela*, para. 9.2 (CCPR/C/121/D/2203/2012, 1 February 2018). See also HRC, Communication No. 2069/2011, 7-31 October 2014, *Shikhmuradova v. Turkmenistan*, para. 6.6 (CCPR/C/112/D/2069/2011, 19 January 2015).

[31]HRC, Communication No. 2203/2012, 20 November 2017, *Gabriel Osío Zamora v. Venezuela* (CCPR/C/121/D/2203/2012, 1 February 2018) and HRC Communication No. 811/1998, 20 July 2004, *Rookmin Mulai v. Guyana*, para. 6.1 (CCPR/C/81/D/811/1998, 18 August 2004).

[32]HRC, General Comment No. 32, para.19.

[33]*Ibid*.

> constitution or the law. The dismissal of judges by the executive, e.g. before the expiry of the term for which they have been appointed, without any specific reasons given to them and without effective judicial protection being available to contest the dismissal is incompatible with the independence of the judiciary. The same is true, for instance, for the dismissal by the executive of judges alleged to be corrupt, without following any of the procedures provided for by the law.[34]

The above-mentioned set of requirements guaranteeing the independence relates to the conditions of judges themselves. However, General Comment No. 32 also deals with the issue of the independence of the judiciary vis-à-vis other State powers. Indeed, it makes clear that:

> States should take specific measures guaranteeing the independence of the judiciary [. . .]. A situation where the functions and competencies of the judiciary and the executive are not clearly distinguishable or where the latter is able to control or direct the former is incompatible with the notion of an independent tribunal.[35]

The concept of the independence of judges is an irreplaceable element of the principle of the separation of powers.[36] It is true that the independence of the judiciary is almost never absolute, since the various branches of the State are often intertwined, as it is the case of those legal systems in which the judges are appointed by the executive power, however, these correlations must be organized in such a way as not to undermine the essence of the principle of independence.[37]

Thus, under Art. 14(1) of the ICCPR States are obliged to protect the institutional independence of the judiciary through structural and function safeguards. The other state bodies have the duty to respect the independence of the judiciary. Tribunals must be politically independent (they must not be controlled or manipulated or influenced by the other State's branches. Moreover, tribunals must be able to fulfil their functions without fear: the judges' independency necessarily fades away if they

---

[34] *Ibid.*, para.20. See also HRC, Communication No. 1376/2005, 24 July 2008, *Soratha Bandaranayake v. Sri Lanka*, para. 7.3 (CCPR/C/93/D/1376/2005, 24 July 2008).

[35] *Ibid.*, para. 19.

[36] See the Report of the Special Rapporteur on the Independence of Judges and Lawyers. Mission to Qatar (A/HRC/29/26/Add. 1, 31 March 2015, para. 45) where it is underlined that: "It is the principle of the separation of powers, together with the rule of law, which opens the way to an administration of justice that provides guarantees of independence, impartiality and transparency. For this reason, there should be clear demarcation between the respective competences of the different branches of power. A situation where the functions and competencies of the judiciary and the executive are not clearly distinguishable, or where the latter is able to control or direct the former, is incompatible with the notion of an independent tribunal."

[37] With reference to HRC, in the case *Eligio Cedeño v. Venezuela* (Communication No. 1940/2010, CCPR/C/106/D/1940/2010, 4 December 2012, para. 7.3), the Committee takes the opportunity to recall that: "States should take specific measures to guarantee the independence of the judiciary, protect judges from any form of political influence, and establish clear procedures and objective criteria for the appointment, remuneration, tenure, promotion, suspension and dismissal of the members of the judiciary and for disciplinary sanctions against them. A situation where the functions and competencies of the judiciary and the executive branch are not clearly distinguishable or where the latter is able to control or direct the former is incompatible with the notion of an independent tribunal." See Shetreet and McCormack (2016) and Sterett and Walker (2019).

face retribution for judgement unfavourable to private parties or governments.[38] Lastly, only an independent judiciary in a constitutional democracy can effectively guarantee human rights and the rule of law.

Indeed, at present, the overwhelming majority of legal systems, in particular through their respective constitutions, is deemed to recognise the principle of the independence of the judiciary.[39] Conversely, the risks stem from failure to comply with the relevant constitutional provisions. These include, for example, the use of measures restricting the independence of judges justified on the basis of emergency situations or widespread practices of corruption or intimidation against judges.

With regard to these phenomena, the HR Committee carries out a careful activity of monitoring and control through the periodic reports requested to States Parties. In this sense, the list of issues submitted very recently by the HR Committee to Ukraine on which the latter will have to respond is enlightening. Among the various issues, particular attention is given to the procedures put in place by Ukraine to ensure the independence of judges from external interference and the progress made in protecting the independence of prosecutors.[40]

[38]See HRC, *Vladislav Kovalev et al. v. Belarus* (CCPR/C/106/D/2120/2011, 27 November 2012). In that case the Committee retains that Art. 14(1) was violated because of the situation of intimidation surrounding the trial since "[. . .] the court was under pressure: the access in the court room, besides police officers, was controlled by other unidentified persons in civilian clothes, who refused to disclose their identity. They were allegedly obviously officers of intelligence services. They were checking the persons entering the court room and could refuse access to or even arrest persons who came to attend the trial. This created an atmosphere of fear and is an indication of the pressure exercised on the court [. . .]." para. 3.4. On the same point see the brief prepared by M Stephenson: "The third characteristic of judicial independence is that the judiciary is free from interference. Parties to a case, or others with an interest in its outcome, cannot influence the judge's decision. In practice, protecting judges from private persons with an interest in the case means preventing judicial corruption and coercion. Insulating judges from officials of other branches of government is often taken to be the most important aspect of judicial independence. Government poses perhaps the most serious threat to judicial independence for two reasons: it has a potential interest in the outcome of myriad cases, and it has so much potential power over judges." World Bank, Judicial Independence: What It Is, How It Can Be Measured, Why It Occurs.

[39]Bartole (2018), pp. 1–20.

[40]See, e.g. List of issues in relation to the eighth periodic report of Ukraine (CCPR/C/UKR/Q/8, 14 November 2019): "(b) Measures taken to secure the independence of judges from any outside interference in their activities, to ensure their safety, and to address effectively the reported incidents of such interference, particularly in conflict-related and other high profile cases, including pressure on judges by parliamentarians and by resorting to criminal law provisions, [. . .] (c) Progress made towards strengthening the independence and impartiality of prosecutors, including with regard to: (i) the work of the joint working group tasked with improving relevant regulations, including the procedure for the appointment and dismissal of the Prosecutor General; (ii) the introduction of random allocation of cases to prosecutors based on strict and objective criteria; (iii) the extension of the statutory limitation for bringing disciplinary sanctions against prosecutors; and (iv) the adequate remuneration of prosecutors." para. 18. See also the List of issues prior to submission of the fourth periodic report of Croatia (CCPR/C/HRV/QPR/4, 25 November 2019): "Please report on measures taken and progress made to ensure adequate safeguards against political influence on the procedure for selecting, appointing and renewing the mandate of the President of the Supreme Court, to

4 Detailing the Principle of the Independence of Judges Through Soft Law

In parallel with the interpretation of the principle of the independency of the judiciary by the HR Committee, attempts have also been made by the UN to substantiate this principle and to identify further components and standards thereto by means of soft law instruments, as it is typically the case in the United Nations. These attempts have a twofold objective: on the one hand, to help UN Member States to codify and develop the principle of the independence of the judiciary in their respective domestic systems and, on the other hand, to create reference standards to which to relate the monitoring of the implementation of the principle by Member States.

Among these soft law instruments, it is worth mentioning the Basic Principles on the Independence of the Judiciary adopted by the Seventh UN Congress on the Prevention of Crime and the Treatment of Offenders in 1985. These principles are described as being declaratory of universally accepted views on this issue by the UN Members States, and they have become an important yardstick in assessing the independence of the judiciary in the work of international monitoring organs and non-governmental organizations.[41]

These principles were endorsed by the UN General Assembly in Resolution 40/32 of 29 November 1985. In the following month, in Resolution 40/146 of 13 December 1985, the General Assembly welcomed the Basic Principles and invited governments "to respect them and to take them into account within the framework of their national legislation and practice". Few years later, the UN Economic and Social Council adopted the Procedures for the Effective Implementation of the Basic Principles on the Independence of the Judiciary (Resolution 1989/60 of 19 May 1989) where UN Member States are asked to adopt and implement in their justice systems the Basic Principles in accordance with their constitutional processes and domestic practice as well as to promote the culture of the independence of the judiciary.[42]

The 1985 Basic Principles, "formulated to assist Member States in their task of securing and promoting the independence of the judiciary", are the following: (a) independence of the judiciary; (b) freedom of expression and association; (c) qualifications, selection and training; (d) conditions of service and tenure; (e) professional secrecy and immunity; and (f) discipline, suspension and removal.

---

improve the efficiency of the judicial system and to address the significant backlog, especially of civil and commercial cases." para. 17.

[41]UN Office of the High Commissioner for Human Rights, Human Rights in the Administration of Justice. A Manual on Human Rights for Judges, Prosecutors and Lawyers (2003). Professional training series N°9. p. 119.

[42]In 1990 the Eight UN Congress on the Prevention of Crime and the Treatment of Offenders, held in Havana, also adopted some Guidelines on the Role of Prosecutors, 27 August to 7 September.

In particular, the Basic Principles list two sets of standards of evaluation: one standard concerns the judiciary *per se*, as a State's branch, while the other concerns every single judge. It has been said that:

> Judicial independence is, therefore, both a state of mind and a set of institutional and operational arrangements. The former is concerned with the judge's independence in fact; the latter with defining the relationships between the judiciary and others, particularly the other branches of government, so as to assure both the reality and the appearance of independence. The relationship between these two aspects of judicial independence is that an individual judge may possess that state of mind, but if the court over which he or she presides is not independent of the other branches of government in what is essential to its functions, the judge cannot be said to be independent.[43]

Concerning institutional independence, it must be guaranteed by law, and possibly be enshrined in the constitution of each State. And it is the responsibility of the State, i.e. all other branches of the State, parliament and executive power, to guarantee such independence. The respect for the judicial authority is crucial for the preservation of the rule of law, and of human rights. For the same reason, judicial decisions, once rendered, must be respected by the parties to the proceedings and the competent authorities must intervene with coercive measures to compensate in case of failure to spontaneously comply.[44]

From this assumption the Basic Principles depicts a number of requirements which pertain to institutional independence of the judiciary.[45] Specifically, the judiciary must be independent with regard to internal matters of judicial administration, including the assignment of cases to judges within the court to which they belong (independence as to administrative matters, contained in Principle 14); the judiciary must have independence in financial matters, and have sufficient funds to carry out its tasks efficiently (independence as to financial matters, contained in Principle 7); the judiciary must be independent with regard to decision-making and its decisions must be respected and observed by both the Government and other institutions (independence as to decision-making, contained in Principle 4);[46] the

[43]UN Office on Drugs and Crime, Commentary on the Bangalore Principles of Judicial Conduct, September 2007, para. 23.

[44]See, e.g. the Report of the Special Rapporteur on the independence of judges and lawyers on his mission to Poland (A/HRC/38/38/Add.1, 5 April 2018), where the UN Special Rapporteur on the Independence of the Judiciary concludes that the non-implementation of judgements, in the specific case of the Polish Constitutional Court "constitutes a flagrant breach of the principles of judicial independence and the separation of powers, as well as a violation of the Polish Constitution. The duty to respect and abide by the judgments and decisions of the judiciary constitutes a necessary corollary of the principle of institutional independence of the judiciary." para. 29. On the perception of the independence of judges in Europe see Van Dijk (2021) pp. 29-51.

[45]For comments on the Principles, see Leckie (1987), pp. 13–28.

[46]This principle entails the prohibition of interference with the work of the judiciary. However, it is not easy to identify the concept of undue interference. Clearly, in a democratic society, the right balance should be reached between the need to protect the judiciary from pressure and interference on the one hand and the interest in an open debate on issues of public interest on the other. The prohibition of interference with the judiciary must not become an immunity from any form of

judiciary must have jurisdictional competence, which means that there must be judicial autonomy in the determination of questions of competence (jurisdictional competence, contained in Principle 3); and, finally, the judiciary has both the right and the duty to ensure fair court proceedings and issue reasoned decisions (Principle 6).[47]

Concerning the independence of individual judges, for the Basic Principles, it is to be understood as the right and duty of each judge to decide cases, even the most vexed, applying the law and without fear of repercussions, reprisals and inappropriate personal criticisms. The means whereby to guarantee the judges' independence in the performance of their professional duties are accurately listed by the Basic Principles and they consist in appointing or electing judges exclusively on the basis of their professional qualifications and personal integrity and without any discrimination (Principle 10);[48] in long-term security of tenure

---

criticism. On this point see the observations from the HR Committee on the independence of the judiciary in Romania: "39. The Committee is concerned about reports of undue attacks on the independence of the judiciary by public officials and the media [. . .]. 40. The State party should continue its efforts to ensure and protect the full independence and impartiality of the judiciary and guarantee that it can carry out its judicial functions without any form of pressure or interference. The State party should also take measures to protect the prosecution against any undue interference [. . .]". Concluding observations on the fifth periodic report of Romania, CCPR/C/ROU/CO/5, 11 December 2017.

[47] As far as the financial independence of the judiciary is concerned, in practice it is conditioned by the fact that the allocation of resources depends on the State budget, which is usually drawn up by the government and adopted by the legislative power. Hence the suggestion of the usefulness of the participation of the judiciary in the determination of its financial needs. On this point, see UN Office of the High Commissioner for Human Rights, Human Rights in the Administration of Justice. A Manual on Human Rights for Judges, Prosecutors and Lawyers (2003). Professional training series N°9, pp. 119–135.

[48] E.g., in 2018 the HR Committee concluded with regard to Algeria that: "39. [. . .] the independence of the judiciary is not sufficiently guaranteed and that the executive plays a significant role in the organization of the judicial branch. The Committee is concerned that, pursuant to Organic Act No. 04-11 of 6 September 2004 on the organization of the judiciary, (a) senior judges can only be appointed by presidential decree; (b) judges are appointed by presidential decree on the recommendation of the Minister of Justice after deliberation in the High Council of the Judiciary; (c) judges become tenured only after serving for 10 years; (d) the judges serving in the prosecution service are entirely under the authority of the Minister of Justice, who may reassign them; and (e) dismissals and compulsory retirements are effected by presidential decree and all other disciplinary measures are ordered by the Minister of Justice. It is equally concerned by allegations of outside interference in decisions of judges and public prosecutors and by reports of collective and mass compulsory retirements of judges and public prosecutors (art. 14). 40. As part of the reform of the justice system it has undertaken, the State party should amend Act No. 04-11 of 6 September 2014 with a view to (a) ensuring that judges and public prosecutors are appointed through an independent process that is based on objective, transparent criteria for assessing candidates' suitability in terms of the required skills, competence and reputation; (b) strengthening the independence and the powers of the High Council of the Judiciary, in particular with regard to assessing judges' qualifications, disciplinary measures, dismissals and compulsory retirements; and (c) guaranteeing the tenure of judges and public prosecutors, the independence of judges and the impartiality of public prosecutors and protecting the workings of the judiciary from any outside interference." Concluding observations on the fourth periodic report of Algeria, CCPR/C/DZA/CO/4, 17 August 2018. On discrimination for gender or religion see the observation adopted by the HR

(Principle 12);[49] in adequate remuneration (Principle 11); in their promotion on the basis of objective factors (Principle 13); in attributing the competence to decide on the accountability of individual judges for unethical professional behaviour to a fully independent and impartial organ ensuring due process of law (Principles 17-20);[50] and, lastly, in recognising the rights of judges to freedom of expression and association which are crucial in a democratic society (Principle 8).

Finally, in order to have truly independent judiciary, also the training and continued education of judges in national and international human rights law is deemed to be essential. On this point, the HR Committee has often underlined the importance of training judges, as well as other legal professions and police officers, in human rights law.[51]

Committee in 1998 on the report of Sudan: "132. The Committee is concerned that [...] very few non-Muslins and women occupy judicial positions at all levels. Therefore measures should be taken to improve the independence and technical competence of the judiciary, including the appointment of qualified judges among women and the minorities." (Report of the Human Rights Committee, UNGA Official Records, Fifty-third Session, Supplement No. 40 (A/53/40)).

[49]Recently, the HR Committee, facing, *inter alia*, the fact that in Vietnam the judges are appointed by the Communist Party based on their loyalty to the fatherland, concluded on the Report presented by that State that: "33. The Committee is concerned regarding the influence on the procuracy and the judiciary of the ruling party, thereby undermining their independence, and the lack of confidence of the public in the justice system. It also remains concerned at judges' lack of security of tenure. 34. The Committee reiterates its recommendation CCPR/CO/75/VNM, 5 August 2002, para. 9 that the State party should take immediate steps to protect the independence and impartiality of the judiciary and the procuracy, guarantee that they are free to operate without interference and ensure transparent and impartial processes for appointments to the judiciary and the procuracy." (Concluding observations on the third periodic report of Vietnam, CCPR/C/VNM/CO/3, 29 August 2019).

[50]See the observations by the HR Committee on the report of Azerbaijan: "26. The Committee is also concerned about the number of disciplinary proceedings that have been instituted against judges in recent years and regrets the lack of information on safeguards in place to ensure that judges cannot be sanctioned for minor infractions or for a controversial interpretation of the law [...]. The Committee is also concerned about the number of disciplinary proceedings that have been instituted against judges in recent years and regrets the lack of information on safeguards in place to ensure that judges cannot be sanctioned for minor infractions or for a controversial interpretation of the law (arts. 2 and 14). 27. The Committee reiterates its previous recommendations (see CCPR/C/AZE/CO/3, para. 12). The State party should take all measures necessary to safeguard, in law and in practice, judicial independence. In particular, it should: [...] (d) Ensure that an independent body is responsible for judicial discipline and that sufficient safeguards are in place to prevent disciplinary actions being taken against judges for minor infractions or for a controversial interpretation of the law." (Concluding observations on the fourth periodic report of Azerbaijan, CCPR/C/AZE/CO/4, 16 November 2016).

[51]See the observations submitted by the HR Committee on the report of the Libyan Araba Jamahiriya in 1999: "134. Training in human rights law should be given to all judges and members of the legal profession." (Report of the Human Rights Committee, UNGA Official Records, Fifty-fourth Session, Supplement No. 40 (A/54/40)). See also the observation adopted in 1998 by the HR Committee on the report of Sudan where the Committee manifests its concern about the technical competence of Sudanese judges and police officers and suggests that: "Training in human rights law should be given to all judges, law enforcement officers and members of the legal profession." (Report of the Human Rights Committee, UNGA Official Records, Fifty-third Session, para. 132).

In conclusion, these principles, though non-binding, have greatly influenced the practice of States in creating and consolidating independent judiciaries, as well as the practice of UN human rights treaty bodies and of the Special Rapporteur on the Independence of Judges and Lawyers. They have also been terms of reference at the regional level.[52] Since the additional parameters relating to the principle of the independence of the judiciary have been provided in the framework of the development and consolidation of human rights and, in particular, the principles of fair trial referred to in Art. 14 of the ICCPR, their purpose is not to define the role and conduct of judges but to clarify the scope and the contents of the rights claimed by individuals in relation to the judiciary.

On the contrary, a completely different approach characterises the Bangalore Principles of Judicial Conduct adopted in 2002 by the Judicial Integrity Group, which is an independent, autonomous, not-for-profit and voluntary entity, whose members are or have been heads of the judiciary or senior judges at domestic, regional or international level.[53] In July 2006, the UN Economic and Social Council adopted Resolution 23,[54] recommended to it by the UN Commission on Crime Prevention and Criminal Justice in which it has recognized the Bangalore Principles as representing a further development of, and as being complementary to, the UN Basic Principles on the Independence of the Judiciary. Accordingly, the UN Economic and Social Council has invited Member States to encourage their judiciaries to take into consideration the Bangalore Principles when reviewing or developing rules with respect to the professional and ethical conduct of members of the judiciary.

What differentiates the Bangalore Principles from the UN Basic Principles is not so much the way in which they were adopted, namely through the interaction between the competent UN bodies and members of the judiciary—at the highest level—of the Member States,[55] as their perspective on the question of the independence of the judiciary. In fact, their objective is not to specify the scope of the rights to a fair trial but to define and substantiate rules of conduct for judges, which could contribute to guaranteeing the independence of the judiciary.

To that end, judges are called to: (a) exercise the judicial function independently on the basis of his/her assessment of the facts and in accordance with a conscientious understanding of the law, free of any extraneous influences, pressures, threats or

[52] Olbourne (2003), p. 107.

[53] For more information, see The Judicial Integrity Group. https://www.judicialintegritygroup.org/images/resources/documents/JIG%202000-2011.pdf. Accessed 11 Nov 2019.

[54] UN Economic and Social Council (ECOSOC), Strengthening Basic Principles of Judicial Conduct, E/RES/2006/23, 27 July 2006.

[55] Other set of principles on the independence of the judiciary were adopted at the level of non-governmental organizations. It is worth reminding the International Bar Association's Code of Minimum Standards of Judicial Independence (IBA Code), adopted in 1982 by the International Bar Association, and the Montreal Universal Declaration on the Independence of Justice (Montreal Declaration), adopted by the First World Conference on the Independence of Justice held in Montreal in 1983.

interference (Value 1(1)); (b) to be independent from society in general and in relation to the particular parties to a dispute which the judge has to adjudicate (value 1(2)); (c) be free from inappropriate connections with, and influence by, the executive and legislative branches of government, but must also appear to a reasonable observer to be free therefrom (Value 1(3)); (d) be independent of judicial colleagues in respect of decisions which the judge is obliged to make independently (Value 1(4)); (e) encourage and uphold safeguards for the discharge of judicial duties in order to maintain and enhance the institutional and operational independence of the judiciary (Value 1(5)); and finally (f) exhibit and promote high standards of judicial conduct in order to reinforce public confidence in the judiciary which is fundamental to the maintenance of judicial independence (Value 1(6)).[56]

From the reading of these principles and their commentary, adopted by the Open-Ended Intergovernmental Expert Group Meeting on Strengthening Basic Principles of Judicial Conduct held in Vienna in 2007, the judge, in the administration of justice, must act at the service of the entire community, because only by acting accordingly, he/she will create in the community itself a sense of full confidence in justice and the judiciary. In other words, the principle of the independence seems to be intended as twofold: on the one hand, it protects judiciary and judges from interference by other state powers, but on the other hand, it also implies that judges act in the knowledge that the independence of the judiciary lies also in their daily good administration of justice.

All the above-mentioned soft law principles are nowadays universally accepted but they still need to be fully implemented and guaranteed. This is confirmed by their insertion in 2016 in the Compendium of UN Standards and Norms in Crime Prevention and Criminal Justice so to reiterate that they should be general standards of judicial conduct.[57]

However, it is also necessary to take into account new risks that may arise for the independence of the judiciary from the evolution of contemporary society and specifically from economic globalization. As entrepreneurial, financial and commercial activities continue to grow, the independence of the judiciary should also be guaranteed from new forms of pressure and interference stemming from the need to secure the interests associated with these activities. Today, the independence of the judiciary means not only that the judiciary must be free from governmental and political pressure, but also that judges must not succumb to the enormous power, wealth and resources of the business and commercial sector which do not necessarily turn into bribery but which can nevertheless turn into multiple forms of pressure.

---

[56]UN Office on Drugs and Crime, Commentary on the Bangalore Principles on Judicial Conduct, September 2007.

[57]UN Office on Drugs and Crime, Compendium of United Nations Standards and Norms in Crime Prevention and Criminal Justice, 2006, in particular, Part 4. Good governance, the independence of the judiciary and the integrity of criminal justice personnel, pp. 343–377.

5 Improving the Principle of Independence of Judges: The Practice of the Special Rapporteur on the Independence of Judges and Lawyers

This wide and developed body of soft law on the independence of judges has offered models for lawmakers, encouraging them to incorporate these international guidelines and standards into their national constitutions and to enact them into law. Many UN Member States have formally adopted the above-mentioned principles and they report regularly to the United Nations on their progress and problems, sometimes seeking help with legal education or the monitoring of procedures. Despite such, this independence has remained extremely vulnerable, under attack or non-existent *de facto* in many parts of the world.

Moreover, the lack of binding mechanisms of controls on the respect of human rights at the UN level further reduces the effectiveness of the above-mentioned prescriptions. The limits of the universal conventional system for the protection of human rights are well known. They consist in the limited incisiveness and effectiveness of the instruments of control provided for to guarantee respect for human rights established by the UN treaties. The powers conferred on UN bodies[58] with regard to the monitoring of the respect of human rights result only in recommended measures, since they are not given any power to settle disputes relating to the violation of these rights on a compulsory basis. If the recommendations of the UN bodies certainly have a high moral and political influence, however, it is not possible to ignore that the UN monitoring mechanisms on the respect of human rights are not able to achieve the standard of effectiveness that is typical of international human rights courts.

Then, the price that the conventional system on the protection of human rights promoted by the United Nations pays in order to achieve a universal scope is the limited effectiveness of its monitoring mechanisms. Indeed the UN human rights treaties, although characterised by a detailed and rather exhaustive definition and declination of human rights, lack of forms of control capable of imposing on State the duty to respect human rights so eroding their domestic jurisdiction in that field.

However, despite these limitations, the UN bodies in the field of human rights seek to exercise their respective mandates as widely as possible and also flexibly. In this context, flexibility also involves the recourse to *ad hoc* mechanisms, in specific cases of particular and serious human rights violations, and/or to 'multi-functional'

[58]E.g., the UN High Commissioner for Human Rights, whose role is to transpose the issue of the protection and development of human rights into every UN programme, as a guarantee for the maintenance of international peace and security; the Human Rights Council whose most important responsibility is the Universal Periodic Review, to which all UN Member States are subject every 4 years to review the fulfilment of their obligations under the various UN human rights treaties; and the HR Committee composed by independent experts which monitors, through different means, most of them to be accepted by States parties, the implementation of the ICCPR by States Parties.

mechanisms, aimed not only at monitoring respect for human rights, through the ascertainment of alleged violations of human rights, but at suggesting legislative, institutional and operational reform to develop and improve respect for human rights.

With regard to the issue of the independence of the judiciary, it is worth reflecting upon the role played by the Special Rapporteur on the Independence of Judges and Lawyers, first established in 1994 by the former UN Commission on Human Rights[59] on the basis of:

> both the increasing frequency of attacks on the independence of judges, lawyers and court officials and the link which exists between the weakening of safeguards for the judiciary and lawyers and the gravity and frequency of violations of human rights.[60]

The Special Rapporteur's mandate is *inter alia*: (a) to inquire into allegations on violations of the independence of the judiciary and lawyers and to report his or her conclusions and recommendations thereon; (b) to identify and record not only attacks on the independence of the judiciary, lawyers and court officials but also progress achieved in protecting and enhancing their independence, and make recommendations, including the provision of advisory services or technical assistance when they are requested by the State concerned; (c) to identify ways and means to improve the judicial system, and make concrete recommendations thereon; (d) to study, for the purpose of making proposals, important and topical questions of principle with a view to protecting and enhancing the independence of the judiciary and lawyers and court officials.[61] Obviously, the Special Rapporteur may not intervene with measures that are binding on the States but he/she sends allegation letters and urgent appeals to concerned Governments to clarify and/or bring these cases to their attention, conducts country visits upon the invitation of the concerned Government and presents annual thematic reports to the UN Human Rights Council and the UN General Assembly.

From the practice of the Special Rapporteur it emerges firstly that the concept of the judiciary and thus the scope of application of the principle of the independence of the judiciary and judges tend to be broadened. Indeed, the monitoring of the respect of this principle has also been extended by the Special Rapporteur to international judges (specifically the International Criminal Court)[62] and to judicial personnel sent

[59]As it is well known, the UN Council of Human Rights is also competent (as the Commission was previously competent) to promote and monitor the respect of human rights in a given State (country mandate) or with reference to specific aspects (thematic mandate) through the so-called special procedures. These special procedures consist in entrusting one or more independent experts (so-called special rapporteurs) with the task of analysing, monitoring and reporting on the human rights situation in that territory or in relation to that particular subject.

[60]Commission on Human Rights, Resolution 1994/41, 4 March 1994. The mandate was extended for 1 year by the Human Rights Council (Decision 2006/102). In June 2008, the mandate was subject to review by the Human Rights Council and every 3 years so far.

[61]UN Human Rights Council, Resolution 8/6, 28 June 2008.

[62]The alleged facts concern some very negative remarks made by the U.S. President's National Security Adviser, against the International Criminal Court which are deemed to constitute: "an

to a given State within the framework of international programmes of State assistance (specifically international judicial personnel sent to assist East Timor).[63]

Secondly, it appears that the category of threats to the independence of the judiciary and the judges is understood in a fairly broad sense, so as to include not only the typical threats—legislative reforms presumably aimed at limiting the independence of the judiciary,[64] influence of the Government,[65] structural lacks or crisis in the administration of justice,[66] negative modifications of the status of judges, *ad hoc* punitive measures towards individual judges or individual threats, etc.[67]—but also speeches against the work of the judiciary[68] or 'advertising' campaign[69] which could interfere with the principle of independence.

---

improper interference with the independence of the ICC and could hinder the ability of ICC judges, prosecutors, and personnel to carry out their professional duties." (Communication AL USA 6/2019, 20 March 2019).

[63]The alleged facts concern resolutions from both Government and Parliament calling for the immediate termination of the contracts of all international judicial personnel and advisers in the justice sector seemingly in connection with a series of court decisions in cases of taxation of foreign oil companies and corruption of Government officials. On the same vein the Government ordered the revocation of the permits to stay in the country of eight members of the international judicial staff (five judges, two prosecutors and one adviser to the Anti-Corruption Commission). These facts raise concern about the apparent interference of the executive and legislative powers in the independence of the judiciary and the deleterious effects that these decisions could have to the administration of justice in East Timor (Communication TLS 1/2014, 17 November 2014, A/HRC/2885, 19 February 2015)).

[64]See, e.g. the Report of the Special Rapporteur on the independence of judges and lawyers on his mission to Poland (A/HRC/38/38/Add.1, 5 April 2018), where the Special Rapporteur identifies a number of infringements to the principle of the independence of the ordinary judiciary in the recent reforms adopted in Poland, respectively with specific reference to new rules for appointing and dismissing court presidents (paras. 47-52) and the procedure for the selection of the judicial members of National Council for Judiciary. See also Communication No. HUN1/2012, 29 February 2012, A/HRC/20/30, 15 June 2012, on the constitutional reform in Hungary allegedly limiting the independence of the judiciary.

[65]See, e.g. the Report of the Special Rapporteur on the independence of judges and lawyers (Mission to Turkey, A/HRC/20/19/Add.3, 4 May 2012), para. 25).

[66]See, e.g. the Report of the Special Rapporteur on the independence of judges and lawyers (Addendum. Report to the mission to Peru, E/CN.4/1998/39/Add.1, 19 February 1998, para. 87).

[67]See, e.g. the Report of the Special Rapporteur on the independence of judges and lawyers (Addendum on Mission to South Africa, E/CN.4/2001/65/Add.2, 25 January 2001, pp. 4–55); Communication UKR 2/2019, 31 May 2019 (concerning alleged threats received by a Ukrainian judge in the Donetsk region, in relation to a court ruling. Communication POL 3/2019, 23 May 2019 (concerning a Polish judge subject to disciplinary proceedings as a consequence of a decision taken in the legitimate exercise of judicial functions).

[68]E.g. Communication ITA/2019, 12 July 2019, concerning alleged threats to the independence of the judiciary arising from public statements by the then Minister of Interior of Italy. According to the Rapporteur: "If confirmed, such attacks would constitute a serious breach to the principle of judicial independence."

[69]See, e.g. the Report of the Special Rapporteur on the independence of judges and lawyers on his mission to Poland (A/HRC/38/38/Add.1, 5 April 2018), where the Special Rapporteur expresses his concerns "at the 'Fair Courts' campaign launched by the Polish National Foundation [...]. The

Thirdly, some concern has also been manifested with regard to judges' duties, in particular the duty to "conduct themselves in a manner which could compromise their independence."[70] The lack of integrity has been seen as particularly dangerous since it "leads to a deterioration of judicial accountability and erodes public trust in the judicial system, creating a breeding ground for attacks and restrictions on judicial independence."[71]

Lastly, the practice of the Special Rapporteur helps to identify a number of areas for action to consolidate and develop the principle of independence of judges. To begin with, it is worth mentioning the concept of accountability of judges.[72] For the Special Rapporteur judicial independence and accountability are two complementary dimensions of an effective justice system, even if tensions exist between the two principles. The tensions result mainly from the lack of an established concept of judicial accountability. Indeed, in general, priority has been given to developing and strengthening the independence of the judiciary to the detriment of the establishment and proper functioning of accountability mechanisms, since it was believed that the strengthening of independence would have a more direct influence on the protection of human rights and the rule of law.[73]

To conclude, according to the Special Rapporteur, immunity for judges should not be absolute; on the contrary the immunity granted to them should be commensurate with the purpose of protecting the independence of justice operators, taking into consideration that judges need to act in accordance with predefined ethical standards and the duties and responsibilities intrinsic to their functions.[74] However, special attention should be given to the accountability mechanisms; it is therefore a crucial issue to clearly establish the actions for which justice operators should be accountable, to whom they should be accountable and through which processes.[75]

Finally, the Special Rapporteur has also focused on another key point which guarantees the independence of the judges: judiciary and judicial career processes which very often are assigned to self-governing judicial bodies, such as judicial

campaign, which sparked controversy due to the lack of transparency about its sponsor and budget, consists of billboards, advertisements on television and social media and a dedicated portal. It provides a distorted image of the judiciary, depicting judges as 'the enemy' of Polish people and an evil in Polish society." para 19.

[70]See, e.g. Report of the Special Rapporteur on the independence of judges and lawyers (Addendum: Preliminary report on the mission to Italy, E/CN.4/2002/72/Add.3, 26 March 2002, paras. 32-34) where the influence of the Minister of Justice in the High Council of Judges and Prosecutors is analyzed.

[71]See the Report of the Special Rapporteur on the independence of judges and lawyers, A/74/176, 16 July 2019, para. 102.

[72]See the Report of the Special Rapporteur on the independence of judges and lawyers, A/HRC/26/32, 28 April 2014.

[73]*Ibid.*, paras. 51–52 and 56.

[74]*Ibid.*, para. 54.

[75]*Ibid.*, paras. 77–96.

councils.[76] These bodies have been very positively considered by the Special Rapporteur which recommends their establishment as well as the development under the UN auspices of a comprehensive set of rules to identify common principles and good practices in relation to the establishment, composition and functioning of such councils.[77] Some *caveats* on their structure and functioning are also suggested, such as to endow judicial councils with the widest powers in the field of selection, promotion, training, professional evaluation and discipline of judges but also:

> in order to avoid excessive concentration of power in one judicial body and the perception of corporatism, the Special Rapporteur considers it good practice to establish different independent bodies competent for specific aspects of judicial administration (e.g. selection, promotion, training and discipline of judges). The composition of these bodies should reflect the particular task entrusted to them.[78]

6 Sustaining the Independence of Judges As a Means Towards Economic Growth: The Assistance by the World Bank

Assistance in establishing judicial independence in developing and transition economies has become a major goal of numerous financial programs including those of the UN and the UN agencies. An independent judiciary is not only one of the fundamental components of the rule of law and a bulwark in defence of human rights, but it is also thought to be important for developing and transition economies because it may facilitate their economic progress. Investment and jobs are more easily achieved in an effective, transparent legal environment, with due process. Laws and contracts must be enforceable and meaningful, which means predictability in decisions; that property and other economic rights are protected and that the access to justice is guaranteed.[79] It is the judiciary which is responsible to settle commercial and economic disputes and to safeguard fair competition, and in doing so contribute to business, commerce and economic growth.

Among the UN agencies, the World Bank is particularly committed to financially supporting the building of accessible, efficient and fair justice institutions which are deemed to be essential in sustainably reducing poverty and increasing shared prosperity (the s.c. World Bank's twin goals). And the independence of the judiciary is considered by the Bank so important for economic development, for fostering a healthy business environment, for enhancing growth, for improving

[76]See the Report of the Special Rapporteur on the independence of judges and lawyers, A/HRC/38/38, 2 May 2018.

[77]*Ibid.*, paras. 89–90.

[78]*Ibid.*, paras. 94–96.

[79]The World Bank Legal and Judicial Reform: Strategic Directions, January 2003, available at: http://documents.worldbank.org/curated/en/218071468779992785/Legal-and-judicial-reform-strategic-directions, Accessed 15 Nov 2019.

access to public services, for countering corruption and for reducing the abuse of power, that it has been included among the indicators of States' competitiveness index.[80]

In particular, the World Bank efforts are aimed, *inter alia*, at enhancing independence, transparency and accountability of the judicial system, thus encouraging good governance. Indeed, no legal and judicial reform can succeed without an independent judiciary. To reach this goal, because of the political nature of justice sector reform, the interests of government and the judiciary must be overcome in order to generate political support for reforms. Moreover, reform measures must be sustainable and involve a long-term commitment by policy makers at governmental, judicial, executive and legislative levels.

The World Bank grounds its projects for judicial reform on the concept of independence of the judiciary, as it has been defined by the ICCPR, and on the practice of the UN treaty bodies as well as of relevant special rapporteurs. According to the Bank, judicial independence "[...] has two functions: one is to limit government power and the other is to protect the rights of individuals." The Bank defines an independent judiciary as:

> one that issues decisions and makes judgments that are respected and enforced by the legislative and executive branches; that receives an adequate appropriation from the legislature; and that is not compromised by political attempts to undermine its impartiality.[81]

At the same time, the World Bank underlines that "[t]he essence of an independent and impartial judge lies in his or her personal integrity."[82]

Around 800 projects have been promoted by the World Bank all around the world over a period of approximately 25 years with the purpose of assisting judicial reforms. Initially, the projects were closely focused on the judicial system, but now they have a broader scope because a more inclusive concept of justice has been developed. In general, the projects are aimed at improving the institutions of justice, the legal empowerment of the weakest and most marginalized individuals and groups, the strengthening of certain regulatory or judicial areas most relevant to economic development. Sometimes judicial independence is only an indirect goal of these projects, on the contrary it is an explicit task in other projects. This was the case of the 1997 Peru Judicial Reform Project which was cancelled because of insufficient government commitment to judicial independence. Other projects are for instance the 2000 Armenia Judicial Reform Project; the 2005 Peru Justice Services

---

[80]See The World Bank's Judicial Independence Indicators, 2016, where a score from 1 to 7 (best) is assigned to each member State in the light of the replies received from respondents to the question: "In your country, how independent is the judicial system from influences of the government, individuals, or companies?" in the period 2012-2016. E.g. New Zealand is given a score of 6.68, Norway of 6.50, Italy of 3.56, South Africa 5.54, Venezuela, 1.13 and India 4.2.

[81]*Ibid.*, p. 26.

[82]*Ibid.*, p. 26. See also the World Bank Study, Judicial Independence: What It Is, How It Can Be Measured, Why It Occurs, available at: http://siteresources.worldbank.org/INTLAWJUSTINST/Resources/JudicialIndependence.pdf. Accessed on 15 Nov 2019.

Modernization Project; the 2006 Sudan Capacity Building of the National Judiciary; and the 2011 Albania Legal and Judicial Reform Project.[83]

To reach its goals in the justice work program, the World Bank uses all the financial instruments available within the World Bank Group, such as investment/project lending, results and policy-based lending, technical assistance, trust funds, grants, partnerships and reimbursable advisory services.

7 Conclusion

The strengthening of judicial systems and, in particular, of the independence of judges, is not expressly mentioned in the Sustainable Development Goals, constituting the Agenda 2013 for the Sustainable Development, signed in 2015 by the Governments of the 193 UN Member States, which have committed themselves to achieve these Goals by 2030.[84] However, among the 17 Sustainable Development Goals (SDGs), SDG 16 on 'Peace, Justice and Strong Institutions' includes the specific target 16.3 which aims at promoting the rule of law at national and international levels and ensuring equal access to justice for all.

It goes without saying that an independent judiciary cannot but be one of the *conditio sine qua non* for an effective and fair justice. There could be no real access to justice if judicial independence lacks or is compromised and when judges are subservient to specific interests. Citizens must be confident that their cases will be heard and decided by impartial judges. So, even if indirectly, the strengthening of an independent and impartial justice is connected with the goal to improve the equal access to justice.

Therefore, in the approach of the Agenda for Sustainable Development, the rule of law takes on a dynamic dimension within this global vision of human societies' development. Then the independence of the judiciary, which is an essential pillar of the principle of the rule of law, is not anymore a result to be achieved *per se* but it assumes a dynamic and holistic role not only exclusively at the legal level but also at the social and economic levels in the mediation between the interests of current generations and those of future generations as well as between competing interests of current generations.

As the Special Rapporteur on the Independence of the Judiciary underlined a few years ago:

> an independent judiciary and legal profession in full conformity with applicable standards contained in international human rights instruments, are essential to the full and

[83]Laver (2012), pp. 183–238, at p. 196; The World Bank: New Directions in Justice Reform, 2012. For the full list of projects in Europe and Central Asia see https://www.worldbank.org/en/region/eca/brief/justice. Accessed on 27 January 2021.

[84]UNGA, Transforming our world: the 2030 Agenda for Sustainable Development, Resolution 70/1 of 25 September 2015.

non-discriminatory realization of human rights and indispensable to the processes of democracy and sustainable development.[85]

References

Bartole S (2018) The contribution of the Venice Commission to the internationalization of the National constitutional law of the organisation of the judiciary. In: Motoc I et al (eds) New developments in constitutional law. Eleven, The Hague, pp 1–20

Chesterman S (2012) Rule of law. In: Wolfrum R (ed) Max Planck encyclopedia of public international law. Oxford University Press, Oxford, pp 1014–1222

Fitschen T (2008) Inventing the rule of law for the United Nations. In: Wolfrum R et al (eds) Max Planck yearbook of United Nations law. Brill/Twelve, Leiden, pp 347–380

Laver R (2012) The World Bank and judicial reform: overcoming 'blind spots' in the approach to judicial independence. Duke J Comp Int Law 22:183–238

Leanza U, Caracciolo I (2010) Il diritto internazionale: Diritto per gli Stati e diritto per gli individui. Parti speciali. Giappichelli, Turin

Leckie S (1987) The UN and the independence of the judges and lawyers. Newsletter 17:13–28

Lehtimaja L, Matti P (1999) Article 10. In: Alfredsson G et al (eds) The Universal declaration of human rights. Nijhoff, Leiden, pp 223–240

Nowak M (2005) U.N. covenant on civil and political rights: CCPR commentary, 2nd edn. N.P. Engel, Kehl am Rhein

Olbourne B (2003) Independence and impartiality: international standards for national judges and courts. Law Pract Int Courts Tribunals 2:97–126

Shetreet S, McCormack W (eds) (2016) The culture of judicial independence in a globalised World. Brill Nijhoff, Leiden

Sterett SM, Walker LD (eds) (2019) Research handbook on law and court. Elgar Publishing, Cheltenham

Van Dijk F (2021) Perceptions of the Independence of Judges in Europe. Palgrave MacMillan, Basingstoke

Zhang J (2009) Fair trial rights in ICCPR. J Politics Law 2:39–43

Ida Caracciolo is a full professor of International Law and President of the MA Course in "International Relations and Organizations", Department of Political Sciences of the University of Campania "Luigi Vanvitelli". Judge of the International Tribunal for the Law of the Sea. Member of the Permanent Court of Arbitration, *ad hoc* Judge at the European Court of Human Rights and Alternate Arbitrator at the OSCE Court of Conciliation and Arbitration. Author of numerous scientific publications in the Law of the Sea, International Criminal Law, International Humanitarian Law and Human Rights Law.

[85]Report of the Special Rapporteur on the independence of judges and lawyers (A/HRC/35/31, 9 June 2017), para. 20.

Social Media Communication by Judges: Assessing Guidelines and New Challenges for Free Speech and Judicial Duties in the Light of the Convention

Jannika Jahn

Contents

1 Introduction 137
2 The Current Jurisprudence of the ECtHR 138
 2.1 Judicial Statements on Pending Proceedings 139
 2.2 Judicial Statements on Questions of Law or Politics 139
 2.3 Judicial Criticism of the Justice System 141
 2.4 In Sum: Criteria Guiding the Balancing Exercise 141
3 Assessment of the Current Approach 142
 3.1 The Necessity for Striking a Balance Between Freedom of Expression and Judicial Duties 142
 3.2 A Functional Approach 144
 3.3 Appearance of Bias or Dependence 144
4 The Challenge of Social Media Communication for Judges 145
 4.1 Specificities of Social Media Communication 146
 4.2 Conflicting Interests 147
5 Striking the Balance Between the Competing Interests Regarding Social Media Communication 148
 5.1 Approaches to Delineating the Duty of Judicial Restraint and Rules of Conduct for Social Media Communication in Germany, England and France 148
 5.2 The Compatibility of These Approaches with the Court's Case Law 150
6 Conclusion 152
References 153

1 Introduction

Judges often have to decide on the right to freedom of expression, on its scope of protection and its limits. However, there are also instances where the freedom of expression of judges themselves comes into conflict with their judicial duties to be independent and impartial, and judges find themselves having to make decisions on

J. Jahn (✉)
Max Planck Institute for Comparative Law and International Law, Heidelberg, Germany

M. Elósegui et al. (eds.), *The Rule of Law in Europe*,
https://doi.org/10.1007/978-3-030-56001-0_9

this tension. This is because, besides speaking through their judgments, judges in Europe also make extrajudicial statements on legal or political issues. This brief chapter will shed some light on this particular area of the conflicting rights and duties of judges in the jurisprudence of the European Court of Human Rights (ECtHR). Based on a brief analysis of the relevant case law, the chapter will highlight how the use of social media challenges established standards of judicial behaviour. Against this background the chapter gives a brief overview of how Germany, France and England define the scope of the duty of judicial restraint and how they have gone about social media communication by judges. Against this background the chapter finally assesses whether the approaches taken are in line with the Court's case law.

2 The Current Jurisprudence of the ECtHR

When assessing whether an infringement of judicial free speech was justified, the Court has to strike a fair balance with the legitimate interest of a democratic State in ensuring that its civil service properly furthers the purposes enumerated in Art. 10 (2) of the European Convention on Human Rights (the Convention).[1] The Court has acknowledged that, like civil servants, judges are subject to the duty of judicial restraint.[2] This is because judges require public confidence in their capacity to be independent and impartial[3] and this confidence is not only derived from judgments actually being delivered impartially but also from the public manifestly seeing these judgments to be delivered without bias or prejudice.[4] Regarding civil servants' right to freedom of expression, the "duties and responsibilities" referred to in Article 10 (2) of the Convention assume a special significance, which has led the Court to acknowledge a certain margin of appreciation for the Convention states in determining whether the impugned interference is proportionate to the aim pursued by the measures taken.[5]

When analysing the Court's case law, certain jurisprudential lines may be identified. Broadly speaking, these divide into cases where judges comment on

---

[1]ECtHR [GC], *Baka v. Hungary*, 27 May 2014, No. 20261/12, para. 162; ECtHR [GC], *Wille v. Liechtenstein,* 28 Oct. 1999, No. 28396/95, para. 64; ECtHR, *Albayrak v. Turkey*, 31 Jan. 2008, No. 38406/97, paras. 41–42.

[2]ECtHR, *Vogt v. Germany,* 26 Sept. 1995, No. 17851/91, para. 53 (concerning civil servants), ECtHR, *Pitkevich v. Russia,* 8 Feb. 2001, No. 47936/99, The Law para. 2 (concerning judges).

[3]ECtHR, *Kudeshkina v. Russia*, 26 Feb. 2009, No. 29492/05, para. 86; ECtHR [GC], *Morice v. France*, 23 Apr. 2015, No. 29369/10, para. 128.

[4]ECtHR, *Delcourt v. Belgium*, 17 Jan. 1970, No. 2689/65, para. 31; ECtHR, *Oleksandr Volkov v. Russia*, 9 Jan. 2013, No. 21722/11, para. 106 (derived from *R v Sussex Justices, ex parte McCarthy* [1924] 1 KB 256).

[5]ECtHR, *Vogt v. Germany,* 26 Sept. 1995, No. 17851/91, para. 53; ECtHR, *Albayrak v. Turkey*, 31 Jan. 2008, No. 38406/97, para. 41; ECtHR [GC], *Baka v. Hungary*, 27 May 2014, No. 20261/12, para. 162.

proceedings and those where judicial comments are not related to specific proceedings. In the latter category of cases, this chapter will focus on comments of a political content and judicial criticism of the administration of justice.

2.1 *Judicial Statements on Pending Proceedings*

Statements that are related to pending proceedings are generally held to be inadmissible. In *Wille v. Liechtenstein* the Court mentioned that Convention states may limit free speech, when judges make remarks on pending proceedings.[6] This is because the ECtHR has recognized that the failure of judges to exercise restraint may curtail the rights of applicants to an impartial tribunal as guaranteed under Article 6 (1) of the Convention. Maximum discretion is required from judges with regard to their own cases in order to preserve their image as impartial arbiters.[7] The yardstick for assessing whether judicial impartiality is impaired or not is whether the judicial conduct caused an apprehension of bias.[8] This is the case if a judge publicly shows a negative attitude towards the person to be judged.[9] In principle, the ECtHR asks whether the chosen terms of the statement suggest that the judge has formed a negative opinion on a party to the proceedings or even indicates the outcome of the proceedings and thus expresses bias or prejudice.[10]

2.2 *Judicial Statements on Questions of Law or Politics*

Statements that do not include remarks on pending proceedings are generally held to be admissible, even if they are of a political nature.[11] However, they have to be reconcilable with the judicial duty of restraint (Art. 10 (2) of the Convention).[12] In cases of conflict, the ECtHR has considered the value of the specific statement in light of its constitutional context in order to assess the level of protection that must be

[6]ECtHR [GC], *Wille v. Liechtenstein,* 28 Oct. 1999, No. 28396/95, para. 67. It further mentioned "severe criticism of persons or public institutions and insults of high officials".

[7]ECtHR [GC], *Baka v. Hungary*, 27 May 2014, No. 20261/12, para. 164.

[8]ECtHR, *Delcourt v. Belgium*, 17 Jan. 1970, No. 2689/65, para. 31; ECtHR, *Oleksandr Volkov v. Russia*, 9 Jan. 2013, No. 21722/11, para. 106.

[9]See e.g. ECtHR, *Olujic v. Croatia*, 5 Feb. 2009, No. 22330/05, paras. 63, 67; cf. ECtHR, *Buscemi v. Italy*, 16 Sept. 1999, No. 29569/95, paras. 65 et seq.

[10]For an overview of the different tests involved, see ECtHR, *Olujic v. Croatia*, 5 Feb. 2009, No. 22330/05, paras. 57 et seq.; exemplarily, see ECtHR, *Lavents v. Latvia,* 28 Nov. 2002, No. 58442/00, paras. 118-119; ECtHR, *Buscemi v. Italy*, 16 Sept. 1999, No. 29569/95, para. 68.

[11]ECtHR [GC], *Wille v. Liechtenstein,* 28 Oct. 1999, No. 28396/95, para. 67.

[12]*Ibid.*

afforded to the statement, the necessary degree of scrutiny regarding the interference, and the margin of appreciation correspondingly granted to the respondent state.[13]

In *Wille v. Liechtenstein,*[14] the Court held that in a democratic society a constitutional judge must generally be allowed to publicly participate in a constitutional debate. In this case, the Prince of Liechtenstein had not reappointed the president of the State Court of Justice, since he had pointed out that the State Court would have the last word on the interpretation of the constitution during a public lecture. In its examination, the Court underlined that this statement was made at a lecture on constitutional law and did not take a constitutionally unacceptable view. The political implications of the statement were inevitable. The Court also stated that an interference with the freedom of expression of such a high-ranking judge must call for close scrutiny,[15] especially when a Convention state sanctions statements on matters of public interest.[16]

In *Baka v. Hungary,*[17] the Court assigned great weight to a statement by the President of the Supreme Court in which he had criticized legislative reforms for affecting the judiciary, especially its independence.[18] The relevance of the statement was further increased by the fact that, as President of the National Council of Judges, the judge was also subject to a statutory duty to defend the interests of the judiciary.[19] Further to the judge's office, the Court took account of the statement and its context in order to assess whether the respondent state had violated the Convention.[20] It found that the statement had not gone beyond mere criticism from a strictly professional perspective so that, applying strict scrutiny to the interference and a narrow margin of appreciation, it found the respondent state's response was out of proportion to the aims pursued.[21]

With *Previti v. Italy (No. 2)*),[22] the Court implies that the value of contributions of judicial expertise to the public discourse on judicial issues may limit the duty of judicial restraint.[23] The Court stated that the public expression of a different political opinion to that of the party involved in the proceedings alone was not a reason to assume bias; a truly biased statement would require the expression of vehement criticism of persons, public institutions or senior civil servants that represented the view of the party to the proceedings.[24]

---

[13]ECtHR [GC], *Baka v. Hungary*, 27 May 2014, No. 20261/12, para. 171.

[14]*Ibid.*

[15]*Ibid*, para. 64.

[16]ECtHR [GC], *Baka v. Hungary*, 27 May 2014, No. 20261/12, para. 165.

[17]ECtHR [GC], *Baka v. Hungary*, 27 May 2014, No. 20261/12.

[18]*Ibid*, paras. 165, 168 et seq.

[19]*Ibid*, paras. 166–171.

[20]*Ibid*, para. 166.

[21]ECtHR [GC], *Baka v. Hungary*, 27 May 2014, No. 20261/12, paras. 171–175.

[22]ECtHR, *Previti v. Italy (No. 2),* 18 Dec. 2009.

[23]*Ibid*, paras. 253–254, 258.

[24]*Ibid.*

2.3 Judicial Criticism of the Justice System

With respect to statements criticizing the administration of justice or other judges, the Court holds that free speech may be curtailed where such statements would harm the authority and the impartiality of the judiciary (cf. Art. 10 (2) of the Convention).[25] Accordingly, judges may be required to desist from destructive attacks against other judges[26] or criticisms of the judiciary's dealing with pending proceedings.[27] Hence, judges shall not improperly imply that other judges lack independence or impartiality. If a judge comments on matters regarding the functioning of the justice system, particular moderation is required even for the dissemination of accurate information.[28]

2.4 In Sum: Criteria Guiding the Balancing Exercise

The ECtHR undertakes a nuanced balancing exercise when considering cases of conflict between judicial freedom of expression and the interest of the respondent states to make sure that judges adhere to their duties under Art. 10 of the Convention, especially to their duty of restraint. Placing them on the same footing as civil servants, the Court recognizes their freedom of expression while affording a margin of appreciation to the Convention states to delineate the specific duties that judges may be subject to. The Court accepts that pending cases should not be publicly commented. Statements that include political assessments or value judgments may, however, not *per se* be held irreconcilable with the duty of judicial restraint. According to the Court, this would not pay due respect to the value such statements may have for the judiciary and the democratic discourse. Limits to judicial free speech should be justified with the negative effect such a statement would have on the performance of the judge's duties or the authority of the judiciary.

---

[25] ECtHR, *Kudeshkina v. Russia*, 26 Feb. 2009, No. 29492/05, para. 86; see also ECtHR [GC], *Wille v. Liechtenstein*, 28 Oct. 1999, No. 28396/95, para. 64; ECtHR [GC], *Baka v. Hungary*, 27 May 2014, No. 20261/12, para. 164.

[26] ECtHR, *Di Giovanni v. Italy*, 9 Jul. 2013, No. 51160/06, para. 81.

[27] ECtHR, *Kudeshkina v. Russia*, 26 Feb. 2009, No. 29492/05, para. 94.

[28] *Ibid*, para. 93.

3 Assessment of the Current Approach

3.1 The Necessity for Striking a Balance Between Freedom of Expression and Judicial Duties

There was a longstanding rule in many Convention states requiring judges to exercise strict restraint in public comments: up until the 1980s in Germany,[29] the end of the twentieth century in England[30] and the beginning of the twenty-first century in France.[31] For different reasons, this rule was relaxed in all three countries, requiring a balance to be struck between freedom of expression and the judicial duty to be and manifestly appear to be independent and impartial.

In balancing the competing interests in its case law, the Court has discarded the primacy of independence because of the recognition that civil servants are endowed with civil rights, even if their conduct relates to their official duties.[32] This central assumption is further supported by aspects that speak in favour of rejecting a primacy of independence over judicial speech.

First, the Court is right to point out that judicial statements may have a particular value for the democratic discourse. Covering judges in a veil of silence would also prevent them from publicly pointing out political practices that may harm judicial independence. Since judges cannot claim an infringement of their independence before the ECtHR, seeing judges freely speak up is an important sign for the Court to assess judges' independence in a given Convention state. This is the case especially for high-ranking judges and those who are in a position to represent other judges. This is why in *Wille v. Liechtenstein* and *Baka v. Hungary* the Court called for close scrutiny of interference with such judicial expressions.[33] Additionally, the

---

[29]See Dürholt (1977), pp. 217, 220. Besides cultural changes within the judiciary, a trigger for this development was also the Federal Constitutional Court's (FCC) decision, in which the Court held that civil servants are also endowed with civil rights, FCC, BVerfGE, 14 March 1972, 33, 1 (9 ff.). As a consequence, the duties of judges were held to be only admissible if they did not unlawfully infringe their civil rights. Hence, the duty of restraint now had to be balanced with the judge's freedom of expression, see FCC, 30 Aug. 1983—2 BvR 1334/82—, NJW 1983, 2691.

[30]Lord Mackay waived the strict duty of restraint in 1987, saying that "judges should be free to speak to the press, or television, subject to being able to do so without prejudicing their performing of the judicial work. [...] Judges should be permitted to speak out" (The Times (London), 4 November 1987, 3).

[31]See Salas (2000), para. 212, "[...] *magistrat reste silencieux dans le débat, secret dans sa délibération et elliptique dans ses motivations.*" Greilsamer and Schneidermann (1992) were the first judges to publicly speak about their work as judges. In 2007 the *Conseil Supérieur de la Magistrature (CSM)* asked judges for a more activist interaction with the public/media, acknowledging, however, that this meant a mental revolution. CSM, Rapport Annuel, 2007, para. 122, see also *CSM*, Communiqués of 15 December 2005 and of 16 February 2006. Legal writer Bussy said in 2010, this revolution had started (Bussy 2010, p. 2526, para. 24).

[32]See also ECtHR, *Vogt v. Germany,* 26 Sept. 1995, No. 17851/91, para. 53.

[33]ECtHR [GC], *Wille v. Liechtenstein,* 28 Oct. 1999, No. 28396/95, para. 64; ECtHR [GC], *Baka v. Hungary*, 27 May 2014, No. 20261/12, paras. 165, 171.

participation in a public debate may also stimulate a judge's self-reflection, hence improving his or her capacity to be impartial. Finally, one might say that it is better to have bias and prejudice in the open than hidden in disguise. This is because if a judge has revealed bias through one of her statements, she may be challenged.

On the other hand, considering the fact that judges are representatives of the state, it proves to be proportionate to require some moderation for judicial statements which are linked to the judge's office and are thus imputable to the state. Moreover, the secrecy of deliberations and the fact that certain judges might otherwise no longer sit in certain proceedings are factors against a primacy of freedom of expression, i.e. an unrestrained freedom of expression. In Germany, the legal order comprises the right to one's lawful judge (Art. 101 (1) 2 German Basic Law). This right guarantees that the sitting judge is determined by law, i.e. by objective criteria which shall serve the independence of the judiciary.[34] It would be quite contrary to this right, if the judiciary had to check which statements a certain judge has made, before assigning him to a certain case. Moreover, in legal orders, where judges are appointed by the Court President, case assignments would become increasingly difficult the more individual judges would no longer be considered apt to deal with certain legal issues because of their publicly disclosed convictions. Either way, the more topics judges cover with their statements, the more they might be held biased in court proceedings. In the long run, this might become problematic for the functioning of the justice system.

Furthermore, arguing—in the tradition of legal realism—for judges to open their personal attitudes and opinions to public scrutiny would not in fact enhance but rather weaken judges' freedom of expression.[35] Judges would feel less free to express themselves publicly, if such statements were to prove their impartiality and independence. By contrast, in the current jurisprudence of the ECtHR,[36] judges' impartiality and independence are presumed. The duty of judicial restraint serves the purpose of preventing judicial behaviour from rebutting this presumption on which public confidence in the judiciary rests.[37] Hence, even if judges are meant to restrain themselves in their contribution to public debates, they are generally free in their expression.

Considering these arguments, it seems proper to balance the competing legal interests, without giving one interest primacy over the other.

[34]FCC, 8 Feb. 1967, BVerfGE 21, 139 (146); FCC, 8 June 1993, BVerfGE 89, 28 (36).

[35]In the tradition of legal realism, German scholars have considered the judicial decision-making process to be a constructive process which should be inter-subjectively comprehensible, pointing out that professional ethics, rules of bias and disciplinary law should not remain "anachronistic" interpretations of the concepts of separation of powers or judicial independence, but should enable an opening up of the judiciary. In their opinion, judges should open their views to public scrutiny in a transparent way by revealing them. Representing this thinking, see Scherer (1979), pp. 177–178.

[36]See ECtHR, *Olujic v. Croatia*, 5 Feb. 2009, No. 22330/05, para. 58; ECtHR, *Hauschildt v. Denmark*, 24 May 1989, No. 10486/83, para. 47.

[37]Cf. ECtHR, *Kudeshkina v. Russia*, 26 Feb. 2009, No. 29492/05, para. 86; FCC, 30 Aug. 1983—2 BvR 1334/82—, NJW 1983, 2691.

3.2 A Functional Approach

The Court has taken a functional approach in interpreting the duty of restraint. For the Court it is decisive whether the judge's impugned conduct impaired the performance of the judicial duties, particularly, during any previous, pending or imminent proceedings.[38] Consequently, the Court found a violation of Art. 10 in *Wille v. Liechtenstein*, where the judge's statement had not compromised the performance of his duties.[39] It also found a violation when no evidence was adduced to show that a judge had behaved in a way that would cause reasonable doubts as to his capacity to deal with cases impartially.[40] Thus, judges are not allowed to comment on pending cases[41] and required to exercise maximum discretion with regard to any topics related to the cases with which they deal in order to preserve their image as impartial arbiters.[42] In the same vein, judges are expected to exercise discretion and circumspection when informing the public about criminal investigations in progress, so as not to violate the presumption of innocence.[43]

3.3 Appearance of Bias or Dependence

The Court developed its jurisprudence on impartiality and independence with reference to the English dictum "justice must not only be done but must manifestly be seen to be done."[44] We also find this approach in other European countries, such as Germany[45] or France.[46] The approach has been criticized in legal scholarship for being part of a power struggle of the judiciary to uphold the image of an autonomous legal system that can only be interpreted by the professional elite of judges.[47] This argument may be countered by two arguments:

---

[38]ECtHR [GC], *Wille v. Liechtenstein,* 28 Oct. 1999, No. 28396/95, para. 69; ECtHR, *Albayrak v. Turkey*, 31 Jan. 2008, No. 38406/97, para. 46.

[39]ECtHR [GC], *Wille v. Liechtenstein,* 28 Oct. 1999, No. 28396/95, para. 69; ECtHR, *Albayrak v. Turkey*, 31 Jan. 2008, No. 38406/97, para. 46.

[40]ECtHR, *Albayrak v. Turkey*, 31 Jan. 2008, No. 38406/97, para. 46.

[41]ECtHR [GC], *Wille v. Liechtenstein,* 28 Oct. 1999, No. 28396/95, para. 67.

[42]ECtHR [GC], *Baka v. Hungary*, 27 May 2014, No. 20261/12, para. 164.

[43]ECtHR, *Fatullayev v. Azerbaijan*, 22. April 2010, No. 40984/07, para. 159.

[44]ECtHR, *Delcourt v. Belgium*, 17 Jan. 1970, No. 2689/65, para. 31; ECtHR, *Oleksandr Volkov v. Russland*, 9 Jan. 2013, No. 21722/11, para. 106 (derived from *R v Sussex Justices, ex parte McCarthy* [1924] 1 KB 256).

[45]FCC, 11 Oct. 2011—2 BvR 1010/10, 2 BvR 1219/10, para. 17 (*Di Fabio*) (bias); FCC, 30 Aug. 1983—2 BvR 1334/82—, NJW 1983, 2691; Federal Administrative Court (FAC), 29 Oct. 1987—BVerwGE 78, 216—, NJW 1988, 1748, 1749 (duty of restraint).

[46]CSM, S 079, 20.07.1994; CSM, Rapport Annuel, 2011, 01.01.2012, pp. 72–73.

[47]Bourdieu (1987), p. 808.

First, in a democratic society, citizens cannot hold judges to account in a way which they do with respect to the political branches of government through their vote. Hence, public trust in the capacity of judges to adhere to the rule of law becomes all the more relevant. The Court acknowledges this finding in its case law by pointing out the importance that judges behave in a way that preserves public confidence in their independence and impartiality.[48]

Second, showing that the judiciary authoritatively rules on questions of law is necessary for conveying that it properly performs the settlement of legal disputes.[49] The Court has recognized this finding in the interpretation of the term "authority of the judiciary" in Art. 10 (2). According to the Court this term denotes, in particular, "that the courts are, and are accepted by the public at large as being, the proper forum for the settlement of legal disputes and for the determination of a person's guilt or innocence on a criminal charge; further, that the public at large have respect for and confidence in the courts' capacity to fulfil that function."[50] For this purpose, the Court requires judges to show restraint when criticizing the administration of justice.[51]

4 The Challenge of Social Media Communication for Judges

The importance of the "appearance"-standard is highlighted by the new challenge to judicial communication posed by the use of social media by judges.[52] This may be best exemplified by a look at a recent case in Germany which can be called the "*facebook*-judge" case. A criminal judge had posted a picture on his publicly accessible *facebook*-page, on which he could be seen with the following T-shirt imprint: "We give your future a home – prison." He had further commented on this picture with the words, "this is my 'when you get out, I will have retired' – look". According to the Federal Court of Justice, this statement raised reasonable apprehension of bias of the criminal judge.[53] This case is not the only example of judicial

[48]ECtHR, *Kudeshkina v. Russia*, 26 Feb. 2009, No. 29492/05, para. 86 with further references.

[49]Heritier, in: Wagner/Sherwin (Hrsg.), Law, Culture and Visual Studies, 2014, p. 25 ff.; Lembcke (2013), p. 49 f.; see also Luhmann (1969), p. 55 ff.

[50]ECtHR, *Worm v. Austria*, 29 August 1997, No. 22714/93, para. 40; ECtHR, *Kudeshkina v. Russia*, 26 Feb. 2009, No. 29492/05, para. 86.

[51]ECtHR, *Kudeshkina v. Russia*, 26 Feb. 2009, No. 29492/05, para. 86.

[52]The following assessment is my own; for a similar assessment, see ENCJ, Justice, Society and the Media Report 2011-2012, p. 9. For an assessment of social media as platform for personal communication, associative activities and self-presentation, see Rowbottom (2006), pp. 489, 498 et seq.; note, that this is a general overview which concentrates on the common challenges of social media use for judges. For specific behavioural guidelines, it might me worthwhile to distinguish between the different platforms and the different types of judges.

[53]FCJ, 12 Jan. 2016—3 StR 482/15.

presence in social media. In other European countries, social media is increasingly used by judges. In France, for example, some judges run their own blogs on which they write about legal developments, advertise events, etc.[54] The new development was also discussed in the European Network of Councils for the Judiciary (ENCJ).[55] Judiciaries in England and France have responded to the new challenges by drafting guidelines for judicial conduct with respect to the use of social media.[56]

4.1 Specificities of Social Media Communication

Against this background, the question arises as to which characteristics particularly distinguish social media communication? Social media is defined as serving, often profile-based, the networking of users and their communication across the Internet.[57] Social media helps people to interact, using text, pictures and tone.[58]

When creating a personal profile, users are motivated to present their personal background, their interests and their political views. Posting content on one's own personal profile suggests that the user personally connects to this content. The private and the professional sphere blend into each other. Concepts of "friendship" or "followers" permeate the social media sphere. While "friendships" imply that communication is personal and responsive, "followers" provoke an aspiration for approval. Hence, instead of maintaining a distance between the commentator and the subject of discussion as well as other discussants, social media strives to establish proximity between the different users as well as between the user and his or her posted content.[59]

Moreover, the pace of communication in social media is rapid. Partly because of the velocity and, partly due to the platform itself, users usually formulate their comments in a short and pointed manner. Taking *Twitter* as an example,

---

[54]*Portelli*, http://chroniquedelhumaniteordinaire.blogs.nouvelobs.com/ (président de chambre près la Cour d'appel de Versailles); *Barella*, http://lajustice.blogs.liberation.fr/; *Bilger*, http://www.philippebilger.com/; *Rosenczveig*, http://www.rosenczveig.com/ (président du tribunal pour enfants de Bobigny) ; *Huyette*, le paroles de juge, http://www.huyette.net/.

[55]ENCJ, Justice Society and the Media, Report 2011–2012, pp. 19–20.

[56]Recueil des obligations déontologiques des magistrats, 2019, Charte de déontologie de la juridiction administrative, 2018; UK Supreme Court (UKSC) Guide to Judicial Conduct, 2019; Guide to Judicial Conduct, 2020, revised; Code of Conduct for the FCC, https://www.bundesverfassungsgericht.de/DE/Richter/Verhaltensleitlinie/Verhaltensleitlinien_node.html.

[57]Gablers Wirtschaftslexikon, "Soziale Medien", last accessed 27 August 2019.

[58]*Ibid.*

[59]With respect to traditional media, communication theory scholars have pointed out that reporting is generally attention-focused which means that it strives for topical information, customer proximity, surprise effects, a confrontational character of reporting and a focus on people and events, These parameters roughly cluster the criteria that Schulz has identified as guiding the media's choice regarding the information they report, Schulz (1976), p. 31 et seq.; ibid, Schulz (1997), p. 70 et seq.; Strohmeier (2004), p. 124; cp. also Meyer (2001), p. 47 et seq.

communication is meant to be quick, pointy and attention-gathering, as it seeks to acquire followers.

Last but not least, individual posts and data that are publicly available on social media channels remain present. They create "digital profiles" on the basis of which technical programs might help to predict decisions of judges in the future.[60]

4.2 Conflicting Interests

While different challenges arise in this context,[61] this article focuses on the challenge for balancing freedom of expression and judicial duties in this context.

Preliminary to addressing the competing interests, it should be assessed under which conditions a profile is seen to be "official" and "public", as only then will a conflict between the interests potentially arise. Hence, the first question to be addressed is how do we separate private and official behaviour? Here, the French Code of conduct for administrative judges says that behaviour is official if the judicial office is disclosed on the profile.[62] It is also official, if a person is publicly known to be a judge.[63] This is convincing. Since the ECtHR has identified the maintenance of the public image of an impartial judiciary to be a legitimate aim for interferences with the judges' freedom of expression, it has to be decisive if a statement is (objectively) perceived to be made by a private person or by a judge. It cannot be decisive if a judge (subjectively) meant a statement to be private.

Furthermore, there must be a definition for when posts are seen to be "public". They are public if they are publicly accessible to anyone. Yet, in social fora a membership of the same forum and sometimes a connection to the commentator are prerequisites for being able to read a comment. In order for a post to acquire relevance for the objective to preserve the public image of an impartial judiciary, it must have been at least accessible to a group of "undefined" followers.[64] This would also be the case, if a connection of users is necessary for a comment to become visible, if the connection can be created unilaterally. On the contrary, if a connection has to be mutually accepted, a comment in such a network would not be public.

Regarding the question of whether judges should be obliged to refrain from having such a publicly accessible official profile and from actively posting their

---

[60]For the possibilities of personal data processing, see Consultative Committee of the Convention for the protection of individuals with regard to automatic processing of personal data, Report on Artificial Intelligence, T-PD(2018)09Rev, 15.10.2018.

[61]It has been discussed what it means for proceedings if a judge is a "friend" with one of the parties to the proceedings or an attorney (Rojahn and Jerger 2014, p. 1147).

[62]Charte de déontologie de la jurisdiction administrative, 16 March 2018, para. 47.

[63]*Ibid.*

[64]*Ibid*, para. 47-1.

views on it, the ECtHR's jurisprudence on the conflict of judges' freedom of expression and their judicial duties entails the requirement to balance the competing interests: Profiles in social networks have an individual value for a judge. Social platforms offer a new space for exercising the right to freedom of expression. They create a new, publicly accessible communicative space. Thus, having a profile is a condition for being able to fully exercise the right to freedom of expression in all existing spaces for public communication. In addition, social media has gained importance for the democratic opinion-forming process, including the sharing of information as well as the exchange of opinions.

On the other hand, social media communication also poses certain risks for preserving the public trust in an independent and impartial judiciary. As analysed above, the Court has so far taken a functional approach to interpreting the duty of judicial restraint. Thus, a judge may not be sanctioned for statements that do not have a negative bearing on the performance of his duty. In other words, the judge should behave in a way that conveys an inner independence from extraneous influences which allows him to decide any case that comes before him without prejudice or bias. Furthermore, the Court requires judges to exercise restraint if a statement could call the judiciary's authority and impartiality into question.

5 Striking the Balance Between the Competing Interests Regarding Social Media Communication

In Germany, England and France the approaches taken to the balancing of judges' freedom of expression and the interest of the state in preserving an independent and impartial judiciary differ slightly; so do the requirements for judges regarding social media communication. While some rules properly tackle the challenges that social media communication poses to judiciaries, rules that prohibit judges to use social media in their professional capacity depart from the level of protection that the Court requires for judicial free speech.

5.1 Approaches to Delineating the Duty of Judicial Restraint and Rules of Conduct for Social Media Communication in Germany, England and France

In England, the duty of restraint is focused on preserving the impartiality of a judge. The Guide to Judicial Conduct mentions the risk that public statements might give rise to concerns regarding bias or pre-judgment in future cases which would most likely be the case if a judge had participated in a political or controversial public discussion.[65] The Guide to Judicial Conduct thus requires judges to avoid expressing opinions in social media which could impair public confidence in their impartiality.[66] The Guide to Judicial Conduct for the UK Supreme Court calls on the Justices to be "wary of publishing online any more personal information than is necessary and [to] exercise extreme caution in discussing both judicial and personal matters."[67] All other judges are required not to mention their profession when using social media.[68]

In France, the duty of judicial restraint is interpreted as an instrument that preserves the image of an independent and impartial judiciary which generally shows restraint in all public statements[69] and never misappropriates public communication in a professional capacity for the purpose of promoting personal interests.[70] Here, Codes of Conduct require strict restraint in judges' social media communication.[71] Judges are asked to make sure that their accounts are not found on public search engines and not to mention their profession.[72] If their profession is evident, judges shall be vigilant when making remarks, refrain from commenting on political or social controversies and exercise strict moderation when commenting on legal issues.[73]

In Germany, the yardstick for delineating the scope of the duty of judicial restraint is the judge's inner independence which includes judicial impartiality, neutrality and objectivity as decisive characteristics (section 39 German Judiciary Act (DRiG)). Further to requiring restraint regarding pending proceedings, section 39 DRiG requires a judge to be moderate in all of her public statements. Judges are also prohibited to use their office for gaining public attention for political statements, so as not to prejudice public confidence in their independence and impartiality.[74] The concept of independence underpinning section 39 DRiG is premised on the consideration that the public would find a judge who shows to be emotionally committed to

---

[65]Guide to Judicial Conduct, March 2018, revised version, p. 14. See also the UKSC Guide to Judicial Conduct, 2019, para. 3.5.

[66]Guide to Judicial Conduct, March 2018, revised version, p. 18.

[67]UKSC Guide to Judicial Conduct, 2019, para. 5.20, also raising the Justices' awareness that communication on social media is "not private, that comments may be copied and have an unintended readership and longevity; and that it is increasingly easy to piece together information on a Justice from a variety of sources."

[68]*Ibid.*

[69]CDP, P013, 09/10/1987; décret no 59-1292, 13 Nov. 1959; Recueil des obligations déontologiques des magistrats, Chapter VIII, para. 10; Charte de déontologie de la jurisdiction administrative, 16 March 2018, para. 44, especially with respect to political or social matters.

[70]Recueil des obligations déontologiques des magistrats, Chapter VIII, para. 8.

[71]Charte de déontologie de la jurisdiction administrative, 16 March 2018, para. 47. Recueil des obligations déontologiques des magistrats, Chapter VIII, para. 14; annex pp. 72–73.

[72]Charte de déontologie de la jurisdiction administrative, 16 March 2018, paras. 47-1, 47-2.

[73]*Ibid*, paras. 47-2, 47-3; Recueil des obligations déontologiques des magistrats, Chapter II, para. 14; annex p. 72-73.

[74]FAC, 29 Oct. 1987—BVerwGE 78, 216 -, NJW 1988, 1748, 1749.

certain personal or political agendas, to be unable to distance himself from these convictions in the individual case. The duty of judicial restraint shall preserve the public trust in a judiciary that adheres to this standard.[75] Specific rules for social media communications by judges have not been enacted. Hence, the above-mentioned rules apply which should leave judges free to use social media unless they fail to meet their obligation of moderation or (mis-)use their office for purely private purposes.

To conclude, while all judges are allowed to use social media,[76] they are subject to different guidelines for the use of social media. In England and France judges are generally asked not to disclose their profession when communicating through social media. For some judges this goes beyond the approach adopted with respect to traditional media, where they are allowed to disclose their profession.[77] Judges are further required to exercise *strict* restraint in social media communication. Although judges in Germany are not subject to a stricter duty of restraint regarding their communication in social media, they are generally asked to preserve restraint in all of their communications and not to conflate private and professional interests.

5.2 The Compatibility of These Approaches with the Court's Case Law

The Court allows judges' freedom of expression to be limited when a statement risks to infringe the right to an impartial judge. In relation to their own cases, the Court has even acknowledged that judges should be required to refrain from using the press.[78] Thus, applying the Court's case law, Convention states should be free to interpret the duty of judicial restraint in a way that prohibits judges to comment their own cases or topics that are related to their own imminent or pending proceedings in social media.

The ECtHR's current case law also permits subjecting judges to *strict* judicial restraint regarding topics that might become relevant for future proceedings, as social media, more than traditional media, entails an increased risk for judges to lose public confidence in their capacity to decide the individual case without prejudice or bias. This is because social media platforms store statements which

[75]FCC, 30 Aug. 1983—2 BvR 1334/82 -, NJW 1983, 2691; FAC, 29 Oct. 1987—BVerwGE 78, 216—, NJW 1988, 1748, 1749. Cf. *Wassermann*, NJW (1995), pp. 1653–1654.

[76]FCJ, 9 Aug. 2006 - 1 StR 50/06, NJW 2006, 3290, 3295, beck para. 51; Scheuten, in: Hannich (eds.), Karlsruher Kommentar zur StPO, 8th ed. 2019, sec. 24 para. 22; UK Guide to Judicial Conduct, March 2018, revised version, p. 17.

[77]UK Guide to Judicial Conduct, March 2020, revised version, pp. 13–15; UKSC Guide to Judicial Conduct, 2019; Recueil des obligations déontologiques des magistrats, Chapter VIII, para. 8. Administrative judges are generally asked to refrain from mentioning their profession when making commenting on matters of a political or social nature, Charte de déontologie de la jurisdiction administrative, 16. March 2018, para. 44.

[78]ECtHR, *Buscemi v. Italy*, 16 Sept. 1999, No. 29569/95, para. 67.

thereby remain “present”. This “presence” of statements prevents an impression of bias or prejudice, which was fuelled by a certain statement, from fading with time. The constant availability of comments could also make it possible to extract a profile of a judge. Here, not only the exact wording of a statement but also the sheer amount of statements expressing the same opinion could compromise the impression that a judge has the capacity to decide the individual case impartially.

Furthermore, the Court’s case law also allows for requiring judges to exercise *strict* restraint with respect to using the characteristic function of social media to engage in interactive discussion with other users. Debates between a judge and other social media users on subject matters that are relevant for the judge’s decision-making practice could not only adversely affect public confidence in the judge’s impartiality but also in the authority of the judiciary, as it might seem that not only the courts but also the public is part of the forum for settling legal disputes.

Despite not being in line with the ECtHR’s current case law, it might fall within the Convention states’ margin of appreciation to require judges to show moderation in all of their social media communications and to demand a high degree of restraint in sharing private information and opinions, irrespective of a specific bearing on the judge’s decision-making practice. Such restrictions on judges’ free speech, as adopted in France and—in view of the current legal situation—possibly also in Germany if rules of judicial conduct for social media communication are adopted, are underpinned by the understanding that social media communication bears a high risk of compromising judicial independence because it collapses the judge’s private and his professional sphere. Underlying such an understanding is a notion of independence that requires judges generally to demonstrate their ability to perform their professional duties independently of private interests. Indeed, this is a lot to ask of judges and it may well be asked why not here as well, public trust in the judge’s capacity to stay professional when exercising her function would have to be presumed, unless a judicial statement could be shown to raise reasonable doubts as to this capacity.[79] However, public confidence may also be affected by a statement that, as in the “*facebook*-judge” case, was made independently of a particular case but that casts doubt on the judge’s general ability to perform his or her judicial duties without prejudice. Not every citizen will differentiate whether a certain comment has a bearing on the judge’s performance of her duties in a particular case or not. Additionally, social media communication is considered to be associative particularly with those who share common views. The affiliation with interest groups might—as context to a certain statement—increase the impression that a judge is so deeply socialised and ingrained in these communities that she will not distance herself from the views that are shared within that community when deciding an individual case. For these reasons the Court might consider a strict restraint in all social media communication to fall within the Convention states’ margin of appreciation for delineating the exact scope of judicial duties under Art. 10 (2) of the Convention.

---

[79]For such an assessment, see Sunstein (2001).

Prohibiting judges to mention their profession in social media communication, however, hardly seems reconcilable with the Court's case law. The same goes for the restriction of commenting political or controversial topics in social media. Such prohibitions do not only prevent judges from using social media to comment on private matters but also on topics of public interest, such as matters concerning the separation of powers and judicial independence. Since social media constitute an important space for public communication, this would considerably limit judicial freedom of expression. Applying the ECtHR's case law, this restriction would lack sufficient justification. As stated above, in assessing the limits drawn by a Convention state to judicial freedom of expression, the Court requires evidence that the judge's impugned conduct impaired the performance of his duties, particularly, during any previous, pending or imminent proceedings.[80] As such evidence is not a condition for the prohibition to apply, the restriction of free speech cannot be considered as necessary in a democratic society.[81]

6 Conclusion

Under the Convention, judges' freedom of expression may be limited in the interest of the proper performance of their professional duties as representatives of the state. In delineating the scope of these duties, especially the duty of restraint, the Court has taken a nuanced approach which focuses on preserving public confidence in the judges' capacity to properly perform the judicial task. Social media communication has prompted some Convention states to issue new rules for judicial behaviour as they perceive social media as a challenge to the public perception of judicial independence and impartiality. Having assessed these rules in light of the Court's case law, some seem to cross the line of what can be deemed compatible with the Convention. This can be explained with the different approaches taken—the Court's approach being focused on the performance of the judicial task, the German and French approaches, for instance, being more focused on preserving the image of a judiciary that generally adheres to the characteristics of impartiality, neutrality and objectivity. Furthermore, Convention states aim at preventing judges to collapse their private and professional sphere. So far, the Court has not had to deal with social media communications by judges. Yet, considering the importance that social media has gained not only for private but also for public interaction and debates between citizens, it will only be a matter of time until the Court will have to deal with the bearing of judges' social media communication on their impartiality and independence.

[80] ECtHR [GC], *Wille v. Liechtenstein,* 28 Oct. 1999, No. 28396/95, para. 69; ECtHR, *Albayrak v. Turkey*, 31 Jan. 2008, No. 38406/97, para. 46.
[81] *Ibid.*

References

Bourdieu P (1987) Die Macht des Rechts. Hastings Law J 38(5):814–853
Bussy F (2010) Justice et Médias. Recueil Dalloz 38:2526–2535
Dürholt K (1977) Richteramt und Meinungsfreiheit. ZRP:217–220
Greilsamer L, Schneidermann D (1992) Les juges parlent. Fayard, Paris
Lembcke O (2013) Autorität der Verfassungsgerichtsbarkeit – eine Skizze in vergleichender Absicht. In: Michael W et al (eds) Die Politik des Verfassungsrechts. Nomos Verlagsgesellschaft mbH & Co. KG, Baden-Baden, pp 37–65
Luhmann N (1969) Legitimation durch Verfahren. Suhrkamp, Berlin
Meyer T (2001) Mediokratie. Suhrkamp, Berlin
Rojahn A, Jerger C (2014) Richterliche Unparteilichkeit und Unabhängigkeit im Zeitalter sozialer Netzwerke. Neue Juristische Wochenschrift 2014:1147–1151
Rowbottom J (2006) Media freedom and political debate in the digital era. Modern Law Rev 69 (4):489–513
Salas D (2000) Le tiers-pouvoir. Hachette, New York
Scherer J (1979) Gerichtsöffentlichkeit als Medienöffentlichkeit. Athenäum, Bodenheim
Schulz W (1976) Die Konstruktion von Realität in den Nachrichtenmedien. Alber Karl, Zürich
Schulz W (1997) Politische Kommunikation. Springer, Berlin
Strohmeier G (2004) Politik und Massenmedien: Eine Einführung. Nomos, Glashütte
Sunstein C (2001) Republic.com 2.0. Princeton University Press, Princeton

Dr. Jannika Jahn is a research assistant at the Max Planck Institute for Comparative Law and International Law (University Heidelberg), where she has also written her PhD thesis. She is attorney at law and worked for a global law firm. She holds an LLB from the University College London and the University of Cologne.

Part III
Freedom of Expression

The Strasbourg Case Law on the Limits of Free Speech: A Few Legal-Theoretical Issues

Krzysztof Wojtyczek

Contents

1 Introduction ... 157
2 The Difficulty of Apprehending Utterances Through Translation ... 158
3 Speech in Natural Language and Its Impact ... 159
4 The Dichotomy of Statements of Facts/Value Judgments ... 161
5 The Variety of Facts and Factual Statements ... 163
6 Free Speech and the Requirements of Clarity and Precision of Legislation ... 165
7 The Difficulties Connected with Speech Denying Mass Human Rights Violations ... 167
8 Offensive Speech and Identity Issues ... 168
9 Conclusion ... 169
References ... 169

1 Introduction

The European Court of Human Rights (ECtHR) has developed a very rich case law concerning the limits of the admissible speech content. This case law may be analyzed from very different perspectives. Most of the commentators approach the question from the viewpoint of political philosophy and ethics, reflecting upon the limits of free speech. However, in order to answer the question whether the limits imposed upon free speech have been set forth correctly, one has to understand the whole situation of the act of speech encompassing the speaker, the persons or persons referred to in the speech, the audience, the content of the speech, as well as its social context. Therefore the case law pertaining to the limits of speech raises also very interesting questions belonging to the field of legal theory, in particular legal semiotics, and more generally questions within the scope of reflection of analytical philosophy. The purpose of the present paper is to offer a short survey

K. Wojtyczek (✉)
Jagiellonian University, Kraków, Poland
e-mail: k.wojtyczek@uj.edu.pl

M. Elósegui et al. (eds.), *The Rule of Law in Europe*,
https://doi.org/10.1007/978-3-030-56001-0_10

of selected legal-theoretical issues which arise in Strasbourg cases concerning the question of free speech limits, without pretending to exhaust the topic.

2 The Difficulty of Apprehending Utterances Through Translation

Freedom of speech cases require to understand all the smallest nuances and all the subtleties of the language spoken. Many of the freedom of speech cases are borderline cases where the small nuances of an utterance may easily tip the balance in one way or another. One of the great difficulties of the freedom of speech cases lies in the fact that international judges or members of treaty bodies usually have to evaluate utterances spoken in languages which they do not understand. For the purpose of international adjudication these utterances are translated into the working language of their courts or treaty bodies. Insults, curses, insinuations and half-truths are very difficult to translate.[1] Most of the linguistic subtleties of such utterances are lost in translation which often either attenuates or reinforces the striking power of the original speech. The English or French version to be assessed says at best only almost the same[2] as the original utterance and sometimes not quite the same. The possible ways of understanding as well as potential hidden connotations of the version submitted by the translators are never exactly the same as in the case of the original utterance. The Strasbourg judges are therefore usually called to assess the case through the prism of utterances which say almost the same as the impugned utterance in its original language.

The difficulty stemming from this fact is further enhanced by a second factor. In most cases, the working languages are not the native tongues of the adjudicators. The vocabulary used in translations is not always part of a vocabulary used by foreign speakers in their daily work and life. The impugned utterances are apprehended through a foreign language which is a factor which may considerably impact the correct assessment of the original speech. The apprehension through a foreign language usually attenuates the striking power of an utterance, playing to some extent in favour of the speaker, not of the person or group insulted by the speech. The domestic authorities are much better placed to understand and interpret speech under litigation. These difficulties are a strong argument for granting a very wide margin of appreciation to domestic authorities in cases in which the issue of free speech limits depends upon linguistic subtleties. Moreover, in such cases the international judge should in principle rely upon the interpretation of utterances established by the domestic authorities.

[1]Compare the considerations in the joint dissenting opinion of Judges Wojtyczek and Kūris appended to the judgment of 5 July 2016 in the case of case of *Ziembiński v. Poland (No. 2)*, application no. 1799/07.

[2]See Eco (2006).

3 Speech in Natural Language and Its Impact

Speech which triggers a criminal reaction is typically everyday speech, often confused and devoid of precision. This fuzziness of the speech may reflect the confusion of the mind. The litigated utterances are frequently open to different interpretations. In many cases, there is a danger that the choice of an interpretation may impact upon the outcome. Moreover, even brief and somewhat confused utterances may simultaneously convey a full bundle of messages of different nature. Under such conditions, it is necessary to devise rules aiming at circumscribing the margin of appreciation left by the very nature of language to an utterance's interpreter. For the purpose of adjudication on the limits of the freedom of speech it is therefore necessary to apprehend a case through the prism of the understanding and reaction of an average member of the actual audience.[3] What matters is how such a person would understand a specific utterance, what conclusions he would draw and what would be his typical reactions.

If a speech is directed at a wide audience it is therefore necessary to apprehend a case through the prism of the understanding and reaction of an average person listening to the speech. If the speech is accessible to a restricted audience only, such as for instance a professional group, it is therefore necessary to take into account the understanding and reaction of an average member of this group. The question to be answered is always how an average member of the actual audience will understand a specific utterance. How does he understand the expression used? What conclusions will he draw from the speech? What will be his reaction?

If the speech is only accessible to a specific group and especially a professional group, its real impact may be completely different from the reaction of the general public. The question may be whether a potentially defamatory statement will be taken seriously as anything more than a mere expression of personal frustrations. Can it really harm the attacked person? One can give here the example of a letter written by an advocate to the superiors of a judge. It is obvious the actual audience in such a context will be particularly critical and will not give credence to statements not supported by sufficient evidence which would make the allegations at least prima facie plausible.[4]

In this context, one has to note that freedom of speech litigation at domestic level often involves expert opinions prepared by linguists on the exact meaning of certain words.[5] Given the requirement to look at contentious speech from the perspective of an average speaker such an approach may justify a certain skepticism. A plaintiff in domestic proceedings who submits expert opinions written by linguists in order to

[3]Compare the views expressed in the joint dissenting opinion of Judges Wojtyczek and Grozev, appended to the judgment ECtHR, *Peruzzi v. Italy*, 30 Jun. 2015, application no. 39294/09, paras. 4 and 5.

[4]*Ibid.*

[5]See for instance ECtHR, *Zybertowicz v. Poland* (No. 2), 17 Jan 2017, application no. 65937/11, para. 13.

persuade the judge that speech attacking him is either insulting or defamatory typically rather weakens his position. Speech becomes problematic when its insulting or defamatory nature is visible on its face to the average audience.

Typically, the audience is a national audience, especially in the case of utterances spoken in a language which is not an international language. If the audience is national, one has to examine its understanding and reaction given the specific meaning of the words used in the language spoken.

In some cases, the actual audience may be an international audience.[6] It may be so even if the words are spoken in a non-international language but the speaker expects that his words will be translated and disseminated abroad, especially if he is a public figure. In that case, this international dimension will have to be taken into account. In such a situation the matter of linguistic subtleties is of lesser importance. What matters is also the reaction among the foreign audience reached through words disseminated in the translation as long as the translation is not misleading or made in bad faith. The translated speech is no longer a mere tool to grasp the original utterance but becomes the heart of the litigation.

Some judgments express views which point to the fact that the Court tries to take into account to some extent the real characteristics of the audience. One can give here the following example:

> Un tel discours est inévitablement de nature à susciter parmi le public, et particulièrement parmi le public le moins averti, des sentiments de mépris, de rejet, voire, pour certains, de haine à l'égard des étrangers.[7]

One has to note here—en passant—that this dictum, which was criticized—rightly—by the judge Sajó in his dissenting opinion,[8] carries with it far-reaching implications for the understanding of democracy which underlies the reasoning of the judgment in question.

The impact of the speech depends inter alia upon the status of the speaker among those who listen to him. Will the speaker be taken sufficiently seriously to cause harm because people give credence to his speech? The answer depends inter alia upon the credibility of the speaker in the eyes of the audience. A recognized and trusted opinion leader has the biggest striking power and the capacity to damage other persons. In defamation cases, the greatest harm comes from a person who is considered to be credible to the audience and is therefore not only listened to by the audience but also trusted by the audience. The worst real damage comes from a person generally considered as trust-worthy but who resorts to lie in homeopathic doses. The impact upon the reputation may be very limited if a speaker is not taken seriously. A person known to be a notorious liar will not have the same pernicious impact on the reputation as a person who is widely considered as truth-telling. This does not mean that being a notorious liar should be considered as a mitigating

[6]See for instance ECtHR [GC], *Perinçek v. Switzerland*, 15 Oct. 2015, application no. 27510/08.

[7]ECtHR, *Feret v. Belgium*, 16 Jul. 2009, application no 15615/07, para. 69.

[8]Separate opinion of judge Sajó joined by judges Zagrebelsky and Tsotsoria appended to ECHR, *Feret v. Belgium*, 16 Jul. 2009, application no 15615/07.

circumstance for the purpose of criminal liability. On the other hand, the status of a recognized opinion leader may be viewed as an aggravating circumstance.

4 The Dichotomy of Statements of Facts/Value Judgments

The ECtHR case law distinguishes two types of utterances: statements of facts and value judgments. The following quote summarizes the classical approach of the Court:

> 46. Moreover, in order to assess the justification of an impugned statement, a distinction needs to be made between statements of fact and value judgments in that, while the existence of facts can be demonstrated, the truth of value judgments is not susceptible to proof. The requirement to prove the truth of a value judgment is impossible to fulfil and infringes freedom of opinion itself, which is a fundamental part of the right secured by Article 10 (see, for example, *Lingens v. Austria*, 8 July 1986, § 46, Series A no. 103; *Oberschlick v. Austria* (no. 1), 23 May 1991, § 63, Series A no. 204). The classification of a statement as a fact or as a value-judgment is a matter which in the first place falls within the margin of appreciation of the national authorities, in particular the domestic courts (see *Prager and Oberschlick* (. . .) § 36). However, even where a statement amounts to a value judgment, there must exist a sufficient factual basis to support it, failing which it will be excessive (see *Jerusalem v. Austria*, no. 26958/95, § 43. . .). As the Court has noted in previous cases, the difference lies in the degree of factual proof which has to be established (see *Scharsach and News Verlagsgesellschaft v. Austria*, no. 39394/98, § 40. . .).[9]

In other words, like a statement of facts a value judgment also requires a rational justification in the light of the facts.

The distinction between statements of facts and value judgments is of limited usefulness for legal analysis. Grammatical sentences in natural languages are rarely logical propositions describing facts. They are also rarely purely evaluative sentences. In natural language many utterances mix descriptive, evaluative and emotive elements.[10] Thus, for instance, the grammatical sentence "Andrew is a bad cop." is simultaneously: (1) a statement of facts conveying the information that Andrew is a policeman, a (2) negative evaluation of his work in the police (a value judgment) and (3) a expression of negative emotion towards Andrew conveyed by the choice of the word "cop".[11] The sentence "Paul's statement is a lie" is both a proposition attributing the value of falsehood to a specific statement, a proposition stating that Paul deliberately told untruth and, given the negative emotional load connected with the word "lie" a value judgment alleging that Paul acted wrongly. The sentence "Martha's dissertation in philosophy deserves an A grade" states the fact that Martha has written a dissertation in philosophy and

[9]ECtHR, *Ungváry and Irodalom Kft. v. Hungary*, 3 Dec. 2013, application No. 64520/10.

[10]On this question see Copi et al. (1998), pp. 89–95.

[11]Compare the remarks in the separate opinion of judge Wojtyczek appended to ECtHR, *Makraduli v. The Former Yugoslav Republic of Macedonia*, 19 Jul. 2018, applications nos. 64659/11 and 24133/13, para. 2.

evaluates the quality of her work as very good. The grammatical sentence "A. caused many problems while directing the administrative department X." states that some unidentified persons (either within or outside the service) have found certain situations—which A. created—as unwelcome. It also expresses the assessment that A. has not performed his duties satisfactorily.

One has to add here another caveat. A logical proposition is a statement which describes with precision facts which occur at a certain place and at a certain moment. It is an idealization. Factual statements in natural language are not identical with logical propositions in this sense.[12] They usually describe in an imprecise way some factual elements, while others are implied and co-defined by the textual and social context. In order to assess their logical value, one has to look at them from the perspective of their addressees: will the addressees have an image reflecting the reality or will the addressees get a distorted image of the reality.

In most cases, speech under litigation constitutes a mix of statements of facts and value judgments.[13] It is neither a pure statement of facts nor a pure value judgment and the proportions of the elements may vary considerably. Thus the question whether a specific utterance or set of utterances should be classified as a statement of facts and/or a value judgment should rather be replaced by the question: what are the factual and evaluative layers in a specific utterance or set of utterances? Only then can one ask the subsequent questions: (1) is the descriptive layer reflecting the facts? and (2) is the evaluative layer supported by a factual basis?

According to the Court's case law on the distinction between statements of fact and value judgments, "the difference lies in the degree of factual proof which has to be established".[14] One has to note that the difference further diminishes in the most recent case law. The requirement for a defendant to prove the veracity of his factual statements may be excessive. This newer approach has been presented by the Court in the following terms:

> Accordingly, the domestic courts applied the so-called "presumption of falsity" (sometimes referred to as the "defence of justification" or the "defence of truth"), under which defendants are required to prove to a reasonable standard that factual allegations are true. The Court has held that such an approach does not, as such, contravene the Convention (see *Rumyana Ivanova v. Bulgaria*, no. 36207/03, §§ 39 and 68, 14 February 2008; *Makarenko v. Russia*, no. 5962/03, § 156, 22 December 2009; and *Rukaj v. Greece* (dec.), no. 2179/08, 21 January 2010)), and has held a lack of effort to make out that defence against applicants (see *Mahmudov and Agazade v. Azerbaijan*, no. 35877/04, § 44, 18 December 2008). However, it has also held that if an applicant is clearly involved in a public debate on an important issue he should not be required to fulfil a more demanding standard than that of due diligence. In such circumstances, the obligation to prove the factual statements may deprive the applicant of the protection afforded by Article 10 (see Kurski v. Poland,

[12] On this issue see: Ziembiński (1976), pp. 67–68 and pp. 73–75.

[13] Compare the above-mentioned separate opinion of judge Wojtyczek appended to ECtHR, *Makraduli v. The Former Yugoslav Republic of Macedonia*, 19 Jul. 2018, applications nos. 64659/11 and 24133/13, para. 2.

[14] ECtHR, *Ungváry and Irodalom Kft. v. Hungary*, 3 Dec. 2013, application No. 64520/10.

no. 26115/10, § 56, 5 July 2016 and Braun v. Poland, no. 30162/10, § 50, 4 November 2014).[15]

The same approach is also reflected i.a. by the following views:

Indeed, in situations where on the one hand a statement of fact is made and insufficient evidence is adduced to prove it, and on the other the journalist is discussing an issue of genuine public interest, verifying whether the journalist has acted professionally and in good faith becomes paramount (see Flux v. Moldova (no. 7), no. 25367/05, § 41, 24 November 2009).

In *Rumyana Ivanova* the Court found that, in view of the nature of the applicant's allegation, the task of researching and demonstrating it was not unreasonable or impossible (see *Rumyana Ivanova*, cited above, §§ 63-65). By contrast, the nature of the allegation in the present case – that a number of irregularities in the admission of students to secondary schools were due to bribe-taking – made it very difficult, if not impossible, for the applicant to provide direct corroboration of it (compare with *Thorgeir Thorgeirson v. Iceland*, 25 June 1992, § 65 in fine, Series A no. 239). That difficulty was demonstrated by, among other things, the reluctance of a witness for the applicant to identify the parents who had told him that they had paid money to get their children admitted to special schools.[16]

This approach may be summarized in the following terms: both the descriptive and evaluative layers of an utterance require a sufficient factual basis.

5 The Variety of Facts and Factual Statements

Facts may be described in different ways.[17] There may utterances describing individual facts: "On 5 August 2019 in the city of A. the car owned by X. crashed with a car owned by Y". There may be utterances describing in a synthetic way whole classes of individual facts: "X. was ill-treated by Y. during a period running from 1 August 2019 until 16 December 2019" or "During the Great Depression which began in 1929 many companies went bankrupt". The question may arise to which extent such a generalization is justified by individual facts. Contentious utterances may pertain to facts which did not happen such as failures to act and to potential causal links between such omissions and other facts (such as "Mr. X. could have been saved").[18]

Facts may belong to natural reality. Such is the death of a particular dog or a solar eclipse occurring at a specific date. Things become more complicated as many facts belong to linguistic reality or social reality.

---

[15]ECtHR, *Makraduli v. The Former Yugoslav Republic of Macedonia*, 19 Jul. 2018, applications nos. 64659/11 and 24133/13.

[16]ECtHR, *Kasabova v. Bulgaria*, 19 Apr. 2011, application No. 22385/03, § 63-64.

[17]Compare Searle (1995), pp. 79–126.

[18]See for instance ECtHR, *Magosso and Brindani v. Italy*, 16 Jan. 2020, application no 59347/11, especially para. 11.

Many disputes about the limits of freedom of speech concern utterances saying that a certain person said this or that.[19] Such utterances about utterances are interpretive utterances explaining or summarizing the meaning of a third person's speech. Manipulation of a person's speech, overinterpretation, interpretation in bad faith or attribution of bad faith to the speaker are common tools used for the purpose of harming the reputation or dignity of a speaker. The questions to be asked are: (1) does the paraphrase or summary reflect faithfully the content of another person's speech?; (2) could the interpreter of the speech interpret in good faith the speech in question in the way he did?

Statements of facts may refer to conventional behaviors which have a special social meaning attributed to them by rules recognized in a specific society.[20] The grammatical sentence "The professor greeted his students as he entered the lecture hall" states the fact that the professor uttered a verbal formula which is socially accepted for the purpose of greeting someone. In order to characterize a certain behavior as a greeting one has to refer to customs observed in the society in question and to conclude these customs have been observed. A certain behavior is observed through the lenses of social conventions.

The sentence "X. has breached the principles of professional ethics" states that X. has acted, undertook certain acts. It also states that these acts may be characterized from the perspective of principles of professional ethics and that the relationship between these acts and the principles is one of non-compliance. In a case in which the principles of professional ethics are not contested as unreasonable, the same sentence is simultaneously a negative assessment (a disproval) of the acts performed.

The sentence "A. sold his apartment in Paris to B." alleges that A. and B. have legal capacity that A. was the owner of an apartment, that the said apartment is located in Paris, that they concluded a sales contract, that the contract contained clauses which enable to classify it as a sale, that the contract did not contain any clause which would make it invalid, that the contract had the form required by French law, that the contract produced legal effects and that as a result of the contract the ownership of the apartment has been transferred to B. The sentence states not only certain facts belonging to social reality but also characterizes them from the viewpoint of law. A certain behavior is described through the prism of legal rules which requires to establish certain social facts and identify their legal meaning and consequences upon the basis of relevant legal rules. The identification of legal meaning and consequences may be based upon very subjective assessments.

In this context the grammatical sentence "A. has not sold his apartment in Paris to B." may express the fact A. and B. have not even tried to conclude any contract, or that they tried to concluded a sales contract but for a certain (unspecified) reason this contract was not valid under the French law.

[19]See for instance ECtHR, *Zybertowicz v. Poland*, 17 Jan. 2017, application no. 59138/10, par. 46.

[20]Compare Nowak et al. (1987), pp. 115–135; Searle (1995), pp. 79–126; see also Grabowski (1999), pp. 63–93.

The sentence "Minister A. violated the provision B. of the Constitution by issuing the regulation C.", states that Minister A. enacted the regulation C., that the regulation is part of the legal system and characterizes the relationship between the content of the regulation and the constitutional provision B. as being one of incompatibility. The latter means either that there is a logical contradiction between the regulation C. and the provision B. or that the regulation C. produces practical effects which—in the view of the speaker—the provision B. forbids to produce.

The sentence "X.'s behavior amounts to corruption" does not only bring a legal and moral characterization of a certain behavior but first and foremost brings a factual statement that X. performed an act or acts which do correspond to what is understood as corruption.

6 Free Speech and the Requirements of Clarity and Precision of Legislation

Regulations restricting fundamental freedoms should be clear and enable their addressees to predict the legal consequences of their actions. It is not an easy task to draft provisions limiting the substance of speech which are clear and predictable in their application. Provisions restricting offensive or defamatory speech directed at individuals have a long history of legal practice and a rich case law which clarified their meaning. Provisions limiting speech directed at groups or classes of individuals are much more recent. The case law of the Court illustrates the difficulty with observing the requirements of clarity and precision while restricting speech affecting groups or classes of persons.

An example of these difficulties is the Belgian legislation criminalizing incitement to discrimination.[21] Discrimination is defined in this legislation in the following way: "any distinction, exclusion, restriction or preference with the aim or effect of destroying, compromising or limiting the recognition, enjoyment or exercise, under the conditions of equality, of human rights and fundamental freedoms in political, economic, social or cultural domain or any other domain of social life".[22]

The ECtHR has adopted the following approach to the principles of equality and non-discrimination:

> 68. The Court has established in its case-law that only differences in treatment based on an identifiable characteristic, or status, are capable of amounting to discrimination within the

---

[21]See ECtHR, *Feret v. Belgium*, 16 Jul. 2009, application no 15615/07: "*Quiconque... incite à la discrimination, à la ségrégation, à la haine ou à la violence à l'égard d'un groupe, d'une communauté ou de leurs membres, en raison de la race, de la couleur, de l'ascendance ou de l'origine nationale ou ethnique de ceux-ci ou de certains d'entre eux.*"

[22]*Ibid.*: "*Toute distinction, exclusion, restriction ou préférence ayant ou pouvant avoir pour but ou pour effet de détruire, de compromettre ou de limiter la reconnaissance, la jouissance ou l'exercice, dans des conditions d'égalité, des droits de l'homme et des libertés fondamentales dans les domaines politique, économique social ou culturel ou dans tout autre domaine de la vie sociale.*"

> meaning of Article 14 (see *Eweida and Others v. the United Kingdom*, nos. 48420/10 and 3 others, § 86, ECHR 2013).
>
> Generally, in order for an issue to arise under Article 14 there must be a difference in the treatment of persons in analogous, or relevantly similar, situations (see *X and Others v. Austria* [GC], no. 19010/07, § 98, ECHR 2013). However, not every difference in treatment will amount to a violation of Article 14. A difference of treatment is discriminatory if it has no objective and reasonable justification; in other words, if it does not pursue a legitimate aim or if there is not a reasonable relationship of proportionality between the means employed and the aim sought to be realised (see *Fabris v. France* [GC], no. 16574/08, § 56...; *Weller v. Hungary*, no. 44399/05, § 27, 31 March 2009; and *Topčić-Rosenberg v. Croatia*, no. 19391/11, § 36, 14 November 2013).[23]

These views should be complemented by the following quote:

> The Court has so far considered that the right under Article 14 not to be discriminated against in the enjoyment of the rights guaranteed under the Convention is violated when States treat differently persons in analogous situations without providing an objective and reasonable justification (see the *Inze* judgment, cited above, p. 18, § 41). However, the Court considers that this is not the only facet of the prohibition of discrimination in Article 14. The right not to be discriminated against in the enjoyment of the rights guaranteed under the Convention is also violated when States without an objective and reasonable justification fail to treat differently persons whose situations are significantly different.[24]

Briefly speaking, the ECHR allows justified differentiations and forbids unjustified differentiations. Ultimately, the issue of discrimination is a matter of axiological choices.[25] Under the ECHR there are differentiations which are excluded by consensus and there are differentiations which may be debated. For instance, whether affirmative action in favor of certain groups is acceptable may be debatable. For some persons promoting substantive equality may be seen a necessary measure while for other persons it may be seen as a discrimination. Is a call in favor of affirmative action an incitement to discrimination? It is not clear. National legislation reserves certain human rights to nationals. In this context, is a call to maintain legislation limiting the right to vote in legislative elections to nationals an incitement to discrimination of non-nationals? Or is it possible to advocate restricting political activities of persons who were granted political asylum? Is advocating parliamentary immunities an incitement to a preference which hinders the exercises of fundamental political rights on an equal footing? The letter of the legislation quoted above does not give a clear answer. The interpreter has to turn to extra-textual and even extra-legal principles and values in order to try to give an answer.

---

[23]ECtHR, 22 March 2016, *Guberina v. Croatia*, no. 23682/13, §§ 68-69.

[24]ECtHR, 6 April 2000, *Thlimmenos v. Greece*, no. 34369/97, § 44.

[25]Sadurski (1985), p. 96.

7 The Difficulties Connected with Speech Denying Mass Human Rights Violations

The case law also brings out the legal difficulties with criminalization of speech denying mass human rights violations. One can give here the example of the case of *Perinçek v. Switzerland*,[26] in which the applicant was punished in the defendant State for his utterances concerning the genocide of Armenians in 1915–1917.

The problem of legislation criminalizing genocide denial is that genocide is a concept of international criminal law which defines with precision the crime of genocide for the purpose of holding criminally liable those who commit the offense described in international law provisions. The definition pertains to acts of individuals. A genocide is always a crime committed by specific individuals acting in a specific manner at a certain place and at a certain time. In this context, the characterization of specific historical "events" as genocide may be understood as an intellectual shortcut and means that during these events specific individuals have committed acts which correspond to the definition of genocide under international law and have been or could have been hold criminally liable for the crime of genocide as defined in international law. In other words, this means that there are sufficient grounds to convict a specific person for the crime of genocide.

In some cases the legal characterization of criminal acts as genocide is obvious as it is the case of Shoah or massacres of Armenians.[27] Both these mass human rights violations were the point of reference for the legal definition of genocide adopted in the 1948 Convention on the Prevention and Punishment of the Crime of Genocide.[28] In other cases, the legal characterization of mass human rights violations may be debatable, especially as the crime of genocide is not easy to prove in judicial proceedings.[29]

The case law concerning hate speech also raises questions concerning the understanding, the interpretation and the impact of utterances. In the above-mentioned case, the applicant's utterances were considered both at domestic level and in Strasbourg as utterances concerning the legal qualification of massacres of Armenians which occurred in 1915–1917. Such an approach which stems from the legal issues arising under the domestic law was, however, problematic for at least two reasons. Firstly, the applicant's utterances seemed to pertain mostly to the facts and suggested that their scope might have been narrower than what is generally believed. In any event, the average members of the public have probably understood the

---

[26]ECtHR [GC], *Perinçek v. Switzerland*, mentioned above.

[27]Compare the views expressed by the judges Spielmann, Casadevall, Berro, De Gaetano, Sicilianos, Silvis and Kūris appended to ECtHR [GC], *Perinçek v. Switzerland*, 15 Oct. 2015, application no. 27510/08, para. 2.

[28]Compare the separate opinion appended to ECtHR, *Perinçek V. Switzerland*, 17 Dec. 2013, application no. 27510/08: Joint Concurring Opinion of Judges Raimondi and Sajó and the Joint Partly Dissenting Opinion of Judges Vučinić and Pinto De Albuquerque, para. 29.

[29]See the remarks of Sands (2017), p. 380, written from the perspective of a practicing lawyer.

applicant's speech as pertaining mainly to facts. Secondly, the applicant's speech negatively stereotyped the national community which was the victim of the massacres by accusing it of spreading an "international lie". Such speech is undeniably painful to the descendents of the victims. As a result of the approach adopted, which consisted in reducing the issues raised by the actual speech to one legal dimension, these essential aspects of the applicant's speech and of the whole communicative situation were left unaddressed.

8 Offensive Speech and Identity Issues

The case law characterizes certain forms of hate speech as attacks on identity. The approach of the ECtHR on this issue may be summarized with the following quote:

> The notion of personal autonomy is an important principle underlying the interpretation of the guarantees provided for by Article 8. It can therefore embrace multiple aspects of the person's physical and social identity. The Court further reiterates that it has accepted in the past that an individual's ethnic identity must be regarded as another such element (see S. and *Marper v. the United Kingdom* [GC], nos. 30562/04 and 30566/04, § 66, ECHR 2008, and *Ciubotaru v. Moldova*, no. 27138/04, § 49, 27 April 2010). In particular, any negative stereotyping of a group, when it reaches a certain level, is capable of impacting on the group's sense of identity and the feelings of self-worth and self-confidence of members of the group. It is in this sense that it can be seen as affecting the private life of members of the group.[30]

In the context of cases concerning hate speech oriented at classes of persons the question of the nature of the class of persons affected arises. A class of persons may be a community, i.e. a class of persons which developed a certain type of social bonds and a common social life. This is the case of ethnic minorities. A class of persons may be defined by certain characteristics whereas the class has not developed any type of social ties nor any common life. Such is for instance the class of persons who belong to a certain personal income tax bracket: they are a set of persons without any types of social bonds between them. Similarly, obese persons belong to class which is not a community in the meaning of sociology.

The distinction between mere classes of persons and communities is important because belonging to a community (like an ethnic or a religious group) engages the human being more profoundly and is usually much more important for the construction of one's identity than the mere fact of having a certain characteristic which is not at the basis of a specific social bonds with other persons sharing the same characteristics, such as obesity. Attacks against communities are typically more painful and harmful than attacks against mere classes of persons.

One has to note also *en passant*, in this context, the specificity of Marxist hate speech directed at certain social classes (especially at the means of production owners) often connected with a negative stereotyping of the groups concerned.

[30] ECtHR [GC], *Aksu v. Turkey*, 15 Mar. 2012, applications nos. 4149/04 and 41029/04, para. 58.

9 Conclusion

The brief panorama of issues arising in the context of freedom of speech litigation shows a certain number of difficulties for the judges dealing with such cases. In particular the dichotomy between statements of facts and value judgments becomes clearly obsolete. Against this backdrop, it seems necessary to refine the methodology applied by the judges, be it at national or international level. Legal semiotics may offer useful tools to conceptualize issues arising in individual cases and to reason the judgments and decisions in a persuasive manner. More generally, analytical legal theory may offer useful tools to describe with precision and clarity the facts under consideration, to explain their legal characterization and to justify in a more persuasive manner the judicial decision applying the European Convention on Human Rights.

References

Copi IM et al (1998) Introduction to logic, 10th edn. Upper Saddle River, Prentice Hall

Eco U (2006) Dire presque la même chose. Expériences de traduction. Grasset, Paris

Grabowski A (1999) Judicial argumentation and pragmatics. Księgarnia Akademicka, Kraków

Nowak L et al (1987) Conventional acts in law. In: Ziembiński Z (ed) Polish contributions to the theory and philosophy of law. Rodopi, Amsterdam, pp 115–136

Sadurski W (1985) Giving desert its due. Social justice and legal theory. D. Reidel Publishing Company, Dordrecht

Sands P (2017) East West Street. Weinfeld & Nicolson, London

Searle J (1995) The construction of social reality. Penguin Books, London

Ziembiński Z (1976) Practical logic. Reidel -PWN, Warszawa

Krzysztof Wojtyczek Academic teacher at the Jagiellonian University since 1991, Full Professor of Law since 2015; Judge of the European Court of Human Rights elected in respect of Poland in 2012; Visiting Fulbright Fellow, George Washington University, Washington, DC, 1996–1997; Visiting Humboldt Scholar, Georg-August-Universität, Göttingen, 2003–2005.

Freedom of Expression, Offences to Religion and Public Morals in Strasbourg Case Law

Javier Martínez-Torrón

Contents

1 Introduction: A Recurrent Issue ... 171
2 The General Principles Established by the European Court ... 174
3 A Case Law in Need of Development ... 177
4 Religious Freedom and Protection of Religious Feelings ... 179
5 Statements of Fact and Subjective Opinions ... 181
6 Manipulation of History and Hate Speech ... 187
7 Public Morals as a Notion That Could Justify Limitations on Freedom of Expression ... 191
8 Towards an Integrating Conception of Human Rights ... 196
References ... 197

1 Introduction: A Recurrent Issue

There is no need to insist that freedom of expression, recognized by Article 10 of the European Convention on Human Rights (the Convention), is one of the fundamental rights that has great significance for the structure and dynamics of democratic societies. And it is well known that some people, when exercising their right to publicly express their own ideas and opinions, do it—intentionally or not—in a manner that is disrespectful for those who hold different views.

The Strasbourg jurisdiction has dealt with this type of situations for a long time. In particular since the *Handyside* judgment, in 1976, which involved the judicial seizure of a book for teenager scholars (*The Little Red Schoolbook*) that British authorities considered contrary to public morals. The book, written by an author of

J. Martínez-Torrón (✉)
Complutense University, Madrid, Spain
e-mail: jmtorron@ucm.es

M. Elósegui et al. (eds.), *The Rule of Law in Europe*,
https://doi.org/10.1007/978-3-030-56001-0_11

philo-maoist orientation, included some obscene passages and some others inciting to rebel against parental authority.[1]

It is relatively frequent that, through a variety of channels of communication, we find a public discourse that is directly offensive against religion; it may be against religion in general or a particular religion—its doctrinal, historical, social or organizational aspects—or against sacred figures or religious symbols. The European Court of Human Rights (ECtHR) has adjudicated on these cases in various occasions since *Otto-Preminger-Institut*, in 1994, concerning the judicial prohibition of a blasphemous film (*Das Liebeskonzil*), which was to be showed in a cinema club in Innsbruck. The film contained a gross mockery of the main characters of Christianity, including God Father, Jesus-Christ and the Virgin Mary.[2]

These situations are far from being solved, as demonstrated by the fact that, only in 2018, the Strasbourg Court delivered four judgments in situations characterized by a confluence between freedom of expression and freedom of religion, with very different profiles.

Sekmadienis[3] regarded an advertising campaign introducing a new clothing line in Lithuania, which used characters and expressions of religious connotation, not explicit but clearly visible. More precisely, the campaign showed the image of a man of unequivocal resemblance with the way Jesus-Christ was traditionally represented in Christian iconography, and a woman with a parallel similarity to customary depictions of the Holy Virgin. In both cases, the images were accompanied by captions that read popular expressions of Christian origin in Lithuania: "Jesus, what trousers!", "Dear Mary, what a dress!", and "Jesus [and] Mary, what are you wearing!" The campaign was prohibited and the textile company was fined, on the ground that the disrespect it showed for symbols of Christianity—the majority religion in Lithuania—was against public morals.

In *Mariya Alekhina*,[4] the applicants were three women belonging to a feminist group of punk music, Pussy Riot, who invaded the Christ the Saviour Orthodox Cathedral in Moscow and began to perform a song that was strongly critical of president Putin and the patriarch of the Russian Orthodox Church. The members of the music band certainly looked for celebrity and visibility; they had invited journalists and broadcast their performance—soon interrupted by security personnel—through a video published in YouTube. They were charged with the aggravated

---

[1]ECtHR, *Handyside v. United Kingdom*, 7 Dec. 1976. For an interesting guide to the Strasbourg case law in this matter, see Oetheimer (2007).

[2]ECtHR, *Otto-Preminger-Institut v. Austria*, 20 Sept. 1994. Two years later, the doctrine contained in this judgment was reaffirmed in ECtHR, *Wingrove v. United Kingdom*, 25 November 1996, a propos of a video that, in its author's words, constituted a pornographic version of St Theresa's ecstasy with homosexual connotations. For further details and bibliographical references on this case law of the ECtHR, see Martínez-Torrón (2007), pp. 233–269. An update of that essay, in Spanish, can be found in Martínez-Torrón (2014), pp. 83–120.

[3]ECtHR, *Sekmadienis v. Lithuania*, 30 Jan. 2018.

[4]ECtHR, *Mariya Alekhina and others v. Russia*, 17 Jul. 2018.

offence of hooliganism motivated by religious hatred and received a two-year prison sentence.

Consequence also of an application against Russia, *Ibragim Ibragimov*[5] regarded a very different issue: an action of the public authorities that restricted the freedom of religious speech. The application was caused by the prohibition and seizure of books written by a Muslim theologian, Said Nursi, which were considered—on unclear grounds—to be extremist writings that incited violence and hostility between believers and non-believers.

The fourth judgment, *E.S. v. Austria*,[6] had its origin in a conflict caused by a seminar entitled "Basic information on Islam", organized by an institute linked to a right-wing party and aimed at young voters. In that seminar, the speaker—a woman—made some references to the history and life of Prophet Muhammad, in particular to his marriage with young Aisha, the third of his wives, suggesting that the central figure of Islam did not deserve to be looked at as a role model because he had committed actions that, from a contemporary perspective, would be revealing of a tendency to paedophilia. The Austrian courts, applying the same legislation used in *Otto-Preminger-Institut*, sentenced the applicant to a fine of 480 euro as guilty of an offence of disparaging an object of veneration of a domestic church or religious society in a manner capable of arousing justified indignation.

It is not my intention to provide in this paper a detailed analysis of the foregoing decisions and the legal reasoning that the ECtHR followed in them (as well as some interesting remarks we can find in separate opinions). However, it is worth noting that, except in the last case, the Court concluded that there had been a violation of the freedom of expression protected by Article 10 of the Convention. The judgment *E. S. v. Austria* is an isolated decision in the context of a tendency of the European Court, since the mid-2000s, to prioritize freedom of expression over the protection of religious feelings when it had to adjudicate on situations of an offensive speech in the public sphere. Indeed, the same section of the Court, in 2019, in another case of anti-Islamic speech, *Tagiyev and Huseynov*, concluded that there had been a violation of the applicants' freedom of expression.[7]

The purpose of these pages is, first, to remind the key criteria established by the Strasbourg jurisdiction for an appropriate legal approach to conflicts deriving from the use of offensive language, including that of anti-religious nature. And second, to emphasize some of the questions that, in such a delicate matter, the case law of the European Court has left without a proper solution; questions that, in my view, would need a more careful elaboration. From the perspective of this paper, among the 2018 aforementioned judgments, *Sekmadienis* and *E.S.* deserve special attention, because they raise issues of interest with regard, respectively, to the notion of public morals and to the competence of State and international courts to enter into historical debates.

[5]ECtHR, *Ibragim Ibragimov v. Russia*, 28 Aug. 2018.

[6]ECtHR, *E.S. v. Austria*, 25 Oct. 2018.

[7]ECtHR, *Tagiyev and Huseynov v. Azerbaijan*, 5 Dec. 2019.

2 The General Principles Established by the European Court

The first of the general principles formulated by the ECtHR in this area, more than 40 years ago, is that freedom of expression, albeit not being of course absolute or unlimited, includes the right to use offensive or scandalous language. For the Court, this right, which is an essential foundation of a society that deserves to be considered democratic, comprises not only the freedom to disseminate ideas that society perceives as reasonable or innocuous, but also those that "shock, offend or disturb."[8] This implies that, although the exercise of freedom of expression can be restricted, the necessity of every restriction must be carefully scrutinized. In this regard, the ECtHR has recognized national authorities a certain margin of discretionary appreciation. However, it has also insisted that such margin is not unlimited and that national authorities' decisions are subject to review by the European Court, especially from the perspective of their proportionality, i.e., if they are proportionate to achieve the legitimate aim pursued by the restrictive measure in question[9] (aim that, besides, must be one of those explicitly mentioned by article 10.2 of the Convention[10]).

Over the years, the European Court has provided some criteria designed to facilitate finding an adequate—and difficult—balance between the States' discretionary power and the Court's competence to review the proportionality of restrictions on free speech. Those criteria can be summarized in the need to contextualize the analysis, taking into account not only the content of the expressions but also the circumstances of the society in which the offensive language has been used as well as those of the offending speaker and the means utilized to disseminate the offensive expressions.[11] In addition, it is important to assess the nature and severity of the sanctions that may have been imposed; thus, the criminal nature of the sanction or its

[8]"Freedom of expression constitutes one of the essential foundations of such a society [democratic society]. . . . it is applicable not only to 'information' or 'ideas' that are favourably received or regarded as inoffensive or as a matter of indifference, but also to those that shock, offend or disturb the State or any sector of the population. Such are the demands of that pluralism, tolerance and broadmindedness without which there is no 'democratic society'." (ECtHR, *Handyside v. United Kingdom*, 7 Dec. 1976, para. 49).

[9]ECtHR, *Handyside v. United Kingdom*, 7 Dec. 1976, para. 49.

[10]That is, national security, territorial integrity, public safety, the prevention of disorder or crime, the protection of health or morals, the protection of the reputation or rights of others, the prevention of the disclosure of information received in confidence, and the maintenance of the authority and impartiality of the judiciary.

[11]A summary description of those criteria can be found in the judgment ECtHR, *Seher Karataş v. Turkey*, 9 Jul. 2002, para. 37; and more recently in the above-mentioned ECtHR, *Mariya Alekhina*, 17 Jul. 2018, para. 217 ff. See also Howard (2018), pp. 99 ff.

economic amount may tip the scales in order to determine whether freedom of expression has been violated or not in a specific case.[12]

Beside the need for a contextual analysis, the ECtHR has held that, in the area of political debate, the speech to be protected must be construed in an especially broad fashion. And, correspondingly, the legitimate limitations on political speech must be interpreted in a particularly restrictive manner, i.e., the State must provide persuasive and convincing reasons to justify an interference with freedom of expression. A similar doctrine must be applied to opinions dealing with issues of general interest to society.[13] Conversely, the State has a broader margin of appreciation to regulate and impose limitations on speech in commercial matters or advertising, on the basis that such speech does not pursue per se the general interest of society and citizens must be shielded from expressions that are confusing or even deceiving.[14]

The broad protection of freedom of expression covers of course the content of the information or opinion in question but also the way chosen to disseminate it. In other words, it guarantees every person's right to choose a particularly offensive or provocative form to transmit a message that could have been expressed in a more respectful manner.[15] Moreover, it protects not only messages that are spread through words but also those conveyed by images, including artistic expressions.[16]

The Court has also stressed the importance of distinguishing between statements of facts and opinions.[17] The former, as they refer to an objective reality, allow a higher control of their truth or falsity, and therefore they leave more space for limitations or sanctions—freedom of expression does not protect a right to lie. Conversely, opinions are subjective and hence, as far as they have some factual support, are less susceptible of being restricted by the State.

A specific and significant case of language is hate speech, which the ECtHR understands in the light of the definitions proposed by other Council of Europe bodies. That is:

> all forms of expression which spread, incite, promote or justify racial hatred, xenophobia, anti-Semitism or other forms of hatred based on intolerance.[18]

---

[12]See ECtHR, *Sürek v. Turkey* (n° 1), 8 Jul. 1999, para. 64; ECtHR, *Chauvy and others v. France*, 29 Jun. 2004, para. 78; and ECtHR, *Paturel v. France*, 22 Dec. 2005, paras. 47–51.

[13]See, for instance, ECtHR, *Lingens v. Austria*, 8 Jul. 1986, para. 42; ECtHR, *Castells v. Spain*, 23 Apr. 1992, para. 46; ECtHR, *Wingrove v. United Kingdom*, 25 Nov. 1996, para. 58; ECtHR [GC], *Fressoz and Roire v. France*, 21 Jan. 1999, para. 45; ECtHR, *Seher Karataş v. Turkey*, 9 Jul. 2002, para. 37.

[14]ECtHR, *Sekmadienis v. Lithuania*, 30 Jan. 2018, paras. 73 and 76.

[15]ECtHR, *Oberschlick v. Austria*, 23 May 1991, para. 57; ECtHR, *Prager and Oberschlick v. Austria*, 26 Apr. 1995, para. 38.

[16]ECtHR, *Müller and others v. Switzerland*, 24 May 1988, para. 27.

[17]ECtHR, *Lingens v. Austria*, 8 Jul. 1986, para. 46.

[18]Committee of Ministers of the Council of Europe, Recommendation No. R (97) 20 on "hate speech", 30 October 1997. In Spain, the issue has been studied by Martín Sánchez (2012), pp. 1–33. From a broader perspective, which includes the initiative against the "defamation of religions" in

The European Court, when it considers that a certain expression qualifies as hate speech, has always stated unambiguously that such expressions are not protected by the European Convention on Human Rights. And often the Court has done it applying not Article 10.2 (legitimate limitations on freedom of expression) but Article 17, which prohibits the abuse of rights.[19] With the consequence that, in those cases, the Court's tendency has been to declare the applications inadmissible as incompatible *ratione materiae* with the Convention (sometimes with a rationale that, in reality, contained a true judgment on the merits, "disguised" as an inadmissibility decision[20]). To put it in different words, in such cases the ECtHR has maintained that hate speech does not constitute a manifestation of freedom of expression that deserves the potential protection of the European Convention. Therefore, once a certain expression is deemed hate speech, there is no need to assess if the restrictions imposed on it by the State were legitimate and proportionate.

This doctrine, naturally, is also applicable to anti-religious hate speech, although the Court has been reluctant so far to accept that any of the situations submitted to its jurisdiction can be characterized as such. In applications that had their origin in offensive language against religion, or against a particular religion, the ECtHR has stated, at the most, that they were "gratuitous offences" against religious feelings. And in this regard, since the judgment *Otto-Preminger-Institut* in 1994, the Court's position has been that, in the absence of a clear European consensus about the limits of State action in such a delicate matter, closely linked to national history and culture, the doctrine of the margin or appreciation has to be generously applied.[21] That is, national authorities must be recognized a broad discretion to decide when and how they can resort to the legitimate limitations on freedom of expression foreseen by Article 10.2 of the Convention.

No doubt, the ECtHR's doctrine on gratuitously offensive expressions against religion leaves a number of important questions in the air and has been often criticized.[22] And nevertheless, the Court has not explicitly modified its general principles, although the practice of the last fifteen years reveals a tendency to prioritize freedom of expression in that type of conflicts.

---

the UN, see Combalía (2009) and Pérez-Madrid (2009). See also the collected papers in the monographic issue of the review "Derecho y Religión" 12 (2017), coord. by I. Cano.

[19]"Article 17 Prohibition of abuse of rights — Nothing in this Convention may be interpreted as implying for any State, group or person any right to engage in any activity or perform any act aimed at the destruction of any of the rights and freedoms set forth herein or at their limitation to a greater extent than is provided for in the Convention".

[20]The most emblematic case is ECtHR, *Roger Garaudy v. France*, 24 Jun. 2003.

[21]For an extensive analysis of the doctrine of the margin of appreciation, formulated explicitly for the first time in ECtHR, *Handyside v. United Kingdom*, 7 Dec. 1976, see Arai-Takahashi (2002). For a brief explanation, with key references to case law, Martínez-Torrón (2005). For an interesting reinterpretation of that doctrine, with suggestions for future development, see Iglesias Vila (2017).

[22]See, for instance, Howard (2018), pp. 28–32; Leigh (2011), p. 71; Cram (2009), pp. 325–327; Martínez-Torrón (2007), pp. 267–269.

3 A Case Law in Need of Development

The above-mentioned principles are not, in general, difficult to accept from a theoretical perspective but they require important precisions and nuances when applied to solve particular cases. And in this respect the judgments of the ECtHR could have been clearer. The Court could have devoted less efforts to the grandiloquent exposition of general principles and have been more concerned about providing precise criteria that could actually serve as guide or orientation to national courts to adjudicate on similar situations.[23]

Indeed, freedom of expression is a matter extremely complex and delicate, which needs a careful and balanced approach. And, when we analyse the Strasbourg decisions, we can easily get the impression that the European Court has not put the necessary energy in defining the boundaries that separate the territory of the margin of national appreciation from the common core of legal criteria that must prevail in all the 47 countries of the Council of Europe. Most often, the Court formulates its principles in a very general fashion, repeating them almost like mantras in every decision, as a sort of wild card that makes possible to decide on a conflict one way or the opposite, sometimes without being patent the reason of those different decisions—and the problem is aggravated by the fact that not all the chambers of the Court apply those general criteria in the same manner.

These dynamics are far from the ideal and leave some important questions without being addressed with sufficient depth. For instance, to mention briefly some issues that I will not examine in detail in the following pages, to what extent the Strasbourg Court should reconsider some aspects of its doctrine on hate speech in the light of the parallel case law of US courts.[24] I am not suggesting that the latter is the paradigm to be followed—indeed, it is significant that US legal literature has included such case law within the so-called "American exceptionalism".[25] But we can probably find interesting middle ground between the US and the European conceptions of which should be the appropriate reaction of the State to that type of abusive language, as well as of the circumstances that can legitimize restrictions on the exercise of freedom of expression, which is an indisputable pillar of democratic societies.[26]

Something similar occurs with regard to the dilemma of whether hate speech situations should be adjudicated under article 17 of the Convention (abuse of rights)

---

[23]In this point I refer to my remarks in Martínez-Torrón (2015), especially pp. 284–288.

[24]Among the immense legal literature in the United States on this issue, see Matsuda (1993); Post (1988), pp. 297–335; Baker (1997), pp. 979–1020; Minow (2000), pp. 1253–1277; O'Neil (2012–2013), pp. 467–498. For an interesting comparison between the US and Canada, Greenawalt (1996); and Tomlins (2013), pp. 44–71.

[25]For a detailed analysis of American exceptionalism by various authors, see Ignatieff (2005). For a firm and reasoned critique to the prevailing attitudes on hate speech in the United States, Waldron (2012).

[26]For an interesting comparison of US and European notions about how hate speech should be dealt with in contemporary societies, see Herz et al. (2012); Hare et al. (2009).

or rather article 10.2 (limitations on freedom of expression). Traditionally, the Strasbourg case law has been inclined to take the first option, which I do not think is the most adequate one, among other reasons because, once some language is labeled as hate speech, public authorities are exempted from providing precise justifications for their restriction on freedom of expression. Nevertheless, the European Court not always has followed easily identifiable criteria, as demonstrated by its position in cases of *negationism*. Thus, situations of denial of the Holocaust of the Jewish people under the Nazi regime have been normally addressed with most severity under article 17;[27] and the same has been done other times with expressions considered as anti-Islamic hate speech.[28] In contrast, the negation of the Armenian genocide perpetrated by the Turkish government in the early twentieth century has been dealt with in a different fashion; the Court has meticulously examined if the restriction on freedom of expression was justified under the limitation clause of article 10.2 (and has concluded, by a narrow majority, that is was not).[29]

Another question that the ECtHR has left without clarification is if, for the purposes of the protection offered by the European Convention, opinions conveyed through private channels should be distinguished from those expressed in public spaces.[30] It is possible that those two types of public language do not deserve the same legal treatment by the courts. And probably it would be appropriate to make further distinctions within the notions of public and private spaces; the public square is not the same as a parliament or a publicly owned radio or TV channel; and private publications or personal Internet blogs are not the same as private TV channels, which are subject to a strict system of public concessions and controls in many European countries. Again, in this area, a comparison with the US judicial doctrine that distinguishes between diverse categories of fora could be useful;[31] not because I think that the Strasbourg case law must be "Americanized", but because the US Supreme Court, irrespective of the opinions we may have of each of its judgments, has put more effort in the elaboration of relatively clear criteria aimed at orientating the future decision of cases by the rest of US courts (as well as, of course, the Supreme Court itself). Conversely, the Strasbourg court sometimes seems more concerned about justifying a particular decision in an unassailable fashion rather than tracing an intelligible itinerary of future adjudication for national courts (as well as, of course, for the European Court itself).

We will turn now more in detail to other questions that, in my view, require attention from the ECtHR.

[27]ECtHR, *Roger Garaudy v. France*, 24 Jun. 2003; also ECtHR, *M'Bala B'Bala v. France*, 20 Oct. 2015.

[28]ECtHR, *Norwood v. United Kingdom*, 16 Nov. 2004.

[29]ECtHR [GC], *Perinçek v. Switzerland*, 15 Oct. 2015. See infra, Section 6 of this paper.

[30]Such question may be addressed by the Court a propos of the case ECtHR, *Asociación de Abogados Cristianos v. Spain*, 20 Jun. 2019.

[31]For a critical explanation of the US judicial doctrine that distinguishes between different fora and its consequences, with abundant bibliographical and case law references, see Lidsky (2011).

4 Religious Freedom and Protection of Religious Feelings

A first and crucial question consists in elucidating if the protection of the religious feelings of the majority or a minority of the population constitutes an integral part of the freedom of religion or belief guaranteed by Article 9 of the Convention. To my judgment, it is problematic to maintain that one of the functions of a legal system is the protection of feelings, be they religious or of any other kind. The reason is that it would put legal guarantees, which should desirably be objective, in an environment of subjectivity, instability and unpredictability, for these characteristics are usually intrinsic to the sphere of sentiments.

In any event, the Strasbourg Court has kept an ambiguous and hesitant position in this regard.[32] On the one hand, on the basis that Article 10 of the Convention protects also those opinions that "shock, offend or disturb",[33] the Court has held that religions cannot reasonably expect to be free from criticism. Indeed, as mentioned above, according to the ECtHR, Article 10 protects the deliberate choice of offensive content, as well as a particularly offensive way to convey that content, and also the resort to some exaggeration and even provocation.[34] But on the other hand, in *Otto-Preminger-Institut*, the Court seemed to declare that religious feelings are included in the scope of protection of religious freedom:

> The respect for the religious feelings of believers as guaranteed in Article 9 (art. 9) can legitimately be thought to have been violated by provocative portrayals of objects of religious veneration; and such portrayals can be regarded as malicious violation of the spirit of tolerance, which must also be a feature of democratic society.[35]

Although the ECtHR has not made clear under which circumstances the protection of religious feelings can prevail over the right to freedom of expression, its tendency has been to interpret that only in extreme cases it is possible to justify limitations or sanctions imposed on anti-religious language that has been intentionally offensive or provocative.[36] At the same time, the Court has emphasized that the doctrine of the margin of appreciation is of importance in this matter; as the European Convention does not impose a uniform criterion about these situations, and in the absence of a European consensus on the issue, national legal systems and

---

[32]For further details, I refer to Martínez-Torrón (2014).

[33]ECtHR, *Handyside v. United Kingdom*, 7 Dec. 1976, para. 49.

[34]See supra, note 14 and accompanying text.

[35]ECtHR, *Otto-Preminger-Institut v. Austria*, 20 Sept. 1994, para. 47.

[36]In Spain there is a specific legal provision to that purpose. Article 525 of the Penal Code criminalizes public derision—orally or in writing—of "tenets, beliefs, rites or ceremonies" of a religious community with the intention to offend the feelings of its members; and it imposes the same penalty to similar conducts with regard to people who profess no religion. This legal provision is almost never applied in practice. On this theme, from a comparative law perspective, see the essays included in the collective book Martínez-Torrón (2014).

authorities have certain discretion to punish those expressions that are deemed "gratuitously offensive" against a religion or its sacred symbols.[37]

The Strasbourg approach is apparently dominated by the notion that the exercise of freedom of religion or belief—by religious or non-religious people—requires an atmosphere of tolerance and respect, free from attacks that may actually inhibit citizens from manifesting their beliefs without intimidation. This is suggested by another of the passages of *Otto-Preminger-Institut*:

> the manner in which religious beliefs and doctrines are opposed or denied is a matter which may engage the responsibility of the State, notably its responsibility to ensure the peaceful enjoyment of the right guaranteed under Article 9 (art. 9) to the holders of those beliefs and doctrines. Indeed, in extreme cases the effect of particular methods of opposing or denying religious beliefs can be such as to inhibit those who hold such beliefs from exercising their freedom to hold and express them.[38]

This, for the rest, is a common feature to all fundamental freedoms. A social environment of free discussion and expression, including the free manifestation of beliefs, is essential to democracy. And vice versa, an ambience of verbal aggression or violence is not the most adequate habitat for the exercise of freedoms. From this perspective, attacks on the ground of religion are not intrinsically different from attacks on the ground of sex, race or national origin; and all those factors are mentioned by Article 14 of the Convention, which prohibits discrimination.[39]

Nevertheless, we should not lose sight of the fact that, according to Article 10, every restriction on freedom of expression, in addition to pursue a legitimate aim, has to be justified as "necessary in a democratic society". Which means that, in the words of the European Court, it must respond to a "pressing social need".[40]

In my view, the analysis of situations that involve offences to religious feelings must depart from a basic principle: the protection of religious feelings, per se, is not an integral part of the guarantee offered by freedom of thought, conscience and religion. Article 9 of the Convention preserves an ambit of freedom but not a space of sentiments or emotions.

The foregoing does not mean that it is not possible to impose legitimate restrictions or sanctions on expressions that are gratuitously offensive in particularly grave cases. More specifically, such possibility exists when abusive language is clearly calumnious; freedom of expression does not protect an alleged right to lie—and

---

[37]ECtHR, *Otto-Preminger-Institut v. Austria*, 20 Sept. 1994, para. 49–50.

[38]ECtHR, *Otto-Preminger-Institut v. Austria*, 20 Sept. 1994, para. 47.

[39]In fact, the possibility to consider that religion constitutes a legitimate ground to restrict freedom of expression was recognized by the three judges who, *Otto-Preminger-Institut*, wrote a joint dissenting opinion and refused to accept that the freedom of religion enshrined in article 9 ECtHR imply an alleged right to the protection of religious feelings. In their precise words, "tolerance works both ways and the democratic character of a society will be affected if violent and abusive attacks on the reputation of a religious group are allowed" (ECtHR, *Otto-Preminger-Institut v. Austria*, 20 Sept. 1994, joint dissenting opinion of Judges Palm, Pekkanen and Makarczyk, para. 6).

[40]ECtHR, *Handyside v. United Kingdom*, 7 Dec. 1976, para. 48.

therefore to calumny. The same applies to language that, even not strictly qualifying as hate speech, can actually lead, because of the circumstances and the context, to a limitation on the freedom of religion of some people. For instance, when the offence in question not only hurts the feelings of some persons but also seriously damages the reputation of a religious group or its members, with the actual possibility of causing situations of discrimination or making difficult for some citizens to freely practice their religion.

This is probably the sense of the ECtHR's allusion to the inhibitory effect that some public speech may have on the freedom of certain people to manifest their beliefs. And it is likely also the intended meaning of the reference of the three dissenting judges in *Otto-Preminger-Institut* to the abusive attacks to the reputation of religious groups.[41] Such situations would not only involve a mere contempt for feelings but an attack to the freedom of others. And this is more likely to occur in the case of attacks to religious minorities, which in general are more vulnerable to the consequences of defamation.

5 Statements of Fact and Subjective Opinions

It has been already mentioned that, for the ECtHR, it is crucial to distinguish between those expressions that consist in statements of fact and those others that contain an opinion, because the veracity or falsity of facts is more susceptible of control. While opinions are subjective and belong to the legitimate diversity of interpretations of reality, the objectivity of facts is verifiable and sometimes measurable. As a consequence, according to the European Court, a subjective opinion is in principle protected by Article 10 as far as it is supported by objective and true facts.

The immediate question that comes to mind is how much factual—true—support is needed for a subjective opinion to benefit from the guarantee of Article 10. The question is especially relevant when an opinion interprets real facts in a far-fetched or disproportionate fashion. Naturally, every person looks at reality from a particular perspective, which includes a certain degree of selection, slant, bias or distortion, even to the extent of manipulation. The important issue is to determine when such views cease to be a mere interpretation of facts, no matter how exaggerated or partial, and becomes a falsification, i.e., a lie. Certainly, it is not an easy question to answer, and even less in the abstract.

Aware that in case of doubt it is preferable to opt for freedom (*in dubio pro libertate*), the Strasbourg case law, as in general the judicature of Western democracies, has tended to a maximalist conception of the freedom to express subjective opinions; these are protected as far as there is a minimum of factual truth, irrespective of how "creative" is the speaker's imagination, and irrespective of

[41] See supra notes 37 and 38 and accompanying text.

how ostensibly such interpretation of reality leaves aside a part of the true facts (even a large part). It is, in my view, a sensible tendency, which is based on the conviction that the hypothetical benefits of correcting the opinions that deform objective facts in an interested way are exceeded by the risks of giving public authorities the power to intervene in the free exchange of ideas to define which is the "orthodox version" of reality—and to illegalize or proscribe all other "heterodox" versions.[42]

If we apply the foregoing to the specific area of offensive expressions against religion, or against a particular religion, which has been the position of the Strasbourg Court? The brief answer would be: irregular. Two examples will serve to illustrate it.

One is the *Giniewski* case, in 2006, originated by a press article against the Catholic Church, which the French courts had considered defamatory.[43] The applicant described himself as a journalist, historian and sociologist who tried, in his work, to encourage an approach between Jews and Christians. In 1994, he published an op-ed piece criticizing the Encyclical *Veritatis Splendor* of Pope John Paul II. In it he affirmed that the Catholic doctrine of the "fulfilment" (*accomplissement*) of the Old Testament in the New Testament lead to anti-Semitism and contained the theological foundations that make possible justifying the extermination of Jews in the Nazi concentration camps. The text suggested a parallelism between the "fulfilment" (*accomplissement*) of the Old Testament and the implementation (*accomplissement*) of the Holocaust.[44] A Christian association brought criminal proceedings against the applicant, accusing him of a crime of racial defamation against the Christian community. The applicant was sentenced in first instance as guilty of publicly defaming a group of persons (Christians) on the ground of membership of a religion. After a subsequent and complex procedural itinerary, the applicant was absolved from criminal charges but the economic sanctions deriving from the civil action were confirmed.

The European Court, in a unanimous judgment, decided in favour of the plaintiff, with a brief assessment of the facts in which, unlike the French courts, concluded that there was no serious offence against Christianity. Where the French courts had

[42]The US Supreme Court expressed this idea vividly long ago, in 1943: "If there is any fixed star in our constitutional constellation, it is that no official, high or petty, can prescribe what shall be orthodox in politics, nationalism, religion, or other matters of opinion, or force citizens to confess by word or act their faith therein." (*West Virginia State Board of Education v. Barnette,* 319 U.S. 624, 642) The case involved the conscientious objection of Jehovah's Witnesses to participate in the flag salute ceremony in public schools.

[43]ECtHR, *Giniewski v. France*, 31 Jan. 2006.

[44]The incriminating passages were considered to be the following: "*L'Église catholique s'auto-institue seule détentrice de la vérité divine et s'arroge le 'devoir' de diffuser sa doctrine comme seule universelle. Elle proclame fortement l'accomplissement de 'l'ancienne' Alliance dans la nouvelle, la supériorité de cette dernière, doctrine qui prolonge 'l'enseignement du mépris' des juifs … De nombreux chrétiens ont reconnu que l'anti-judaïsme scripturaire et la 'doctrine de l'accomplissement' de l'ancienne par la nouvelle Alliance, conduisent à l'antisémitisme et ont formé le terrain où ont germé l'idée et l'accomplissement d'Auschwitz*". The full text of the article can be found in *ibid*., para. 23.

seen a grave accusation of anti-Semitism directed against Catholics, and a statement that their doctrine was partly responsible for the massacres perpetrated by the Nazis, the ECtHR only saw the exposition of a thesis about the causes of the persecution of Jews in Europe.[45] For the Court, the applicant's press article did not contain any gratuitous attack against religious beliefs as such but rather some thoughts that, even if they could be hurtful for many, focused on a subject of indubitable significance in our recent history.[46]

The Court remarked that the search for historical truth is an integral part of freedom of expression and that it was not the Court's role or competence to take sides in a historical controversial issue.[47] Indeed, the Court's succinct analysis of the contentious text revealed its intention to refrain from making any judgment about the actual foundation of the author's opinion. The European Court also emphasized that, when an author communicates his opinions on issues of general interest, limitations on freedom of expression must be construed narrowly; the threat of a legally imposed sanction—even a reduced economic penalty—could have a deterrent effect and could inhibit the press, or the authors, from freely disseminating their ideas and intervening in public debates on important issues.[48] Such restrictions would be justifiable only in the case of opinions that were gratuitously offensive to the religious beliefs of others, incited to hatred or lack of respect, or denied well-established historical facts.[49]

It is worth comparing the ECtHR's position on *Giniewski*[50] with a recent decision: the aforementioned *E.S. v. Austria*.[51] As I explained at the beginning of this chapter, the conflict had its origin in statements that strongly criticized Prophet Muhammad, which had been expressed by a person giving a seminar entitled "Basic information on Islam". The seminar was organized by an institute run by the Freedom Party of Austria (*Freiheitliche Partei Österreichs*, FPÖ), characterized by a political nationalist orientation, a conservative and liberal approach in economic issues, and a restrictive stance on immigration matters, especially with regard to Muslims, which the party declares to be based on its interest in preserving Austrian cultural identity. The seminar was held in Vienna and was directed not only at party members and their invitees but also at young voters in general; indeed, it had been

[45] *Ibid.*, para. 50.

[46] *Ibid.*, para. 51.

[47] *Ibid.*, para. 51, with explicit reference to ECtHR, *Chauvy and others v. France*, 29 Jun. 2004, para. 69.

[48] *Ibid*, para. 35.

[49] *Ibid.*, para. 52, with explicit reference to ECtHR, *Roger Garaudy v. France*, 24 Jun. 2003, *En droit*, para. 1. The mention of the *Garaudy* decision is particularly significant, for the case involved the delicate issue of anti-Semitism in Europe, more precisely its expression through "negationism", i.e., expression of opinions aimed at denying the existence or the dimension of the Holocaust.

[50] Shortly before, in ECtHR, *Paturel c. France*, 22 Dec. 2005, a different chamber of the Court had adopted an approach similar to that in ECtHR, *Giniewski v. France*, 31 Jan. 2006, but with an interesting separate opinion adding nuances to the Court's rationale.

[51] ECtHR, *E.S. v. Austria*, 25 Oct. 2018.

publicized in the institute's web pages. Among the approximately thirty attendees there was an undercover journalist, who later asked the Vienna Public Prosecutor's Office to bring criminal proceedings against the speaker at the seminar.

The applicant was initially accused of incitement to hatred but, because of doubts about the exact expressions she had used, she was finally convicted of disparaging religious doctrines pursuant to art. 188 of the Austrian Criminal Code; she was ordered to pay the cost of the proceedings as well as a fine of 480 euro.[52] The court found her guilty of publicly disparaging an object of veneration of a domestic church or religious society, namely Prophet Muhammad, in a manner "likely to arouse justified indignation."[53] The statements that the court found incriminating affirmed that Muhammad was far from being an ideal man or a role model, and that it was incomprehensible that the central prophet of Islam was a warrior who had several wives; especially considering that he married one of them—Aisha—when he was more than 50 years old and she only six, and that he had sexual intercourse with her when she had hardly turned nine years old. The last fact, added the speaker, would qualify today as paedophilia.[54] For the Austrian courts, such statements were intentionally provocative, contained an abusive attack and a gratuitous offence to a religious community, and did not contribute at all to a debate of general interest—they were just aimed at defaming Muhammad. Moreover, the courts refused to recognize any relevance to one of the applicant's allegations, namely that all participants in the seminar knew of her critical approach and it was therefore very doubtful that anyone could feel offended; for the Austrian courts, at least one of the participants had felt offended, as her complaints had led to the applicant's prosecution.[55]

The ECtHR, in its judgment, dispatched as irrelevant—without providing any concrete reason—the circumstance that the seminar had been attended only by about 30 people. The Court also completely deferred to the national authorities the assessment of how much the "religious peace" of the country could be endangered. And, most significantly, the Court approached the content of the applicant's statements in a totally different way in comparison with *Giniewski*.[56]

[52]A day-fine of four euros for a period of 120 days, which would result in 60 days' imprisonment in the event of default.

[53]Article 188 of the Austrian Criminal Code is part of a section that contains, inter alia, offences against religious peace. This is its text: "Whoever, in circumstances where his or her behaviour is likely to arouse justified indignation, publicly disparages or insults a person who, or an object which, is an object of veneration of a church or religious community established within the country, or a dogma, a lawful custom or a lawful institution of such a church or religious community, shall be liable to up to six months' imprisonment or a day-fine for a period of up to 360 days." (translation provided by the Court in ECtHR, *E.S. v. Austria*, 25 Oct. 2018, para. 24).

[54]ECtHR, *E.S. v. Austria*, 25 Oct. 2018, para. 13.

[55]For a detailed description of the judicial itinerary and rationale used by the Austrian courts, see *ibid.*, paras. 14–22.

[56]*Ibid.*, paras. 50–57.

On the one hand, the Court emphasized the obvious offensive and provocative nature of the statements, recalling at the same time that, as such, this does not justify limitations on freedom of expression; Article 10 of the Convention not only protects the dissemination of ideas "that are favourably received or regarded as inoffensive or as a matter of indifference, but also . . . those that offend, shock or disturb".[57] And on the other hand, and above all, the judgment went into a relatively detailed assessment of the historical rigour and accuracy of the applicant's statements; concluding, and underscoring, that they "they had not been made in an objective manner",[58] and that the applicant "failed to neutrally inform her audience of the historical background, which consequently did not allow for a serious debate on that issue".[59] That is, the ECtHR not only centred its judgment on the characterization of the tone of the applicant's speech as offensive, provocative, insulting and hurtful; it also took a position about the substance of the debate, thus acting as censor of what is or not intellectually or historically accurate. In addition, the Court declared that the criminal sanction imposed on the applicant (480 euro or 60 days of imprisonment) was moderate and not disproportionate,[60] when in *Giniewski* it had considered excessive, and with a deterrent effect on freedom of expression, to order the applicant to pay 1 franc (=0.15 euro) as civil damages (there was no criminal conviction) and to publish a notice of the ruling in a national newspaper at his own expense.[61]

It is not my intention to analyse here in detail the ECtHR's case law on freedom of expression and offences against religion,[62] but it is worth noting the contradiction between the approaches of the European Court in *Giniewski* and in *E.S.*, respectively. If we compare the rationale of these two judgments, the result is puzzling. If a Pope, then alive, is accused in a press article published in a national newspaper of endorsing a doctrine that, for the journalist, is in the origins of anti-Semitism and the Nazi extermination camps, the Court holds that it is a contribution about a historical issue of general interest for society. The Court refrains from evaluating how well-grounded the journalist's opinion was—notwithstanding the fact that most likely it would appear absurd to anyone who knows something about the life of John Paul II and his relationships with the Jewish communities. Conversely, if in the context of a seminar attended by hardly 30 people the speaker accuses a person who died centuries ago, but is venerated by millions of Muslims, of having sexual relationships which today would be deemed as paedophilia, then the Court makes a pronouncement on a historical question—objectively of much lesser significance

---

[57] *Ibid.*, para. 42.

[58] *Ibid.*, para. 52.

[59] *Ibid.*, para. 54.

[60] *Ibid.*, para. 56.

[61] ECtHR, *Giniewski v. France*, 31 Jan. 2006, para. 55. In ECtHR, *Aydin Tatlav v. Turkey*, 2 May 2006, para. 30, the Court had considered disproportionate, and inhibiting for the exercise of freedom of expression, a criminal sanction consisting in a fine of 10 euros.

[62] I have already done it in other writings, previously cited. More recently, including some comparative remark regarding the US law, see Martínez-Torrón (2017).

even though it is emotionally important for many—in spite of the fact that, in reality, the relationships of Muhammad with Aisha, and her age when she married the Prophet, are the subject of a historical debate.

Why such a different attitude of the ECtHR? It has been suggested that, even if the Court could have wished to modify its doctrine about gratuitous offences to religious feelings as expressed in *Otto-Preminger-Institut*, the case of *E.S.* was not probably the adequate opportunity to do so; it could lead to the wrong perception that Strasbourg justifies the legal punishment of insults against Christianity but delegitimizes an equivalent punishment of disparagement of Islam.[63] It is an interesting conjecture but I am not entirely persuaded by it. Among other reasons, because it does not look like the European Court has the least intention to change its general principles on this matter—which the Court could likely have done in *E.S.* without the need to alter the outcome, especially considering the manifold ways in which it has applied those principles in the past.

Was perhaps this different approach caused by the fact that in *Giniewski* the targeted religion was Catholicism—i.e., the major church in France—while in *E.S.* it was Islam, a more "vulnerable" minority in a society, as Austria, that is predominantly Catholic? In reality, it is not easy to find a clear reason, and even less in the light of Strasbourg precedents. It is true that in *I.A. v. Turkey*, which involved an offensive book against Muhammad and Islam, the Court took the same position as in *E.S.*, but it was a controversial judgment adopted by a divided chamber—four votes against three.[64] And a few months later, in *Aydin Tatlav*,[65] the same chamber of the Court, unanimously, affirmed that freedom of expression had to prevail in a case regarding another book containing statements that were openly offensive against Islam (for instance, that Islam is of "barbaric violence", or that Muhammad founded his main policies on violence and promised men a paradise with "the true parasitic life of an aristocrat").[66]

What is striking and raises particular concern in the rationale of the *E.S.* judgment is the fact that the Strasbourg Court decided to assess the "objectivity", "neutrality" and "rigour" of the statements made by the applicant. The Court had not done it before, and even less in such a detailed way. Not even in *Otto-Preminger-Institut* or in *Wingrove*, whose outcome was also favourable to the protection of religious feelings, the Court made reference to the historical accuracy of a ridiculing depiction of Jesus-Christ and the Virgin Mary, or of St Theresa's ecstasy. Its arguments focused on the fact that the audio-visual expressions in question were unnecessarily offensive and provocative, without judging their truth or their correctness.

---

[63]See Smet (2018).

[64]ECtHR, *I.A. v. Turkey*, 13 Sept. 2005. The three judges of the minority wrote a joint dissenting opinion with a vigorous reasoning against the judgment's rationale.

[65]ECtHR, *Aydin Tatlav v. Turkey*, 2 May 2006. Nevertheless, the composition of the Second Chamber, had changed: only five of the seven judges were the same as in *I.A v. Turkey*.

[66]*Ibid.*, para. 12.

Without going into the particulars of the judgment, I do not deny that, in the circumstances of the *E.S.* case, the European Court could have justified the applicant's conviction by the Austrian courts. But, if that is what the Court thought it was the fair thing to do, it should have used different arguments. Intervening in a debate—ongoing in the Islamic world—about the precise facts of the relationship between Muhammad and Aisha, and about her actual age when she married, is not the courts' competence, including the ECtHR, as the Court itself has recognized.[67] And, with regard to the argument that the offence was "likely to arouse justified indignation", the only person that appeared to have been "indignant" at the words of the applicant was an undercover journalist that attended the seminar with the presumable purpose of finding grounds to attack the institute of the Freedom Party of Austria. If there were actually any indignation, it would have been triggered not by the applicant's speech but rather by the publicity that the journalist—intentionally—gave to it.

6 Manipulation of History and Hate Speech

We could conjecture that, in *E.S.*, the European Court of Human Rights intended—like the Austrian courts—to avoid that a political party disseminated, under the guise of a purported historical critique, an image of Muslims as irrational and fanatical people who profess beliefs that are irreconcilable with Western values. If this were the case, in my opinion resorting to the concepts of disparagement of religion or likely justified indignation was not the right approach. The Court should have rather analysed the situation in the light of hate speech, i.e., incitation to hatred, violence or discrimination. Otherwise, there is the risk to open the door to the possibility that the European Court decides to assume the role of arbiter in intellectual or historical disputations—a role that, so far, it has rejected. One of the consequences of it would be that the Court might justify new patterns of censorship of provocative expressions that question core aspects of some religions. That would be most unfortunate because, leaving aside the possible inappropriate tone of such critiques, the debate about those issues is of general interest for society.

The foregoing leads us to raise a third important question: when, and under which circumstances, can we say that the manipulation or falsification of historical truth, by disseminating false information or by hiding relevant true data, are actually a subtler form of hate speech? In other words, when can be conclude that the apparent intellectual or historical debate in reality conceals a discourse that is aimed at promoting hostility towards a particular group of persons?

This is precisely the case of the so-called negationism, whose actual purpose is not to determine accurately historical data but rather to use them, manipulated or just fabricated, to spread a subliminal message. The most well-known type of

[67] See note 46 and accompanying text.

negationism refers to the intended extermination of the Jewish people perpetrated by the Nazi regime, questioning the true intention or the dimension or such crime, and sometimes its very existence. The publications of such orientation are not aimed at revising or refining the knowledge we have of that tragic episode of our recent history. Its aim is, by undermining the credibility of historical testimonies (including those of the survivors), to transmit a message of anti-Semitism, namely that the Jews are a cunning and parasitic people that have no scruples to distort the reality and present themselves as victims as a strategy for their benefit.

The ECtHR's position has been normally very clear when it has adjudicated on cases relating to anti-Semitic negationism. Two decisions are particularly well known. One is *Roger Garaudy*,[68] which involved the criminal conviction of a notorious French public figure for negation of crimes against humanity and incitement to hatred. The European Court, in a long inadmissibility decision,[69] held that the criminal sentence was justified by Article 17 of the Convention. In the Court's view, the work of Mr. Garaudy not only contained a critique of Israeli policies but also, and above all, a denial of historical facts that were well established and proven. For the Court, his work was aimed at the rehabilitation of the Nazi regime through a falsification of history and a negation of crimes against humanity, which in turn was an unequivocal form of hate speech.[70] Identical approach permeated another large inadmissibility decision, *M'Bala*,[71] about a popular French comedian (his artistic name is "Dieudonné") who had been sentenced to an economic penalty for using in his shows sarcastic expressions of anti-Semitic, negationist and offensive nature. After reminding that freedom of expression also applies to satire—with all it involves of caricature and provocative exaggeration—the ECtHR made clear that this freedom does not protect speech against the fundamental values of the European Convention on Human Rights, as is the case of the denial of Shoah.[72]

A similar approach inspired *Norwood*, another—shorter—inadmissibility decision concerning a curious form of anti-Islamic expression which, rather than "negationist", should qualify as "attributionist", i.e., unfounded and indiscriminate attribution of acts of violence to a religious community as a whole.[73] Despite the brevity of its reasoning, *Norwood* has had a remarkable impact on North-American

[68]ECtHR, *Roger Garaudy v. France*, 24 Jun. 2003.

[69]The official French text has 40 pages. Such a length reveals that the case deserved a judgment on the merits and not an inadmissibility decision as "manifestly ill-founded". The decision states that it was adopted unanimously.

[70]See ECtHR, *Roger Garaudy v. France*, 24 Jun. 2003, *En droit*, para. 1.i.

[71]ECtHR, *M'Bala B'Bala v. France*, 20 Oct. 2015. This time, it was a majority decision of 18 pages. Many scholars have criticized the fact that such important issues have been ended with inadmissibility decisions that are actually, by their length and approach, judgments on the merits. This does not help the transparency of the Court; inadmissibility decisions do not enjoy the same publicity as judgments; in addition, in non-unanimous decisions, it is not known how many judges are in the minority side and these cannot write dissenting opinions.

[72]See ECtHR, *M'Bala B'Bala v. France*, 20 Oct. 2015, paras. 31–33.

[73]ECtHR, *Norwood v. United Kingdom*, 16 Nov. 2004.

legal literature, perhaps because it involved a case emerged in other common law country (United Kingdom), and because the legal solution given to the case was in overt contrast with the usual criteria followed by the US judicature. The applicant was a regional organiser for an extreme right wing political party (BNP) who had been sentenced to pay a fine of 300 pounds for having displayed in the window of his flat, for two months, a large poster with a picture of the Twin Towers in flames, together with the sentence "Islam out of Britain – Protect the British People" and a prohibition sign with the symbol of a crescent inside. With a very laconic reasoning based on Article 17 of the Convention, the European Court held that:

> Such a general, vehement attack against a religious group, linking the group as a whole with a grave act of terrorism, is incompatible with the values proclaimed and guaranteed by the Convention, notably tolerance, social peace and non-discrimination.[74]

Nevertheless, four years later, the ECtHR, in *Soulas*,[75] rendered a new decision—this time a judgment—concerning anti-Islamic speech apropos of a book against immigration, whose publisher and author had been sentenced to the payment of a fine of 7500 euro each. The French courts held that some passages of the book contained incitation to hatred and violence against Muslim communities of African origin. The European Court's judgment is confusing and far from the approach taken in *Norwood*. The Court reminded the importance of fighting against racial discrimination and agreed that part of the text transmits a negative stereotyping of those communities, but it did not describe it as hate speech. For the ECtHR, the circumstances were not sufficiently grave as to justify the application of Article 17 of the Convention but they were serious enough to conclude that the restriction of freedom of expression by French authorities was well founded and the sanctions imposed were proportionate.[76] This leads to wonder to what extent the European Court's position on this issue is erratic; a poster in a window is deemed grave enough to invoke Article 17 but the publication of a book is not, even though that work, under the guise of a socio-political analysis, is aimed at stigmatizing a part of the population.

On the other hand, the clarity of the criteria followed in cases of anti-Semitic speech is in overt contrast with the more tepid posture of the ECtHR in another case concerning negationism, *Perinçek*,[77] with regard to the Armenian genocide at the hands of the Ottoman Empire. The applicant was the leader of a Turkish political party (the Workers' Party[78]) who, in several public events held in Switzerland, denied that any genocide of Armenians by the Turks ever existed and described it as "an international lie". The Swiss courts sentenced the applicant to pay the costs of the proceedings (10,000 Swiss francs), an additional payment of 1000 francs as

---

[74]ECtHR, *Norwood v. United Kingdom*, 16 Nov. 2004, para. The law.

[75]ECtHR, *Soulas and others v. France*, 10 Jul. 2008.

[76]See ECtHR, *Soulas and others v. France*, 10 Jul. 2008, paras. 41–48.

[77]ECtHR [GC], *Perinçek v. Switzerland*, 15 Oct. 2015.

[78]This party dissolved in 2015 and was succeeded by the Patriotic Party, also led by Perinçek. Its ideology is a curious mix of socialism, left-wing populism and nationalism.

compensation to the Switzerland-Armenia Association, and a fine of 3000 francs. He was also warned that, if in the future he incurred a similar conduct in Swiss territory, he would receive a prison sentence. It is not my intention to discuss here the outcome of the case or to analyse the complex and long judgment of the Grand Chamber (122 pages, plus other 12 pages of separate opinions of the seven dissenting judges), but it is worth noting three aspects of it.

First, unlike the aforementioned cases of anti-Semitic negationism, the application in *Perinçek* ended with a judgment on the merits and not with a mere decision of inadmissibility as ill-founded (in reality there were two judgments, one by a chamber and other by the Grand Chamber). Second, also unlike those other decisions, the case was judged in the light of Article 10.2 of the Convention (limitations on freedom of expression) instead of Article 17 (abuse of rights), which the Court affirmed must be applied only "on an exceptional basis and in extreme cases".[79] This difference is significant, for an approach based on Article 10.2 requires determining if the penalties imposed on the applicant can be deemed "necessary in a democratic society" to achieve some of the legitimate purposes enumerated in that article of the Convention. And third, precisely because of it, the Court examined carefully and in detail the factual circumstances and the context of the applicant's statements on the Armenian genocide (including the international notion of genocide and the actual impact of the public events in which the applicant spoke) in order to ascertain whether the interference with the applicant's freedom of expression was justifiable and proportionate. And the Court concluded, by ten votes against seven, that it was not, and therefore there had been a violation of Article 10 of the Convention.

I am not in principle against any of those three aspects: either deciding the application by a judgment, examining it under Article 10.2 of the Convention, or performing a detailed analysis of the factual circumstances. Just the opposite, I think this is the right way to proceed. What I do not understand is the reason why the ECtHR applied in *Perinçek* criteria that were different from those inspiring the aforementioned cases of anti-Semitic and anti-Islamic speech, without any indication at all that it had the wish to change its jurisprudence.[80] To begin with, *Garaudy*, *M'Bala* and *Norwood* were decided under Article 17, and certainly it is not easy to accept that they were "extreme cases" that required exceptional action on the part of the European Court. As I said, it is not my intention to discuss here if the Court's decisions in these four cases was the right one or not. However, it is difficult not to get the impression that, in comparison with the decisions on conflicts generated by expressions of anti-Semitic negationism, the Court applied different and less strict

[79]ECtHR [GC], *Perinçek v. Switzerland*, 15 Oct. 2015, para. 114.

[80]It is true that para. 114 of *Perinçek* refers to a "recent" position of the Court. However, although *Garaudy* and *Norwood* are of 2003 and 2004 respectively, *M'Bala* was decided five days after *Perinçek*. And those three cases are cited repeatedly in *Perinçek* without any indication that the Court had the intention to introduce a new jurisprudence (indeed, it looks quite the opposite).

standards to the speech against Armenian genocide.[81] And, in such a delicate matter, it is essential to keep homogeneous criteria and justify very persuasively any inequality in the treatment of apparently comparable situations.

7 Public Morals as a Notion That Could Justify Limitations on Freedom of Expression

I would like to refer now to some questions that relate to the protection of public morals, which is mentioned by Article 10.2 of the Convention among the aims that may justify restrictions on freedom of expression—and on other rights recognized by the European Convention.[82] In this regard, it should be borne in mind that, to be acceptable, it is not sufficient that limitations or sanctions on the exercise of freedom of expression are based on the concept of public morals in the abstract; they must be measures specifically "prescribed by law" (with the aim of the protection of public morals).[83]

Of the various notions enumerated by the European Convention to justify limitations on freedoms, public morals are probably the most ethereal one, the one that is most difficult to apply and to apprehend in its precise details. It is likely also the one that makes jurists feel less at ease and takes them out of their comfort zone. In fact, so far it has been only rarely used by the Strasbourg Court, thus evincing a reluctance that is shared by many European jurisdictions.[84]

---

[81]As the German judge Angelica Nussberger noted in her separate opinion, the explanation provided by the ECtHR to distinguish those situations, in ECtHR [GC], *Perinçek v. Switzerland*, 15 Oct. 2015, paras. 209–212 and 242–250, is not very convincing.

[82]In reality, Article 10.2 ECtHR mentions just "morals", but the comparison with other articles of the Convention—including Article 9, on religious freedom—leaves no doubt about the fact that it is the protection of public morals, and not private morals, what could justify the application of restrictive measures to the exercise of freedom of expression. Morals are mentioned specifically in articles 6, 8, 9, 10 and 11 of the European Convention.

[83]As is well-known, the reference to the "law" must be interpreted as comprising not only legislation but also case law, regulations and administrative praxis. The requirement of being "prescribed by law" is inspired by legal certainty, so that citizens can reasonably foresee the consequences of their actions. For a more detailed explanation of it, with references, see Martínez-Torrón (2005), pp. 597–598.

[84]One of the most indicative cases in Strasbourg in this regard is ECtHR, *Gough v. United Kingdom*, 28 Oct. 2014, concerning public nudity. The applicant was a British citizen who, convinced of the benefits of public nudity, attempted to promote it by walking totally naked in various places, earning the nickname "the naked rambler", which made him arrested in multiple occasions. Significantly, the cause used by the British authorities for his detention and subsequent trial was "breach of the peace". The issue of public morals was virtually not mentioned by the British courts (at least in the version given by the ECtHR). And the references that the European Court itself made to public morals in its judgment were few and formulaic. The Court concluded that neither Article 8 nor Article 10 had been violated.

It is perhaps revealing that a number of the few judgments that have made reference to public morals involve either the protection of the life of the unborn[85] or limitations on adoption by persons of non-traditional sexual orientation.[86] With regard to freedom of expression, prior to *Sekmadienis*, in 2018, we find three main judgments: *Handyside* (1976),[87] *Müller* (1988),[88] and *Mouvement Raëlien* (2012).[89] As mentioned at the beginning of this paper, *Handyside* defined some key principles on the guarantee of freedom of expression; the application has its origin in the judicial prohibition and seizure of a book aimed at teenagers, which was deemed to be against public morals because it contained some obscene passages and some others of anarchist orientation, inciting to rebellion against authority within the family. *Müller* concerned the confiscation, ordered by the Swiss courts, of three large paintings that contained gross obscene representations that included scenes of sodomy, fellatio and bestiality; the paintings were to be displayed in an exhibition, of free access, held as part of the celebrations of the 500th anniversary of the Canton of Fribourg's entry into the Swiss Confederation. *Mouvement Raëlien* involved the prohibition of a poster campaign programmed by the Raëlian movement, which described itself as religious, aimed at attracting new followers; the campaign was to be developed in the public spaces of the Swiss town of Neuchâtel but the Swiss authorities considered the campaign immoral and against the public order, based on the references of the Raëlians' doctrine to "geniocracy", human cloning, eugenics and "sensual meditation" (the latter, according to the Swiss authorities, could lead to abuse of children, which in some of the group's sources were described as "privileged sexual objects"). In those three judgments, the ECtHR held that there was no violation of freedom of expression and gave priority to the national margin of appreciation to determine the reach and consequences of the protection of public morals. *Handyside* and *Müller* were adopted by a large majority of the judges, and *Mouvement Raëlien* was decided by a divided Grand Chamber: nine votes to eight.

If we turn now to *Sekmadienis*, probably the most interesting aspect of this judgment is the relationship between public morals, freedom of expression and religious freedom, especially on account of the reason alleged by Lithuanian authorities to justify the limitation on freedom of expression. As mentioned above,[90] and without any intention to go into the details of the judgment more than is strictly necessary, the case involved an advertising campaign to introduce a new clothing

[85]See ECtHR [GC], *A, B and C v. Ireland*, 16 Dec. 2010; ECtHR [GC], *Evans v. United Kingdom*, 10 Apr. 2007; ECtHR [GC], *Vo v. France*, 8 Jul. 2004; ECtHR, *Open Door and Dublin Well Woman v. Ireland*, 29 Oct. 1992. Indicative of the significance that the Court recognized to those cases is the fact that all of them were decided by the Grand Chamber (or by the Court in plenary session, which was the approximate equivalent before the reform of the Court in 1998).

[86]ECtHR, *Fretté v. France*, 26 Feb. 2002; ECtHR [GC], *X, Y and Z v. United Kingdom*, 22 Apr. 1997.

[87]ECtHR, *Handyside v. United Kingdom*, 7 Dec. 1976.

[88]ECtHR, *Müller and others v. Switzerland*, 24 May 1988.

[89]ECtHR [GC], *Mouvement Raëlien Suisse v. Switzerland*, 13 Jul. 2012.

[90]See supra note 3 and accompanying text.

line, which displayed three advertisements in twenty hoardings in public areas of Vilnius, using humorously some characters and words of implicit, but clear, religious connotation. Following the complaints of a number of citizens, the State bodies for consumer protection and regulation of commercial publicity initiated review proceedings and concluded that, because of its frivolous attitude towards central figures of Christianity, the advertising campaign had gone beyond the limits of decency that public morals imposed. Having been consulted, the Catholic Bishops Conference of Lithuania expressed the same opinion, declaring that the advertisements degraded sacred persons and offended the feelings of Christians. The removal of the campaign was ordered (it had been active only a few weeks in Vilnius) and a moderate fine (less than 600 euros) was imposed on the company.

When we compare the facts in *Sekmadienis* with those in other judgments mentioned above, the most distinctive factor is that the national law considered that respect for the religious beliefs and feelings of others was an integral part of public morals. In *Handyside* and *Müller*, the notion of morals—which was no doubt operative in British and Swiss law—appeared dissociated from religious elements. The same occurred in *Mouvement Raëlien*: the circumstance that the protagonist of the vetoed campaign was a group self-described as religious is accidental; the action of the Swiss authorities would have been the same whatever was the nature (real or apparent) of the group involved. In *Otto-Preminger-Institut*, as in other subsequent cases decided in Strasbourg (including *Giniewski* and *E.S.*), the national authorities alleged that certain sanctions on the exercise of freedom of expression were justified as necessary to ensure respect for religious feelings, which they understood was a part of the freedom of religion protected by Article 9 of the Convention. Such restrictive measures, therefore, were legitimate as their aim was the protection of the rights of others.

In *Sekmadienis*, the approach of the national authorities was different. They did not affirm that citizens have the right to have their religious feelings protected; what they asserted is that the State must ensure the maintenance of public morals, which include the preservation of an atmosphere of religious tolerance. Lithuanian law envisages the prohibition of advertisements that infringe public morals;[91] and both the courts and administrative practice interpret the law in the sense that public morals demands that every form of expression respects the religious beliefs and feelings of the population. The Supreme Administrative Court was especially clear about this when it declared that religion contributes to the moral development of society and therefore the inappropriate use of religious symbols is contrary to commonly accepted moral norms.[92] The same court also observed that such principle is particularly applicable to expressions that have a purely commercial purpose and are not intended to contribute to any public debate about religion, its symbols, and its proper place in civil society.[93]

[91]See ECtHR, *Sekmadienis v. Lithuania*, 30 Jan. 2018, paras. 34–35.

[92]*Ibid.*, para. 25.

[93]*Ibid.*, para. 29.

If we turn to the judgment of the Court of Strasbourg, probably it is not difficult to agree with its outcome. The Court held that, in the specific circumstances of the case, the restriction on freedom of expression was not sufficiently justified (which on the other hand, according to a separate concurring opinion of one of the judges, should not be understood as giving carte blanche to offend religious symbols in public[94]). However, it is more difficult to share the rationale of the Court, which focussed on a summary and almost formulaic account of general principles and passed like on tiptoe through the important issues, beginning with the very notion of public morals.

Indeed, the ECtHR has been reluctant so far to go into the concept of public morals in depth and has merely referred to it in the minimum possible terms when it was indispensable to justify its decision. It would appear as it the Court felt uncomfortable talking of public morals, perhaps assuming that a secular judge must not speak about morals—this would be a mistake, because public morals, in the sense that it is used by the European Convention as well as by many national laws, are a legal and not a moral notion. As a matter of fact, since *Handyside*—and *Sekmadienis* is no exception—the ECtHR's position on public morals has been characterized by its lack of definition, in spite of how important this concept is, like all concepts that can be used to legitimize limitations on fundamental freedoms. In the few times the Court has referred to public morals, normally it has just reiterated some general statements: that the notion of public morals is unprecise and continuously changing;[95] that it is part of the general interest; and that this is a matter in which, not existing a European consensus, a broad margin of appreciation must be recognized to national authorities (in the traditional formulation of the margin of appreciation doctrine by the Court, the less consensus there is among European countries on a particular issue, the bigger is the national margin of appreciation, and vice versa[96]). Certainly not much.

I am afraid that, in *Sekmadienis*, the ECtHR has lost another opportunity to introduce new nuances in some of its old doctrines. In a number of prior judgments, the Court could have said more about the function of the European consensus vis-à-vis the national margin of appreciation[97]—which would have been very welcome in order to avoid surprisingly odd interpretations of that doctrine, as the ones provided in *Leyla Şahin* or *S.A.S.*[98] In *Mouvement Raëlien*, the Court missed the chance to elaborate on an important aspect of freedom of expression: if the limitations enumerated in Article 10.2 of the Convention, including public morals, must be construed differently depending on whether the speech in question goes through private channels or through spaces or media that are controlled and managed

[94]Concurring opinion of the Maltese judge Vincent de Gaetano.

[95]See ECtHR, *Handyside v. United Kingdom*, 7 Dec. 1976, para. 48.

[96]See supra note 20.

[97]In this regard, see the interesting remarks of the ad hoc Irish judge Mary Finlay Geoghegan in her concurring opinion to the judgment ECtHR [GC], *A, B and C v. Ireland*, 16 Dec. 2010.

[98]ECtHR [GC], *Leyla Şahin v. Turkey*, 10 Nov. 2005; ECtHR [GC], *S.A.S. v. France*, 1 Jul. 2014.

by public authorities or institutions.[99] And, also in *Mouvement Raëlien*, it would had been desirable that the Court enunciated clearer criteria to distinguish when a speech can be deemed predominantly commercial despite coming from a religious group (real or alleged); this is a very significant issue characterized by the convergence of proselytism, religious freedom and freedom of expression.

In *Sekmadienis*, perhaps the most important issue that the ECtHR left aside was the relationship between public morals and religion, in a double sense. On the one hand, to what extent the notion of public morals used by State law may include elements deriving from secularized religious principles (this issue is only incidentally alluded by the judgments, in the light of some unclear references to tensions between majority and minority[100]). And on the other hand, if a national legal system can adopt the position that public morals involve respect for the religious feelings of people. This was precisely the approach taken by the Lithuanian authorities and it is not per se an unreasonable idea. It needs, however, to be carefully elaborated to avoid the risk that a notion that is valid in itself is transformed in practice into an instrument of moral authoritarianism, thus hindering legitimate expressions of discrepancy with regard to ethical values held by the majority, which would be to the detriment of one of the central freedoms guaranteed by the European Convention. Ultimately, these are questions that connect with the broader theme of the relationships between religion and culture, and which is the role of those relationships in the context of a society that must protect both freedom of expression and freedom of religion—i.e., a society not characterized by the political predominance of a majority religion (even if it is socially predominant).

In my view, *Sekmadienis* was an "easy case" from the perspective of which its fair outcome should be. Nevertheless, because of the importance of the questions it raised, it should have received more attention by the Strasbourg Court. Certainly, we cannot expect from the European Court a treatise on religion and public morals, but some more clear guidance in this area would have been advisable. The Court could—and probably should—have provided criteria that could serve as points of reference for State laws to avoid two mistakes: to eradicate moral dissent from society; and to misread the *Sekmadienis* judgment—as one of the judges warned—as a sort of carte blanche to trivialize public offences against religious symbols in a society which has decided that such offences run counter the ambiance of tolerance and respect required for the peaceful exercise of freedoms.

---

[99]The separate opinions of some judges paid much more attention than the judgment to this issue, which in my view is of the utmost importance.

[100]See ECtHR, *Sekmadienis v. Lithuania*, 30 Jan. 2018, paras. 80–82.

8 Towards an Integrating Conception of Human Rights

One of the main challenges that contemporary democratic societies must face is to mark itineraries that facilitate adequate and reasonable solutions of conflicts between the exercise of fundamental rights by different persons. The proliferation of such situations is a fact that can be read in various ways. Among the reasons that may explain the increase in this type of conflicts there are two which, in my view, are of particular significance.

In the first place, a progressively extensive interpretation of human rights. There is a tendency to enlarge the range of conducts, identities and life attitudes which are included within the protectable content of human rights. And, in parallel, new rights have been added to classic rights, sometimes in a controversial fashion—and not always in binding legal or international documents but often in the political discourse, at least in the West. Such expansion of the legal protection of certain human characteristics and choices naturally multiplies the possibilities of negative interaction between the exercise of fundamental freedoms by different people, especially when there is a remarkable disparity between each other's conception of which is the prevailing or more legitimate claim in case of clash.

In the second place, such negative interaction becomes more frequent as fundamental rights are increasingly exercised from the perspective of a purely individualist position. The beginning of the culture of human rights had its centre of gravity in the recognition of the dignity of human beings, which is intrinsically linked to their moral dimension, with all it implies of ethical responsibility—not only individual but also social responsibility. The success of the movement in favour of human rights came in the twentieth century, after two devastating world wars that injected into our culture the conviction that reconstructing societies based on peace and justice was only possible if they were founded on human dignity and human rights. A few generations later, however, the same societies, being chronologically and emotionally distanced from those tragedies, have ended up accentuating what human rights have of individual claim in the legislative and judicial realm, and in parallel blurring what human rights have of contribution to social harmony and cohesion. The notion of the essentiality of human rights has been preserved but we have lost sight of why they are essential. This paves the way for an implicit social legitimation of any exercise of rights, even though it does not have any other purpose than the instant interest—here and now—of the individual exercising those rights.

If there is a fundamental freedom whose exercise from a strictly individualist perspective is susceptible of causing conflicts, this is freedom of expression, and even more in the Internet era. It is a freedom easy to exercise, and its negative effects are not normally either immediate or tangible, and hence there is a tendency to accept them as the "reasonable price" we must pay for freedom in a democracy. No doubt, such tendency is based on sensible grounds but at the same time we should not underestimate the power—sometimes destructive—of words.

Social conflicts that have freedom of expression as protagonist require a careful legal treatment, by legislation and especially by the courts; this applies also to conflicts involving the sensitive realm of religion and beliefs. The purpose of this paper has been to point out some elements that I think should be taken into account in the debate about the criteria that must define such legal treatment. In any event, we should bear in mind that solving this type of conflicts is a responsibility of the entire society and not only of the law and the State institutions. The pernicious effects of excessive or abusive free speech could be often remedied with a spontaneous and vigorous social response more efficiently than with the use of legal instruments.

Furthermore, if we look beyond conflicts generated by the exercise of freedom of expression, it is urgent to retrieve the meaning of human dignity as a central notion around which we can build societies based on the respect for the human rights of everyone, and not only the rights of the majority that gets hold of political power—or the control of the media. In ideologically and culturally plural societies, it is natural that competing notions of human rights are bound to coexist. The real challenge is to make possible for those notions to live together, with the maximum degree of mutual respect, instead of having the dominant position trying to banish or conquer the competitor.[101]

References

Arai-Takahashi Y (2002) The margin of appreciation Doctrine and the principle of proportionality in the Jurisprudence of the ECtHR. Intersentia, Antwerp

Baker CE (1997) Harm, liberty, and free speech. South Calif Law Rev 70:979–1020

Combalía Z (2009) Libertad de expresión y difamación de las religiones: el debate en Naciones Unidas a propósito del conflicto de las caricaturas de Mahoma. Revista General de Derecho Canónico y Derecho Eclesiástico del Estado 19:2–5

Cram I (2009) The Danish cartoons, offensive expression, and democratic legitimacy. In: Hare I et al (eds) Extreme speech and democracy. Oxford University Press, Oxford, pp 311–330

Greenawalt K (1996) Fighting words: individuals, communities and liberties of speech. Princeton University Press

Hare I et al (2009) Extreme speech and democracy. Oxford University Press, Oxford

Herz M et al (2012) The content and context of hate speech. Rethinking regulation and responses. Cambridge University Press, Cambridge

Howard E (2018) Freedom of expression and religious hate speech in Europe. Routledge, New York

Iglesias Vila M (2017) Subsidiarity, margin of appreciation and international adjudication within a cooperative conception of human rights. Int J Const Law 15:393–413

Ignatieff M (2005) American exceptionalism and human rights. Princeton University Press

Leigh I (2011) Damned if they do, damned if they don't: the European Court of Human Rights and the protection of religion from attack. Res Publica 17(1):55–73

Lidsky L (2011) Public Forum 2.0. Boston Univ Law Rev 91:1975–2028

[101]Some interesting initiatives with this orientation have recently emerged in scholarly circles. For instance, the project "Human Dignity for Everyone Everywhere", which has produced a text already translated into several languages: the "Punta del Este Declaration on Human Dignity for Everyone Everywhere". See https://www.dignityforeveryone.org (accessed on 30 January 2021).

Martín Sánchez I (2012) El discurso del odio en el ámbito del Consejo de Europa. Revista General de Derecho Canónico y Derecho Eclesiástico del Estado 28:1–33
Martínez-Torrón J (2005) Limitations on religious freedom in the case law of the European Court of Human Rights. Emory Int Law Rev 19:587–636
Martínez-Torrón J (2007) Freedom of expression versus freedom of religion in the European Court of human Rights. In: Sajó A (ed) Censorial sensitivities: free speech and religion in a fundamentalist world. Eleven International, Utrecht, pp 233–269
Martínez-Torrón J (2014) ¿Libertad de expresión amordazada? Libertad de expresión y libertad de religión en la jurisprudencia de Estrasburgo. In: Martínez-Torrón J & Cañamares S (eds) Tensiones entre libertad de expresión y libertad religiosa. Tirant lo Blanch, Valencia, pp 83–120
Martínez-Torrón J (2015) Strasbourg's approach to religion in the pluralist democracies of Europe. In: Griffith-Jones R & Hill M (eds) Magna Carta, religion and the rule of law. Cambridge University, Cambridge, pp 281–300
Martínez-Torrón J (2017) Hate speech, libertad de expresión y sentimientos religiosos. Estudios Eclesiásticos 92:749–767
Matsuda M et al (1993) Words that wound. Westview Press, Boulder
Minow M (2000) Regulating hatred: whose speech, whose crimes, whose power? – an Essay for Kenneth Karst. UCLA Law Rev 47:1253–1277
Oetheimer M (2007) Freedom of expression in Europe: case-law concerning Article 10 of the European Convention on Human Rights. Council of Europe, Strasbourg
O'Neil RM (2012–2013) Hate speech, fighting words, and beyond—why American law is unique. Albany Law Rev 76:467–498
Pérez-Madrid F (2009) Incitación al odio religioso o "hate speech" y libertad de expresión. Revista General de Derecho Canónico y Derecho Eclesiástico del Estado 19:1–28
Post RC (1988) Cultural heterogeneity and law: pornography, blasphemy, and the first amendment. Calif Law Rev 76:297–335
Smet S (2018) E.S. v. Austria: Freedom of Expression versus Religious Feelings. The Sequel. Strasbourg Observers
Tomlins S (2013) The freedom to offend? How the "Mohammad Cartoon Controversy" has influenced public debate on Canada's hate speech regulation. J Church State 57:44–71
Waldron J (2012) The Harm in Hate speech. Harvard University Press, Cambridge

Javier Martínez-Torrón is a Professor of Law at Complutense University and Titular Member of the International Academy of Comparative Law. Visiting professor, lecturer and researcher in numerous Universities and institutions in the five continents (among them Stanford, Cambridge, Oxford, Chicago, Columbia, Berkeley, Harvard, Freiburg, Strasbourg, Turin, Messina, Haifa, UNAM (Mexico), and National University of Colombia). His academic work focuses on the legal analysis of freedom of religion or belief and its interactions with other fundamental rights, from a comparative and international perspective. His writings, published in 28 countries and in 13 languages, include 25 books as author, co-author or editor, and more than 130 essays in legal periodicals or collective volumes. His recent books include Law, Religion, and Freedom: Conceptualizing a Common Right (co-ed., Routledge, 2021); COVID-19 y libertad religiosa (co-ed. Iustel, 2021); Religion and Law in Spain (2d ed, Wolters-Kluwer, 2018); Great Christian Jurists in Spanish History (co-ed., Cambridge U.P., 2018).

The Responsibility of Internet Portal Providers for Readers' Comments. Argumentation and Balancing in the Case of *Delfi AS v. Estonia*

Robert Alexy

Contents

1 Introduction 199
2 The Main Elements of Principles Theory 200
2.1 Rules and Principles 200
2.2 Proportionality 201
2.2.1 Suitability 201
2.2.2 Necessity 202
2.2.3 Proportionality in the Narrower Sense 202
2.2.4 Weight Formula 203
3 An Analysis of the *Delfi* Case on the Basis of Principles Theory 205
3.1 The Facts 205
3.2 The Collision 205
3.2.1 The Subsumption of the Activity of *Delfi* under the Scope of Article 10 ECHR 206
3.2.2 The Internet Triangle 207
3.3 The Abstract Weight Variable and the Reliability Variable 208
4 The Intensities of the Interferences 208
4.1 The Intensity of the Interference with B's Personality Rights 208
4.2 The Proportionality of the Interference with C's Freedom of Expression 210
4.2.1 Necessity 210
4.2.2 Proportionality in the Narrower Sense: Weight Formula 211
References 213

I should like to thank Stanley L. Paulson for suggestions and advice on matters of English style.

R. Alexy (✉)
University of Kiel, Kiel, Germany
e-mail: alexy@law.uni-kiel.de

M. Elósegui et al. (eds.), *The Rule of Law in Europe*,
https://doi.org/10.1007/978-3-030-56001-0_12

1 Introduction

The *Delfi* Grand Chamber judgement of the European Court of Human Rights (ECtHR) concerns the question of the liability of the provider of an internet portal, in our case *Delfi*, on which articles are published in connection with the call to add comments—be they anonymously or not—on these articles. In the *Delfi* case, a goodly number of comments were published anonymously, among them some that constituted hate speech and incitement to violence.[1] The Estonian Supreme Court held the provider of the portal, *Delfi*, liable for the comments of the commentators.[2] The Grand Chamber followed this line. With this, a considerable step in a great new field has been taken.

New experiments and new discoveries are challenges for theories in the natural sciences. Something analogous is true of law. New cases present challenges to theories in law. My question is: can principles theory meet the challenges presented by the *Delfi* case? In order to answer this question I will present first the main elements of principles theory, which will then be applied in an analysis of the *Delfi* case.

2 The Main Elements of Principles Theory

2.1 Rules and Principles

Principles theory begins with the norm-theoretic distinction between rules and principles.[3] Rules are norms that require something definitively. They are definitive commands. Their form of application is subsumption. If a rule is valid and if its conditions of application are fulfilled, it is definitively required that exactly what it demands be done. If this is done, the rule is complied with; if this is not done, the rule is not complied with. By contrast, principles are optimization requirements. As such, they demand that something be realized "to the greatest extent possible given the legal and factual possibilities".[4] Rules aside, the legal possibilities are determined essentially by opposing principles. For this reason, principles, each taken alone, always comprise a merely prima facie requirement. The determination of the appropriate degree of satisfaction of one principle relative to the requirements of other principles is brought about by balancing. Thus, balancing is the specific form of application of principles.

[1]ECtHR [GC], *Delfi AS vs. Estonia*, 16 Jun. 2015, No. 64569/09, para.18.

[2]*Ibid.*, para. 30–1.

[3]See Alexy (1985), pp. 47–49.

[4]*Ibid.*, p. 47.

2.2 *Proportionality*

The nature of principles as optimization requirements leads straightaway to a necessary connection between principles and proportionality. The principle of proportionality (*Verhältnismäßigkeitsgrundsatz*) consists of three sub-principles: the principles of suitability, of necessity, and of proportionality in the narrower sense. Principles *qua* optimization requirements require optimization relative both to what is factually possible and to what is legally possible. The principles of suitability and necessity refer to optimization relative to the factual possibilities. The principle of proportionality in the narrower sense concerns optimization relative to the legal possibilities.

2.2.1 Suitability

The first sub-principle, the principle of suitability, precludes the adoption of means that obstruct the realization of at least one principle without promoting any principle or goal for which it has been adopted. If a means M, adopted in order to promote the principle P_1, is not suitable for this purpose, but obstructs the realization of P_2, then there are no costs either to P_1 or P_2 if M is omitted, but there are costs to P_2 if M is adopted. Thus, P_1 and P_2 taken together may be realized to a higher degree relative to what is factually possible if M is abandoned. P_1 and P_2, when *taken together*—that is, as elements of a single system—proscribe the use of M. This shows that the principle of suitability is nothing other than an expression of the idea of Pareto-optimality. One position can be improved without detriment to the other.

An example of the violation of the principle of suitability is found in a decision of the German Federal Constitutional Court. The law in question required that not only persons who apply for a general hunting licence have to pass a weapons examination but also persons who apply exclusively for a falconry licence. The Court argued that the weapons examination for falconers is not suitable for promoting the "proper exercise of these activities as intended by the legislator".[5] Therefore, "no substantially clear reason"[6] existed for the infringement of the general freedom of action on the part of the falconer, as guaranteed by Article 2 Paragraph 1 of the Basic Law. For that reason, the regulation was declared disproportional[7] and, consequently, unconstitutional.

---

[5]Decisions of the Federal Constitutional Court (*Entscheidungen des Bundesverfassungsgerichts*; hereafter: BVerfGE) 55, 159 (166).

[6]BVerfGE 55, 159 (167).

[7]BVerfGE 55, 159 (166).

2.2.2 Necessity

Cases in which laws are declared unconstitutional for reasons of unsuitability are rare. Normally the measure applied by the legislator will at least promote his aims to a certain degree. This suffices for suitability. For this reason, the practical relevance of the sub-principle of suitability is rather low. The situation is completely different where the second sub-principle of the principle of proportionality, the principle of necessity, is concerned. This principle requires that of two means promoting P_1 that are, broadly speaking, equally suitable, the one that interferes less intensively with P_2 has to be chosen. If there exists a less intensively interfering and equally suitable means, one position can be improved at no cost to the other.[8] Under this condition, P_1 and P_2, *taken together*, require that the less intensively interfering means be applied. This is, again, a case of Pareto-optimality.

An example is the decision of the Federal Constitutional Court on sweets, especially in the form of Easter rabbits and Santa Claus-figures that consist of puffed rice. In order to protect consumers from mistakenly taking those puffed rice sweets to be chocolate products, a ban on puffed rice sweets was issued. The Court argued that consumer protection could be achieved "in an equally effective but less incisive way by a duty of labelling".[9] For this reason, the ban was declared to be a violation of the principle of necessity and, therefore, disproportional.

2.2.3 Proportionality in the Narrower Sense

Just as with the principle of suitability, the principle of necessity concerns optimization relative to the factual possibilities. Optimization relative to the factual possibilities consists in avoiding avoidable costs. Costs, however, are unavoidable when principles collide. Then balancing becomes necessary. Balancing is the subject of the third sub-principle of the principle of proportionality, the principle of proportionality in the narrower sense. This principle tells us what optimization relative to the legal possibilities is. In the1985 *A Theory of Constitutional Rights* I expressed the requirement of optimization relative to the legal possibilities by means of a rule that I called the "Law of Balancing".[10] This rule states:

> The greater the degree of non-satisfaction of, or detriment to, one principle, the greater must be the importance of satisfying the other.

---

[8]Where the question of whether the less or the more intensively interfering means is chosen arises, the principle of necessity presupposes that all other principles or goals are indifferent with respect to this choice. If, however, there exists a third principle or goal, P_3, that is affected negatively by the adoption of the means interfering less intensively with P_2, then the case cannot be decided by considerations concerning Pareto-optimality. When costs are unavoidable, balancing becomes necessary.

[9]BVerfGE 53, 135 (146).

[10]Alexy (1985), p. 102.

The Law of Balancing excludes, inter alia, an intensive interference with principle P_1 that is justified only by a low importance assigned to the satisfaction of the colliding principle P_2. Such a solution would not be an optimization of P_1 *together with* P_2.

2.2.4 Weight Formula

The Law of Balancing has been criticized by Aharon Barak for considering on the side of the limited right only "the extent of the constitutional right's limitation,"[11] that is, "the degree of its limitation,"[12] whereas on the side of the justification of the limitation or interference the importance of the colliding principle is to be found. He is, without any doubt, correct. The formulation of the Law of Balancing has been developed with an eye to a standard situation that appears with great frequency.[13] For a deeper, more precise and complete analysis, the Law of Balancing has to be elaborated further. This further elaboration amounts to the Weight Formula.[14] The Weight Formula defines the weight of a principle P_i in a concrete case, that is, the concrete weight of P_i relative to a colliding principle P_j ($W_{i,j}$), as the quotient, first, of the product of the intensity of the interference with P_i (I_i) and the abstract weight of P_i (W_i) and the degree of reliability of the assumptions concerning what the measure in question means for the non-realization of P_i (R_i), and, second, the product of the corresponding values with respect to P_j, now related to the realization of P_j. It runs as follows:

$$W_{i,j} = \frac{I_i \cdot W_i \cdot R_i}{I_j \cdot W_j \cdot R_j}$$

It appears that Barak's "importance of preventing the limitation of the constitutional right"[15] is the same as the product of I_i and W_i, whereas his "importance of the proper purpose"[16] is the same as the product of I_j and W_j. If this should be the case, Barak's critique applies to the original formulation of the Law of Balancing but not to its elaboration by means of the Weight Formula.[17]

---

[11]Barak (2012), p. 6.

[12]*Ibid.*, p. 364.

[13]See Alexy (2007), pp. 15–17.

[14]See Alexy (2003), pp. 443–448.

[15]Barak (2012), p. 6.

[16]*Ibid.*

[17]A further element in Barak's reconstruction of balancing is probability; ibid., p. 362. It is a deep question as to whether probability has to be distinguished from reliability or certainty (R) as an epistemic modality, or whether each of them can be reduced to the other. If, as I assume, they cannot be reduced to each other, it is conceivable that probability is exclusively an element of I_i and of I_j and that the variable "R" refers exclusively to reliability as an epistemic modality. The latter would give sense to sentences like: "It is clear that the danger for the right is 20 percent", "It is plausible that the danger for the right is 20 percent", and "It is not excluded that the danger for the right is 20 percent."

A formula like the Weight Formula, which expresses a quotient of two products, is sensible only if all of the factors can be represented by numbers. This is the problem of graduation. Elsewhere,[18] I have proposed a discrete, that is, a non-continuous triadic scale, in which geometric sequences are implemented. This scale assigns the values "light" (*l*), "moderate" or "medium" (*m*), and "serious" (*s*) to the intensity of interference and to the abstract weights. These values are expressed by the numbers 2^0, 2^1, and 2^2, that is, by 1, 2, and 4. Where the epistemic side is concerned, that is, R_i and R_j, one can work with the stages "reliable" or "certain" (*r*), "plausible" (*p*), and "not evidently false" (*e*), to which the numbers 2^0, 2^{-1}, and 2^{-2}, that is, 1, ½, and ¼, are to be assigned.[19] By means of these triads, most of the decisions of constitutional courts can be grasped. Where they do not suffice, that is, where one has to introduce still more attenuated graduations, they can be extended to double-triadic scales.[20]

The epistemic variables R_i and R_j refer to empirical premises as well as to normative premises. This can be expressed by the following equation:

$$R_i = R_i^e \cdot R_i^n$$

This equation might be called the "reliability equation". In cases in which both empirical and normative reliability are in question, for R_i and R_j one must substitute the respective products on the right side of the reliability equation. In this way, a refined version of the Weight Formula[21] appears on stage:

$$W_{i,j} = \frac{I_i \cdot W_i \cdot R_i^e \cdot R_i^n}{I_j \cdot W_j \cdot R_j^e \cdot R_j^n}$$

The two Weight Formulas show how many constellations are possible in balancing. If one takes the refined Weight Formula with four variables on each side, that is, with eight variables altogether, one acquires, on the basis of the two triadic scales, 3^8, that is, 6561 constellations.[22] In case of the elementary Weight Formula with three variables on each side, one acquires, again on the basis of the two triadic scales, 3^6, that is, 729 constellations. It is an important point concerning the rationality of balancing that this diversity has a well-ordered, not a chaotic, character. This plays a great role in the answer to the question of whether at least some constitutional rights, such as human dignity, have an absolute character.[23]

[18] Alexy (2007), pp. 20–26.

[19] *Ibid.*, p. 25.

[20] *Ibid.*, pp. 22–23.

[21] See on this Alexy (2014), pp. 513–515.

[22] *Ibid.*, p. 522.

[23] Alexy (2015), p. 511.

3 An Analysis of the *Delfi* Case on the Basis of Principles Theory

3.1 The Facts

In Estonia in the winter, ice roads are used in order to cross the frozen sea as connections between the mainland and certain islands. In January 2006, *Delfi* published on its portal an article with the title "SLK Destroyed Planned Ice Road". SLK is a company that provides a public ferry transport service between the mainland and certain islands. L. was the leading person in this company. The article attracted a great number of comments. In a considerable number of them, L. was insulted, some even constituted hate speech and incitement to violence. After L.'s lawyers had become engaged, the offensive comments were delated by *Delfi*. This was six weeks after their publication.

3.2 The Collision

The Court begins its assessment with the remark that the *Delfi* case concerns a new situation defined by "conflicting realities".[24] "[U]ser-generated expressive activity on the internet provides an unprecedented platform for the exercise of freedom of expression."[25] But this new freedom is connected with new dangers.

> Defamatory and other types of clearly unlawful speech, including hate speech and speech inciting violence, can be disseminated like never before, worldwide, in a matter of seconds, and sometimes remain persistently available online.[26]

These two realities are new, without any question. But the norms that have to be applied to them are old: freedom of expression, as guaranteed by Article 10 ECHR, and personality rights, as guaranteed in Article 8 ECHR.[27] With this, the door is opened to classify the *Delfi* problem as a problem of a collision between freedom of expression and protection of personality.

---

[24]ECtHR [GC], *Delfi AS vs. Estonia*, 16 Jun. 2015, No. 64569/09, para. 110.

[25]*Ibid.*

[26]*Ibid.*

[27]*Ibid.*

3.2.1 The Subsumption of the Activity of *Delfi* under the Scope of Article 10 ECHR

This general view on the new "conflicting realities",[28] on the one side, and Article 10 and Article 8 ECHR, on the other side, is, however, correct only if the activity of *Delfi* falls within the scope (*Tatbestand*) or in the protected area (*Schutzbereich*)[29] of Article 10 ECHR. This is the case if the activity of *Delfi* is an exercise of freedom of expression, that is, if *Delfi's* activities can be subsumed[30] under the concept of exercising freedom of expression.

This is the most important question of the decision.[31] There is no doubt that the authors of the comments fall within the scope of freedom of expression.[32] But that is not the issue of the case. The issue is whether *Delfi* as the provider of the internet portal, that is, as the initiator and promotor of the comments, falls within the scope of freedom of expression, too. The Court answers this in an affirmative way. Its main claim is:

> [T]he applicant company's involvement in making public the comments on its news articles on the Delfi news portal went beyond that of a passive, purely technical service provider.[33]

The publishing of news and comments on an internet portal is classified, following the line of the Estonian Supreme Court, as a kind of "journalistic activity", in spite of the fact that there exist considerable differences between a portal operator and a traditional publisher.[34]

Normally, the subsumption within the scope of a freedom right enhances freedom. Here, the opposite is the case. It restricts freedom. This happens by imposing liability on *Delfi* for the comments made by "third parties".[35] This is an ascription of comments that violate personality rights made by third parties to *Delfi*. *Delfi* is made

---

[28] *Ibid.*

[29] See on this Alexy (1985), pp. 196–200.

[30] On the relation between balancing and subsumption see Alexy (2003), pp. 433–449.

[31] As a different construction, there seems to exist in principle an alternative to subsuming *Delfi's* activity under freedom of expression. If one considers the activity of *Delfi* as a pure performance of economic activities, and if one has a constitutional provision like Article 12 German Basic Law, which protects freedom of profession, one can nevertheless connect free speech responsibilities resulting from the protection of personality rights with this economic activity. Economic activity that interferes with personality rights cannot be considered without taking both aspects into account. Economic activity as such has, for instance, nothing to do with protection of environment. But the proportionality of the economic activity can profoundly depend on its environmental effects. Even if *Delfi's* activity were considered as only economic, all points attributed to it under the aspect of freedom of expression could nevertheless be captured. They would appear as the subjects of the principle of personality as countervailing or opposing principle.

[32] ECtHR [GC], *Delfi AS vs. Estonia*, 16 Jun. 2015, No. 64569/09, para. 140.

[33] *Ibid*, para. 146.

[34] *Ibid*, para. 112.

[35] *Ibid*, para. 140.

responsible for comments that do not stem from it, but would not have been possible without *Delfi's* activities. One might call this the "ascription thesis".

3.2.2 The Internet Triangle

The ascription thesis, resulting from the subsumption of the internet portal provider *Delfi* under freedom of expression as provided by Article 10 ECHR, leads to a structure that might be called the "internet triangle". Three legal subjects are connected in this triangle by requirements of human rights. The classical case of a connection of three legal subjects by human or constitutional rights results from the horizontal effect of these rights.[36] This classical horizontal effect concerns a triangle with two private subjects at the base and the state at the top. In the internet triangle all three subjects are private subjects. This non-classical conception of the horizontal effect places a private subject, the provider of the internet portal, in our case *Delfi*, at the position traditionally held by the state. It is contested whether such altogether private triangles are compatible with the principles of a democratic constitutional state at all, and, if they are compatible, at which point the state has to be reintroduced in one way or other. The answers to these questions depend essentially on the answer to the question of whether a completely private internet triangle can provide a rational way to solve collisions of the rights connected in it. That shall be our theme. In order to provide an answer a closer look at the structure of the private internet triangle is necessary.

At the base of the triangle the two private subjects directly involved are to be found, the commentator, we can call him "*A*", and the victim of the comment, we can call him "*B*". In our case this is L., the leading person in the public ferry company. At the top we find the provider of the internet portal, in our case *Delfi*. This position might be called "*C*". *B* has a right against *A* not to be violated in his personality rights, and a right against *C* to be protected against violations committed by *A*. *C* has a right against *A* to interfere with his freedom of speech in order to prevent violations of *B's* personality rights. On the other hand, *A* has a right against *C* that *C* respect his freedom of expression.

All this could be elaborated a great deal more. But this is not necessary for our purposes. The central problem of the *Delfi* decision is the responsibility of the internet portal provider for reader's comments. That concerns the relation between *B* and C in the triangle. It is of importance for the analysis of relations in the internet triangle that this analysis can begin with just one relation. In our case this is the relation between the victim and the provider, that is, between *B* and *C*.

---

[36]See on this Alexy (1985), pp. 351–365.

3.3 *The Abstract Weight Variable and the Reliability Variable*

The Weight Formula has, in its basic form, on each side three variables, the intensity of interference variable (I_i, I_j), the abstract weight variable (W_i, W_j), and the reliability variable (R_i, R_j). In the *Delfi* decision the abstract weights of the colliding principles are explicitly determined as equal: "Article 10 and 8 of the Convention deserve equal respect".[37] This implies that the abstract weight variables can be canceled. The reliability variables play no role in the argumentation of the Court. To be sure, the decision depends on many empirical assumptions. But questions concerning the quality of the empirical knowledge employed are not a theme here. Thus, the reliability variable is not explicitly in play. This means that in our case, as is so often the case, all depends on the intensities of the interferences, that is, on I_i and I_j.

4 The Intensities of the Interferences

4.1 *The Intensity of the Interference with B's Personality Rights*

L., the leading person in the public ferry company, in our case *B*, has claimed compensation for non-pecuniary damages with respect to 20 comments.[38] The Grand Chamber focuses on two things: "hate speech and incitement to violence",[39] "against L.".[40] Both are qualified many times as "clearly unlawful".[41] A closer analysis is explicitly classified as unnecessary.

> Thus, the establishment of their unlawful nature did not require any linguistic or legal analysis since the remarks were on their face manifestly unlawful.[42]

One might think that with this, we have left the field of balancing and principles theory. This, however, is not the case.

The thesis of the unlawfulness of hate speech and incitement to violence counts as a solution in the relation between the commentator and the victim of the comment, that is, between *A* and *B*, but not in the relation between the victim of the comment and the provider of the internet portal, that is, between *B* and *C*. This relation is the subject of the *Delfi* decision. As soon as the Court takes this into consideration, the argumentation surrounding proportionality becomes very intensive.

---

[37] ECtHR [GC], *Delfi AS vs. Estonia*, 16 Jun. 2015, No. 64569/09, para. 110. See also para. 139.

[38] *Ibid*, para. 18.

[39] *Ibid*, para. 115.

[40] *Ibid*, para. 114.

[41] *Ibid*, paras. 114, 115 and 140.

[42] *Ibid*, para. 117.

With this, we have a strong asymmetry in the proportionality analysis. On the one side only a thesis, the thesis of unlawfulness, and on the other side an abundance of arguments. This, however, does not mean that we have no classification of the intensity of interference with the personality rights of the victim of the comments. This classification is not explicitly formulated, but is implicit in the unlawfulness thesis. It says that hate speech and incitement to violence are serious (*s*) interferences—perhaps even very serious interferences as expressed by the double-triadic scale. The intensity of interference, accordingly, has to receive at least the value 4. This is supported by the general remark that:

> the ease, scope and speed of the dissemination of information on the Internet, and the persistence of the information once disclosed, which may considerably aggravate the effects of unlawful speech on the Internet compared to traditional media.[43]

The verb "aggravate" has a clear reference to the intensity of interference in the Weight Formula.

Another point ought to be added. The prohibition of hate speech and incitement to violence is without any doubt a rule. But it is nevertheless connected with principles, the principles of freedom of speech and the protection of personality. If one follows the wide theory of the scope of constitutional and human rights—which is far more closely connected with the rationality of legal argumentation than the narrow theory of the scope[44]—then the rule that prohibits hate speech and incitement to violence is the result of balancing freedom of speech against protection of personality. In the presentation of the main elements of principles theory, only one of the two laws of principles theory has been considered, the Law of Balancing as explicated by the Weight Formula. This law is intrinsically connected[45] with the second law of principles theory, the "Law of Colliding Principles".[46] It says, in non-technical terms:

> The circumstances under which one principle takes precedence over another constitute the conditions of a rule which has the same legal consequences as the principle taking precedence.[47]

In the circumstances *C*, hate speech and incitement to violence, the protection of personality takes precedence over freedom of speech. The protection of personality requires that both be forbidden. Therefore, the precedence, as result of balancing, implies the rule that hate speech and incitement to violence are forbidden.

---

[43] *Ibid*, para. 147.

[44] Alexy (1985), pp. 200–217.

[45] Alexy (2017), pp. 26–28.

[46] Alexy (1985), pp. 50–54.

[47] Ibid., p. 54. A more technical formulation of this law runs as follows: If principle P_1 takes precedence over principle P_2 in circumstances C: $(P_1 \mathbf{P} P_2)C$, and if P_1 gives rise to legal consequences Q in circumstances C, then a valid rule applies which has C as its protasis and Q as its apodosis: $C \rightarrow Q$; ibid.

4.2 The Proportionality of the Interference with C's Freedom of Expression

Principles theory and proportionality are closely connected. The one implies the other, and vice versa. Proportionality analysis comprises not only balancing, that is, optimization relative to the legal or normative possibilities, but also, as stated above, optimization relative to the factual possibilities. This is the subject of the first two sub-principles of the principle of proportionality, the principles of suitability and of necessity. In practice, the principle of suitability is, as already indicated, of low importance. The situation is completely different where the principle of necessity is concerned. In its general formulation the principle of necessity requires that of two means for promoting P_1 that are, broadly speaking, equally suitable, the one that interferes less intensively with P_2 has to be chosen. If there exists a less intensively interfering and equally suitable means, one position can be improved at no cost to the other.

4.2.1 Necessity

In our case, the constellation is more complex. This is due to the fact that the triangle brings three persons into play. With this, the question arises of whether one involved party can claim that an interference with another party's rights would render an interference with its rights unnecessary. In our case this is the question of whether an interference on the side of the author of the comment would render an interference on the side of the provider of the internet portal, *Delfi*, unnecessary.

The Court speaks in this context about:

> the question whether the liability of the actual authors of the comments could serve as a sensible alternative to the liability of the Internet news portal in a case like the present one.[48]

In connection with this, it stresses the importance of anonymity for freedom of speech.[49] Then it comes to the decisive point, that of "uncertain effectiveness".

> [T]he uncertain effectiveness of measures allowing the identity of the authors of the comments to be established, coupled with the lack of instruments put in place by the applicant company for the same purpose[50]

is declared—along with other points, for instance the "better financial position"[51] of the media company—to justify "shifting the risk"[52] to the Internet news portal. With this, the liability of the commentators is declared not to be an equally suited

[48] ECtHR [GC], *Delfi AS vs. Estonia*, 16 Jun. 2015, No. 64569/09, para. 147.

[49] *Ibid.*, paras. 147 and 149.

[50] *Ibid.*, para. 151.

[51] *Ibid.*

[52] *Ibid.*, para. 147.

alternative. This means that it is disproportional according to the second sub-principle of proportionality, the principle of necessity.

4.2.2 Proportionality in the Narrower Sense: Weight Formula

Cases that cannot be resolved by optimization relative to the factual possibilities, that is, by the sub-principles of suitability and necessity, must be resolved by the sub-principle of proportionality in the narrower sense, that is, by balancing according to the Weight Formula. In our case the result of the Weight Formula depends on the intensity of interference on both sides. The intensity of the interference with the personality rights of the victim of the comments (I_i) has already been classified as serious (s) if the triadic scale is used. It receives the value 4. Now the intensity of interference with the freedom of expression of the provider of the internet portal, *Delfi*, by imposing liability for comments made by "third parties"[53] (I_j), has to be determined.

The answer to this question essentially depends on what is to be understood under the liability imposed to the internet portal. The court puts this in the following words:

> [T]he Court does not consider that the imposition on the applicant company of an obligation to remove from its website, without delay after publication, comments that amounted to hate speech and incitements to violence, and were thus clearly lawless on their face, amounted, in principle, to a disproportionate interference with its freedom of expression.[54]

A simpler formulation is to be found at the end of the Court's assessment: "Therefore, the measure did not constitute a disproportionate restriction on the applicant company's right to freedom of expression."[55]

What is not disproportional is proportional.[56] In the light of the value serious (s) on the side of the interference with the personality right of the victim, the interference with *Delfi's* freedom of expression would be proportional if the intensity of this interference (I_j) were not higher than moderate or medium (m). The sentence "The interference with *Delfi's* freedom of expression is moderate" is what I have called a "classification proposition".[57] Authors like Habermas,[58] Schlink,[59] and Poscher[60] who conceive balancing as arbitrary, pure decision, or a matter of intuition are

---

[53]*Ibid.*, para. 140.

[54]*Ibid.*, para. 153.

[55]*Ibid.*, para. 162.

[56]The question of whether this sentence has to be further qualified with respect to stalemates which lead to discretion or a margin of appreciation shall not be considered here. See on this Alexy (1985), pp. 410–412.

[57]Alexy (2017), p. 22.

[58]Habermas (1992), p. 259.

[59]Schlink (1984), p. 462.

[60]Poscher (2012), p. 241.

compelled to deny the justifiability of classification propositions.[61] In response, I have set out the argumentation thesis, which says that propositions about the intensity of interferences lend themselves to rational justification. The argumentation thesis leads to an intrinsic connection between mathematically reconstructed balancing and legal argumentation.

In the light of this background I want to close with a look at the arguments of the Grand Chamber concerning the intensity of interference with *Delfi's* freedom of expression. *Delfi* is qualified as a "professionally managed Internet news portal" that runs "on a commercial basis".[62] It is interested in as large a "number of comments on news articles published by it", because "the revenue earned from advertisement" "depended on the number of visits".[63] And it is the greatest internet portal in Estonia.[64] The Court concedes that *Delfi's* "automatic word-based filter"[65] is still of limited efficiency.[66] But it lays emphasis on the fact that *Delfi* had meanwhile "set up a dedicated team of moderators".[67] In addition, the compensation *Delfi* was obligated to pay for non-pecuniary damage is rather low, 320 euros.[68] All this runs in the direction of the general judgement "that it does not appear that the applicant company had to change its business model."[69] One does not have to agree with this. But one must grant that these are arguments. And they are arguments supporting the classification proposition "The interference with *Delfi's* freedom of expression is medium". With this we have arrived at our aim.

Only the variables of the Weight Formula concerning the intensity of interference, I_i and I_j, are relevant in our case. The abstract values, W_i and W_j, cancel each other, and the variables concerning the epistemic reliability, R_i and R_j, play no role in the argumentation of the Court. I_i has the value 4, I_j the value 2. This implies that the concrete weight of the protection of personality, $W_{i,j}$, is 2. When a principle has a value greater than 1 it takes precedence over the colliding principle.[70] Thus, the interference with *Delfi's* freedom of expression is proportional and therefore lawful.

[61] Alexy (2017), p. 22.

[62] ECtHR [GC], *Delfi AS vs. Estonia*, 16 Jun. 2015, No. 64569/09, para. 144.

[63] *Ibid.*

[64] *Ibid.*, para. 83.

[65] *Ibid.*, para. 156.

[66] On the possibilities to use artificial intelligence in the control of the internet see Alexy (2019), pp. 213–220.

[67] ECtHR [GC], *Delfi AS vs. Estonia*, 16 Jun. 2015, No. 64569/09, para. 157.

[68] *Ibid.*, para. 160.

[69] *Ibid.*, para. 161.

[70] Alexy (2017), p. 26.

References

Alexy R (1985) A theory of constitutional rights (trans: Rivers J). Oxford University Press, Oxford

Alexy R (2003) On balancing and subsumption. Ratio Juris 16:433–449

Alexy R (2007) The weight formula. In: Stelmach J et al (eds) Frontiers of the economic analysis of law. Jagiellonian University Press, Krakow, pp 9–27

Alexy R (2014) Formal principles: some replies to critics. Int J Const Law 12:511–524

Alexy R (2015) Menschenwürde und Verhältnismäßigkeit. Archiv des öffentlichen Rechts 140:497–513

Alexy R (2017) Proportionality and rationality. In: Jackson VC et al (eds) Proportionality. New frontiers, new challenges. Cambridge University Press, Cambridge, pp 13–29

Alexy R (2019) Mart Susi's internet balancing formula. Eur Law J 25:213–220

Barak A (2012) Proportionality: constitutional rights and their limitation. Cambridge University Press, Cambridge

Habermas J (1992) Between facts and norms: contributions to a discourse theory of law and democracy (trans: Rehg W). Polity Press, Cambridge

Poscher R (2012) The principles theory: how many theories and what is their merit? In: Klatt M (ed) Institutionalized reason: the Jurisprudence of Robert Alexy. Oxford University Press, Oxford, pp 218–247

Schlink B (1984) Freiheit durch Eingriffsabwehr – Rekonstruktion der klassischen Grundrechtsfunktion. Europäische GRUNDRECHTE-Zeitschrift 11:457–468

Robert Alexy is a jurist and a legal philosopher. He studied law and philosophy at the University of Göttingen. He received his PhD in 1976 with the dissertation *A Theory of Legal Argumentation*, and he achieved his Habilitation in 1984 with *A Theory of Constitutional Rights*. He is a professor at the University of Kiel and in 2002 he was appointed to the Academy of Sciences in Göttingen. In 2010 he was awarded the Order of Merit of the Federal Republic of Germany.

Axel Springer AG v. Germany, or: How to Perform Limited Review

Martin Borowski

Contents

1 Introduction 215
2 The Facts of the Case 216
2.1 The Prior Conviction and the Arrest 216
2.2 The First Article in September 2004 217
2.3 The Second Article in July 2005 217
2.4 Proceedings Before German Courts 217
3 Proceedings Before the European Court of Human Rights (ECtHR) 218
3.1 Admissibility and Submissions 218
3.2 The Standard of Review of Balancing in Springer v. Germany 219
3.2.1 One Case, the Claim to Correctness, and Six Panels of Judges 219
3.2.2 On the Reconstruction of Limited Review 220
3.2.3 Two Strategies to Present Limited Review 222
3.2.4 The Review of the Result and of the Process Leading to the Result 223
3.2.5 The Set of Balancing Criteria 223
3.2.6 Balancing "in Conformity" with the Criteria 223
3.2.7 The Application of the Criteria for Balancing 224
4 Under-review and Over-review (*Unterkontrolle und Überkontrolle*) 228
5 The 15th Protocol Amending the ECtHR 228

1 Introduction

In the decision of the Grand Chamber *Axel Springer AG* v. *Germany*[1] from 2012, freedom of expression by the press according to Article 10 of the European Convention on Human Rights (ECtHR) competes with the right to protection of the private life according to Article 8 ECtHR. It is a case of *Drittwirkung* or horizontal

[1]ECtHR [GC], *Axel Springer AG v. Germany*, 7 Feb. 2012, No. 39954/08.

M. Borowski (✉)
Heidelberg University, Heidelberg, Germany
e-mail: borowski@jurs.uni-heidelberg.de

M. Elósegui et al. (eds.), *The Rule of Law in Europe*,
https://doi.org/10.1007/978-3-030-56001-0_13

effect of constitutional and Convention rights. Germany's courts sanctioned the applicant, the public limited company Axel Springer, for publishing in their newspaper "Bild" two articles that revealed the circumstances, first, in which an actor was arrested at the Munich *Oktoberfest* in the possession of a small amount of cocaine in July 2004 and, second, nine months later, the fact that the actor confessed in court and received a fine. Despite the "margin of appreciation", a majority of twelve judges of the Grand Chamber regarded the sanctions for the articles not justified and found a violation of freedom of expression by Germany. A dissenting opinion supported by five judges disagreed with the majority to the effect that the decisions of the German courts met the relevant standard of review.

This case has been widely discussed and raises, among other issues, the notoriously difficult problem of how to perform limited review.

2 The Facts of the Case

2.1 The Prior Conviction and the Arrest

An actor, called X in the judgment, played the part of the police superintendent Balko in around one hundred episodes of a television series broadcast in the German branch of the commercial channel *RTL* from 1998 to 2005. With an average audience rating of just below 20% this series proved to be quite popular. In 2003 the influential newspaper "Bild" happened to receive the information that X had been convicted of the possession of four grams of cocaine recently, found at his home, and that he had received a suspended prison sentence of five months and had to pay 5000 Euros. Owing to warnings from X, "Bild" initially refrained from publishing this information.

At the end of September 2004, X came out of the toilet next to the *Käfer* tent at the *Oktoberfest* in Munich and tapped his nose, which was regarded to be a suspicious movement by plain-clothes police officers present at the scene. He was searched and a small envelope containing circa 0.2 grams of cocaine was found in his possession. X was immediately arrested for possession of illegal drugs. What then happened with an eye to the prosecution authority remained contested. The applicant, Springer, claimed that its journalists received the information from the prosecution authority by means of a statement and a press conference prior to the publication of their first article.[2] By contrast, the German government disputed that the information was publicly or otherwise provided by the prosecution authority and that it was only publicly confirmed after it had been published in the applicant's newspaper. The Grand Chamber found no evidence in the file as to whether a press conference by the prosecution authority was held prior to the publication of the first article in "Bild". It relied, however, on a sworn statement of a journalist from the applicant—which was

[2] *Ibid.*, paras. 11–12, 102–104.

not contested the German Government—that the information was received from the Munich prosecution authority prior to the publication of the first article.[3]

2.2 *The First Article in September 2004*

The first article in "Bild" in September 2004 revealed the fact that X was caught in possession of cocaine at the mentioned scene, revealing his real name and the name of the role he played, referring to the prosecution authority and a legal expert that made a prediction of the punishment awaiting X, referring also to the earlier conviction. On the day the first article was published in "Bild", other news outlets reported the story, in part referring to the "Bild" article.

2.3 *The Second Article in July 2005*

In July 2005 a second article was published in "Bild", in which the confession of X was reported along with his fine of 18,000 euros.

2.4 *Proceedings Before German Courts*

X brought legal proceedings against the publication of both articles on the ground that his right to personal life had been violated, according to section 823, paragraph 1, BGB (Civil Code) in conjunction with 1004, section 1, BGB. He sought and gained an injunction against the publication of the first article before the *Landgericht Hamburg* (Regional Court). In the main proceedings the *Landgericht* held that X's personality rights were violated by the articles and ordered a penalty of 5,000 euros. This was justified by means of a rather comprehensive and detailed weighing of relevant factors in proportionality analysis. The Grand Chamber Judgment gives a detailed report of this justification in ten marginal numbers over three pages.

The *Oberlandesgericht Hamburg* (Court of Appeal) basically upheld the judgement of the *Landgericht*, significantly reducing the amount of the penalty to 1,000 euros. It referred to the factors for weighing the interests in such cases as established by the case law of the *Bundesgerichtshof* (Federal Court of Justice). There was some disagreement with the *Landgericht* as to whether there was a public interest in X's person. While the *Landgericht* answered this in the negative, the *Oberlandesgericht* went somewhat into a positive direction—it did not, however, regard this difference as decisive. The reason for significantly reducing the penalty was rather the trust

[3]*Ibid.*, para. 104.

established by the statement of the Munich prosecution authority, in the light of which there was only minor negligence on the part of Springer and its employees.

The *Bundesgerichtshof* (Federal Court of Justice) refused leave to appeal on points of law (*Revisionszulassung*), for there was neither a question of fundamental importance nor an issue with the uniformity of the case-law—the statutory reasons for such leave to appeal on points of law. They saw no indication that the relevant criteria for balancing the two rights at stake had been disregarded to a relevant extent, considered against the backdrop of its own case law.

Finally, the *Bundesverfassungsgericht* (German Federal Constitutional Court) ruled by means of a *Kammerbeschluss* (decision by a three judge panel) that there was no violation of a constitutional right provided for in the German Constitution. As is actually the rule rather than the exception in a *Kammerbeschluss*, it refrained from giving explicit substantive reasons to justify its conclusion.

3 Proceedings Before the European Court of Human Rights (ECtHR)

Springer filed an individual complaint according to Article 34 ECtHR. The Fifth Section of the Court decided to join the *Springer* case to the case *von Hannover* v. *Germany II*[4] and to relinquish jurisdiction in favour of the Grand Chamber in March 2010, but disjoined later the *von Hannover II* Case from the *Springer* case. Owing to this particular procedural history, we have a Grand Chamber Judgment without a prior judgment of a Section of the Court.

3.1 Admissibility and Submissions

The Grand Chamber quickly declares the application admissible.[5] As usual, the evaluation of the merits commences with the submissions of the parties. In their submission the German Government emphasized the margin of appreciation that the Member States enjoy. These submissions mention important aspects of the nature of limited review, drawing on Germany's experience with limited review in constitutional law.[6] Nevertheless, these aspects found little, if any, reflection in the reasoning of the Grand Chamber. Springer challenged the evaluation of certain factors in the balancing undertaken by the *Landgericht* and *Oberlandesgericht*.

[4]ECtHR [GC], *von Hannover* v. *Germany n°2*, 7 Feb. 2012, Nos. 40660/08 and 60641/08.
[5]ECtHR [GC], *Axel Springer AG v. Germany*, 7 Feb. 2012, No. 39954/08, para. 54.
[6]*Ibid.*, paras. 56–64.

3.2 The Standard of Review of Balancing in *Springer v. Germany*

There is no doubt that there is an interference with Springer's freedom of expression[7] and that, owing to Germany's domestic statutory law, this interference is "prescribed by law".[8] The only issue is proportionality or, in the wording of the Convention, whether the interference is "necessary in a democratic society".

The assessment begins with the usual phrases stressing the importance of freedom of expression. The Court highlights the functional importance of free expression for a democratic society. Unlike other freedoms, freedom of expression is not merely undergirded by the individual's interest to express oneself, it is also undergirded by a weighty collective good, namely, the functioning of a democratic debate. This is to say that the individual right is supported by a collective good—more supported in the case of a genuine political debate, less supported in an entertainment context or cases of purely commercial speech. This functional approach is mentioned by the Grand Chamber as the justification of the press for reporting all matters of "public interest".[9] To be sure, this is only convincing if the interpretation of this expression has a democratic-functional overtone. The Court then goes on to characterize the right to respect for private life according to Article 8 ECtHR as a potential limiting reason.

In what follows, the Court refers to the margin of appreciation that Member States enjoy, in the framework of European supervision.[10] To use my own expression, the task of the Court is "limited review" of the decisions of German courts. What, however, is precisely "limited review"?

3.2.1 One Case, the Claim to Correctness, and Six Panels of Judges

A case such as *Springer AG* v. *Germany* is typically subject to decisions up to no fewer than six panels of judges. At any rate, it is not the case that every higher panel undertakes strict review of the preceding decision. The *Landgericht* decides the case on the basis of German statutory law, interpreted against the backdrop of the German constitution and the ECtHR. The *Oberlandesgericht* undertakes strict review of the decision of the *Landgericht*. The *Bundesgerichtshof* (Federal Court of Justice) undertakes only review on points of law, not facts, and this only under certain procedural or substantive circumstances—this review is actually in several respects limited, but in a different sense compared to "limited review" of balancing decisions. What is more, the *Bundesverfassungsgericht* reviews only the constitutionality of

[7] *Ibid*., para. 75.

[8] *Ibid*., para. 77.

[9] *Ibid*., para. 79.

[10] *Ibid*., paras. 85–86.

decisions of German ordinary courts (*Fachgerichte*), not whether statutory law as such was interpreted correctly. The review of the balancing of constitutional rights undertaken by ordinary courts is only subject to limited review. Finally, a section of the European Court of Human rights and/or the Grand Chamber undertakes limited review of the final decision of the courts of the Member States.

It is also worth mentioning that the legal instruments for the protection of human rights applied by these six panels of judges—rights of the German constitution and Convention rights—may be different to some extent, but that the instruments themselves and every legal decision applying them raises the claim to moral correctness, namely, the claim that the respective legal decision counts as an expression of human rights as moral rights. Owing to differences in space and time, the positive morality, the factual interpretation of what human rights as moral rights require in a case at hand may differ somewhat. Human rights as moral rights are, however, the vanishing point (*Fluchtpunkt*) undergirding all legal judgments on national or international fundamental rights.

In short, limited review is a phenomenon that arises owing to epistemic uncertainty on what human rights—moral rights that have been transformed into legal rights—require and the division of labour in authoritative structures in the municipal and international legal system. The international level of the protection of human rights is subsidiary to the national level. Limited review in the sense of the margin of appreciation is an expression of this subsidiarity.

3.2.2 On the Reconstruction of Limited Review

The Two Core Phrases on the Review Standard

Coming back to the case at hand, before one analyzes the justification given by the Grand Chamber in greater detail, it is well to have a look at the dissenting opinions of five judges. The core criticism here is that the Grand Chamber misjudged the margin of appreciation and assumed the role of the competent national courts. The core sentence reads:

> In order to exercise this Court's powers of review without becoming a fourth instance, our task in guaranteeing respect for Convention rights in this type of case is essentially to verify whether the domestic courts have duly balanced the conflicting rights and have taken into account the relevant criteria established in our case-law without any manifest error or omission of any important factor.[11]

The dissenting vote then goes on to explain that the decisions of German courts met this standard.

The limited nature of review is reflected in the wording of the Court's reasoning, where one reads that "the Court's task is not to take the place of the national

[11] *Ibid.*, Dissenting Opinion of Judge Lopez Guerra joined by Judges Jungwiert, Jäger, Villiger and Poealunghi.

courts".[12] The standard applied here seems to be, however, far stricter, requiring not merely application of the arguments "without any manifest error or omission of any important factor" (as the dissenting vote states) but application "in conformity with the criteria laid down in the Court's case-law"—this latter phrase might indicate strict review rather than limited review.

Strict and Limited Review

What, then, is precisely the difference between "strict review" and "limited review"? In the case of strict review, a review organ applies the substantive law itself and then simply compares as to whether the decision to be reviewed arrives at the same result. If yes, the decision to be reviewed is upheld. If not, the decision to be reviewed is rescinded and replaced by the decision of the review organ with a different result.

This is fundamentally different in limited review. The decision to be reviewed in a limited fashion can involve balancing, subsumption, or both. Since in *Springer AG* v. *Germany* the review of a proportionality judgment takes centre stage, I shall focus on balancing.

A paradigmatic level of intensity of review in limited review is "plausibility review" (*Vertretbarkeitskontrolle*). Plausibility review means that the review organ refrains from imposing the result it regards to be the correct balancing of the competing substantive rights—here freedom of expression and respect for private life. Rather, it merely asks as to whether the decision to be reviewed arrives at a "plausible" result. Unlike in the case of strict review, there are not only two outcomes—correct result/wrong result—, there are, however, three possible outcomes: (i) substantively fully correct result, (ii) not substantively fully correct, but plausible result, (iii) result is neither fully substantively correct nor plausible. In "plausibility review", the decision to be reviewed passes review if it is substantively fully correct or at least substantively plausible. To put a sharp edge on it, the decision to be reviewed may well be "not fully substantively correct"—in this sense substantively incorrect—and at the same time "correct" from the point of view of plausibility review. This is to say that two different levels of correctness can be distinguished—purely substantive correctness on the one hand and correctness based on balancing substantive rights and goods under epistemic uncertainty in a situation one the other, in which there are reasons to give relative deference to a preceding decision.

The potential difference between these two levels is the more pronounced the more limited the review that is undertaken. It is greater, for example, if one asks whether a decision to be reviewed is "not arbitrary"—the phrase "without any manifest error or omission of any important factor" in the dissenting vote goes in this direction. The review is the more limited the greater the epistemic uncertainty.

[12] *Ibid.*, para. 86.

3.2.3 Two Strategies to Present Limited Review

There are two different strategies for the review organ for presenting "plausibility review".

The Open Strategy

The first strategy consists in, first, balancing all competing substantive rights—establishing substantive correctness—and then, second, determining in the light of this result whether the decision to be reviewed departs from this result only to such an extent that it can be regarded as "plausible". I shall call this the "open strategy".

The Hidden Strategy

The second strategy presents the comprehensive assessment by immediately asking whether a decision to be reviewed is "plausible", without revealing whether the review organ, if they were to decide the substantive merits of the case, would arrive at a different conclusion. I shall call this the "hidden strategy". It might seem to be an advantage of this hidden strategy is that it avoids the confusion that may arise with an eye to two different levels of "correctness" as explained above. How can one admit that a decision to be reviewed is substantively incorrect, but passes the relevant review standard?

There can, however, be little doubt that one can evaluate the "plausibility" of a decision to be reviewed only after balancing the substantive merits from one's own point of view. Even if the "hidden strategy" is chosen for presenting the issue, in performing plausibility review the review organ has to go at least implicitly through three steps: (i) balancing the substantive merits of the case, (ii) compare this with the result of the decision to be reviewed, and—in cases the two results differ—evaluate whether, considering the extent of difference between the two results, the decision to be reviewed counts as "plausible" or not. The advantage of the open strategy is that it presents a much clearer justification in terms of legal argumentation and a much clearer precedent for future cases. Legal certainty and, more generally, legal argumentation require the open strategy.

This is to say that it is perfectly legitimate in limited review if the review organ evaluates the substantive merits of balancing the competing rights from their own point of view. This needs, however, to be sufficiently placed in perspective considering the epistemic uncertainty and the weight of reasons to defer to a preceding decision, and preferably explicitly in the sense of the open strategy.

3.2.4 The Review of the Result and of the Process Leading to the Result

The Grand Chamber acknowledges at the outset that it is not supposed to take the place of the national courts.[13] It concretizes its standard of review in the following key sentence:

> Where the balancing exercise between those two rights has been undertaken by the national authorities in conformity with the criteria laid down in the Court's case-law, the Court would require strong reasons to substitute its view for that of the domestic courts.[14]

The first issue is that this requires a certain process rather than merely a certain result. In the case of the review of court decisions, it may suggest itself to require that a certain process of legal argumentation has actually taken place (*Vorgangskontrolle*). This is, however, less clear in the context of review of parliamentary statutes. If a directly democratically legitimated parliament enacts a certain statute that objectively represents a plausible compromise between two competing Convention rights, would the Grand Chamber require that parliament go through the process of using the criteria from the Court's case law for arriving at the statute? If that process did not take place, is this procedural defect alone sufficient to pronounce a violation of the Convention? Or would a correct result be sufficient, independent from the process that led to this result (*Ergebniskontrolle*)? I shall just flag up this difficult issue for legislation and note that both the Grand Chamber and the dissenting vote require to a certain extent review of both the process and the result of judicial decisions.

3.2.5 The Set of Balancing Criteria

The second issue is that the Grand Chamber seems to insist on the Court's very own set of criteria for the balancing. To be sure, there may well be reasonable disagreement as to what the relevant set of balancing criteria is. The dissenting opinion is far more tolerant in this respect, for it requires, first, that the balancing be undertaken without an "omission of any important factor"—indicating that some of the Court's criteria may be, in a concrete case, "not important" and, second, merely the application of the criteria "without any manifest error" rather than "in conformity".

3.2.6 Balancing "in Conformity" with the Criteria

The third issue is that it is not clear what it means to undertake a "balancing exercise [...] in conformity with the criteria laid down in the Court's case-law". Does it only mean that these criteria—no fewer and no more—are mentioned in the justification

[13] *Ibid.*, para. 86.

[14] *Ibid.*, para. 88.

of the balancing? Or does it mean that these and only these criteria are used with the fully correct weight? If that is meant, however, why would then still "strong reasons" justify replacing the national courts' balancing result with the Grand Chamber's balancing result? If one uses the fully correct set of balancing criteria with the fully correct weight, the result is necessarily identical. This might suggest that "in conformity" permits some degree of reasonable disagreement in terms of weight of the criteria for balancing. This is not, however, fully clear, and even if this is true, we are completely left in the dark what extent of reasonable disagreement the Grand Chamber is willing to accept—somewhat limited review in the form of "plausibility review" or severely limited review in the form of "non-arbitrariness review"?

3.2.7 The Application of the Criteria for Balancing

The Grand Chamber gives a general introduction into and illustration of the criteria for balancing of cases involving a competition between freedom of expression and respect for private life, namely, the contribution to a debate of general interest,[15] how well known the person concerned is and what the subject of the report is,[16] the prior conduct of the person concerned,[17] the method of obtaining the information and its veracity,[18] the content, form and consequences of the publication,[19] and finally the severity of the sanction imposed.[20]

The Contribution to a Debate of General Interest

In limited review, you would expect the Court to refer to the balancing of national courts and apply a standard of limited review such as "plausible" or "not arbitrary". The Court, however, simply evaluates the merits of the contribution of the articles to a debate of general interest from its very own point of view, arriving at a carefully positive, but vague result: It "may be considered to present a degree of general interest"[21] that a TV actor was arrested on the suspicion of possessing illegal drugs. To be sure, from the functional point of view of facilitating democratic deliberation, access to this kind of information relating to an entertainment celebrity is hardly relevant. What is more, it remains the secret of the Grand Chamber whether "general interest" should be understood empirically or normatively.

[15] *Ibid.*, para. 90.
[16] *Ibid.*, para. 91.
[17] *Ibid.*, para. 92.
[18] *Ibid.*, para. 93.
[19] *Ibid.*, para. 94.
[20] *Ibid.*, para. 95.
[21] *Ibid.*, para. 96.

How Well Known Is the Person Concerned and What Is the Subject of the Report?

In assessing the next criterion "how well known is the person concerned and what is the subject of the report?" the Grand Chamber actually refers to the national courts. It does so, however, merely for supporting its own point of view. Generally, the relevant national assessment is the one stemming from the highest national court that has explicitly addressed the substantive issue. This is the *Oberlandesgericht* (Court of Appeal). Instead of applying a standard of limited review, the Grand Chamber emphasizes from the outset that the Regional Court (*Landgericht*) and the Court of Appeal (*Oberlandesgericht*) disagreed on that count. That is true, but hardly relevant. Pretending a limitation of review, the Grand Chamber emphasizes that it was for domestic courts to determine how well known an actor is in a certain member state—a sociological issue intimately linked to the culture and the contemporary celebrity culture of a nation—but then goes on to support the conclusion that X had the status of a "public figure", by arguing basically on its behalf the view of the Court of Appeal (*Oberlandesgericht*), but putting a much stronger spin on this—the Court of Appeal actually agreed that there was some limited interest in whether X was arrested and sentenced, but that he was not a role model, so that this interest changed not the outcome of balancing.[22] To be blunt, the Grand Chamber's reference to the two judgments of German courts is purely strategic to orchestrate the substantive result the Grand Chamber preferred themselves.

X's Conduct Prior to Publication of the Impugned Articles

With an eye to X's prior conduct the Grand Chamber remarks that he revealed details about his private life in a number of interviews. We learn that this,[i]n the Court's view',[23] reduced his legitimate interest in protecting details from his private life. Is this to say that you have to reveal everything if you had revealed anything beforehand? It is precisely the point of a liberty that you are free what to reveal and what not, and this ought not to be undermined by means of attributing weight propositions in balancing the liberty. The evaluation of this issue by the *Oberlandesgericht*,[24] which is more skeptical than the one presented by the *Landgericht*[25] is not even mentioned.

---

[22] *Ibid.*, para. 33.

[23] *Ibid.*, para. 101.

[24] *Ibid.*, para. 34.

[25] *Ibid.*, para. 23.

The Method of Obtaining the Information and Its Veracity

There are also problems with an eye to considering the "method of obtaining the information and its veracity". The *Oberlandesgericht* assumed that the "Bild" journalists obtained the information on X from the Munich prosecution authority and the Grand Chamber agreed. The *Landgericht* had held, however, that a newspaper has the obligation of balancing the competing rights at stake and refrain from publication if competing rights outweigh the press' freedom of expression.[26] The Grand Chamber simply states: "In the Court's opinion, there is nothing to suggest that such a balancing exercise was not undertaken."[27] This refers to a process—how does the Grand Chamber justify this conclusion? They hold that, considering the weight of the balancing criteria in this case, "the applicant company [...] did not have sufficiently strong grounds for believing that it should preserve X's anonymity"[28]—this is the justification of a result. This mistaken equalization of process and result is further aggravated by adding the unclear statement that the applicant company did not "act in bad faith",[29] which appends an unclear subjective dimension to the objective criteria of process and result.

Finally, coming back to the structure of limited review, it is not the task of the Grand Chamber to simply state whether the "balancing exercise"—whatever this precisely means—of the applicant company was correct. It is their task to review the national decisions, which, in turn, reviewed the actions of the applicant company. This may sound hair-splitting, it has, however, an important practical consequence: In the first case the margin of appreciation for the Member State gets lost, while it is—deservedly—considered in the second.

Content, Form and Consequences of the Publication

With an eye to the consequences of the publication, the Grand Chamber explains that the articles did rather little harm to X.[30] This is true, there was, however, very little legitimate interest in spreading the information about him.

Severity of the Sanction Imposed

Finally, the Grand Chamber admits that the sanction imposed was lenient. Indeed, 1,000 euros for a big publishing house such as Springer is, in relation, less than parking fine of ten euros for an individual. Springer finds itself regularly before the

---

[26] *Ibid.*, paras. 27–30.

[27] *Ibid.*, para. 107.

[28] *Ibid.*, para. 107.

[29] *Ibid.*, para. 107.

[30] *Ibid.*, para. 108.

courts for testing the legal boundaries of what can be written in newspaper articles. The Grand Chamber's reference to the chilling effect[31] sounds rather abstract and hollow in these circumstances—do they really want to have us believe that hard-boiled professional journalists with enormous financial firepower in the background are "chilled" by the prospect of a fine of 1,000 euros? Such less than convincing reference to the "chilling effect" is, in my view, unfortunate and even dangerous, for it undermines its argumentative force in cases in which it is truly needed.

The Severity of the Interference and the Intensity of Review

This is to say that we have a light interference with light limiting reasons at best, if not very light. If the severity of the interference with the Convention right counts as a criterion for the intensity of review—this criterion has crystallized as the leitmotif in German constitutional law for determining the intensity of review vis-à-vis the democratically directly legitimated parliament and vis-à-vis ordinary courts—, this suggests even "non-arbitrariness review" (*Willkürkontrolle*) rather than plausibility review (*Vertretbarkeitskontrolle*). Why does the Grand Chamber spend so much time and effort on rather strict review in such a case? The key task of the ECtHR is to sanction severe violations of human rights in cases, in which domestic courts failed to protect them. For both normative and factual reasons it is not the Court's task to second-guess decisions of domestic courts in everyday cases, which involve only light interferences and in which one can reasonably disagree on the outcome of the balancing. This is neither the role of an international human rights court nor does the ECtHR have the capacity to undertake strict review of domestic courts of 47 member states.

The Conclusion

Finally the Court concludes that "the grounds advanced by the Member State [. . .] are not sufficient to establish that the interference complained of was necessary in a democratic society".[32] In other words, in the Grand Chamber's own view, the interference is not proportionate. This is the case, it continues, "[d]espite the margin of appreciation". One who expected any justification for this conclusion is only disappointed. There is no attempt at justifying or even explaining how far the margin extends and why this case is beyond its boundaries.

[31] *Ibid.*, para. 109.

[32] *Ibid.*, para. 110.

4 Under-review and Over-review (*Unterkontrolle und Überkontrolle*)

In conclusion, it suggests itself that the Grand Chamber decision in *Springer AG* v. *Germany* counts as an instance of overreview (*Überkontrolle*). The danger of underreview (*Unterkontrolle*), a violation of human rights without judicial redress, is obvious. By contrast, at first glance there seems to be little harm done in cases of overreview. To the extent that there are, however, good reasons to limit the review by the ECtHR, but the Court overreviews, then the legal competence of the domestic courts to finally review the balancing is violated. Usually the domestic courts are far better equipped to determine the positive morality in their own Member State. Decisions from "Strasbourg" going against important aspects of the positive morality of a Member State of the ECtHR undermine the perceived legitimacy of its case law in this member state. Wrongly and needlessly stirring up opposition by Member States who are generally compliant with reasonable human rights standards is neither legally justified nor politically a good idea.

5 The 15th Protocol Amending the ECtHR

The "margin of appreciation" has been a device in the Court's case law for more than four decades since *Handyside*. *Axel Springer AG* v. *Germany* was decided in 2012 and the member states agreed the 15th Protocol to the ECtHR in 2013, which, among other changes, amends the Preamble to the effect that the "margin of appreciation" is now emphasized in the text. With this Protocol the Member States have given emphasis that they and their courts are not subject to strict review by the ECtHR. To be sure, this Protocol will only come into effect after ratification by all Member States and currently only the ratification of Italy is outstanding. It may well be that looking, with an eye to limited review, at *Axel Springer AG* v. *Germany* is actually a look into the past. It may well be that the Court, anticipating the 15th Protocol coming into effect, has become more circumspect with an eye to limited review. There is, however, quite some way to go before we arrive at a clear and coherent reconstruction of limited review by the ECtHR and the key arguments for determining the appropriate intensity of review in different cases.

Martin Borowski is a Professor at the University of Heidelberg. He worked as a research assistant to Robert Alexy at the University of Kiel. In 2004, Borowski obtained his habilitated at the Faculty of Law at the University of Kiel with the thesis on "Die Glaubens- und Gewissensfreiheit des Grundgesetzes." He was subsequently granted teaching authorization in public law, European law and philosophy of law by the Senate of the Christian-Albrechts-Universität zu Kiel. From 2005 to 2006 he was a visiting researcher in United States with a Humboldt research fellowship and from 2007 to 2012 Senior Lecturer and Reader at the University of Birmingham (UK). Since 2012, he has held the Chair of Public Law, Constitutional Theory and Philosophy of Law at the University of Heidelberg.

Satakunnan Markkinapörssi Oy and Satamedia Oy v. Finland, Conflict of Rights, and the Notion of Responsible Journalism

Peggy Ducoulombier

Contents

1 Introduction 229
2 The Jurisprudential Context: The *Magyar Helsinki Bizottság v. Hungary* Case 232
3 The Solution Found to the Conflict Between Articles 10 and 8 ECHR in the *Satakunnan* Case 234
4 The *Satakunnan* Case in Light of the Notion of Responsible Journalism and Its Impact on the Balance Between Articles 10 and 8 ECHR 244
References 248

1 Introduction

The case of *Satakunnan Markkinapörssi Oy and Satamedia Oy v. Finland*[1] (the *Satakunnan* case) is an interesting case of a conflict[2] between Article 10 and Article 8 of the European Convention on Human Rights (the ECHR).[3] In addition, this case involves important themes which have been running in the European Court of Human Rights' case-law (the Court or the ECtHR) for a few years now, such as the development of transparency exigencies in democratic societies and the notion of responsible journalism.

In order to fully appreciate the questions raised by the *Satakunnan* case, it is interesting to compare it with other cases from the Court's jurisprudence. The manner in which the Court solved the *Satakunnan* case will be assessed in light of Grand Chamber cases such as *Von Hannover v. Germany (n°2)* and *Axel Springer*

[1]ECtHR, GC, *Satakunnan Markkinapörssi Oy and Satamedia Oy v. Finland*, 27 June 2017, app. 931/13.

[2]On the subject of conflict of ECtHR rights, see Ducoulombier (2008), pp. 217–247.

[3]Aspects related to Article 6 ECtHR will not be covered.

P. Ducoulombier (✉)
University of Strasbourg, Strasbourg, France
e-mail: ducoulombier@unistra.fr

M. Elósegui et al. (eds.), *The Rule of Law in Europe*,
https://doi.org/10.1007/978-3-030-56001-0_14

AG v. Germany, *Magyar Helsinki Bizottság v. Hungary* and cases developing the notion of responsible journalism, in particular *Bédat v. Switzerland* and *Pentikäinen v. Finland.*[4]

Nowadays conflicting demands regarding transparency and privacy require the Court to achieve a difficult balance between competing rights and interests, even more when European Union Law (EU Law) considerations are added to the mix. One may wonder whether, in the specific case of *Satakunnan*, the Court managed to achieve that delicate balance. The answer to that question is not a simple one.

On the one hand, one may welcome the fact that the Court draws some boundaries as to the mass publication of personal data, even if the information published is in the public domain and does not belong to the core of an individual's privacy. On the other hand, the reasoning of the Court may be criticized on several points. Indeed, it is difficult to ignore the objections raised by the minority, as to what it reveals of the recent case-law of the Court on the degree of protection afforded to journalists. Put into a wider context, the *Satakunnan* case raises some legitimate concerns. However, in the specific circumstances of the case, it may be propounded that the Court found the right balance between Articles 10 and 8 ECHR.

Let us recall briefly the facts of the *Satakunnan* case. The two applicant companies collected data from the tax authorities with the aim of publishing information about persons' taxable income and assets in a newspaper. It is important to stress that the information was accessible to the public, pursuant to Finnish Law, and had been obtained lawfully.[5] The data published comprised the names of approximately 1.2 million persons whose annual taxable income exceeded certain thresholds, as well as their incomes and taxable assets.

Then these companies moved from paper publication to electronic communication of this information. One company transferred personal data published in the newspaper to the second applicant company which, with a mobile telephone operator, started a text-messaging service, making it possible, by sending a person's name to a service number, to obtain taxation information regarding that person.

The activities of the companies attracted the attention of public authorities. Following some requests for information by the companies, as well as an opinion by the Data Protection Ombudsman, the Finnish National Board of Taxation notified the companies that the information could no longer be given if they continued to publish the information in such an extensive manner. The companies then decided to pay individuals to collect the data manually at the local tax offices.

The Ombudsman then contacted the companies and asked them to stop the publication of the information in this unedited version, which the companies refused

---

[4]ECtHR, GC, *Von Hannover v. Germany (n°2),* 7 February 2012, app. 40660/08 and 60641/08; ECtHR, GC, *Axel Springer AG v. Germany*, 7 February 2012, app. 39954/08; ECtHR, GC, *Magyar Helsinki Bizottság v. Hungary*, 8 Nov. 2016, app. 18030/11; ECtHR, *Bédat v. Switzerland,* 29 March 2016, app. 56925/08; ECtHR, GC, *Pentikäinen v. Finland*, 20 Oct. 2015, app. 11882/10.

[5]Compare with ECtHR, GC, *Fressoz and Roire v. France,* 21 January 1999, app. 29183/95. Although some fiscal information was available to the public, in this case, the journalists had infringed the principle of secrecy of fiscal information.

to do. This led the Ombudsman to ask the Data Protection Board to prohibit the companies from continuing this activity. He argued that under the Personal Data Act the companies had no right to collect, store or pass on personal data and that the derogation provided by the Act regarding journalism did not apply to their situation. The Ombudsman considered that there was no journalistic purpose in this activity which rather resembled processing of personal data. This argument is indeed central to the case. As we will see, the heart of the reasoning of the Court is whether this indiscriminate, automatic publication of personal information could be considered as journalism. However, before the board, the Ombudsman failed and decided to bring the case to the Helsinki Administrative Court. Once again the application failed. According to the Administrative Court, the Act should not be construed as being too detrimental to freedom of expression. The Administrative Court considered that the companies had a journalistic purpose and that the publication of the information, which was already in the public domain, was in the public interest.

The case then reached the Supreme Administrative Court which requested a preliminary ruling from the European Court of Justice (ECJ) on the interpretation of the Data Protection directive.[6] The ECJ considered that the activities described were processing of personal data. It also considered that:

> activities such as those involved in the domestic proceedings, relating to data from documents which were in the public domain under domestic legislation, may be classified as 'journalistic activities' if their object is the disclosure to the public of information, opinions or ideas, irrespective of the medium which is used to transmit them.[7]

However, even with a large interpretation of the notion of journalism, it was also necessary to protect the conflicting right of privacy and therefore derogations to the protection had to apply only insofar as strictly necessary. In any case, the ECJ left to the domestic courts the task of deciding whether activities, such as those involved in the proceedings, could be classified as "journalistic activities".

The Supreme Administrative Court then decided to quash the decisions of the Board and the Administrative Court and to refer the case back to the Board, requesting that it prohibited the processing of taxation data by the applicant companies, which the Board did in 2009. The applicants complained to the Administrative Court about the decision, complaint which was dismissed and the decision was then upheld by the Supreme Administrative Court.

Following these decisions, the SMS service was shut down. Publication in paper version continued briefly but then stopped, although it is unclear whether some information was still available on the internet. The companies brought their case to

---

[6]Directive 95/46/EC of the European Parliament and of the Council of 24 October 1995 on the protection of individuals with regard to the processing of personal data and on the free movement of such data, repealed as of 25 May 2018 by Regulation (EU) 2016/679 of the European Parliament and Council on the protection of natural persons with regard to the processing of personal data and on the free movement of such data.

[7]ECJ, GC, *Tietosuojavaltuutettu v Satakunnan Markkinapörssi Oy and Satamedia Oy*, 16 December 2008, Case C-73/07, ECLI:EU:C:2008:727, pt 61.

the ECtHR, arguing that the domestic decisions had breached their right to freedom of expression.

The chamber decided, by six votes to one, that there was no violation of Article 10 ECHR,[8] which was confirmed by the Grand chamber by 15 votes to two. In order to understand the controversy created by this case it is important to put it first in its jurisprudential context (Sect. 1), before turning to the reasoning of the Grand chamber (Sect. 2) and then assess its impact on the conflict between Articles 10 and 8 ECHR, in light of the development of the notion of responsible journalism (Sect. 3).

2 The Jurisprudential Context: The *Magyar Helsinki Bizottság v. Hungary* Case

Indeed, the interest of *Satakunnan* is best understood if one mentions another case which raised some concerns about the scope of freedom of expression and its potential impact on the protection of the right to privacy, namely the Grand Chamber case of *Magyar Helsinki Bizottság v. Hungary*, decided in 2016. In this case, the Court had to clarify its case-law on the right to obtain information held by public authorities. Compared to similar provisions in the American Convention on Human Rights[9] or the International Covenant on Civil and Political Rights,[10] Article 10 ECHR does not expressly mention this right. However, in the ECtHR's case-law several chamber judgments started to recognize this right, under certain circumstances, in a way which was difficult to reconcile with the precedents of *Leander v. Sweden*[11] or *Guerra and others v. Italy.*[12] Thus, the Grand Chamber felt necessary to clarify the law in this area, although in a cautious manner. As a result, the Court ruled that although:

> Article 10 does not confer on the individual a right of access to information held by a public authority nor oblige the Government to impart such information to the individual [. . .], such a right or obligation may arise, firstly, where disclosure of the information has been imposed by a judicial order which has gained legal force (which is not an issue in the present case) and, secondly, in circumstances where access to the information is instrumental for the individual's exercise of his or her right to freedom of expression, in particular 'the freedom to receive and impart information' and where its denial constitutes an interference with that right.[13]

[8]ECtHR, *Satakunnan Markkinapörssi Oy and Satamedia Oy v. Finland*, 21 July 2015, app. 931/13.
[9]See Article 13.1 ACHR.
[10]See Article 19.2 ICCPR.
[11]ECtHR, *Leander v. Sweden*, 26 March 1987, app. 9248/81.
[12]ECtHR, GC, *Guerra and others v. Italy*, 19 February 1998, app. 14967/89.
[13]See para. 156 of the *Magyar Helsinki Bizottság* case.

The Court held that there had been a violation of Article 10 ECHR in this case, where a Non-Governmental Organization (NGO) had been denied access to information on lawyers being appointed by the police as public defenders in order to research the efficiency of the system. The Court considered that the disclosure of the information, personal data related to professional activities and more precisely the names of public defenders and the number of times they had been appointed to act as counsel in certain jurisdictions, by their nature and degree would not affect individuals' right to privacy.[14] It must be stressed that the Court applied the idea that, when it comes to Article 8 ECHR, the seriousness of the interference must reach a particular threshold before the provision can be applied. This idea was developed in *Von Hannover (n°2)* and *Axel Springer AG v. Germany* regarding the protection of reputation, a facet of Article 8 ECHR which was not involved in *Magyar Helsinki Bizottság*. Thus, the Court denied the existence of a conflict between Articles 10 and 8 ECHR. It held that the information requested contributed to a debate of public interest and was necessary to the exercise by the NGO of its public watchdog function. This ruling thus contributes to the development of a right to transparency, although a qualified one, in the Court's case-law.

However, this decision created some controversy within the Court. Although the division was mainly based on the subject of the interpretation of the Convention, in his dissenting opinion, Judge Spano, joined by Judge Kjølbro, also worried about the practical consequences of the decision on domestic legislation protecting personal data. He worried:

> that member States of the Council of Europe may now have to change fundamentally their national freedom-of-information laws [...and] have to reconcile those requirements with national and EU data-protection legislation.[15]

Judge Spano also criticized the majority's position regarding the refusal to consider the personal data involved in the case as protected by Article 8 ECHR.[16]

As a result, concerns were expressed that privacy could be damaged by the principles developed in the case of *Magyar Helsinki Bizottság* and the demands of freedom of expression.[17] The *Satakunnan* case alleviates these fears although raising new ones.

---

[14]See para. 196 of the *Magyar Helsinki Bizottság* case.

[15]See para. 40 of the dissenting opinion.

[16]See para. 41 of the dissenting opinion.

[17]However, the subsequent case-law of the ECtHR illustrates that the solution found in *Magyar Helsinki Bizottság* is limited to specific circumstances and that the right to receive State-held information is far from being absolute. See for instance, ECtHR, *Studio monitori and others v. Georgia*, 30 January 2020, app. 44920/09 and 8942/10, where the Court found no violation of Article 10 ECtHR. In this case, three applicants, an NGO, a journalist and a lawyer, requested full disclosure of specific criminal files, some of them involving prominent public figures. Their requests were denied by domestic courts. The Court considered that the applicants failed to sufficiently explain why the disclosure was necessary for the exercise of their freedom of expression and stressed that, despite having been denied access to the material, the two first applicants were able to publish the results of their investigation, thus demonstrating that the disclosure requested

3 The Solution Found to the Conflict Between Articles 10 and 8 ECHR in the *Satakunnan* Case

A major difference between *Satakunnan* and *Magyar Helsinki Bizottság* is that in *Satakunnan*, the Court considers that there is a conflict between two Convention rights,[18] which influences the framework applied for solving the case.

Indeed, in case of a conflict between Convention rights, the ordinary rules of interpretation of the Convention are more difficult or even impossible to apply. The principle according to which restrictions to Convention rights must be construed strictly, that preference must be given to rights over restrictions, cannot be applied, despite being recalled by the Court in the general principles part of its ruling,[19] as there is no reason to favour one right over the other.

The method used is the balancing of the two conflicting rights which, in the specific case, must be given equal respect by the Court.[20] Indeed, these two rights are both derogable and qualified rights, therefore, as the Court recalls, they carry equal weight. Since the case of *Chassagnou and others v. France*, where the Court explained its position towards conflicts of rights, the idea of hierarchy as a method to solve conflicts was put aside in favour of the balancing of the competing rights.[21]

---

was not instrumental to the exercise of their right. As far as the third applicant is concerned, the Court considered that he failed to explain how he could further the public access to news or facilitate the dissemination of information in the interest of public governance.

[18]See para. 122 of the *Satakunnan* case: "Given this context and the fact that at the heart of the present case lies the question whether the correct balance was struck between that right [freedom of expression] and the right to privacy [. . .] it is necessary, at the outset, to outline some of the general principles deriving from the Court's case-law on Article 10 [. . .] and Article 8 [. . .]". See also para. 163.

[19]See para. 124 of the *Satakunnan* case.

[20]See para. 123: "Bearing in mind the need to protect the values underlying the Convention and considering that the rights under Articles 10 and 8 of the Convention deserve equal respect [. . .]".

[21]ECtHR, GC, *Chassagnou and others v. France*, 29 April 1999, app. 25088/94, 28331/95 and 28443/95, para. 113: "In the present case the only aim invoked by the Government to justify the interference complained of was 'protection of the rights and freedoms of others'. *Where these 'rights and freedoms' are themselves among those guaranteed by the Convention or its Protocols, it must be accepted that the need to protect them may lead States to restrict other rights or freedoms likewise set forth in the Convention. It is precisely this constant search for a balance between the fundamental rights of each individual which constitutes the foundation of a 'democratic society'. The balancing of individual interests that may well be contradictory is a difficult matter, and Contracting States must have a broad margin of appreciation in this respect,* since the national authorities are in principle better placed than the European Court to assess whether or not there is a 'pressing social need' capable of justifying interference with one of the rights guaranteed by the Convention. It is a different matter where restrictions are imposed on a right or freedom guaranteed by the Convention in order to protect 'rights and freedoms' not, as such, enunciated therein. In such a case only indisputable imperatives can justify interference with enjoyment of a Convention right", emphasis added.

It does not mean that the idea of hierarchy is not present in the field of Human Rights or in the Court's case-law,[22] but simply that hierarchy is not the method used to solve conflict between rights[23] although balancing rights requires that a weight is ascribed to each of them.[24]

The Court also adds, in *Satakunnan*, that the same principle must be applied, in particular regarding the scope of the margin of appreciation, regardless of whether the case is analyzed through the prism of Article 10 or Article 8 ECHR.[25]

In addition, in *Satakunnan*, the Court alludes to the idea of practical concordance when stating that, in case of a conflict between rights, national authorities must thrive to "retain the essence of both".[26] However, if this is a clear way to put aside an abstract hierarchical reasoning and to stress the fact that balancing requires compromise rather than the sacrifice of one right to the other,[27] at the end of the day, one right will prevail over the other in light of the concrete circumstances of each case. This implicit reference to practical concordance therefore does not change the methodology applied for solving the case.

Despite this presentation, the existence of a conflict between convention rights could be debated in light of the *Magyar Helsinki Bizottság* case, in which the Court considered that, although personal data was involved, the information required by the NGO did not have the potential to affect the right to privacy to an extent which entailed the involvement of Article 8 ECHR. On the contrary, the Court in *Satakunnan* goes the extra mile to bring fiscal information, which is available to the public in Finland, under Article 8 ECHR so as to frame the case as a conflict between two Convention rights. Using its case-law on data protection, the Court recalls that personal data is "any information relating to an identified or identifiable individual",[28] that the fact that information is already in the public domain does not necessarily exclude the application of Article 8 ECHR and stresses that the prevalence of Article 10 ECHR in the case of *Magyar Helsinki Bizottság* was based on the insufficient consideration given by domestic authorities to the demands of freedom of expression.[29]

Therefore, what brings the Court to recognizing the existence of a conflict between two rights is not so much the fact that the information affects a particularly

---

[22]For instance, see the difference between absolute and qualified rights.

[23]One exception to this principle is when an absolute right is involved in a conflict, although in this instance framing the case as a conflict between rights may be disputed. In such a case, the absolute right should automatically prevail over the other right. See, for instance, ECtHR [GC], *Gäfgen v. Germany*, 1st June 2010, app. 22978/05.

[24]On the subject of conflicts of rights and hierarchy of rights, see Ducoulombier (2015), pp. 39–51.

[25]See para. 163 of the *Satakunnan* case.

[26]See para. 123 of the *Satakunnan* case.

[27]See, for instance, ECtHR, *Öllinger v. Austria*, 29 June 2006, app. 76900/01. For an express reference to this notion in a joint opinion, see *Pfeifer v. Austria*, 15 November 2007, app. 12556/03.

[28]See ECtHR, GC, *Amann v. Switzerland*, 16 February 2000, app. 27798/95.

[29]See *Magyar Helsinki Bizottság v. Hungary*, *op. cit.*, para. 176; but this solution was also based on the fact that the information requested was in possession of the authorities and did not sufficiently impact the right to privacy.

private aspect of an individual's life but rather the manner in which this personal data has been processed and published, beyond what can be considered as normally foreseeable.[30] *Satakunnan* is rather a case of data protection than a case of protection of privacy. The Court uses its case-law on DNA collection and retention to recall that "the protection of personal data is of fundamental importance to a person's enjoyment of his or her right to respect for private and family life."[31] The fact that the information processed does not belong to the core of Article 8 ECHR does not have a major bearing on the case in which form prevails over substance. As the Court explains:

> Article 8 of the Convention thus provides for the right to a form of informational self-determination, allowing individuals to rely on their right to privacy as regards data which, albeit neutral, are collected, processed and disseminated collectively and in such as form or manner that their Article 8 rights may be engaged.[32]

As to the framework applied to the case, an interesting argument is made by the applicants when reviewing the legitimate aim pursued by the State's interference, which could have had an impact on the manner in which the conflict could have been solved. The applicants stress that:

> the need to protect privacy in the instant case was abstract and hypothetical. Any threat to privacy had been practically non-existent and, in any event, the case was not at all about the privacy of isolated individuals.[33]

This would indicate the presence of an asymmetrical conflict, where the right which conflicts with the applicant's right is not held by an identified right-holder, which could then impact its concrete weight in the balance.[34] It could be indeed legitimate to consider that the right which is actually interfered with should carry more weight than the opposing right, when this right is not held by any identified right-holder but rather protected as an abstract value. This does not mean that, at the end of the balancing exercise, the applicant's right will necessarily prevail, but it will start the balancing exercise with an advantage. However this argument is dismissed by the Court, who reframes the conflict as a symmetrical conflict, by recalling that:

> it emerges clearly from the case file that the Data Protection Ombudsman acted on the basis of concrete complaints from individuals claiming that the publication of taxation data [...] infringed their right to privacy.[35]

This symmetrical nature of the conflict guarantees that both rights are indeed given an equal consideration at the beginning of the balancing exercise.

---

[30] See para. 136 of the *Satakunnan* case.

[31] See para. 137 of the *Satakunnan* case.

[32] *Idem.*

[33] See para. 156 of the *Satakunnan* case.

[34] See Ducoulombier (2008), pp. 219–225.

[35] See para. 157 of the *Satakunnan* case. Although a paragraph later the Court seems to analyze the case from the abstract prism of the conciliation between the rights operated by the legislator.

When it comes to solving conflicts between Articles 10 and 8 ECHR, the Court has devised a specific methodology to be followed by domestic courts. This methodology was developed in the twin Grand Chamber cases of *Von Hannover v. Germany (n°2)* and *Axel Springer AG v. Germany*. In *Von Hannover (n°2)*, the Grand Chamber stressed that, if the methodology and case-law of the Court were followed by domestic courts, respect for the subsidiarity principle meant that very strong reasons would be needed before the European Court could contemplate replacing the domestic courts' decision by its own assessment of the solution to be given to the conflict.[36] However, as mentioned in the subsequent case of *Aksu v. Turkey*:

> if the balance struck by the national authorities was unsatisfactory, in particular because the importance or scope of one of the rights at stake was not duly considered, the margin of appreciation would be a narrow one.[37]

This means that if domestic authorities do apply the methodology and criteria of the European Court, the margin of appreciation allocated to them should be a wide one, in line with the principle laid down in the *Chassagnou* case. However, the scope of the margin of appreciation in cases of conflicts between rights, in particular when Article 10 conflicts with Article 8 ECHR, has failed to be allocated in a consistent and coherent manner, as demonstrated for instance by the dissenting opinion in the Grand Chamber case of *Axel Springer AG v. Germany*.[38] In *Satakunnan*, the Court does not immediately clarify the scope of the margin of appreciation and simply recalls the general principle laid down in *Von Hannover (n°2)*.[39] However, in line with the reference to the subsidiarity principle, the Court's analysis relies heavily on the arguments of the Finnish Supreme Administrative Court, which applied the *Von Hannover (n°2)* criteria to the case.

---

[36]See para. 107 of the *Von Hannover (n°2)* case: "Where the balancing exercise has been undertaken by the national authorities in conformity with the criteria laid down in the Court's case-law, the Court would require strong reasons to substitute its view for that of the domestic courts".

[37]ECtHR, GC, *Aksu v. Turkey*, 15 March 2012, app. 4149/04 and 41029/04, para. 67.

[38]See the dissenting opinion of Judge López Guerra joined by Judges Jungwiert, Jaeger, Villiger and Poalelungi: "[...] none of the grounds which would justify a review by this Court of the judgments of the domestic courts are present in this case. The domestic courts did not fail to balance the conflicting interests or to apply the relevant criteria in doing so. They made no manifest error of appreciation; nor did they fail to consider all the relevant factors. Nevertheless, on this occasion and instead of concentrating its assessment on whether the domestic courts applied the above-mentioned criteria effectively, the Grand Chamber has chosen to re-examine the same facts that were brought before the national courts. And this was done in spite of the national courts having extensively assessed the circumstances of the case in a way that was not manifestly unreasonable, and with the added benefit of their direct examination of the context in which the events occurred. Analysing the same facts and using the same criteria and same balancing approach as the domestic courts, the Grand Chamber came to a different conclusion, giving more weight to the protection of the right to freedom of expression than to the protection of the right to privacy. But that is precisely what the case-law of this Court has established is not our task, that is, to set ourselves up as a fourth instance to repeat anew assessments duly performed by the domestic courts [...]".

[39]See para. 198 of the *Satakunnan* case.

The application of the *Von Hannover* methodology to the case may already call for some questioning, as the dissenting opinion of judge Tsotsoria in the chamber case illustrates, in which she doubted that it was pertinent to apply the *Von Hannover*'s framework to *Satakunnan*. Indeed, the case is quite different from the German case as no intimate information is concerned in *Satakunnan*. Although elaborated for a particular conflict involving the right to reputation and privacy, the Court has found it pertinent to apply this methodology, *mutatis mutandis*, to other cases. However, it seems that it was necessary for the Court to apply these criteria in order to support the conclusion that there was no violation of Article 10 ECHR in *Satakunnan*, by using other arguments than the mere quantity of information published as we will see.

The *Von Hannover* criteria that the Court found pertinent to transpose, as far as it was possible to do so, to the *Satakunnan* case are as follows: the contribution to a debate of public interest, the degree of notoriety of the person affected, the subject of the news report, the prior conduct of the person concerned, the content, form and consequences of the publication and the circumstances in which the photographs were taken. In addition, when cases are lodged before the Court on the basis of an alleged infringement of Article 10 ECHR, the Court must have regard for the way in which the information was obtained, its veracity and the seriousness of the penalty imposed on the applicant.

Coming back to the margin of appreciation, in *Satakunnan* the Court allocates a wide margin of appreciation to the State. The scope of the margin of appreciation is clarified at a late stage in the reasoning of the Court and stems from the application of the *Von Hannover* criteria that must be used to solve the conflict between Articles 10 and 8 of the Convention, which in the case of *Satakunnan* are strongly connected to one another.

First, the Court tackles the central issue of whether the publication interfered with contributes to a debate of public interest.[40] Usually, in the Court's case-law, interference with journalist work in this area is highly suspicious and calls for a narrow margin of appreciation.[41] It was therefore necessary for the majority to demonstrate that the indiscriminate publication of fiscal information did not belong to this highly protected category, without contradicting its own general principles, such as the fact that it is not for domestic authorities nor the Court to issue value judgments on editorial choices made by journalists as to the reporting techniques, or the fact that, in previous case-law, the Court did say that publication of fiscal information was a

[40]The manner in which the Grand Chamber reaches the conclusion that there is no violation of Article 10 ECtHR is quite different from that of the chamber that considered that the information contributed to a debate of general interest, that no professional ethical question was engaged, but that there was no reason to substitute its views for that of the domestic courts. The Grand Chamber is much more severe towards the applicants' behaviour.

[41]See para. 167 of the *Satakunnan* case.

matter of public interest[42] as well as the importance given in its case-law to new technologies and the internet.[43]

The specific question under scrutiny in *Satakunnan* is particularly interesting to our modern society where major scandals are revealed thanks to the large publication of materials online. The problem for the courts involved in this case was that it was necessary for them, in order to follow the ECJ case-law, to demonstrate that the sole object of the publication was not the disclosure to the public of information, opinions or ideas, irrespective of the medium used to transmit them. It is true that it is difficult to understand how the domestic courts and the ECtHR concluded that this was not the case. The choice they made was to rule that the information published did not contribute to a debate of general interest. This may be open to discussion although, it can also be argued that journalism, even data journalism, requires more than collecting and publishing raw information. Indeed, this is the line of reasoning that is followed by the Court. What is fundamental in the Court's reasoning is the fact that collecting information is part of journalist work but the same cannot be said of the indiscriminate publication of the data. It therefore distinguishes between the public interest in giving access to the data and the public interest in disseminating the data.[44] The manner and form of the publication is what hurt the applicants. The Court even goes as far as classifying the publication done by the applicants as voyeurism, which therefore allows it to deny the high degree of protection it usually grants to journalists.[45]

Even if the original purpose of the Finnish law is transparency, so as to encourage debates on matters of public interest, the Court stresses that the publication did not focus on particular public figures which brings us to the second *Von Hannover* criterion: the notoriety of the persons concerned by the publication. The Court emphasizes that among the 1.2 million persons affected, very few were public-figures or well-known personalities for whom publication of fiscal information could, under certain circumstances, be considered as contributing to a debate of public interest and for whom the degree of protection offered to their right to privacy is lower than the protection afforded to ordinary citizens.[46] Indeed, the level of protection offered by certain Convention rights in the Court's case-law depends on the status of the right-holder. For instance, political actors or journalists usually enjoy a high level of protection of their freedom of expression due to their role in a democratic society, while civil servants or judges enjoy a lower level of protection due to their duty of loyalty towards the State. When it comes to Article 8 ECHR, on the contrary, political actors or public figures enjoy a lower level of protection of their privacy than ordinary citizens do, as they chose a public life and must accept a higher level of scrutiny from the media and the public at large. However, the Court

[42]See, for instance, ECtHR, GC, *Fressoz and Roire v. France, op. cit.*, para. 50.

[43]See, for instance, ECtHR, *Ahmet Yıldırım v. Turkey,* 18 December 2012, app. 3111/10.

[44]See para. 175 of the *Satakunnan* case.

[45]See para. 177–178 of the *Satakunnan* case.

[46]See para. 179–180 of the *Satakunnan* case.

stresses that the publication did not target public figures, as other publications did. The applicants try to defend themselves by stressing that too much information kills the information and that massive publication of information may contribute to a certain form of anonymity for the persons involved. Although interesting, the argument fails, the Court insisting on the abuse of the originally legitimate purpose of transparency pursued by Finnish law.

Moving on to the method of obtaining the information, although the applicants did nothing illegal, the Court targets their behaviour and in particular the fact that they hired individuals to collect information when they came under the radar of the authorities. According to the Court, this tends to indicate that the applicants tried to "[circumvent] the normal channels" for getting the information, in contradiction with the ethics of journalism. This is stressed by the Court in order to undermine the good faith of the applicants which is a requirement of responsible journalism.[47]

Then the Court analyzes other elements related to the content, form and consequences of the publication and goes back to previous issues such as the fact that the information published was already available to the public. But once again, the nature of the information is not as important as its treatment and the Court recalls that this is a case of processing of personal data, thus leading to a high degree of protection to the benefit of Article 8 ECHR. In addition, the Court recalls that the weight given to Article 8 ECHR for information available to the public is not consistent in its case-law and depends on the circumstances of each case. Linked to the manner in which the information was accessible and could been obtained, this demonstrates for the Court that the nature of publicly available information does not run counter to specific safeguards for the right to privacy, in particular when it comes to publication of an unlimited extent. The publicly available nature of the information must be therefore distinguished from its publication, in particular without consent, similarly to what the ECJ ruled in *Volker und Markus Schecke GbR*.[48] The Court considers that the original intent of the legislator had been abused by the applicants. The balancing exercise achieved by the legislator, under judicial review, must therefore be given special consideration which leads to the allocation of a wide margin of appreciation to the State, as becomes more and more common in the Court's case-law, even when Article 10 ECHR is involved such as in the case of *Animal Defenders International v. the United Kingdom*.[49] Finally, in light of the limited restriction imposed on the applicants, the Court rules by 15 to two votes that there had been no violation of Article 10 ECHR.

If one may think that the *Satakunnan* case achieves the right balance between Article 10 and Article 8 ECHR, several criticisms may be raised regarding the reasoning of the Court.

---

[47] See para. 185 of the *Satakunnan* case.

[48] ECJ, GC, *Volker und Markus Schecke GbR and Hartmut Eifert*, 9 November 2010, Cases C-92/09 and C-93/09, ECLI:EU:C:2010:662.

[49] See ECtHR, GC, *Animal Defenders International v. the United Kingdom*, 22 April 2013, app. 48876/08.

First, we may recall what we said about framing the case as a conflict between two convention rights. The case can be contrasted with *Magyar Helsinki Bizottság v. Hungary* where the Court found that there was no conflict between Articles 10 and 8 ECHR. One could also argue that it should have been the case in *Satakunnan* due to the content of the information published and its public nature. Had the case been analyzed solely under the prism of Article 10 ECHR, the solution may have been different.

In addition, the weight given to both rights, which has an impact on the margin of appreciation allocated to the domestic authorities, may also be subject to criticism. It is true that the scope of the margin of association is always subject to controversy. There is no hierarchy between the various factors determining the scope of the margin of appreciation, these factors may pull in different directions and this is even truer in case of a conflict between rights. In our case, one may object that even if fiscal information is protected by Article 8 ECHR, it represents an interest which lies at the periphery of the right to privacy as opposed for instance to information regarding health or sexual orientation, while freedom of the press lies at the core of Article 10 ECHR. Although we said that hierarchy was not a method to solve conflicts between rights, balancing is not opposed to the idea of hierarchy. Indeed, weights must be ascribed to rights and we know that in the Court's case-law certain rights, or certain aspects within rights, are afforded different level of protection.

However, it is also true that, even if fiscal information is not considered as a core aspect of Article 8 ECHR, there is a consensus in Europe regarding the protection of its confidentiality. Normally, when there is a consensus in Europe on a subject, this leads the Court to the conclusion that a narrow margin of appreciation should be allocated to the State whose decision contradicts the existing consensus. Therefore, the decision of the Court may seem, at first glance, contradictory. However, this is not the case because even if Finland authorizes, to a certain extent, disclosure of fiscal information, the national courts' decision limited this publication and therefore was in line with the existing European consensus protecting confidentiality of fiscal information.[50]

On this point the dissenting opinion of judge Sajó and judge Karakaş is interesting. The dissenters criticized the scope of the margin of appreciation and the balancing of the competing rights. They argued that it was contradictory to grant, at the same time, a wide margin of appreciation to the legislator to favour transparency and a wide margin of appreciation to domestic courts to contradict this objective by protecting privacy, thus stressing the confusion of the doctrine of the margin of appreciation.[51] It is true that this part of the case is far from being clear.

On the balancing, the dissenters criticized the fact that domestic courts failed to give due consideration to both rights. This criticism seems excessive, although the domestic courts could have expanded their references to the European case-law to

[50]See para. 81–82 of the *Satakunnan* case for the comparative law material. At para. 120, the Court stresses that the case is unusual in that respect.

[51]See para. 19–20 of their dissenting opinion.

other cases besides *Von Hannover (n°2)*. It is true that extensive space is dedicated to the analysis of privacy considerations, in particular by the ECtHR when it reviews the ECJ case-law, and that the right of the public to receive information is left in the shadows since the information is not considered as contributing to a debate of general interest. This can lead to the criticism that there is in fact no real balancing between Articles 10 and 8 ECHR. The dissenters stress the various elements supporting Article 10 ECHR that the majority should have taken into consideration. However, the majority *did* take them into consideration and this is why it was necessary to find arguments to support the idea that no journalist activity was involved, otherwise the judgment would have been in blatant contradiction with the traditional Court's case-law. A convincing argument propounded by the dissenters is that the Court, when balancing rights, must take into account the seriousness of the interference suffered by the rights involved, in particular in this case Article 8 ECHR.[52] This would have been in coherence with its case-law on conflicts between freedom of expression and reputation, which emphasizes that, in order for Article 8 ECHR to be engaged, the interference it suffers must be serious enough, must reach a minimum threshold.[53] However, this element is absolutely not mentioned in *Satakunnan* while the importance of the interference with Article 10 ECHR is downplayed. The analysis of the sanction imposed on the applicants, focusing on the fact they were not prohibited from publishing fiscal information as long as they complied with Finnish and EU legal rules, misses the point that the applicants stopped their activities and that the first company went bankrupt. The lack of concrete analysis of the seriousness of the harm suffered by the right to privacy seems to support the applicants' argument that the conflict was indeed an asymmetrical conflict, which should have had an impact on the balancing exercise made by the Court.

It could also be objected to the majority that the case is contrary to the general principles of the Court's own case-law as the core of what is criticized in the applicants' behaviour is the manner and form of their publication. In that regard, the arguments developed by the dissenting opinion are also interesting. Indeed, they consider that the majority's judgment weakens, without foundation, the "robust protection" usually offered to journalists by the Court. They criticize first the fact that the majority considers that the applicants were not engaged in journalist activities. There is, indeed, a major division between the majority and the minority about the kind of work required by journalist activity. In addition, it is also important to stress that the ECJ ruled that, due to the importance of freedom of expression in a democratic society, the notion of journalism should be interpreted in a large manner, in light of the evolution of the profession and of technologies. The position of the

[52]See para. 26 of their dissenting opinion.

[53]See, for instance, ECtHR, GC, *Axel Springer AG v. Germany*, *op. cit.*, para. 83: "In order for Article 8 to come into play, [...] an attack on a person's reputation must attain a certain level of seriousness and in a manner causing prejudice to personal enjoyment of the right to respect for private life."

domestic courts and of the European Court does not seem to be in line with this recommendation. For the majority, if the collection of data is part of journalist work, it is a preamble to real journalist activity which needs an added value, "an analytical input" as the Court says,[54] to be characterized as such. For the minority, this is a novelty in the Court's case-law, especially as we mentioned that the Court reiterates that it is not its place nor that of the authorities to "substitute its own views for those of the press as to what technique of reporting should be adopted".[55] It is interesting to stress that, for the dissenters, "Journalism is first and foremost the collection and presentation of facts and not 'analytical' input. Fact takes precedence over opinion".[56] If this statement seems excessive as journalism may require some sort of analysis, following the majority's reasoning, one can wonder whether leakers will be treated as journalists and will be protected as such (and as much). In addition, the Court's decision raises interesting questions about who decides who is or is not a journalist. However, one may hope that, in other cases, the content of the information linked may prevail over the form of the dissemination, so as to offer leakers a higher level of protection in light of the case-law of the ECtHR on whistle blowers.

The minority also criticized the fact that the Court needed to argue that the original intent of the legislator had been abused, by focusing on the extent of the publication, to demonstrate that the publication of fiscal information did not contribute to a debate of public interest, in contradiction with the underlying principle of the Finnish legislation. They also criticized the parallel made between this publication and tabloid press, which is indeed excessive as the nature of the information published is not intimate. In addition, as rightly pointed out by the dissenters, it is not less voyeuristic to publish fiscal information about the richest people.[57]

If the majority's reasoning may seem fragile on certain aspects, it is not without merit to emphasize that there is a difference between accessibility of an information to the public and dissemination of this information on the internet. The means used for the dissemination of information have always had an impact on the analysis of the Court with regard to Article 10 ECHR.[58]

The worries expressed by the dissenters in *Satakunnan* may not be completely convincing but they hit several sore points, in particular when the case is read in light of the wider case-law on the notion of responsible journalism.

Indeed, the parallel is drawn by the dissenters between the margin of appreciation given to domestic courts to assess what a journalist activity is with the margin of appreciation given to domestic courts in order to analyze the requirements of

---

[54] See para. 175 of the *Satakunnan* case.

[55] See para. 8 of Judge Sajó and Judge Karakaş's dissenting opinion, quoting from *Axel Springer AG v. Germany, op. cit.*

[56] See para. 8 of the dissenting opinion.

[57] See para. 12 of the dissenting opinion.

[58] See, for instance, ECtHR, *Radio France and Others v. France*, 30 March 2004, app. 53984/00, para. 39: "[...] in considering the 'duties and responsibilities' of a journalist, the potential impact of the medium concerned is an important factor, and it is commonly acknowledged that the audiovisual media have often a much more immediate and powerful effect than the print media [...]".

responsible journalism.[59] In both instances, these notions have been used to "allow a less strict analysis of the balancing performed by the State and the proportionality of the measure adopted".[60] Although one must be careful not to paint too grim a picture of the recent Court's case-law on Article 10 ECHR, as the Court still remains highly protective of several aspects of freedom of expression such as secrecy of sources, on other aspects the case-law may be worrisome.

4 The *Satakunnan* Case in Light of the Notion of Responsible Journalism and Its Impact on the Balance Between Articles 10 and 8 ECHR

If one may agree on the substance of the *Satakunnan* case, it must be stressed that the fears expressed by the dissenters when it comes to the protection of freedom of expression by the Court are not without foundation. Indeed, when this case is put in perspective with several other cases, in particular *Pentikäinen v. Finland* and *Bédat v. Switzerland*, concerns may be raised as to the impact of the development of the notion of responsible journalism on the protection afforded to article 10 ECHR. As stressed by the dissenters citing these two cases, "'Responsible journalism' has recently been used as one of the factors to grant a wider margin of appreciation, resulting in undermining the freedom of the press".[61]

The *Bédat* case is interesting as it involves a conflict between articles 10 and 8 ECHR, in which the Grand chamber concluded, in a debatable manner, that the applicant's conviction at the domestic level for publishing information covered by the secrecy of criminal investigations did not breach article 10 ECHR.[62] The applicant had published an article on a tragic event, involving a driver who appeared to have voluntarily killed and injured people on a Lausanne's bridge, containing information pertaining to the ongoing criminal investigation and to the mental health of the perpetrator.

First, the Court recalled that the protection afforded by article 10 ECHR to journalists is subject to the proviso that they act in good faith in order to provide

[59]See para. 21 of the dissenting opinion.

[60]*Idem.*

[61]See para. 21 of the dissenting opinion.

[62]On the contrary, the chamber ruled by four to three votes that there had been a violation of Article 10. In particular, the chamber, according to us, rightly played down the importance of Article 6 ECHR (right to a fair hearing and presumption of innocence) and of Article 8 ECHR (since the applicant did not use the remedies available to defend his privacy). See ECtHR, *A.B. v. Switzerland*, 1 July 2014, app. 56925/08.

accurate and reliable information in accordance with the tenets of responsible journalism.[63]

Linked to the idea that the use of freedom of expression entails "duties and responsibilities", the development of the notion of responsible journalism may be traced back to the Grand Chamber case of *Stoll v. Switzerland*, in which the Court stated that:

> notwithstanding the vital role played by the press in a democratic society, journalists cannot, in principle, be released from their duty to obey the ordinary criminal law on the basis that Article 10 ECHR affords them protection [...].[64]

Coming back to the application of these ideas in *Bédat* and to the balance made between Articles 10, 8 and 6 ECHR, several assertions of the Court may be disputed, as illustrated by judge López Guerra[65] and judge Yudikvska's dissenting opinions. The chamber's judgment reflected a more precise assessment of the value to be given to the concrete competing rights and interests at stake.

First, as to the form, the content of the article and the contribution to a debate of general interest, relying heavily on the domestic court's ruling, the Court stressed the negative, even mocking, tone of the article. It is difficult to see why this choice in the reporting was questioned by the domestic court and the ECtHR, while the Court's case-law reiterates that it is not for courts to impose a particular editorial style to journalists.[66] In light of *Stoll*, *Bédat* or *Satakunnan*, one may wonder what befalls of this principle. In any case, as recalled by judge López Guerra, this should not have any bearing on the assessment of the article's contribution to a debate of public interest.[67] The Court considered that the incident itself was a matter of public interest but denied, without sufficient ground, that the article contributed to a debate of public interest on this issue. It is necessary to recall that the article questioned the sanity of a man who had killed three people and injured eight others without providing any reasons to the police during questioning. Once again, the Court simply and wrongly deferred to the position of the domestic court.

Then, as to the weight given to Articles 6 and 8 ECHR, the Grand Chamber first considered that the publication of the article in itself ran the risk of influencing the course of justice. It did not accept the argument, which had been followed by the chamber, that a single article could not influence a trial which would not begin before several months and would take place in front of professional judges. As to Article

[63]See ECtHR, GC, *Stoll v. Switzerland*, 10 December 2007, app. 69698/01, para. 103: "Hence, the safeguard afforded by Article 10 to journalists in relation to reporting on issues of general interest is subject to the proviso that they are acting in good faith and on an accurate factual basis and provide 'reliable and precise' information in accordance with the ethics of journalism".

[64]See para. 102 of the *Stoll* case.

[65]The judge was, however, in the majority in the *Satakunnan* case.

[66]For instance, in ECtHR, GC, *Jersild v. Denmark*, 23 September 1994, app. 69698/01, para. 31, the Court recalled that the "protection of Article 10 extends not only to the substance of the ideas and information expressed but also to the form in which they are conveyed".

[67]See para. 7 of Judge López Guerra's dissenting opinion in *Bédat*.

8 ECHR, the Grand Chamber also ignored the pertinent argument of the abstract involvement of the right to privacy which, without depriving this right of protection, could have led to the reduction of its concrete weight in the balancing exercise.

The Court chose to put the emphasis on the positive obligations of the State to protect privacy by instituting criminal proceedings in lieu of the accused, as well as on the personal nature of the information published. However, even the publication of sensitive personal information may give way to the interest of the public to be informed. Although personal, the information published was clearly connected to the subject of general interest of the article.

However, the decision to grant a high level of protection to an accused's right to privacy is quite traditional in the Court's case-law.[68] The Court considers that the status of the right-holder involved in a criminal incident is not equivalent to that of a public figure, insisting on his or her particular vulnerability. On the contrary, it could be argued that individuals committing crimes have taken the risk to put themselves under the scrutiny of the media and the public at large, thus leading to the protection afforded to their right to privacy being rightly reduced. Therefore, even if certain information pertains to private aspects of the accused's life, their publication, when contributing to the clarification of the event (as to the context, the motive etc.), should be considered as contributing to a debate of general interest and should lead to the preeminence of Article 10 ECHR over Article 8 ECHR, in particular when the individual concerned had not seen fit to institute proceedings to protect his privacy against the journalist, illustrating the rather asymmetrical nature of the conflict.

This controversial trend in the Court's case law, diminishing the protection afforded to the press, is also to be found in the case of *Pentikäinen v. Finland*. This case is not related to a conflict between Articles 10 and 8 ECHR. However, the idea of responsible journalism is applied beyond its traditional scope, to journalists' actions and behaviours[69] and it may contribute to explaining why certain judges are worried for the protection of freedom of expression.

The applicant had been arrested, prosecuted and convicted for refusing to comply with a police order to leave the scene of a demonstration. In addition, as a result of his detention, he was unable to transmit his work on the demonstration during more than 17 h, while the Court has often stressed that time is essential in imparting

[68]See, for instance, ECtHR, *Egeland and Hanseid v. Norway,* 16 April 2009, app. 34438/04.

[69]See para. 90 of the *Pentikäinen* case: "[...] the concept of responsible journalism, as a professional activity which enjoys the protection of Article 10 of the Convention, is not confined to the content of information which is collected and/or disseminated by journalistic means. That concept also embraces, inter alia, the lawfulness of the conduct of a journalist, including, and of relevance to the instant case, his or her public interaction with the authorities when exercising journalistic functions. The fact that a journalist has breached the law in that connection is a most relevant, albeit not decisive, consideration when determining whether he or she has acted responsibly."

information.[70] Although journalists are not above the law,[71] it is difficult to expect them to leave the scene of a demonstration at the request of the police while their function is to report on such major events, in particular as these events often turn violent, which then may lead to the use of force by the police. If peaceful journalists are forced to leave under these circumstances, who is going to report on these events, who is going to perform the role of public watchdogs? It is quite shocking that, in this case, the majority found no violation of Article 10 ECHR,[72] which seems to contradict the principle it recalled about the role of the press when covering demonstration and the fact that "any attempt to remove journalists from the scene of demonstration must [...] be subject to strict scrutiny".[73] If it could be accepted that the arrest was necessary in a democratic society, it is difficult to understand how the majority can consider that the length of the detention or the need to prosecute and convict the journalist, although no penalty was imposed, was necessary in a democratic society and may not have any chilling effect on journalists. What was the pressing social need for these specific actions from the domestic authorities?[74] This restrictive trend in the Court's case-law is even more complex to understand than its position on conflicts of rights cases, where competing legitimate interests must be balanced and the solution found may find support in plausible arguments, which as far as I am concerned are lacking from the Court's reasoning in *Pentikäinen.*

To conclude, one may stress that the Court's case-law on conflict between Articles 10 and 8 ECHR has greatly varied over the years. In the past, it was exceptional for the Court to recognize the existence of a conflict, in particular when reputation was involved as it was not considered as a facet of Article 8 ECHR. Then reputation was expressly included from 2004 onwards in Article

---

[70]See, for instance, ECtHR, *Observer and Guardian v. the United Kingdom*, 26 November 1991, app. 13585/88, para. 60: "[...] news is a perishable commodity and to delay its publication, even for a short period, may well deprive it of all its value and interest".

[71]See para. 91 of the *Pentikäinen* case: "[...] It is to be noted in this connection that paragraph 2 of Article 10 does not guarantee a wholly unrestricted freedom of expression even with respect to media coverage of matters of serious public concern. In particular, and notwithstanding the vital role played by the media in a democratic society, *journalists cannot, in principle, be released from their duty to obey the ordinary criminal law on the basis that, as journalists, Article 10 affords them a cast-iron defence* [...]. In other words, a journalist cannot claim an exclusive immunity from criminal liability for the sole reason that, unlike other individuals exercising the right to freedom of expression, the offence in question was committed during the performance of his or her journalistic functions", emphasis added.

[72]By 13 votes to four. The chamber (judgment from February the 4th 2014) found that there had been no violation of Article 10 ECtHR by five votes to two.

[73]See para. 89 of the *Pentikäinen* case: "The 'watchdog' role of the media assumes particular importance in such contexts since their presence is a guarantee that the authorities can be held to account for their conduct vis-à-vis the demonstrators and the public at large when it comes to the policing of large gatherings, including the methods used to control or disperse protesters or to preserve public order. Any attempt to remove journalists from the scene of demonstrations must therefore be subject to strict scrutiny."

[74]On this question, see the dissenting opinion of Judge Spano, joined by Judge Spielmann, Lemmens and Dedov.

8 ECHR,[75] impacting the Court's case-law by reinforcing the weight given to Article 8 ECHR when conflicting with Article 10 ECHR, disrupting the traditional pre-eminence of freedom of expression. Then, the cases of *Von Hannover (n°2)* and *Axel Springer AG*, where the Court presented in a pedagogical manner the criteria to be used to solve a conflict between Articles 10 and 8 ECHR, were considered as re-establishing Article 10 ECHR in its predominant position. However, this interpretation of the Court's case-law was short lived and in the past few years, although it may be more and more difficult to decipher the position of the Court towards freedom of expression, it seems clear enough that the manner in which the Court solves a conflict between Articles 10 and 8 of ECHR is heavily influenced by the principle of subsidiarity. Added to worries regarding the impact of new technologies on individuals' lives, this leaves the protection of freedom of expression being more and more eroded, raising in turn new concerns for the protection of a democratic society.

References

Ducoulombier P (2008) Conflicts between fundamental rights and the European Court of Human Rights: an overview. In: Brems E (ed) Conflicts between fundamental rights. Intersentia, Antwerp, pp 217–247

Ducoulombier P (2015) Interaction between human rights: are all human rights equal? In: Geiger C (ed) Research handbook on human rights and intellectual property. Edward Elgar Publishing, pp 39–51

Peggy Ducoulombier is Professor of Public Law at the University of Strasbourg. She holds a PhD from the University of Strasbourg. She previously worked as a Lecturer for the University of Keele (UK), Aberdeen (UK) and as Professor at the University of Perpignan (France). Her main area of expertise is the European Convention on Human Rights. She is the author of *Les conflits de droits fondamentaux devant la Cour européenne des droits de l'Homme*, published by Bruylant, in 2011.

[75] See, for instance, ECtHR, *Radio France and others v. France*, 30 March 2004, app. 53984/00, para. 31: "[. . .] The Court would observe that the right to protection of one's reputation is of course one of the rights guaranteed by Article 8 of the Convention, as one element of the right to respect for private life."

The Right to Respect for a Journalist's Private Life: Combined Analysis of Articles 8 and 10 of the Convention. Case *Khadija Ismayilova v. Azerbaijan*

Beata Jurik

Contents

1 Introduction 249
2 The Facts of the Case 250
2.1 Threatening Letter and Publication of Videos Depicting the Applicant's Intimate Life 250
2.2 Criminal Investigation 251
3 The Strict Examination of the Obligations Under Article 8 in Light of Article 10 252
3.1 Positive Obligation Under Article 8: The State Has to Secure Respect for Private Life of a Journalist 253
3.2 The Serious and Unjustifiable Breach of the Applicant's Privacy by the Prosecutor's Disclosure of Information About Her Private and Family Life 256
4 Analysis of the Positive Obligation Under Article 10 and Recognition of the Inherent Link with Article 8 257
4.1 A Cumulative Examination of the Human Rights Violations Invoked in the Present Case 257
4.2 Required Clarification on the Content of the Positive Obligation Under Article 10 . 261
5 Conclusion 263

1 Introduction

Articles 8 and 10 of the European Convention on Human Rights, which respectively provide the right to respect for private and family right and the freedom of expression, are traditionally balanced by the Court. In fact, it is because they often come into conflict and the European Court of Human Rights (ECtHR) must choose which of these fundamental rights prevails over the other. Generally, if we are in presence of Articles 8 and 10 in the case involving a journalist, it is because he violated a person's right to respect for private life, for example by disclosing their personal information or data. The victim lodges a complaint against the journalist who defends himself by invoking his freedom of expression and the necessity to inform

B. Jurik (✉)
University of Strasbourg, Center of International and European Studies, Strasbourg, France

M. Elósegui et al. (eds.), *The Rule of Law in Europe*,
https://doi.org/10.1007/978-3-030-56001-0_15

the public. In other cases, where journalists are on the other side of the stand, i.e. when they are victims of violations of their rights, they face notably arrests, bad treatments in jail, suffer abuse by the police or in the worst cases they are murdered. In most cases investigations are not effective. Commonly the ECtHR has to hear these cases in the light of Articles 2, 3 or 6.

In the case *Khadija Ismayilova v. Azerbaijan*,[1] a well-known journalist is victim of attacks on her private life, attacks that she would have never faced if she was not a journalist.

Several reasons explain this choice to analyze it here: firstly, the case is original because it is the first time that the Court examines a violation of the right to respect for private and family right of a journalist. This judgment is a recent case. It comes in a particular context of hatred towards journalists, and attacks not only against them but against the press and the freedom of expression in general are increasing in many European countries.

Another reason is that this judgment provides a new and necessary approach by the Court: both the right to private life and the freedom of expression are invoked by the applicant and examined by the Court both successively and in a concomitant way, through cross-references for the determination of their scope. In fact, these rights do not enter in conflict in this case and so the Court did not proceed to their balancing: on the contrary, the Strasbourg judges combined Articles 8 and 10, analyzed one in the light of the other as if they were complementary. The Court did not rule just on the right which we can qualify as "the principal one" and use the "not necessary formula" for the other one. This new approach of the Court allowed it to embrace fully and entirely all violations of human rights in the case.

2 The Facts of the Case

2.1 Threatening Letter and Publication of Videos Depicting the Applicant's Intimate Life

Ms. Khadija Ismayilova is a prominent investigative journalist from Azerbaijan working especially on corruption and violations of human rights. In the present case she claimed to be victim of a campaign of discrediting and intimidation, especially after her revelations about the Azerbaijani President's family during 2010–2012. Following her numerous publications about the family's suspicious economic activities she has been threatened and intimidated in various ways. In March 2012 she received a letter asking her to cease her journalistic activities. In case she would refuse to do so, the anonymous author of the letter promised to ruin her reputation by publishing a video showing her involved in sexual intercourse with her boyfriend. The letter contained various images from the video taken in her

[1] ECtHR, *Khadija Ismayilova v. Azerbaijan*, 10 Jan. 2019, Nos. 65286/13 and 57270/14.

apartment by hidden cameras that she discovered later. Ms. Ismayilova did not only publicly refuse to stop her professional activities, she also lodged a complaint and asked national authorities for protection.

As a result, the video from the letter was posted online on a website named musavat.tv[2] and reprinted by newspapers close to the government,[3] accusing her of immorality. More than one year later, while investigations in connection with the letter and the first video were underway, another similar video of the applicant (or a woman meant to resemble her) was posted on a fictive website in a relation with Səs.[4]

2.2 *Criminal Investigation*

In her complaint in 2012, the applicant asked the prosecution authorities to ensure her safety, to investigate on the letter and on the publication of videos and to hold those responsible for the threat accountable. Criminal proceedings were launched a few days later and the authorities took some limited steps to advance the investigations.[5] The applicant, persuaded that authorities were not doing everything they could, publicly accused the Baku City Prosecutor's Office of ineffectiveness and slowness of investigations.

Following the press release by the applicant, the Prosecutor decided to answer by a public statement in which a large part of personal information relating to the applicant and her relatives[6] were disclosed. The Prosecutor justified this divulgation by his will to inform the public of the outcome of investigations and to respond to the applicant's accusations about the inactivity of authorities responsible for investigating.

The applicant alleged the breach of her rights under Articles 6, 8, 10 and 13 of the Convention. The Court's answer to those accusations is particularly interesting. The ECtHR carried out a review of two articles: Article 8 and Article 10 of the Convention. It did not examine the right to a fair trial and the right to an effective remedy. In fact, the judges proceeded on a combined analysis of the right to respect for private life and the freedom of expression. Firstly, the Court held a particularly strict examination of obligations under Article 8. During this review the Court

[2]*Ibid.*, para. 15: The domain name "musavat.tv" was apparently chosen to create the suggestion of a link with the Musavat parti or its newspaper, Yeni Musavat.

[3]Three newspapers published articles about the intimate videos: the newspaper Səs published an article titled "Not surprising" and "Who should Khadija sue?" and two others Yeni Azerbaycan, Iki Sahil were also particularly offensive against her. All three are State-controlled and not independent, operating as media organs of the party in power—YAP.

[4]Səs is a newspaper owned by one of the founders of YAP, the ruling party.

[5]Including the hearing of the applicant and her friends, visit of her apartment without any other significant investigations.

[6]Full names, home addresses, contacts, professions, nature of relationship with the applicant.

insisted on the link with Article 10 of the Convention. Then, the judges from the fifth Chamber made a brave and particularly expected step: they continued the analysis of violations of the applicant's rights by an examination of a potential breach of obligations under Article 10. The positive obligation under Article 10 in this case necessarily resulted in serious and flagrant violations of the rights of Article 8.

3 The Strict Examination of the Obligations Under Article 8 in Light of Article 10

The Court recalled throughout its reasoning that the applicant is not just an ordinary victim, but a prominent investigative journalist.[7] It doesn't mean that the Court gave some privilege to the applicant: it only means that judges necessarily kept in mind that an interference with the exercise of rights in Article 8 alleged by the applicant appears to be intimately related to the practice of her profession.

This link between the "human being" of the journalist and her function was important in the reasoning, to the point that the Court carried out a particularly strict control, always keeping an eye on the link between the alleged facts and the professional quality of the victim.

The Strasbourg judges realized a fairly detailed examination of the alleged violations of Article 8. They divided the reasoning in two parts, dealing first with the issue of the threatening letter and the disclosure of the videos before addressing the revelations made by the Baku Prosecutor. This Court's choice is very pedagogical. On the one hand, concerning the first set of allegations, the Court encountered the impossibility to identify the author of the interference. Thus, it was not possible to sanction the State in terms of negative obligation, "[a]s no evidence permitted to identify any State official as the author of violation, or even to make any connection between the author and the State, the violation could not be amputated to Azerbaijanis authorities. Hence, it could not be considered to have violated the applicant's right."[8] On the other hand, concerning the disclosure by the Prosecutor of the applicant's personal information, the State was not only the direct author of the incident in question, but this interference was so serious that its justification by the government was impossible and it deserved to be pointed out.

The Court found a double violation of the State's obligations under Article 8. At first, it recalled that the States have to secure respect of private life of a

---

[7]ECtHR, *Khadija Ismayilova v. Azerbaijan*, 10 Jan. 2019, Nos. 65286/13 and 57270/14, paras. 105, 116 and 128.

[8]*Ibid.*, para. 85: contrary to the demand of the applicant who argued that the State had breached not only the positive obligation (to protect her right to respect for her home and private life), but also the negative obligation (because there had been an unjustified breach with her right to respect for her home and private life by what she qualified "public authorities" as they were linked institutionally and operationally to the State.

journalist. Then, the ECtHR condemned the State for a serious and unjustifiable breach of the negative obligation under Article 8.

3.1 Positive Obligation Under Article 8: The State Has to Secure Respect for Private Life of a Journalist

Concerning the threatening letter and the publication of the videos, their authors were not identified, even though there were some suspicions. Ms. Ismayilova claimed that the State is directly responsible of the above-mentioned incidents. She provided a series of evidence[9] against the State and argued that these violations fall under both types of obligations—positive and negative.

The negative one, because the State interfered in her right through its own agents or through private entities under its control, and the positive because it failed to protect her private life and to investigate effectively on her allegations.

The government submitted that there was no interference by the State with the applicant's rights under Article 8. It considered that the authors could not be identified because there was no evidence and rejected all accusations of the applicant about the campaign of intimidation because of her recent journalistic findings.[10] The government argued, in a rather dismissive way, that the applicant was a public figure and so she could not be surprised if other newspapers revealed information about her private life.[11] To justify the fact that there was no breach of a positive obligation under Article 8 of the Convention, the government said it had taken all necessary investigative steps and provided a short list of those without any further detail[12] or evidence.

The Court did not accept the argument of the applicant, based on the presumption of guilt of the State and a direct violation of Article 8. In the title of point b. of the Court's assessment, the judges posed a clear alternative between "positive or negative obligations".

Therefore, the Court did not examine both types of obligations, it gave the State the benefit of the doubt, but in front of all the evidence provided by the applicant and because of the weak defense of the State, this "gift" made by the Court to Azerbaijani authorities resembled in the end to a Trojan horse. The Court turned the so-called impossibility of identification of the author against the State.

---

[9]*Ibid.*, paras. 86–90 of the judgment: "material evidence"—phone line, additional wires and hidden cameras were installed by an employee of ATS belonging to Baktelekom, a company fully owned and controlled by the State or "motives" of the State to discredit the applicant because of her work.

[10]*Ibid.*, paras. 101–102.

[11]*Ibid.*, para. 103.

[12]*Ibid.*, para. 104.

The Court actually extended the positive obligation for the State to secure the respect for a private life in the sphere of individual relationships[13] to "questions relating to the effectiveness of the criminal investigations".[14] This matter is not new for the Court, which already considered numerous cases concerning the States' obligation to investigate criminal matters where journalists are victims.[15] The Court pointed out that these cases were different, because they do not involve the same rights as the present case,[16] but there is one essentially similar point: the acts were committed against well-known journalists.[17] There is once again a reference to Ms. Ismayilova's profession. Article 8 is clearly examined in the light of Article 10.

The Court questioned whether the State had done everything it could to identify the author of these interferences. In other words, the question was whether the State had fulfilled its positive obligation to conduct an effective investigation and to protect the journalist's private life.

In their concurring opinion in the *Mazepa* case[18] concerning the assassination of the Russian journalist Anna Politkovskaya, judges Jaderblom and Keller, while agreeing with the majority's conclusion, regretted that the Court had missed the opportunity to explain what an effective investigation was and what the criteria and elements to meet the required parameters would be. According to both judges, the Court should have verified the existence of four criteria: the adequacy of investigative measures, the timeliness of procedure, the involvement of family members in the investigation and the independence of investigations. In the *Ismayilova* case the Court did not engage in such a clarification, which would have been all the more welcome since, unlike in the previous cases involving journalists, which led the Court to analyze the violation of their rights under Articles 2 or 3, this was the first time that allegations were based on Article 8. It would have been interesting for the Court to give its assessment of the relevant factors to assess the positive obligation to protect the privacy of a journalist by conducting an effective investigation. The Court identified some concrete elements to be taken into consideration without delivering any general guideline.

Firstly, the Court pointed out to the margin of discretion of the State in the conduct of investigations. Nevertheless, it noted that the allegations in question were very serious and particularly prejudicial to human dignity[19] and so the margin

---

[13]See ECtHR [GC], *Soderman v. Sweden*, 12 Nov. 2013, No. 5786/08.

[14]ECtHR, *Khadija Ismayilova v. Azerbaïdjan*, 10 Jan. 2019, Nos. 65286/13 and 57270/14, para. 115.

[15]See ECtHR, *Gongadze v. Ukraine*, 8 Nov. 2005, No. 34056/02; ECtHR, *Uzeyir Jafarov v. Azerbaijan*, 29 Jan. 2015, No. 54204/08; ECtHR, *Huseynova v. Azerbaijan*, 13 Apr. 2017, No. 10653/10.

[16]In these cases, Articles 2 and 3 were invoked.

[17]ECtHR, *Khadija Ismayilova v. Azerbaïdjan*, 10 Jan. 2019, Nos. 65286/13 and 57270/14, para. 119.

[18]See ECtHR, *Mazepa and Others v. Russia*, 17 Jul. 2018, No. 15086/07.

[19]ECtHR, *Khadija Ismayilova v. Azerbaïdjan*, 10 Jan. 2019, Nos. 65286/13 and 57270/14, para. 116.

allowed to the State was narrowed.[20] The Court recalled that the obligation to conduct an effective investigation was not an obligation of result, but of means.[21] In other words, the State's obligation was not to find the author of the act, but to make all efforts to identify him. The Court brought out the "significant flaw" test, according to which its task was

> to determine whether the alleged shortcomings in the investigation had such significant flaws as to amount to a breach of the respondent State's positive obligations under Article 8 of the Convention.[22]

The Court repeated it was not concerned with allegations of minor errors or isolated omissions in the investigation because it could (and did not want) to replace domestic judges in their assessment of the facts of the case.[23] The ECtHR is not a third-degree jurisdiction.

Nevertheless, in the present case, the Court considered that the investigative authorities should not have ignored the connection between the Applicant's profession and the facts of which she was a victim.[24]

The letter sent clearly referred to the journalist's work, and the videos were intended to discredit her. If the applicant had not been a journalist, she would probably never have suffered these attacks. The link between her professional activity and the violations she was victim of could not be ignored by the authorities, who should have investigated this trail and devoted more attention to it because the freedom of expression was also at stake.

The Court did not find the government's justification convincing. In its control, it went so far as to indicate to the State what it could have concretely done for its investigation to be considered effective. For example, concerning the identification of the author of the letter, investigators could have requested international help from their Russian colleagues.[25] Also concerning the videos, a quick investigation could have enabled the identification of the hosts as well as links with the newspapers held by the political authorities.[26]

Therefore, the Court sanctioned the manner in which authorities had investigated the case and the delay of the investigations. Out of the four criteria proposed by judges Jaderblom and Keller in their common opinion in the *Mazepa* case,[27] the Court only examined two: the adequacy of the investigative measures and the timeliness. Neither the involvement of the applicant and her relatives in the

---

[20]See ECtHR [GC], *Soderman v. Sweden*, 12 Nov. 2013, No. 5786/08.

[21]ECtHR, *Khadija Ismayilova v. Azerbaïdjan*, 10 Jan. 2019, Nos. 65286/13 and 57270/14, para. 118.

[22]*Ibid.*, para. 118.

[23]See ECtHR, *M.C. v. Bulgaria*, 4 Dec. 2003, No. 39272/98.

[24]The same element can be found in the analysis under Article 10, paras. 162–163.

[25]ECtHR, *Khadija Ismayilova v. Azerbaijan*, Nos. 65286/13 and 57270/14, 10 Jan. 2019, para. 126.

[26]*Ibid.*, para. 127.

[27]ECtHR, *Mazepa and Others v. Russia*, 17 Jul. 2018, No. 15086/07.

procedure, nor the independence of the investigations were developed in the present case, whereas the applicant had produced a number of elements in this direction.

The Court nevertheless considered that Azerbaijani authorities had not fulfilled their positive obligation under Article 8 to protect the privacy of Ms. Ismayilova due to significant deficiencies in the investigation, and the duration of the investigation and the overall procedure in his case.

3.2 The Serious and Unjustifiable Breach of the Applicant's Privacy by the Prosecutor's Disclosure of Information About Her Private and Family Life

The applicant considered that the disclosure constituted an interference with her privacy and was contrary to national law prohibiting such disclosure.[28] Furthermore this interference had not pursued any of the legitimate aims admitted under Article 8§2 and was not necessary. Thus, it could not be justified.

The government answered[29] that the Baka's Prosecutor only reacted to the applicant's public statement accusing authorities of ineffectiveness in the procedure and so his aim was to inform the public about the progress in the investigations.

There is a negative obligation under Article 8 relating to the police and prosecution authorities' specific obligations to protect personal information that they have obtained in the course of their investigation.[30] The Court characterized the facts as falling under the concept of privacy, which covers both the physical and the psychological integrity of the person, as well as many aspects of physical and social identity. Thus, the Court intended to protect not only the inner sphere, but also the social relations of the person. In a rather surprising way, the Court did not qualify all the information disclosed as "personal data". The Strasbourg judges seemed to prefer to restrict the use of this term to cases involving the use of internet services.

The Court concluded that the public disclosure of private information constituted an interference with the right to privacy. Nevertheless, in this case the classic triad analysis (suitability, necessity and proportionality) was minimalist since the government itself did not address any of the three requirements. It merely reiterated that the Prosecutor simply wanted to inform the public of the outcome of the case because Ms. Ismayilova had publicly accused authorities of passivity. Thus, the government did not explain whether the interference was provided by law, whether it pursued one of the legitimate aims of Article 8§2 and why it was necessary in a democratic society. That is why the Court did not dwell on it either; it passed rather quickly on

[28] *Ibid.*, paras. 135–137.

[29] *Ibid.*, para. 138.

[30] See ECtHR [GC], *Rotaru v. Romania*, 4 May 2000, No. 28341/95.

the first condition, namely "provided by law"[31] considering that "in any event it lacked justification on other grounds".

Then the Court also turned very briefly to the question of the necessity and proportionality of the interference. According to the Court, the authorities could have informed the public of the progress of investigation. Nevertheless, the way they chose to do so was completely inappropriate and could not be justified. Actually, publishing details of Ms. Ismayilova's private life in the circumstances of the case compounded the already existing breach of the applicant's privacy.[32] In the context of the present case the situation required special vigilance on their part since the investigation in question dealt precisely with serious and flagrant breaches of privacy.[33] The manner in which the authorities acted actually aggravated the violation of this right and the damage to the applicant.

Thus, the Court considered that the interference could not be justified and that there was a second violation of Article 8.

4 Analysis of the Positive Obligation Under Article 10 and Recognition of the Inherent Link with Article 8

The Court examined the same incidents as a possible violation of Article 10 (freedom of expression),[34] however, unlike its analysis under Article 8, it made no longer the distinction between acts underlying the violation of the negative obligations and those constituting a violation of the positive obligations.

4.1 A Cumulative Examination of the Human Rights Violations Invoked in the Present Case

In the *Ismayilova* case the Court did not stop with the double violation of Article 8, which seemed rather obvious. The Court also accepted to rule on Article 10 of the Convention. Could it have stopped at Article 8 and said that there is no need to examine allegations under Article 10? It could have certainly relied on the famous "not necessary formula" in the present case, as it usually does when it considers that the recognition of violations of the first article alleged by the applicant is sufficient. This is how the Court proceeded in almost all cases involving killings or acts of violence against independent journalists.

[31] ECtHR, *Khadija Ismayilova v. Azerbaijan*, 10 Jan. 2019, Nos. 65286/13 and 57270/14, para. 146.

[32] *Ibid.*, para. 148.

[33] *Ibid.*

[34] *Ibid.*, para. 151.

For example in *Jafarov v. Azerbaijan*,[35] the Court observed that:

> the only issue raised by the applicant's complaint under Article 10 of the Convention is that of establishing whether or not the applicant's right to freedom of expression had been violated on account of the domestic authorities' failure to conduct an effective investigation into the attack on him.[36]

Having already found a violation of Article 3 under its procedural limb (the ineffectiveness of the investigation into the attack on the applicant), the Court refrained from examining a potential violation of Article 10. For the Court, the allegations of the applicant under Article 10 were the same as those under Article 3 and did not raise any separate issue.

In *Huseynova v. Azerbaijan*[37] concerning the murder of a well-known journalist, the Court also refused to analyze the case under Article 10. The ECtHR judges observed that there was a difference between that case and the previous ones[38] in which it had found violations of Articles 2 or 3 of the Convention. In those cases the Court concluded on violations under the substantive limb of the articles, because the State had failed to protect the right to life of a journalist, or a journalist was subjected to the use of force by a State agent. In the *Huseynova* case the Court found a violation of Article 2 under its procedural limb, because of the ineffectiveness of the investigation into the killing of the applicant's husband,[39] but it could not be established that the State was at the origin of the murder.[40] Consequently, the Court considered that the only question remaining under Article 10 of the Convention was

> that of establishing whether or not the right to freedom of expression was violated on account of the domestic authorities' failure to conduct an effective investigation into the killing of the applicant's husband.

As the applicant's allegations under Article 10 were based on the same facts as those examined under Article 2 of the Convention, the Court refused to proceed on a separate examination.

In their partly dissenting opinion under the *Huseynova* case, judges Nussberger and Vehabovic regretted the use of the "not necessary formula" in the judgment. In their opinion, the separate analysis of Article 2, without going on the terrain of Article 10, meant to "fail to fully identify the violations of human rights and democracy". In fact, the judges proposed that, in cases involving journalists, the Court should not examine these provisions separately, but try to articulate them, since the principal motive in this case was "the wish to silence a critical voice in a

[35]See ECtHR, *Uzeyir Jafarov v. Azerbaijan*, 29 Jan. 2015, No. 54204/08.

[36]*Ibid.*

[37]See ECtHR, *Huseynova v. Azerbaijan*, 13 Apr. 2017, No. 10653/10.

[38]See for example ECtHR, *Dink v. Turkey*, 14 Sept. 2010, Nos 2668/07, 6102/08, 30079/08, 7072/09 et 7124/09.

[39]ECtHR, *Khadija Ismayilova v. Azerbaijan*, 10 Jan. 2019, Nos. 65286/13 and 57270/14, para. 116.

[40]*Ibid.*, para. 121.

country."[41] To put it differently, if the States do not lead an effective investigations of criminal acts against journalists, there might be a chilling effect on the exercise of the freedom of expression. Judges Nussberger and Vehabovic welcomed the effort of the majority to take into account the chilling effect of the murder in this case and agreed that it was the duty of the authorities "to explore with particular diligence whether the murder, which appears to have been carefully planned, could be linked to Mr Huseynov's journalistic activities."[42] Therefore, they considered that the Court needed to emphasize the link between the professional activity of the victim and the acts perpetrated against them. The only possibility to do so was to examine a potential violation under Article 10.

In the *Mazepa* case,[43] relatives of the assassinated Russian journalist Anna Politkovskaya argued the breach of Article 2 in its procedural limb, but did not invoke Article 10. Thus, the Court did not examine a potential violation of the freedom of expression, but in paragraph 73 of the judgment[44] it recalled the necessity for the State to investigate on the link between the professional activity of the journalist and the murder.

In the present case, the applicant argued that the State of Azerbaijan breached both obligations under Article 10: the negative one, because, according to her, the incidents proved an interference with her freedom of expression committed by the State, or entities dependent or owned by the State. Also, the State violated the positive obligation to take steps to protect her from the campaign against her.

The government simply reiterated the arguments made under Article 8: there was no proof that the State was the author of the alleged interferences and that the threats against Ms. Ismayilova were linked to her professional activities.[45] Nevertheless, such a simplistic justification ignored all the evidence, especially the threatening letter which asked her to stop her journalistic activities. Concerning the divulgation of personal information by the Prosecutor, according to the government, its only aim was to inform the public about the progress of the investigation.[46]

---

[41] ECtHR, *Huseynova v. Azerbaijan*, 13 Apr. 2017, No. 10653/10, para. 9.

[42] *Ibid.*, para. 96.

[43] See ECtHR, *Mazepa and Others v. Russia*, 17 Jul. 2018, No. 15086/07.

[44] *Ibid.*, para. 73: "The Court observes that the pivotal issue in the present case is the respondent State's compliance with its obligation to carry out an effective investigation into the contract killing of an investigative journalist. The Court would reiterate that, in cases where the victim of a killing is a journalist, it is of utmost importance to check a possible connection of the crime to the journalist's professional activity. In this connection, the Court would also refer to Recommendation CM/Rec (2016) 4 on the protection of journalism and safety of journalists and other media actors, in which the Committee of Ministers recommended in paragraph 19 that the conclusions of an investigation must be based on a thorough, objective and impartial analysis of all the relevant elements, including the establishment of whether there is a connection between the threats and violence against journalists and other media actors and the exercise of journalistic activities or contributing in similar ways to public debate."

[45] ECtHR, *Khadija Ismayilova v. Azerbaijan*, 10 Jan. 2019, Nos. 65286/13 and 57270/14, para. 156.

[46] *Ibid.*, para. 157.

In the third-party submission the interveners[47] also called the Court to proceed with a double analysis, which reminds of the proposals made by judges Nussberger and Vehabovic in the *Huseynova* case. According to the interveners,

> the combined effect of the above-mentioned case-law was that, where the privacy of journalists was interfered with as a result of their journalistic work, a member State's obligations under both Articles 8 and 10 were engaged.[48]

The interveners also argued that:

> positive obligations under Article 10 must necessarily extend to actual or threatened breaches of Article 8 rights, and the positive obligations under Article 8 must be subjected to particularly close review by the Court where Article 10 rights were engaged.[49]

This is exactly what the Court did in the *Ismayilova* judgment. The ECtHR proceeded on a separate and combined analysis of both articles to cover all human rights violations. The choice to examine both articles was particularly important in the present-day context of attacks upon journalists and against the freedom of the press, which has become a more general problem. The ECtHR sends a clear message to the States. This approach can be compared with the reasoning in cases of racial discrimination, where the Court found that "a violation of Article 2 of the Convention [was] not sufficient to adequately reflect the wrong-doing and the intensity of the human-rights violation."[50] According to the Court, ignoring the discriminatory element of some acts of violence "would be to turn a blind eye to the specific nature of acts which are particularly destructive of fundamental rights."[51]

Even if the Court already affirmed that there was a positive obligation under Article 10 to take necessary measures to prevent and investigate conducts designed to restrict journalistic activities,[52] especially in the context of preventing violence against journalists, the positive obligations under Article 10 have not been sufficiently developed yet.

---

[47]PEN International, Privacy International, Article 19, Committee to Protect Journalists, Index on Censorship, International Media Support, the Institute for Reporters' Freedom and Safety, International Partnership for Human Rights, PEN American Center, Front Line Defenders, Canadian Journalists for Free Expression, International Federation for Human Rights, World Organisation Against Torture, Norwegian Helsinki Committee, and Human Rights House Foundation.

[48]ECtHR, *Khadija Ismayilova v. Azerbaijan*, 10 Jan. 2019, Nos. 65286/13 and 57270/14, para. 80.

[49]*Ibid.*, para. 81.

[50]See ECtHR [GC], *Nachova and others v. Bulgaria*, 6 Jul. 2006, Nos. 43577/98 and 43579/98.

[51]*Ibid.*

[52]See ECtHR [GC], *Palomo Sanchez and Others v. Spain*, 12 Sept. 2011, No. 28871/95.

4.2 *Required Clarification on the Content of the Positive Obligation Under Article 10*

The Strasbourg judges first recalled the importance of the freedom of expression in democracy, as well as the valuable role of the press.[53] This may seem a classic reminder, but one which was necessary in the context of the new approach developed in this judgment. Any interference with this fundamental freedom can indeed have a "chilling effect" on its exercise, hence the need for States to investigate seriously the allegations reported by journalists.

States are bound not only by their negative obligation not to interfere with the freedom of expression but also by their positive obligation to protect journalists. This obligation also applies in the sphere of individual relationships.[54] This means that the State has to provide an effective system of protection of journalism and consequently to create a favorable environment for journalism. This is not new; the Court already mentioned the coexistence of both obligations in *Dink v. Turkey*.[55] In the present judgment the Court simply specifies its content.

What is the new is the cumulative examination of Articles 8 and 10. The Court's insistence on the necessity to carry out the investigations, while taking into account the possible link between the applicant's profession and the crime she was a victim of, was also new. This link on which the Court had already insisted during the examination of the Article 8, led it to rule on the violation of Article 10 in more detail.

The Court based its reasoning on two elements: first, it provided an overview of the general situation of independent journalists in Azerbaijan, mainly based on third-party submissions.[56] According to a report, Azerbaijan has "one of the most restrictive environments for freedom of expression in the world."[57] The State is involved in the repression of journalists critical of the government.[58] Journalists are arrested, convicted and jailed on political charges. The State and the private entities under the control of the State are involved in this systemic repression. The submissions

[53]ECtHR, *Khadija Ismayilova v. Azerbaijan*, 10 Jan. 2019, Nos. 65286/13 and 57270/14, para. 158.

[54]*Ibid.* para. 158.

[55]See ECtHR, *Dink v. Turkey*, 14 Sept. 2010, Nos 2668/07, 6102/08, 30079/08, 7072/09 et 7124/09.

[56]ECtHR, *Khadija Ismayilova v. Azerbaijan*, 10 Jan. 2019, Nos. 65286/13 and 57270/14, paras. 72–81: observations were received by the Court from numerous charities and NGOs defending freedom of expression and journalist's rights such as Committee to Protect Journalists, International Federation for Human rights, PEN International, Human Rights Foundation and others.

[57]*Ibid.*, para. 74.

[58]See the new case of intimidating and threatening of journalist Osmanqizi (May 2019), the condemnation of journalist Elchin Ismayili (November 2018) or Emin Huseynov (October 2018): https://www.coe.int/fr/web/media-freedom.

specifically mentioned the cases of *Jafarov*,[59] *Khalil*,[60] and *Huseynov*,[61] but also other cases where journalists were ill-treated, and no effective investigation was carried out. All these elements proved that Azerbaijan have not created "an environment protective of journalism" but on the contrary "a climate of impunity",[62] where journalists rather than their attackers are considered like criminals. Furthermore, the applicant herself, Ms. Ismayilova, was arrested in 2014 and in 2015[63] after she engaged the procedure that gave place to this judgement.[64]

Then, the judges took into consideration the particular circumstances of the case; they reiterated that the applicant was not an ordinary person but a well-known investigative journalist, who received a number of international awards. The same elements were used to highlight the specific character of the crime and the passivity of the authorities: the acts were apparently linked to her journalistic activity,[65] there was no other plausible motive for the harassment she faced. Ms. Ismayilova had brought her fear of public humiliation and of an unwarranted invasion of her privacy to the authorities' attention, and these elements should have been considered as such by the investigators.

The Court considered that, although the authorities had launched a criminal investigation in connection with the acts committed against the applicant, there were significant flaws and delays in the way they investigated the case.[66] The Court referred here directly to its reasoning concerning the violation of Article 8 in its procedural limb.[67] The ECtHR also reproached the State that it did not protect the journalist against the articles published in the newspapers. The unjustified public disclosure of Ms. Ismayilova's personal information relating to her and her relatives' life by the authorities during the investigation, contrary to the spirit of a save environment for journalists.[68]

---

[59]See ECtHR, *Uzeyir Jafarov v. Azerbaijan*, 29 Jan. 2015, No. 54204/08.

[60]See ECtHR, *Khalil v. Azerbaijan*, (dec.), 6 Oct. 2010, No. 60659/08.

[61]See ECtHR, *Emin Huseynov v. Azerbaijan*, 7 May 2015, No. 59135/09.

[62]ECtHR, *Khadija Ismayilova v. Azerbaïdjan*, 10 Jan. 2019, Nos. 65286/13 and 57270/14, para. 77.

[63]First for inciting a colleague to commit a suicide and then for a large-scale misappropriation, illegal entrepreneurship, large-scale tax evasion and abuse of power as a director of the independent radio Azadliq Radio.

[64]These allegations gave place to the separate judgment. See ECtHR, *Ismayilova v. Azerbaijan* (No. 2), 27 Feb. 2002, No. 30778/15.

[65]ECtHR, *Khadija Ismayilova v. Azerbaijan*, 10 Jan. 2019, Nos. 65286/13 and 57270/14, para. 119.

[66]*Ibid.*, para. 165.

[67]*Ibid.*, para. 131.

[68]*Ibid.*, para. 165.

5 Conclusion

Rather than balancing Articles 8 and 10, the Court analyzed them successively and also in a combined approach, in order to provide a full view of all the violations committed by the defendant State. In addition to its positive obligation under Article 8 of the Convention to protect the journalist from interference in his/her private life, there is a positive obligation under Article 10 of the Convention which requires the respondent State to take all measures to protect the applicant's journalistic freedom of expression.[69] Such a conclusion applies beyond the facts of the *Ismayilova* case.

This judgment, which became definitive on 10 April 2019 without being subject to an appeal, is nevertheless a strong sign sent by the Court to all European States, in the current context where intimidation, threats and even murders of journalists are trying to destroy democracy.[70] Indeed, as the Court points out, journalists are "watchdogs of democracy" and consequently they deserve appropriate protection by the States.

Beata Jurik is a fellow at University of Strasbourg, Center of International and European Studies, Assistant professor at Faculty of Law, University of Strasbourg. Thesis on Children in EU Law jointly directed by Mr I. BOEV (Associate professor in Public Law, University of Strasbourg) and Mr O. Dubos (Professor of Law, University of Bordeaux). Publications in EU Law, Human Rights and Children's Rights.

[69] *Ibid*., para. 164.

[70] For example, the recent murders of investigative journalists Daphne Caruana Galizia in Malta and Jan Kuciak and his fiancée in Slovakia.

Freedom of Expression, Sliding-Scales, and Fake News

Alessio Sardo

Contents

1 Introduction 265
2 Freedom of Expression in the Balance 267
3 The Sliding Scale Approach 270
4 Fake News: A New Challenge 279
5 Conclusion 286
References 286

1 Introduction

Freedom of expression has been often described as a necessary presupposition for the construction of a democratic legal order and for the implementation of an effective system of human rights. It seems impossible for a democracy to function if citizens are not granted the fundamental right to express their political views.[1] Similarly, the rule of law would become an empty notion when the freedom of

The Author remains grateful to the Alexander von Humboldt Foundation for sponsoring this research, which is part of a larger project hosted by the University of Heidelberg, Institut für Staatsrecht, Verfassungslehre und Rechtsphilosophie. The Author wishes to express his gratitude also to his host, Professor Martin Borowksi, for precious advice.

[1]This proposition has been explicitly endorsed also by the ECtHR. See, for instance, ECtHR, *Lingens v. Austria*, 8 Jul. 1986, No. 9815/82; ECtHR, *Şener v. Turkey*, 18 Jul. 2000, No. 26680/95; ECtHR, *Thoma v. Luxembourg*, 29 Mar. 2001*;* ECtHR, *Marônek v. Slovakia*, 19 Apr. 2001, No. 32686/96; ECtHR, *Dichand and Others v. Austria*, 26 Feb. 2002 No. 29271/95). See also ECtHR, *Handyside v. the United Kingdom*, 7 Dec. 1976 No. 5493/72, para. 49: "supervisory functions oblige it to pay the utmost attention to the principles characterizing a "democratic society". Freedom of expression constitutes one of the essential foundations of such a society, one of the basic conditions for its progress and for the development of every man."

A. Sardo (✉)
Heidelberg University, Heidelberg, Germany

M. Elósegui et al. (eds.), *The Rule of Law in Europe*,
https://doi.org/10.1007/978-3-030-56001-0_16

expression does not protect the impartial, autonomous, judgments of the courts.[2] In this connection, Akhil R. Amar of Yale argued that free speech—the paradigmatic case of freedom of expression—existed even before the First Amendment:[3] the very act of enacting the U.S. Constitution presupposed, so the argument goes, that the constituent power was already granted extensive freedom of (political) speech during the process of adoption of the Federal Constitution. This freedom was rooted in the normative practices of "We, the people". In a similar vein, in Europe, no less authority than Robert Alexy pointed out that the ultimate justification for the existence of human rights beyond positive law stems from the very possibility of a universal, institutionalized, rational discourse where every participant can ask and offer reasons.[4] The word 'discourse' denotes precisely the rational practice of asserting, asking, arguing. While Amar relies on a structural argument with a "historical twist", Robert Alexy makes a more philosophical point. Despite this difference, the main claim raised by the two leading constitutional scholars is the same: The institutional act of enacting a constitution and the existence of human rights presupposes a certain amount of freedom of expression, pace Larry Alexander's skeptical take.[5]

On these premises it would be tempting to infer that freedom of expression is the most fundamental political right, not from an axiological perspective (namely, the moral ranking of human and fundamental rights), but from a purely justificatory and conceptual standpoint.[6] Is it not the case that the European Court of Human Rights (ECtHR) stressed in the landmark decision *Handyside* that freedom of expression constitutes "one of the essential foundations" (namely, a necessary, although not sufficient, condition) for the existence and implementation of any other right, and for "the development of every man"?[7]

---

[2]Frowein (2004).

[3]Amar (2010), p. 513: "To put the point a slightly different way, perhaps the enactment argument can be seen as the ultimate textual argument an interpretation of the tiny but all-important workhorse word "do" in the Preamble. The argument from enactment prompts us to understand what exactly the people did through the very process of ordaining and establishing the Constitution. And what was done, I submit, was a remarkable embodiment of free speech, speech that was inextricably intertwined with the very deed of ordainment itself." On the role that freedom of expression plays in spreading a liberal form of constitutionalism, see Ronsenfeld et al. (2006), p. 146; Bollinger (1986).

[4]Alexy (2012), pp. 2ff.

[5]Alexander (2012).

[6]Gilmore (2011), pp. 517ff. The author argues that expression is fundamental for our self-realization. For a sociological inquiry on this issue, see Nickel (1989), pp. 281–293.

[7]ECtHR, *Handyside v. The United Kingdom,* 7 Dec. 1976 No. 5493/72. For a general analysis of the European Convention of Human Rights (ECtHR), which was signed in Rome on 4 November 1950, see Council of Europe Publishing, Introduction to European Convention of Human Rights – Collected Texts, 1994. The present essay assumes that the reader possesses already a basic knowledge of the Convention. It is worth stressing that the precedents of the European Court of Human Rights (ECtHR) have binding force for European Member States. The ECtHR has the final word on the interpretation of the text of the Convention; however, the Court can be accessed only as

> Freedom of expression constitutes one of the essential foundations of such a society, one of the basic conditions for its progress and for the development of every man. Subject to paragraph 2 of Article 10 (art. 10-2), it is applicable not only to 'information' or 'ideas' that are favorably received or regarded as inoffensive or as a matter of indifference, but also to those that offend, shock or disturb the State or any sector of the population. Such are the demands of that pluralism, tolerance and broadmindedness without which there is no 'democratic society'.[8]

The main goal of this essay is to explore the method used by the European Court of Human Rights for balancing freedom of expression with competing rights, with an eye to the problem of fake news. Section 2 offers a minimal reconstruction of the framework established by Art. 10 ECHR. Section 3 explains how the Court's method for weighing freedom of expression with competing rights is much more than an *ad hoc*, case by case, balancing, for it is instead a sliding-scale approach oriented by the general principle of proportionality. Section 4 deals with the challenge of fake news. The final Sect. 5 contains a summary of the arguments developed in the essay and a short conclusion.

2 Freedom of Expression in the Balance

The contours of the notion of freedom of expression are not easy to define. A first, major issue is the risk of conflating freedom of expression with a general right to liberty or autonomy;[9] a second puzzle concerns judicial balancing, and the idea that freedom of expression is not an absolute right, for it can be derogated by other competing rights and interests. Striking the right balance is perceived as necessary, for the following reason: the absolute protection of freedom of expression might lead to a disproportional compression of other human rights.[10] Every jurist knows that principles that ground human rights tend to collide in specific cases: within the European Convention of Human Rights (ECHR) system, it is easy to imagine a potential normative conflict between free speech and private property, or between artistic expression and the general interest to avoid obscenity. However, the main area of conflict seems the common ground of intersection between freedom of

---

the last resort, when all internal remedies have run out. The so-called doctrine of the domestic margin of appreciation plays a fundamental role for the vertical separation of powers between ECtHR and member States, and in establishing the degree of deference that might be granted to national governments; in general, the Court considered that there must subsist strong reasons to substitute its own view to the State's view.

[8]ECtHR, *Handyside v. the United Kingdom*, 7 Dec. 1976 No. 5493/72; ECtHR, *Vereinigung Bildender Künstler v. Austria*, 25 Jan. 2007 No. 68354/01.

[9]Schauer (1982), pp. 5ff.

[10]Flauss (2009), p. 813: "If freedom of expression occupies a primordial place within the body of rights and freedoms guaranteed by the Convention, it still must simultaneously coexist with other concurrent, and at times conflicting, rights and freedoms."

expression (Art. 10 of the Convention) and the right to respect private life (Art. 8 of the Convention).[11]

The balancing between freedom of expression and the right to respect private life involves a number of delicate issues, which have both a practical and theoretical dimension. As explained by the Court:

> The concept of 'private life' is a broad term not susceptible to exhaustive definition, which covers the physical and psychological integrity of a person and can therefore embrace multiple aspects of a person's identity, such as gender identification and sexual orientation, name or elements relating to a person's right to their image.[12]

Now, if also the notion of freedom of expression were constructed in equally broad terms, it would inevitably overlap and conflate with the very notion of private life. In this way, any conflict between Art. 8 and Art. 10 would become an intra-right conflict (namely, a clash between the same right), which is particularly nasty to resolve. Freedom of expression and privacy would become mere instantiations of a general right to liberty (or autonomy), that is to say, both rights would be grounded on a more general concept. The European Court of Human Rights has always avoided this risk by designing a well-tailored notion of free expression through a series of categorical balancing operations. I will return to categories in Sect. 3. However, I can already anticipate that the expression "categorical balancing" denotes the combination of two approaches for resolving a conflict between rights: the categorical approach, which establishes what counts as freedom of expression and what does not count as freedom of expression through precise definitions, and the balancing approach, which proceeds case by case. Categorical balancing is an attempt in rational systematization: balancing operates through categories and sets down rules that define the content of a right.[13]

The European Court of Human Rights, on the one hand, endorses a broad reading of the notion of expression and, on the other hand, relies on balancing *qua* method for introducing a limited number of exceptions outside the core of this human right. This strategy finds textual support in the ECHR. The ECtHR proclaims the right to freedom of expression at Art. 10, which has a two-paragraphs structure. The article reads as follows:

> 1. Everyone has the right to freedom of expression. This right shall include freedom to hold opinions and to receive and impart information and ideas without interference by public authority and regardless of frontiers. This Article shall not prevent States from requiring the licensing of broadcasting, television or cinema enterprises.
> 2. The exercise of these freedoms, since it carries with it duties and responsibilities, may be subject to such formalities, conditions, restrictions or penalties as are prescribed by law and are necessary in a democratic society, in the interests of national security, territorial integrity or public safety, for the prevention of disorder or crime, for the protection of health or morals, for the protection of the reputation or rights of others, for preventing the

[11]ECtHR, *Chauvy and Others v. France*, 29 Sept. 2004, No. 64915/01, para. 70; ECtHR, *Polanco Torres and Movilla Polanco v. Spain* 21 Sept. 2010 No. 34147/06, para. 40.

[12]ECtHR [GC], *Axel Springer v. Germany*, 7 Feb. 2012, No. 39954/08, para. 82.

[13]Blocher (2009), p. 375ff.

disclosure of information received in confidence, or for maintaining the authority and impartiality of the judiciary.

The Court's interpretation of this article goes beyond the literal, plain meaning of the legal provision. In fact, the ECtHR defends a broader reading of Art. 10, to wit: freedom of expression is not limited to free speech—narrowly understood as the liberty of holding, sharing, receiving information and ideas through speech acts,[14] without interference by the legal authority—for it also includes: (i) the freedom to produce, exhibit, and distribute artworks; (ii) the liberty of realizing a public artistic performance;[15] (iii) the access to relevant public information;[16] (iv) the liberty of showing pictures, icons, images,[17] and religious or political symbols;[18] (v) a good number of other situations, such as preserving cultural heritage,[19] broadcasting,[20] satirical expression;[21] (vi) last but not least, the protection against self-incrimination.[22] The sphere of protection granted to the freedom of the press is even more comprehensive, for it also includes that information and ideas that "offend, shock or disturb";[23] what is more, if applied to the press, the restrictions established by the Second Paragraph of Article 10 shall be "construed narrowly."[24] A peculiarity of the Court's approach is the inclusion of the right to receive information and ideas by the public within the notion of freedom of expression.[25]

Sure enough, the Court allows the possibility of restricting freedom of expression by giving precedence to Member State's interests—such as national security, public safety, and the protection of morals—or to other, conflicting, human rights, such as the right to privacy.[26] In cases of conflicts between rights, the Court must strike a

[14]Austin (1962) and Searle (1969).

[15]ECtHR, *Müller and Others v. Switzerland*, 24 May 1998, No. 10737/84.

[16]ECtHR, *Leander v. Sweden*, 26 Mar. 1987 No. 9248/8.

[17]ECtHR, *Müller and Others v. Switzerland*, 24 May 1988, No. 10737/84; ECtHR, *Chorherr v. Austria*, 25 Aug. 1993, No. 13308/87.

[18]ECtHR, *Vajnai v. Hungary*, 8 Jul. 2008 No. 33629/06.

[19]ECtHR, *Stevens v. the United Kingdom*, 9 Sept. 1989 No. 29576/95.

[20]ECtHR, *Groppera Radio AG and Others v. Switzerland*, 28 Mar. 1990 No. 10890/84.

[21]ECtHR, *Eon v. France*, 14 Mar. 2013 No. 26118/10.

[22]ECtHR, *K. v. Austria*, 13 Oct. 1992, No. 16002/90.

[23]ECtHR [GC], *Axel Springer v. Germany*, 7 Feb. 2012, No. 39954/08.

[24]ECtHR, *Handyside v. the United Kingdom*, 7 Dec.1976, No. 5493/72, para. 49.

[25]ECtHR, *Campos Dâmaso v. Portugal*, 24 Apr. 2008, No. 17107/05, para. 31.

[26]The most common forms of restriction and interference with freedom of speech include criminal convictions, censorship, order to pay damages, prohibition to exercise the profession of journalist, refusal to grant broadcasting license, denial to disclose information. The ECtHR considers that the enumeration of possible restrictions and interference is an open list. See ECtHR, *Barfod v. Denmark*, 22 Feb. 1989 No. 11508/85); ECtHR, *The Sunday Times v. the United Kingdom*, 26 Nov. 1991 No. 13166/8); ECtHR, *Observer and Guardian v. the United Kingdom*, 26 Nov. 1991 No. 13585/88); ECtHR, *Handyside v. the United Kingdom*, 7 Dec. 1976 No. 5493/72; ECtHR, *Müller and Others v. Switzerland*, 24 May 1988 No. 10737/84; ECtHR, *Frankowicz v. Poland*, 16 Dec. 2008 No. 53025/99.

balance, in order to determine which right or interest takes precedence over the other, by specifying under which conditions the relation of precedence holds. The following point shall be stressed from the outset: the very idea of balancing implies that rights are not absolute, for they must be subject to limitations in case of conflict with other rights or interests. In shaping the relations of precedence, the Court has relied on an evolutionary approach, based on a form of "living constitutionalism":[27] The ECtHR does not interpret Art. 10 according to its original public meaning, or according to the intentions of the drafters, ratifiers, and framers of the Convention; by contrast, the Court considered that the content of Art. 10 shall be the result of a "dynamic update", which takes into account the current constellations of values as well as the current normative an factual context, both from the internal perspective—which correspond to the position of the participant, the legal subject, of a Member State's)—and from the external perspective (looking at national systems from a broader, European, perspective).[28]

3 The Sliding Scale Approach

If my understanding is correct, the Court's method for weighing principles is much more complex than a sheer *ad hoc*, freewheeling, balancing of competing interests,[29] for the ECtHR relies on a process of categorization and on a sliding-scale approach to set down the rules that solve a conflict between freedom of expression and other human rights.[30] In fact, the Court decides according to clusters of rules establishing different levels of scrutiny and burdens of proof that the arguments in favor of the challenged law or action must satisfy for being justified. For instance, a slight degree of justification is generally required for interference with commercial expression.[31] In contrast, an extremely strong argument shall be produced for justifying a compression of the freedom of the press. In parallel, the levels of scrutiny range from a very low threshold, such as the one required for commercial expression, to a very high threshold, such as the one imposed by the strict scrutiny normally used for the freedom of the press. The level of scrutiny obviously plays a key-role in determining the outcome of a case, and the strength of protection of a human right as well, something that might eventually lead to a separation between strongly protected classes of cases and weakly protected classes of cases.

[27]Strauss (2010).

[28]Hart (1994), pp. 91ff.

[29]Frantz (1963), pp. 732ff. Frantz asks whether a case-by-case approach to balancing is really necessary for freedom of expression, or whether it is possible to set down rules applicable to entire classes of cases.

[30]Farber (2009) and Zoller (2009).

[31]The Court has carved the notion of 'commercial expression' in a series of precedents. So, for instance, ECtHR, *Casado Coca v. Spain*, 24 Feb. 1994 No. 15450/89) established that the distribution of advertising materials by a barrister counts as commercial expression.

One might plausibly claim that the Court has gradually developed a full array of balancing tests, which operate in every single corner of the ECtHR system, and especially in the field of freedom of expression; proportionality, reasonableness, and strict scrutiny are just a few of them.

On many occasions, the Court used proportionality as a method for resolving conflicts between freedom of expression and other rights. A disclaimer is in order here. One has to distinguish between two different legal meanings of the word 'proportionality': proportionality as a three pronged-test and proportionality as a (meta-)principle that underpins every operation of balancing.[32] In the first instance, proportionality denotes a three-step method for resolving conflict between rights: the first step checks the suitability of the measure; the second step ascertains the necessity of the measure; the final phase determines the relation of precedence between the competing rights, or principles.[33] In the second occurrence, proportionality is understood as a broad, rational principle that prescribes that any interference with a right must be proportioned to the legitimate objective pursued. If the proportionality test is used only for specific categories of speech, the proportionality *qua* meta-principle orientates every single balancing operation of the ECtHR.

The Court relied on the three-pronged proportionality test for resolving conflicts between freedom of expression and national security,[34] or between freedom of expression and essentially contested moral concepts (e.g. the right to defend abortion).[35] Proportionality is frequently used also to resolve the conflicts between Art. 10 and Art. 8, where the test is normally coupled with strict scrutiny for those classes of cases that require the highest protection. That is to say that, for specific categories of expression, the burdens of argumentation imposed on Member's States for the compression of Art. 10 are heightened with respect to the standard application of proportionality. So, for instance, in *Observer and Guardian v. United Kingdom*, the Court held that:

> the dangers inherent in prior restraints are such that they call for the most careful scrutiny on the part of the Court. This is especially so as far as the press is concerned, for news is a perishable commodity and to delay its publication, even for a short period, may well deprive it of all its value and interest.[36]

---

[32]Böckenförde (2017), p. 254.

[33]Alexy (2014), pp. 51ff.

[34]ECtHR, *Hadjianastassiou v. Greece*, 16 Dec. 1992 No. 12945/87, paras. 45–47; ECtHR [GC], *Stoll v. Switzerland*, 10 Dec. 2007, No. 69698/01, para. 151.

[35]ECtHR, *Open Door and Dublin Well Woman v. Ireland*, 29 Oct. 1992, No. 14234/88, where the Court held that a total ban on the distribution of brochure informing pregnant women about the possibilities of abortion abroad was disproportionate despite the strong commitment to Catholic values of the Irish Constitution after the anti-abortion amendments.

[36]ECtHR, *Observer and Guardian v. United*, 26 Nov. 1991, No. 13585/88, para. 60.

In spite of the ubiquity of the proportionality test,[37] the most used balancing method seems to be an altogether different kind of three-pronged test, which we might label "the necessity test".[38] The three-pronged necessity test finds textual support in the second paragraph of Art. 10 (2), and requires the fulfillment of three conditions for a justified interference with the exercise of freedom of expression:[39] first, the interference shall be prescribed by (formal) law; second, the interference shall be aimed at protecting significant interests, such as territorial integrity, public safety, prevention of disorder or crime, protection of health, reputation or rights of others, preventing the disclosure of information received in confidence, and maintaining the authority and impartiality of the judiciary; third, the interference shall be considered as necessary for a democratic society. Determining the meaning of the notion of 'necessity', which is central both in the proportionality test, as a first step, and in the three-pronged necessity test, as an overarching standard, was perhaps one of the hardest tasks that the ECtHR had to fulfill. As explained in *Observer and The Guardian v. the United Kingdom,* the Court considers that a measure is 'necessary' only if a 'pressing social need' exists.[40]

The Court, apparently, confines the use of a third test, a form of rational basis "with bite"[41]—which is the least protective test, among the ones used with Art. 10—to cases involving commercial speech. The rational basis with bite, which considers admissible those measures that are suitable to pursue the goal that the legislator wished to pursue, according to a means/ends analysis, is often combined with a high standard of deference towards national States, by granting them a wide margin of appreciation. Under extenuating conditions, even the publication of true descriptions of real events might be banned.[42] However, this does not mean that a State can arbitrarily choose what ends might be taken as underlying reasons for justifying the

---

[37]ECtHR, *Gawęda v. Poland*, 14 Mar. 2002, No. 26229/95; ECtHR, *The Sunday Times v. the United Kingdom*, 26 Apr. 1979, No. 6538/74; ECtHR, *Observer and Guardian v. the United Kingdom*, 26 Nov. 1991, No. 13585/88.

[38]Flauss (2009), p. 813: "Serving as standards, or as a form of control of the 'necessity' of restrictive measures introduced or tolerated by states relative to the freedom of expression, 'discretionary powers' are by definition a means of favoring –in casu (in case of extreme necessity)– the Strasbourg Court's freedom of assessment and, consequently, authorizing its possible manipulation. [. . .] The multiplicity of variables analyzed in order to balance restrictions placed on the freedom of expression effectively offers the European judge wide powers of flexibility in terms of the interests at issue, especially within the framework of a jurisprudential and jurisdictional policy based on the 'special case.'"

[39]See Bychawska-Siniarska (2017), p. 32f. In my view, the author's approach is over-reductionist, insofar as it reduces all the varieties of balancing tests used by the ECtHR to the three-pronged necessity test, which the author labels the "three-part test".

[40]ECtHR, *Observer and Guardian v. the United Kingdom*, 26 Nov.1991 No. 13585/88, para. 59; ECtHR, *Hertel v. Switzerland*, 25 Aug. 1998 No. 25181/94, para. 46.

[41]Pettinga (1985), pp. 780ff.

[42]ECtHR, *Markt intern Verlag GmbH and Klaus Beermann v. Germany*, 20 Nov. 1989, No. 10572/83, para. 35.

compression of freedom of expression,[43] to wit: the State shall choose among the legitimate ends mentioned by the Second Paragraph of Art. 10, which, in turn, the Court understands as indefeasible, insofar as the list of exceptions enumerated by Art. 10 cannot be derogated, and, therefore, no implicit exception is allowed. The metaphor of the "bite" is here used precisely for grasping the resistance to implicit exceptions, which strengthens the means/ends rationality requirement. The rational basis test—like the other tests that we have mentioned above (the proportionality test and the necessity test)—is coupled with the requirement that the Member States shall rule through laws: any interference with freedom of expression shall be grounded on a written, public, national law. In this case, the Court granted only one notable exception for British Common Law rules, considering that they were so precise, adequately accessible, and foreseeable with certainty as to count as 'law'.[44]

So far so good, but the Court has also designed more specific tests for freedom of expression, in several landmark cases: *Axel Springer v. Germany,*[45] *von Hannover v. Germany,*[46] and *Perinçek v. Switzerland.*[47] These tests are examples of what I have called "definitional balancing": the Court is not treating the case at hand as a case of first impression; on the contrary, it relies on categories of expressions, a set of procedural rules orienting the deliberative process, and specific burdens of justification, which are applicable to a class of cases.

The Grand Chamber's judgment of *Axel Springer* concerns the publication of two articles revealing that Mr. X, a well-known actor who played the role of Police Superintendent Y in a television series, had been convicted of unlawful possession of drugs. These articles were published by the German newspaper *Bild,* which has a large circulation, under satirical titles, accompanied by three pictures of the TV star.

In order to reach a decision, as the tightly argued analysis of Martin Borowski points out, the ECtHR relied on a multi-pronged test that takes into account the following criteria: (i) the general interest of the debate; (ii) how well known the person concerned is; (iii) the subject of the report; (iv) the prior standard of conduct of the person concerned; (v) the method for obtaining the information and its veracity; and (vi) the consequences of publications, including the sanction eventually imposed.[48]

The case of *von Hannover*, decided by the Fifth Section, introduces analogous criteria for the publication of photographs; these criteria have been analytically isolated by Peggy Ducoulombier in her insightful essay: (i) the degree of the

---

[43]Schauer (1995), pp. 633ff.

[44]ECtHR, *The Sunday Times v. the United Kingdom* 26 Nov. 1991 No. 13166/87.

[45]ECtHR [GC], *Axel Springer AG v. Germany*, 7 Feb. 2012 No. 39954/08.

[46]ECtHR [GC], *von Hannover v. Germany*, 17 Feb. 2014 No. 40660/08.

[47]ECtHR [GC], *Perinçek v. Switzerland,* 15 Oct. 2015 No. 27510/08.

[48]Borowski M., *Axel Springer AG v. Germany, or: How to Perform Limited Review*. Published in the present volume. Borowski is obviously right in considering that these criteria can be considered as a further specification of the proportionality principle, and that they operate at a lower level of abstraction.

notoriety of the person affected; (ii) the subject of the picture; (iii) the prior conduct of the person concerned; and, (iv) the consequence caused by the publication of the photos.[49] Finally, *Perinçek*—a case concerning the denial of the Armenian Genocide, decided by the Grand Chamber—counts as an attempt in systematization, too. The Honorable Judges analytically isolate eight factors that shall be considered for those balancing cases involving hate speech: (i) the nature of the statements; (ii) the geographical, historical, and temporal context; (iii) the extent to which the statement affects the competing rights; (iv) the existence of a consensus; (v) the possibility that the interference can be regarded as required by the international obligation assumed by the State; (vi) the method employed by the State to justify the conviction; (vii) the severity of the interference; (viii) the final weighing of freedom of expression against the right to private life.

Coming full circle, a more traditional form of strict scrutiny applies to freedom of the press. As the Court made clear in *Jersild v. Denmark*,[50] and in a number of other decisions,

> the punishment of a journalist for assisting in the dissemination of statements made by another person in an interview would seriously hamper the contribution of the press to discussion of matters of public interest and should not be envisaged unless there are particularly strong reasons for doing so.[51]

Freedom of the press is not immune from liability but triggers strict scrutiny, provided that the journalist is acting in good fate, and communicates reliable information. With an eye to potential conflicts with Art. 8, the Court also clarifies that the protection of personal reputation come into play only if the attack is severe and is made in a manner causing a deliberate prejudice in the exercise of the right to private life.[52]

Overall, the jurisprudence of the ECtHR on matters of freedom of expression seems to follow a sliding-scale approach, similar to the one that was advocated by Justice Thurgood Marshall of the Supreme Court of the United States of America, to whom scholars often refer as both the 'precise test master', and the 'civil rights crusader'.[53] By "sliding-scale" I mean a balancing approach that associates a continuum of available levels of scrutiny to different classes, kinds, categories of (more specific) cases, and that, under certain conditions, can be adjusted ad hoc with respect to the peculiarities of the case at hand. A category, in turn, is a bundle of interrelated properties and principles that define, by denoting, a class of objects, entities, actions.[54] As clarifies:

[49]See Ducoulombier P., *Satakunnan Markkinapörssi Oy and Satamedia Oy v. Finland* and the notion of responsible journalism. Published in the present volume.

[50]ECtHR [GC], *Jersild v. Denmark,* 23 Sept. 1994 No. 15890/89).

[51]ECtHR, *Verlagsgruppe News GmbH v. Austria*, 14 Dec. 2016, No. 8017/11, para. 31.

[52]ECtHR [GC], *Axel Springer v. Germany* 7 Feb. 2012 (App No. 39954/08) para. 83.

[53]Starks et al. (2012).

[54]Schauer (1981), pp. 277ff.

> On a sliding scale, the operative degree of scrutiny depends on a mix of factors: the nature of the classification in question, the constitutional and societal importance of the individual interest adversely affected, and the strength of the state interest asserted in support of the law under consideration. By gauging the level of scrutiny by degrees rather than two or three tiers, the sliding scale offers a more flexible mode of review that eliminates the rigidity of the tiered system.

The Court has a certain margin of maneuver in selecting the appropriate burden of justification for the case at hand; usually, the case is brought under a category of expression (freedom of the press, commercial speech, and military protests, for instance) which had been previously isolated. The margin of appreciation varies accordingly, to wit: a lower burden of justification grants national States with more considerable discretion. The effects of the sliding-scale approach are exemplified by the ECtHR in *Wingrove v. The United Kingdom* (1996), where the majority affirmed: "[W]hereas there is little scope under Article 10 para. 2 [. . .] for restrictions on political speech or on the debate of questions of public interest, [. . .] a wider margin of appreciation is generally available to the Contracting States when regulating freedom of expression in relation to matters liable to offend intimate personal convictions within the sphere of morals or, especially, religion."[55]

Sure enough, the ECtHR does not establish any sort of *a priori* ranking between rights, or any kind of lexical order that confers to freedom of expression the title of the 'ace of trumps' in the hierarchy of human rights.[56] However, the heightened scrutiny generally associated with freedom of expression tendentially places this right at the top of the list, perhaps above reputation,[57] and right below property rights. The absence of a lexicographical priority and the constant reference to the broad idea of proportionality, suggests that the latter orientates the application of every balancing test, and not only the three-pronged proportionality test. The tests endorsed by the Court, as well as the sliding-scale approach, are the result of a "grand theory" for applying human rights developed by the ECtHR over the years.

As hinted above, the Court's sliding-scale approach involves a process of categorization:[58] the court builds up different classes, categories of expression, then

---

[55]ECtHR, *Wingrove v. the United Kingdom*, 25 Nov. 1996 No. 17419/90) para. 58. See also Howard (2017), pp. 22ff., 71ff.

[56]Rawls (2001).

[57]See, for instance, ECtHR, *Pfeifer v. Austria*, 15 Nov. 2007 No. 12556/03). Privacy and reputation normally prevail when the content of expression does not make a significant contribution to the public debate. See, for instance, ECtHR, *Prisma Press v. France*, 1 Jul. 2003, No. 66910/01.

[58]On this specific point, I disagree with the analysis offered in Flauss (2009), p. 810: "Beyond guiding principles, litigation surrounding freedom of speech is similar to a branching case-study tree (far removed from the method of categorization practiced by the United States Supreme Court). Under these conditions, an author could rightly evoke the image of "a tightrope walker using democratic society as his point of reference yet whose characteristics are defined by the court in reality on a case-by-case basis through its legal case law."' The opposition between the US tradition and the EU tradition is not so radical as it appears at first glance, and this has also an historical explanation. As Flauss himself notices: "The attachment to this ideological stance has grown stronger since the middle of the 1980s, notably with the presence inside the court of judges elected

associated with different levels of protection and to different methods for weighing principles.[59] The highest degree of protection is always ascribed to the acts of the judiciary, and to the freedom of expression of the press.[60]

This high level of protection is clearly justified by the principle of the separation of powers, and by the essential role that this "watchdog" plays in implementing the rule of law, and in preserving democracy. It is correct to say that the rights of the press, on many occasions, resemble what Robert Nozick used to call "side-constraints", namely, absolute, deontological constraints.[61] However, this does not mean that the "essential role" of "public watchdog" can overstep certain boundaries implied by other rights, *in primis* the protection of the reputation and privacy. Journalistic freedom is the most extended, for it also covers possible recourses to exaggeration or provocation,[62] and every limitation to journalistic freedom shall be submitted to strict scrutiny. This consideration also holds for those cases of conflict between freedom of expression and protection of private life. As illustrated by the Court in *Axel Springer vs. Germany*:

> In order for Article 8 to come into play, however, an attack on a person's reputation must attain a certain level of seriousness and in a manner causing prejudice to personal enjoyment of the right to respect for private life.[63]

If the categories of judges and journalists are at the top of the scale of protection, the categories of militaries and civil servants are placed right at the bottom. Their exercise of the freedom of expression is much more narrow: under normal conditions, they are not even allowed to distribute written materials where they criticize their superiors, and surely they are not permitted to disclose confidential information.[64] However, this does not entail that the protections of Art. 10 do not apply to militaries at all, especially as far as their private speech is concerned. Commercial expression, too, is placed towards the lowest level of the scale, for it is associated to the less strict tests (such as the rationality with bite).

On several occasions, the Court relied on what we might call "content-based categorization", namely, a classification based on the type of content expressed. This type of categorization pursues two main goals: (i) the goal of leaving certain forms of expression outside of the protection of Art. 10; (ii) the goal of specifying sub-categories within a larger category, in order to treat them differently. The most

---

on account of 'new European democracies.' The judges, often having diplomas from American universities and sometimes even academic experience overseas, have promoted the legal precedents set by the United States Supreme Court relating to "freedom of expression" to a preferential source of inspiration (211)."

[59]Schauer (1982), p. 32f.

[60]ECtHR, *Castells v. Spain*, 23 Apr. 1992, No. 11798/85.

[61]Nozick (1974), pp. 28–33.

[62]ECtHR [GC], *Pedersen and Baadsgaard v. Denmark,* 19 Jun. 2003, No. 49017/99, para. 71.

[63]ECtHR [GC], *Axel Springer AG v. Germany*, 7 Feb. 2012, No. 39954/08, para. 82.

[64]ECtHR, *Vereinigung demokratischer Soldaten Österreichs and Gubi v. Austria*, 19 Dec. 1994, No. 15153/89, para. 38.

striking example of the former strategy is the Holocaust denial, which is a conceptual category carefully isolated by the Court, and situated outside the very notion of freedom of expression.[65]

A fine example of the second strategy, instead, is offered by those decisions where the Court differentiates several sub-categories of freedom of the press, which are associated with different burdens of justifications.[66] In his lecture, Martin Borowski offers an insightful and tightly argued reconstruction of this second approach, when he shows how the court differentiates between four maxi-categories of speech: description of facts (namely, state of affairs which are presented as true), value judgments, opinions, and insults. Value judgements, due to their intrinsic subjective nature, benefit broad protection.[67] The meaning of a value-judgment is nothing else than the expression of a positive or negative attitude (being for/being against) towards a particular action, item, or state of affairs.[68] Concerning opinions and descriptions, the possibility of their restriction depends on the general interest for the public debate:

> The extent of the state's recognized power of restriction structurally dependents on the contribution the speech or message makes to a general interest or public debate. The existence of a general interest debate leads ipso facto to a strengthening of European control. The same goes for political discourse.[69]

Another example of sub-categorization might be the distinction between (simple) information, confidential information, and secret information, which intersects the dichotomic distinction between undisclosed and previously disclosed information. According to the ECtHR, the press might publish secret information that was previously undisclosed, confidential information that was previously undisclosed, or secret information that was already made public. However, the threshold of justification required by the ban of a piece of information classified as confidential that was already made public is much higher than the threshold required for justifying the ban of secret information that had not been already disclosed.

Sure enough, freedom of expression offers a reason for imposing waves of duties and responsibilities on those States that signed the ECtHR.[70] However, the fact that the court relies on categories of expression, allows the possibility of isolating a "core" of the right. Within the core of freedom of expression, the Court also included the privilege to receive information and ideas, which is associated with the correlative duty of the State of not interfering, or even of facilitating, the uptake of a piece of communication: the State shall not interrupt or limit a communicative exchange

---

[65]ECtHR, *Garaudy v. France*, 24 Jun. 2003, No. 65831/01.

[66]ECtHR, *Observer and Guardian v. the United Kingdom*, 26 Nov. 1991, No.13585/88; ECtHR, *Vereniging Weekblad Bluf! v. the Netherlands*, 9 Feb. 1995, No.16616/90, para. 9.

[67]ECtHR, *Lepojic v. Serbia*, 6 Nov. 2007 No. 13909/05.

[68]Schroeder (2008), pp. 1ff.

[69]Flauss (2009), pp. 816ff.

[70]Waldron (1989), pp. 503ff.

unless there is a compelling reason for that.[71] The right to have access to pertinent, public information is also placed within the core of freedom of expression.[72]

It is worth stressing that not every kind of speech act is included within the boundaries of Art. 10; this remark is not limited to the core, for it also holds for the fringe. For instance, hate-speech,[73] incitement to violence,[74] and Holocaust denial are clearly speech acts—they are ways of doing things with words—with specific content, and illocutionary force, and with potential perlocutionary effects. The content is the thought expressed by the utterance (for instance the idea that the Holocaust did not take place); the illocutionary force is, so to speak, the "use" of this content (for instance the thought that the Holocaust did not take place is presented as an assertion); the perlocutionary effects are the effects caused by the utterance (for instance the audience's dignity is violated). However, they fall outside of the protection conferred by Art. 10. For instance, in *Leroy v. France*,[75] the Court considered that a satirical cartoon representing the attack to the World Trade Center coupled with the caption "We have all dreamt of it. . .Hamas did it!" did not deserve freedom of expression coverage and protection thereof, for it was clearly a justification of terrorism's enormous violence. Holocaust denial, incitement to violence, hate-speech cannot be the object of balancing, for they are always excluded, even when cloaked as (pseudo-)artistic products or activities. These categories of speech are situated beyond the boundaries of the right to free expression.

Indeed, there are several overlaps between the content that the ECtHR ascribes to Art. 10 and the right to privacy. For instance, in *Vogt v. Germany* the Court considered that freedom of expression includes the freedom of not being compelled or forced to communicate one's own opinions.[76] However, the fact that the two rights are, so to speak, "jammed" and they might eventually overlap does not imply that the notion of freedom of expression and privacy are "merged"; in other words, as the jurisprudence of the ECtHR clearly shows, the freedom of expression is not simply a form of exercising a right to privacy, and, vice versa, the notion of privacy goes beyond the idea of expressing ourselves as individuals.

As hinted above, the ECtHR has also contributed to fight hate speech effectively. In the Age of Social Networks, hate speech has become a pervasive, global phenomenon. The European institutions have endorsed several measures to fight hate speech,[77] first and foremost, Recommendation No. R. (97) 20 of the Committee of

---

[71]ECtHR, *Lingens v. Austria*, 8 Jul. 1986 No. 9815/82) para. 41; ECtHR, *Şener v. Turkey*, 18 Jul. 2000, No. 26680/95; ECtHR, *Markt intern Verlag GmbH and Klaus Beermann v. Germany*, 20 Nov. 1989 no. 10572/83).

[72]ECtHR, *Österreichische Vereinigung zur Erhaltung, Stärkung und Schaffung v. Austria*, 28 Nov. 2013, No. 32968/11, para. 41.

[73]ECtHR [GC], *Norwood v. the United Kingdom*, 16 Nov. 2004, No. 23131/03.

[74]ECtHR [GC], *Sürek v. Turkey*, 8 Jul. 1999, No. 24735/94, para. 40.

[75]ECtHR, *Leroy v. France*, 2 Oct. 2008, No. 36109/03.

[76]ECtHR [GC], *Vogt v. Germany*, 26 Sept. 1995, No. 17851/91.

[77]Bakalis (2015).

Ministers to the Member States on "Hate Speech" (Adopted by the Committee of Ministers on 30 October 1997) and the ECRI General Policy Recommendation No. 15 on combating Hate Speech (Adopted on 8 December 2015). The European Court of Human Rights has started to grapple with these issues in several important judicial decisions, such as *Belkacem v Belgium* (2017). However, the definition and identification of hate speech is not smooth sailing.[78] As Gottlob Frege clarified, two expressions might have the same semantic content (i.e., the descriptive part of an utterance) and a different tone (i.e., the expressive part of the utterance).[79] Hate speech is often a matter of tone rather than a matter of semantic content. This peculiarity of hate speech poses a new challenge to the traditional accounts of torts of defamation (libel) and private information.

4 Fake News: A New Challenge

In the last few years, freedom of expression has started to face new challenges, coming from the world wide web: the dissemination of bad quality information and pervasive use of hate speech on social networks.[80] As the Court explains in *Shtekel v Ukraine*, the Internet can be both an instrument for increasing freedom of expression and a danger for the protection of the other human rights:

> The risk of harm posed by content and communications on the Internet to the exercise and enjoyment of human rights and freedoms, particularly the right to respect for private life, is certainly higher than that posed by the press. Therefore, the policies governing reproduction of material from the printed media and the Internet may differ. The latter undeniably have to be adjusted according to technology's specific features in order to secure the protection and promotion of the rights and freedoms concerned.[81]

The weakening of the barriers to enter the media market and the increasing dissemination of bad quality information through social media underscore the growing importance of the issue. The reasons for the dissemination of fake news are mainly two: the advertising revenue connected to the amount of people accessing the information, and the ideological and political strategy of disinformation.[82] The ECtHR must necessarily play a fundamental role in supervising the filtering and take-down practices adopted by the Member States', in order to prevent gross

[78] *Belkacem v Belgium*, 20 July 2017, No. 34367/14.

[79] Frege (1897).

[80] Gillespie (2014); Magee (2002), pp. 275–284; Tsesis (2001), pp. 818ff.; Waldron (2012); Nikoltchev and McGonagle (2011); Murphy and Cuinn (2010).

[81] ECtHR, *Shtekel v. Ukraine,* 5 May 2011, No. 33014/05, para. 63. This does not mean that, when a legal issue involves freedom of expression on the internet, the other, competing rights take always priority, for, also in this case, no right shall be considered as absolute and exempt from balancing thereof. The point was stressed by the Court in ECtHR, *KU v. Finland*, 2 Dec. 2008 No. 2872/02) and ECtHR, *Ahmet Yildirim v Turkey*, 18 Dec. 2012 No. 3111/10.

[82] Allcott et al. (2017), p. 214; Bernal (2018), p. 513.

violations of the right to privacy and to remove inequalities.[83] The dangers of the expression on the web are not limited to defamatory materials, although this category represents the most striking and urgent case. To be sure, one might contend that the internet is the new "marketplace of ideas" and, therefore, the Court should not impose restrictions; but this argument is affected by a major flaw. Up until now, the ECtHR has always acted in a market which was already regulated by the Members' State, in order to check whether national entities respect the ECtHR constraints.

As the recent comparative inquiry of the Council of Europe shows, most European States have promulgated targeted regulations which prescribe the removal from webpages and social networks of illegal content concerning child abuse material, terrorism, hate crimes, intellectual property, copyright, and contents that, although *in abstracto* legal, constitute a threat for national security. The main trend is to impose a procedure of 'notice and take-down' for defamatory content, as well as for other contents that violate privacy rights. According to the notice and take-down procedure, the content is removed after publication. However, many systems also require internet hosts, social networks, and providers to act *ex ante*, by filtering and blocking the material which is submitted for publication. The legal issues connected to these practices are extremely delicate for the following reasons. First, the expression on the internet requires the cooperation of two or more actors: the "speaker" who posts the content, and the host who provides a domain-based platform (Facebook, Twitter, Word-Press). Both of them could be considered responsible for the very same act. Second, several hosts act as publishers, making a profit out of what users publish on their platforms, but, strictly speaking, they are not publishers, for the lack of the legal status of the profession of the publisher. In other words, they act only as *de facto* publishers, and, precisely for this reason, their liabilities are not clearly determined.[84] Any reductionist approaches fall short: it is quite evident that entities like Facebook do not operate on the digital market simply as advertisement companies—although they might claim that—for they play a fundamental role in amplifying the speaker's messages at a global level, breaking through the physical borders of the Westphalian States.[85] The threats to the privacy of the citizens abound.

Now, we might wonder whether the approach based on categorization and sliding-scale is suitable for dealing with these novel issues. Have we already reached such a radical change in our ways of expressing ourselves, as "digital" speakers, that requires the abandonment of the more traditional categories for balancing Art. 10 ECHR with other human rights, first and foremost, the right to privacy,

---

[83]Council of Europe, Comparative Study on Blocking, Filtering and Take-Down of Illegal Internet Content, January 2017. See Ó Fathaigh (2019) on the first occurrence of the term 'fake news' in a ECtHR committee judgment.

[84]McGonagle (2019), pp. 227ff.

[85]In recent times, EU law has endorsed several measures for dealing with the "hybrid" legal status of web platforms and social networks. In this respect, the EU Regulation 2019/1150 and the so-called EU Copyright Directive (Directive 2019/790) are perhaps the most striking examples.

established by Art. 8 ECHR? The potential perils coming from social networks are well-known.[86] These platforms make immediately available bad quality information to the global audience; furthermore, if the 'fake news' is a category of expression, at what level of the scale should it be placed? At the bottom, with commercial speech, or at a higher level? With an eye cast to the future, are we able to make any plausible predictions about the path that the ECtHR might take in this respect?

From the outset, there are good reasons to think that the Court might stick to the categorical approach, for this seems to be the strategy also preferred by Member States'. National regulations tend to split freedom of expression on the web into various sub-categories—child pornography, illegal online gambling, intellectual property, and personal data protection—ascribing different levels of protection to each one of these clusters of cases. Accordingly, the ECtHR might decide to associate each category of "web-speech" with a specific balancing test, coupled with a specific burden of justification, and obtain a different level of protection thereof. So, for instance, the most demanding tests and, accordingly, the highest level of protection might be granted to the professional press, whereas the lowest level of protection and, consequently, the least strict tests might be associated with commercial speech. Then, with systematic effort, every category of "web-speech" may be placed at different levels of the scale. In effect, there are some decisions of the ECtHR that, apparently, go in this direction. For instance, in *Pirate Bay* the Court upheld a Swedish ban to a peer-to-peer downloading system that violates copyright according to an "intermediate scrutiny": the ban was deemed proportional with respect to the legitimate aim pursued by the legislator.[87] Now, in my perspective, this is a promising strategy, but it does not resolve the main issues connected to freedom of expression on the web.

First of all, the ECtHR must necessarily check whether the procedures of blocking and notice and take-down yield to a form of political censorship. The ECtHR effectively pursued this strategy in the recent case *Cengiz and Others v. Turkey*,[88] considering the Turkish government's restrictions on YouTube broadcasting were aimed at affecting the right to receive information of the citizens (although, on that occasion, the threshold seemed too low, and the governmental measure was surprisingly considered legitimate, for it was grounded on a duly enacted statute). The practice of blocking and filtering internet contents is even more dilemmatic, due to the fact that this kind of measure is much more radical than the notice and take-down procedure, for it operates *ex ante*. Blocking seems more appropriate to personal data protection but seems far less appropriate when it comes to commercial speech. The opportunity for mandatory filtering systems deserves close attention, too. There is an actual risk that, in order to avoid sanctions, internet

[86] Sunstein (2007).

[87] ECtHR, *Fredrik Neij and Peter Sunde Kolmisoppi (The Pirate Bay) v. Sweden*, 19 Feb. 2013, No. 40397/12.

[88] ECtHR, *Cengiz and Others v. Turkey*, 1 Dec. 2015, No. 48226/10.

providers would start to apply themselves a policy of strict filtering, which frustrates the freedom of expression.

The ECtHR took important steps on many of these issues in a number of recent cases, including inter alia the recent decisions *Delfi v. Estonia,* which has been analyzed by Robert Alexy's contribution to the present volume, and *MTE Index v. Hungary.*[89] There are no reasons to abandon this path. Both in *Delfi*, and in *MTE Index v. Hungary*, the ECtHR played a fundamental role in protecting not only Art. 8 ECHR, but also the right of citizens to be (correctly) informed. In *Delfi*, the Grand Chamber held with a striking majority (15 to 2) that companies are liable for the late removal of unlawful, offensive, vulgar, violent contents from their website. In this case, the Court emphasized the commercial nature of the portal and, correspondingly, the economic interest of the company in the posting of comments.

The Court considered that *Delfi* was not acting merely as a passive service provider, for it allowed the posting of comments that were clearly not protected by freedom of expression—threats, insults, obscene expressions, and all sorts of hate speech—in order to get economic benefits. In this way, the Court substantially equated the company's liability to the liability of a journalistic publisher, in consideration the fact that the company was operating de facto as a discloser of information. This is an important and most welcome achievement.

In *MTE Index V. Hungary* the EtCHR applied the same principle, which, in this case, led to the opposite solution for the facts were radically different: MTE is a non-profit service provider. Therefore, it was not economically interested in the number of comments; furthermore, the negative comments that were published on the MTE's platform did not count as hate speech or incitements to violence.[90]

Second, the Court might try to solve a genuine philosophical puzzle related more closely to fake-news. Within the last few years, the problem of fake news acquired a significant political, social, and legal dimension, and represents one of the main challenges for any normative theory of freedom of expression. Most of our knowledge does not come from direct observation of facts, for we tend to rely on reports and testimony. In this respect, the actual structure of the Web represents a real risk, for it spreads too often bad quality information on a global audience. Social networks are often misunderstood as a genuine source of knowledge, even when they express beliefs that are not justified. If this is state of the art, Member States might worry that this informational overload paradoxically frustrates the right of the citizens to be informed, which is part and parcel of the freedom of expression. Finally, the risk that fake news might be spread on the web for manipulating elections and other institutional act is a real danger for Western democracies.[91]

On the one hand, as the ECtHR explained, internet fosters freedom of expression, for it allows to store and share a large amount of information, enhancing public

---

[89]ECtHR, *MTE Index V. Hungary*, 2 Feb. 2016. See van der Sloot (2016), p. 448; 2015, pp. 212ff.; Synodinou (2015), p. 63; Gasser et al. (2015); Perry et al. (2014).

[90]Weinert (2016).

[91]Allcott et al. (2017), pp. 211–213.

access to news and ideas.[92] On the other hand, the risk of harming other fundamental liberties, such as privacy, is considerable, for it is even higher than the risk connected to the shortcomings of the traditional press,[93] due to a number of problematic factors that have been considered in the ECtHR case law: the more powerful effect of multimedia contents,[94] the possibility of a certain degree of anonymity of the users, and of the persistence of the information on the web.[95] However, national measures against fake-news and bad quality information might easily yield to illiberal consequences, to wit: the battle against fake news might become as a pretext for censorship, especially if the notion of fake news is defined in vague and broad term, such as "unreliable information" that can represent a threat to life, public order, public safety, health, and vital elements of social and transportation structure.[96] What is more, the potential social costs of bad quality information—less accurate and mistaken beliefs, skepticism toward news producers, and unreliable information regarding the political process—shall be balanced with the interests of the news consumers in enjoying the reading of fake news, as a sheer form of entertainment.[97]

These concerns have already emerged in Europe, where the Member States have started to issue network enforcement acts and legislations against fake news. In France, the so-called "law against the manipulation of information", which introduced three new articles (L. 112, L. 163-1 et L. 163-2) in the Electoral Code (*Code Électoral*), was challenged in Court. These new legal provisions prohibit the divulgation of fake news related to the political process during the three months that precede the elections, prescribing sanctions for those providers that publish false information of public interest that might orientate the voter's preferences. The French legislator was clearly worried that cyberattacks analogous to the ones that influenced the last American elections (one might recall the Cambridge Analytica scandal) could have also affected the French elections. It turns out that the French network enforcement act was upheld by the *Conseil Constitutionnel.* The judiciary considered that the compression of the freedom of expression was not disproportioned, for it was limited to the time of the elections and concerned information of public interest.[98] What is more, according to the *Conseil*

[92] ECtHR, *Ahmet Yildirim v. Turkey,* 18 Dec. 2012, No. 3111/10, para. 48.

[93] ECtHR, *Editorial Board of Pravoye Delo and Shtekel v. Ukraine,* 5 May 2011 No. 33014/05) para. 63; ECtHR [GC], *Delfi v. Estonia,* 10 Oct. 2012 No. 64569/09, para. 132.

[94] ECtHR [GC], *Jersild v. Denmark,* 23 Sept. 1994 No. 15890/89, para. 31; ECtHR [GC], *Delfi v. Estonia,* 10 Oct. 2012 No. 64569/09, para. 132.

[95] See also CJEU, *Google Spain SL, Google Inc. v Agencia Española de Protección de Datos, Mario Costeja González* 2014, C-131/12.

[96] Federal Law of 18.03.2019 No. 31-FZ On Amendments to Article 15-3 of the Federal Law on Information, Information Technologies and on Information Protection); Federal Law of 18.03.2019 No. 30-FZ On Amending the Federal Law on Information, Information Technologies and Information Protection.

[97] Levy (2017), p. 22; Allcott et al. (2017), p. 214.

[98] *Conseil Constitutionnel, Décision n° 2018-773 DC* of 20 Dec. 2018.

Constitutionnel, the new law was aimed at protecting the right to vote, which is a necessary condition for a democratic regime.

Now, also the ECtHR might be called to take a stance on these fundamental issues and, as hinted above, it is not so easy to elaborate a precise working definition of 'fake news', which neatly isolates this new category of speech, along with the several sub-species of 'fake news'. What is more, not every fake news is harmful per se; therefore, one should carefully distinguish between protected, unharmful, fake news, and unprotected, harmful, fake news. Evidently, this distinction cannot rely on the traditional criteria for identifying harmful speech, due to the peculiarities of expression through the Internet. To be sure, one might contend that information disorder becomes a pseudo-problem if we endorse the belief in the existence of an epistemic democracy:[99] the belief that every opinion is just as authoritative as another. Accordingly, any sort of speech on the web shall be protected, and this would inevitably lead to a compression of other human rights, *in primis* the right to privacy. In this connection, I think that the notion of epistemic authority might face a more fundamental objection that—as the linguist and philosopher Diego Marconi explains—[100] leads to the abandonment of this ill-formed notion. One should reckon that different subjects have different "epistemic credentials"; nobody is universally authoritative, but each field of knowledge has its own experts that bear an "alethic right" to be acknowledged as reliable sources. In determining the most fundamental truths of natural sciences, social sciences, language, law, and so forth, the experts in the respective fields should have a privileged position.

If we leave aside the problem of epistemic democracy for the moment, and return to the more technical issue of the legal definition of fake news, we might consider that, as plausibly suggested by Romy Jaster and David Lanius, the best solution, perhaps, is to start with a minimalist two-fold notion of "news" as "newly received or noteworthy information, especially about recent events" and, in a more specific usage, as a "broadcast or published report of news."[101] Then, one can add that the qualification "fake" means that the news is, alternatively: (a) false; (b) true but highly misleading; (c) made without any intention of seeking the truth. In this way, it is possible to distinguish fake news from journalistic errors gone viral. Fake news is either false reports or misleading information; they are divulgated either with the intention to deceive the audience or with an utter disregard of the truth.[102] As the very Court considered, journalistic errors should be effectively protected by Art. 10 if the information, although false, concerns an issue of general interest, and was obtained bona fide on accurate research. Journalistic error deserves a higher level of protection, for, otherwise, excessive constraints imposed on professional journalists,

[99]The label 'information disorder' is introduced in Wardle et al. (2017).

[100]Marconi (2019).

[101]Jaster et al. (2018), p. 207.

[102]Fake news can be regarded, to some extent, as lies; lies, in turn, can be consider as morally wrong when they are intentional source of deception. See Shiffrin (2014), p. 12; Fricker (2007), Chapter VI.

acting bona fide, might frustrate their fundamental role as watchdogs of the democracy. As the *Stoll* case clearly shows, the ECtHR is perfectly aware of this risk.[103] It is hard to see how amatorial bloggers might fall within the scope of journalistic activity. If so, they should also be subject to the same duties and responsibilities of professional journalists.

It is worth stressing that fake news is not always straightforwardly false and that all false news is not necessarily a piece of fake news. Sensational, satirical, purely fictional stories, although clearly false, are not fake news if they are presented as not real, namely, as a pure source of entertainment.[104] Accordingly, websites that deliberately and unabashedly offer purely fictional stories, presented to the audience as such, are not spreading, strictly speaking, fake news. Finally, since the times of Aristophanes, satirical expressions have a fundamental role in promoting the political debate. Purely fictional political contents might become harmful only when they are misleadingly used to fool the audience. Therefore, the fictional character of the content shall be clearly stated; for instance, a disclaimer shall be included in the article, and not only on the website, something that, for instance, the webpage 'wtoenews5.com' intentionally avoided when it reported the fake news that Pope Benedict supported Donald Trump for the presidential elections.[105] By contrast, there can also be misleading statements which, despite being literally true, can be associated to an implicit false content and, therefore, misrepresent some facts (what we might dub "distorted news").[106] Instead, journalistic errors that have gone viral are issued with bona fide; the speaker genuinely believes in the truth of what she *says* (i.e., the speaker is truthful, although the content is not true), and her conclusion is supported by evidence. Last but not least, according to the proposed definition, fake news includes those statements made without any concern for the truth, where the content is picked up, made up, by the speaker only to shape the beliefs of her audience. As adumbrated above, not all fake news is necessarily dangerous or harmful. For instance, it is hard to see how the latest fake-news about the lunch Chiara Ferragni (the world-famous Italian fashion blogger) can cause harm or can be considered as a threat posed to democracy.

To close the square, we can say that fake news includes lies (false statements made with the intention of deceiving), true but (intentionally) misleading statements, and statements made without any concern for the truth. The common feature that keeps these notions together is the lack of truthfulness of the speaker. Not every fake news is harmful per se, but some of them might fall outside of the boundaries of Art. 10 ECHR, not least because, by sharing bad quality information, not supported by evidence, they might end up harming the right to be informed.

The Court might rely on the traditional sliding-scale approach, but this presupposes a clear and minimal definition of fake news, which shall then split into

[103]ECtHR [GC], *Stoll v. Switzerland*, 10 Dec. 2007 No. 69698/01, pp. 103–104.

[104]Dentith (2017), pp. 66f.

[105]Allcott et al. (2017), p. 214.

[106]Bennet et al. (2018), p. 124; Benkler et al. (2018), p. 6.

sub-categories. What is more, the ECtHR might wish to finally enter deep water: the possibility of relying extensively, for the first time, on what we might call "epistemic entitlement tests"—a balancing test that determines whether the content of the expression is justified—and "intention-based tests"—a balancing test that evaluates the intentions that underpin the communicative exchange. As mentioned earlier, the content-based approach is an assessment of the quality of the information. We have also said that a necessary condition for the notion of fake news is the insincerity of the speaker: the speaker communicates a purported truth with the intention of deceiving the audience. Now, communication is by large a matter of intention, and the notion of intention plays a central role in the definition of fake news. Therefore, in order to ascertain if a certain piece of communication falls under the protection of Art. 10, the ECtHR might start an inquiry into the communicative intentions of the speaker, which, in turn, can be identified through an analysis of her linguistic behavior. What is more, the Court might submit to close scrutiny the "epistemic entitlements" of the speaker, namely, the quality of the knowledge and expertise of the persons that disseminate bad quality information.

5 Conclusion

The present essay has explored the tests for balancing used by the ECtHR in matters of freedom of expression and the new challenges related to fake-news and bad quality information disseminated on the web. I have suggested that, when dealing with the freedom of expression, the Court relies on a sophisticated sliding-scale approach, and not on a sheer, ad hoc, balancing. Proportionality as a general principle orientates the balancing operations of the ECtHR. Furthermore, the Court combines balancing with an analytic distinction of different categories of speech. I have also considered that bad quality information raises new challenges to freedom of expression, and that the ECtHR has already started to tackle this issue. I have suggested that a precise definition of 'fake news' is fundamental. Not every fake news is harmful *per se*; therefore, the notion of fake news shall be divided into subcategories. Finally, I have briefly addressed the opportunity of an intention-based test.

References

Alexander L (2012) Is there a right of freedom of expression? Cambridge University Press, Cambridge

Alexy R (2012) Law, morality, and the existence of human rights. Ratio Juris 25(1):2–14

Alexy R (2014) Constitutional rights and proportionality. J Constit Theory Philos Law 22:51–65

Allcott H et al (2017) Social media and fake news in the 2016 election. J Econ Perspect 31 (2):211–236

Amar AR (2010) How America's constitution affirmed freedom of speech even before the first amendment. Cap Univ Law Rev 38:502–515
Austin JL (1962) How to do things with words. Clarendon Press, Oxford
Bakalis C (2015) Cyberhate: an issue of continued concern for the Council of Europe's Anti-Racism Commission. Report for the Council of Europe, Strasbourg, pp 1–20
Benkler Y et al (2018) Network propaganda: manipulation, disinformation and radicalisation in American politics. Oxford University Press, Oxford
Bennet WL et al (2018) The disinformation order: disruptive communication and the decline of democratic institutions. Eur J Commun 33(2):122–139
Bernal P (2018) Fakebook: why facebook makes the fake news problem inevitable. North Ireland Leg Q 69(4):513–530
Blocher J (2009) Categoricalism and balancing in first and second amendment analysis. N Y Univ Law Rev 84(2):375–439
Böckenförde E-W (2017) Constitutional and political theory. Selected writings. Oxford University Press, Oxford
Bollinger LC (1986) The tolerant society: freedom of speech and extremist speech in America. Oxford University Press, Oxford
Bychawska-Siniarska D (2017) Protecting the right to freedom of expression under the European Convention of Human Rights. A handbook for legal practitioners. Council of Europe, Strasbourg
Dentith MRX (2017) The problem of fake news. Public Reason 8(1/2):65–69
Farber DA (2009) The categorical approach to protecting speech in American constitutional law. Indiana Law J 84(3):917–938
Flauss J-F (2009) The European Court of Human Rights and the freedom of expression. Indiana Law J 84(3):809–849
Frantz LB (1963) Is the first amendment law? A reply to Professor Mendelson. Calif Law Rev 51 (4):729–754
Frege G (1897) Logik. In: Hermes H, Kambartel F, Kaulbach F (eds) Frege Gottlob 1969: Nachgelassene Schriften. Felix Meiner, Hamburg, pp 137–163
Fricker M (2007) Epistemic injustice. Oxford University Press, Oxford
Frowein JA (2004) Freedom of expression under the European Convention on Human Rights. Monitor/Inf (97) 3:1–61
Gasser U et al (2015) Governance of online intermediaries observations from a series of national case studies. The Berkman Center for Internet & Society Research Publication Series No. 2015-5. Berkman Center, Harvard/Hamburg
Gillespie, Alisdair A. 2014. Hate and harm: the law on hate speech. In Research handbook on EU internet law. Trzaskowski, Jan et al (eds) 488-507. Cheltenham: Edward Elgar Publishing.
Gilmore J (2011) Expression as realization: Speaker's interest in freedom of speech. Law Philos 30 (5):517–539
Hart HLA (1994) The concept of law, 2nd edn. Clarendon Press, Oxford
Howard E (2017) Freedom of expression and religious hate speech in Europe. Routledge, London/New York
Jaster R et al (2018) What is fake news. Versus 127(2):207–227
Levy N (2017) The bad news about fake news. Soc Epistemol Rev 6(8):20–36
Magee J (2002) Freedom of expression. Greenwood Publishing, Westport (Connecticut)
Marconi D (2019) Fake news, the crisis of deference and epistemic democracy. In: Condello A et al (eds) Post-truth, philosophy and the law. Routledge, London, pp 86–92
McGonagle T (2019) The Council of Europe and internet intermediaries: a case study of tentative posturing. In: Jørgensen RF (ed) Human rights in the age of platforms. The MIT Press, Cambridge, pp 227–253
Murphy T, Cuinn GÓ (2010) Works in progress: new technologies and the European Court of Human Rights. Hum Rights Law Rev 10(4):601–638
Nickel JW (1988/1989) Freedom of expression in a pluralistic society. Law Philos 7(3):281–293

Nikoltchev S, McGonagle T (eds) (2011) Freedom of expression and the media: standard-setting by the Council of Europe, (I) Committee of Ministers - IRIS Themes. European Audiovisual Observatory, Strasbourg

Nozick R (1974) Anarchy, State, Utopia. Basic Books, New York

Ó Fathaigh R. Brzeziński v. Poland: fine over 'false' information during election campaign violated Article 10. Strasburg Observers (August 8, 2019). <https://strasbourgobservers.com/2019/08/08/brzezinski-v-poland-fine-over-false-information-during-election-campaign-violated-article-10/>

Perry R et al (2014) Liability for online anonymous speech: comparative and economic analyses. J Eur Tort Law 5(2):205–256

Pettinga GL (1985) Rational basis with bite: intermediate scrutiny by any other name. Indiana Law J 62(3):779–803

Rawls J (2001) Justice as fairness. A restatement. Belknap Press, Cambridge (MA)

Ronsenfeld M et al (2006) Spreading liberal constitutionalism: an inquiry into the fate of free speech in new democracies. In: Choudhry S (ed) The migration of constitutional ideas. Cambridge University Press, Cambridge, pp 156–177

Schauer F (1981) Categories and the first amendment: a play in three acts. Vanderbilt Law Rev 34:265–307

Schauer F (1982) Free speech: a philosophical enquiry. Cambridge University Press, Cambridge

Schauer F (1995) Giving reasons. Stanford Law Rev 47(4):633–659

Schroeder M (2008) Being for. Oxford University Press, Oxford

Searle J (1969) Speech acts. Cambridge University Press, Cambridge

Shiffrin SV (2014) Speech matters: on lying, morality, and the law. Princeton University Press, Princeton

Starks GL et al (2012) Thurgood Marshall: a biography. Greenwood, Santa Barbara

Strauss DA (2010) The living constitution. Oxford University Press, Oxford

Sunstein C (2007) Republic.com 2.0. Revenge of the Blogs. Princeton University Press, Princeton

Synodinou TE (2015) 'Intermediaries' liability for online copyright infringement in the EU: evolutions and confusions. Comput Law Secur Rev 31(1):57–67

Tsesis A (2001) Hate in cyberspace: regulating hate speech on the internet. San Diego Law Rev 38:818–874

van der Sloot B (2015) Welcome to the Jungle: the liability of internet intermediaries for privacy violations in Europe. J Intellect Prop Inf Technol Electron Commerce Law 6:211–228

van der Sloot B (2016) The practical and theoretical problems with 'balancing'. Delfi, Coty and the Redundancy of the Human Rights Framework. Maastricht J Eur Comp Law 23(3):439–459

Waldron J (1989) Rights in conflict. Ethics 99(3):503–519

Waldron J (2012) The harm in hate speech. Harvard University Press, Cambridge (MA)

Wardle C et al (2017) Information disorder: toward an interdisciplinary framework for Weinert E (2016) MET v Hungary: the first European Court of Human Rights ruling on liability for user comments after Delfi AS v Estonia. Entertain Law Rev 27(4):135–139

Zoller E (2009) The United States Supreme Court and the freedom of expression. Indiana Law J 84 (3):885–916

Alessio Sardo (B.A., M.A, Trieste; PhD, Genoa, 2015) is Alexander von Humboldt Fellow at the University of Heidelberg, Department of Public Law, Constitutional Theory and Philosophy of Law. He is also member of the Tarello Institute (Genoa). His research interests include legal theory, comparative constitutional law, general jurisprudence, and human rights. Alessio Sardo's essays have appeared on *The Modern Law Review, Rechtstheorie, The American Journal of Jurisprudence, Archiv für Rechts und Sozialphilosophie*, and *The Kanazawa Law Journal.*

The manufacturer's authorised representative in the EU is Springer Nature Customer Service Centre GmbH, Europaplatz 3, 69115 Heidelberg, Germany. If you have any concerns regarding our products, please contact ProductSafety@springernature.com

Printed and bound by CPI Group (UK) Ltd, Croydon, CR0 4YY
30/09/2026
02225661-0018